THE NINE WAYS OF BON

Excerpts from *gZi-brjid*

Edited and Translated

by

DAVID L. SNELLGROVE

Professor of Tibetan

in the University of London

PRAJÑĀ PRESS

BOULDER 1980

PRAJÑĀ PRESS
Great Eastern Book Company
P.O. Box 271
Boulder, Colorado 80306

ISBN 0-87773-739-8

This reprint has been authorized by the Oxford University Press.

Printed in the United States of America

LIBRARY OF CONGRESS CATALOGING IN PUBLICATION DATA

Gzi, brjid. English. Selections.
The nine ways of bon.

Reprint of the ed. published by Oxford University Press, London, New York, which was issued as v. 18 of London oriental series.
Includes bibliographical references.
I. Snellgrove, David L. II. Title. III. Series: London oriental series; v. 18
BL1943.B6G9213 1978 299'.54 78-13010
ISBN 0-87773-739-8

PREFACE

MY first interest in BON dates from 1956, when in the course of a long journey on foot through the remote Tibetan speaking regions of north-west Nepal, I discovered the old *bon* monastery of Samling in Dolpo. I spent a month in the monastery on that first occasion and collected with the help of the head lama *Shes-rab* a number of interesting manuscripts. Although quite unknown to the non-Tibetan world, Samling was well known to Tibetan *bonpos*, and thus on a return visit to Dolpo in 1960, I met in Tarap the Abbot of *gYuṅ-druṅ-gliṅ* and Geshey Sangye Tenzin Jongdong on their way back from Samling with several loads of books that they had borrowed from the nephew of Lama *Shes-rab*. Now that Tibet is occupied by Chinese Communist forces, Samling has become the main source of books for the few knowledgeable *bonpo* monks who are living as exiles in India.

In 1961 the Rockefeller Foundation kindly offered funds to those universities in Europe, the U.S.A., and Japan which already had a developing interest in Tibetan studies, so as to enable them to invite for a three-year period a few selected scholars from among the many Tibetan refugees in India and Nepal. I took advantage of this opportunity to invite three qualified *bonpo* monks to England, Lopön Tenzin Namdak, formerly of *sMan-ri* Monastery, and Geshey Sangye Tenzin Jongdong and Geshey Samten Gyaltsen Karmay of *gYuṅ-druṅ-gliṅ*. (Both these monasteries are a few days' journey west from Shigatse in Tsang Province.)

Working in conjunction with contemporary *bonpos*, I have readily accepted (with certain reservations) their own interpretation of their religion, and the present work is an attempt to provide a survey of the whole range of their teachings, as formulated certainly not later than the twelfth century and may be even two or three centuries earlier. It has been our intention at this stage to let the texts speak for themselves as much as possible, so that there may be no risk of others accusing us of putting forward exaggerated ideas of what BON is all about.

The present work represents the first attempt to let the *bonpos* themselves give some account of their own religion. Lopön Tenzin Namdak was mainly responsible for the selection of the extracts, and he and I worked on them side by side, resolving textual difficulties as well as we could. The English translation has been entirely my responsibility, for works such as these require a type of English vocabulary with which no Tibetan, however intelligent, is yet sufficiently familiar. Since Tenzin Namdak returned to India in September 1964, where he has been busily reprinting *bonpo* works, I have checked through the whole Tibetan text again with Samten Gyaltsen

Karmay and added a few extra excerpts. I would like to express my thanks publicly to these two knowledgeable *bonpo* monks, who have played so large a part in making this pioneering work a sufficiently safe venture. Likewise I acknowledge with thanks the great assistance that I have received from Professor Walter Simon, who has looked through this whole work for me and patiently checked the terms listed in the glossary. In the long and laborious work of preparing the glossary for publication I have had the continual assistance of Samten Gyaltsen Karmay, and I owe him very special thanks for this.

Thanks are due also to the Trustees of the Rockefeller Foundation who made it possible for me to invite these monks to England. Finally thanks are due (as always) to the School of Oriental and African Studies in the University of London, which continues to make possible my own journeys to India and Nepal in the search of new materials, and which has now by a generous subvention made possible the publication of this present work.

Berkhamsted DAVID L. SNELLGROVE
21 September 1966

CONTENTS

INTRODUCTION

To practising *bonpos*—and nowadays it has become comparatively easy to meet them if one knows where to look among the many tens of thousands of Tibetans who have arrived as refugees in India and Nepal—BON simply means the true religion of Tibet. To the far greater number of other Tibetans, who are not *bonpos*, BON refers to the false teachings and practices that were prevalent in Tibet before Buddhism finally succeeded in gaining a firm hold on the country. *Bonpos* are regarded as pagans—and as such they have suffered serious hostility in the past—and nowadays others take as little account of their existence as possible. By western scholars BON is generally understood as referring to the pre-Buddhist beliefs and practices of the Tibetans. Several scholars have discussed the actual meaning of the term.[1] By the few *bonpos* who know their texts well BON is explained as the Tibetan equivalent of the '*Źaṅ-źuṅ* term' GYER which means 'chant'. Textual 'evidence' can be shown for this in the titles of works said to be translated from the language of *Źaṅ-źuṅ* into Tibetan. Here *bon* is regularly glossed by *gyer*. This is the original meaning they say, for they know that *bon* now covers all the meanings of the Tibetan Buddhist term *chos*. As is well known, *chos* simply translates Sanskrit *dharma* in all its Buddhist meanings. There is no word for 'Buddhism' in Tibetan. Tibetans are either *chos-pa* (followers of *chos*) or *bon-po* (followers of *bon*). They both use the term *saṅs-rgyas* (literally: 'amply purified') to define a perfected sage, a *buddha*. Thus in translation of *bonpo* texts I continue to use such terms as 'buddha' and 'buddhahood'. Any readers who are new to the subject will therefore assume that BON is a form of Buddhism, and that it has certainly developed as such there is no doubt. In this work I am bound to understand BON in the full *bonpo* sense and that includes all their gradual adaptation of Buddhist doctrine and practice.[2] They themselves

[1] See Helmut Hoffmann, *Quellen zur Geschichte der tibetischen Bon-Religion*, Verlag der Akademie der Wissenschaften und der Literatur in Mainz, 1950, p. 137. See Simon, 'A Note on Tibetan *Bon*' in *Asia Major*, v, 1956, pp. 5–8. See Uray, 'The Old Tibetan Verb BON' in *Acta Orientalia Academiae Scientiarum Hungaricae*, xvii, 1964, pp. 323–34. This discussion would seem to leave us with at least two homonyms *bon*, (i) meaning 'invoke' and 'invoker' of which Simon (followed by Uray) understands the original meaning to be 'entreat' or 'invite', and (ii) meaning 'seed'. There remains always the possibility of *Bon* as an alternative for *Bod* (Tibet), but this merely invites inquiry into the origin of the term *Bod*, so far attempted by none. See p. 20, fn. 2.

[2] In his *The Religions of Tibet*, London, 1961, Hoffmann distinguishes between 'The Old *Bon* Religion' (Chapter I) and 'The Systematized *Bon* Religion' (Chapter V). Such a distinction is perhaps helpful, so long as we do not think in the clear-cut terms of pure indigenous *bon* and Buddhist-influenced *bon*. The historical development of *bon* has been far more complex. It is a composite growth where native and foreign elements of all kinds are mingled together.

do not acknowledge these Buddhist elements as adaptations. Lacking the necessary historical sense, they persist in claiming that all their teachings and doctrines are the true original BON, partly promulgated direct in Tibet by *gŚen-rab*, their founder, but mainly received through translations from the language of *Źaṅ-źuṅ* of ancient western Tibet. The ultimate source of their teachings is *sTag-gzigs*, a country situated rather vaguely still further to the west. They would claim that it is the *chos-pa*, the 'Buddhists' of Tibet, who are the adapters and the plagiarists. Without accepting their claims, we are nevertheless bound to accept their interpretation of terms in presenting an account of their teachings and practices, and this is the primary intention of the present volume. In giving an account of any religion we cannot ignore what the practisers have to say about themselves. Thus in giving an historical account of Buddhism itself, we cannot ignore, for example, the eighty-four *Siddhas*, however different their doctrines and practices may be from those of the early Buddhists. We cannot deny the term Buddhist to the Newars of the Nepal Valley, however much they may seem to be influenced by Brahmanical practice. We can merely observe that their form of Buddhism represents a very special development of this religion. Likewise in the case of the *bonpos* we have to accept them and understand them as they are, while still trying to unravel the historical developments of their religion. An understanding of them on their own terms is all the more important nowadays, because we need the assistance of their few remaining scholars in order to understand something of their early texts. Tibetans who can help with these texts are now very rare indeed. Educated *bonpo* monks are brought up in the *dGe-lugs-pa* ('Yellow Hat') Way, trained in conventional Buddhist philosophy and logic and receiving after examination by debate the academic degree of *dGe-bśes*. They know their monastic liturgies and the names of their own *bonpo* gods, but very rarely indeed are they at all experienced in reading the sort of *bonpo* texts in which we most need assistance, namely material which represents 'pre-Buddhist' traditions. This lack of familiarity on the part of present-day *bonpos* with what Western scholars would regard as real *bon* material, may come as a disappointment. It also explains why there still remain terms and ideas not yet properly interpreted in this present work.

Among the three *bonpo* monks who accompanied me to England in 1961 was Tenzin Namdak, once Lopön (*slob-dpon*), best translated as 'Chief Teacher', at sMan-ri.[1] Tenzin Namdak, who has now returned to India after three years in England, is a devoted *bonpo*, firm in his doctrines as well as his vows. Initiated primarily in a threefold *bon* tantra, the

[1] The only existing survey of *bonpo* monasteries to date is in Hoffmann's *Quellen*, p. 236. *sMan-ri*, until recently a large monastery with about 200 monks, is not mentioned, but there is reference to the neighbouring *bonpo* monastery *gYuṅ-druṅ-gliṅ* (p. 238), whose abbot is now a refugee in India.

Ma-rgyud saṅs-rgyas rgyud gsum, he was practised in the meditations and teachings of the VIIIth Way. Remaining celibate, he continued to adhere to the rules of the VIth Way, or rather he adhered to them as far as possible in a foreign western setting. We have read through many texts together, and it was on his suggestion that we set to work to produce a concise account of the 'Nine Ways of *Bon*', and it was he who selected the extracts which serve as the substance of the present account.

The source of these extracts is a work entitled *ḥdus-pa rin-po-che dri-ma med-pa gzi-brjid rab-tu ḥbar-baḥi mdo* 'The Precious Compendium the Blazing *Sūtra* Immaculate and Glorious', in short referred to simply as *gZi-brjid* 'The Glorious'. This work seems to be quite unknown outside Tibet. *gŚen-rab*'s 'biography' is written in three versions, one long, one of medium length, and one short. *gZi-brjid* in twelve volumes is the long version. *gZer-mig* in two volumes is the medium version. *mDo-ḥdus* in one volume is the short one. *gZer-mig* is known of by Western scholars since A. H. Francke edited and translated the first seven chapters, which are published in *Asia Major*, 1924, 1926, 1927, 1930, and 1939. Professor Hoffmann has also used *gZer-mig* for the brief account that he gives of *gŚen-rab*'s life in his *The Religions of Tibet* (pp. 85–97). *mDo-ḥdus* remains unknown in the West, although there may be a copy somewhere in India.

These three works are all classed by the *bonpos* as 'Kanjur' (the term is borrowed from the Buddhists), that is to say as the inspired word of their early sages as translated from the language of *Žaṅ-žuṅ*. *gZi-brjid* is further classed as 'oral tradition' (*sñan-rgyud*). It is believed that *rTaṅ-chen mu-tsha-gyer-med*, a disciple of the sage *Dran-pa nam-mkhaḥ* (eighth century), transmitted it in a vision to *Blo-ldan sñiṅ-po*, who compiled it in its present form.[1] The 'Great Incarnation' (*mchog-sprul*) *Blo-ldan sñiṅ-po* of *Khyuṅ-po* in *Khams* is a well-known literary figure of the *bonpos*. He was a close contemporary of *Tsoṅ-kha-pa*, for he was born about A.D. 1360. He is said to have died in his twenty-fifth year.[2]

Thus *gZi-brjid* would seem to have been compiled towards the end of the fourteenth century, and the contents of the work bear out this tradition. By that time the *bonpos* had absorbed the vast variety of Indian Buddhist

[1] The *bonpos*, like the *rñiṅ-ma-pas*, were busy 'rediscovering' their 'original' teachings, which had been hidden or lost during the persecutions of the eighth century. The main sources of this process of rediscovery were the 'hidden texts' (*gter-ma*) which were now brought to light (*gZer-mig* belongs to this category), and the visionary revelations through which lost texts were 'passed on orally' (*sñan-rgyud*).

[2] This information concerning the authorship of *gZi-brjid* derives from oral information of my *bonpo* assistants here in London. The date A.D. 1360 is calculated from the *bstan-rtsis* ('Doctrinal Dates') of *Ñi-ma bstan-ḥdzin*, once abbot of *sMan-ri*. This useful little work has just been published (1964), thanks to Tenzin Namdak, together with a *Žaṅ-žuṅ* word-list, at the Lahore Press, Jama Masjid, Delhi 6.

teachings, and so were able to restate them as the substance of their higher doctrines of the 'Nine Ways' with the conviction that can only come from that experience and knowledge that is based upon well learned lessons combined with practical experience. At the same time they had preserved through their own oral and literary traditions large quantities of indigenous material which goes back to the eighth century and earlier. But by the fourteenth century *bonpos* had long since forgotten the meanings of many of the earlier names and terms. From the manner in which he orders his material in the first two 'Ways', it is clear that the compiler was by no means so sure of himself as when he was dealing with the later Buddhist material.

The copy of *gZi-brjid* used by us came from Samling Monastery in Dolpo.[1] According to its brief colophon, the lama responsible for our manuscript was *Yaṅ-ston Nam-mkhaḥ rin-chen* and it was written at *Klu-brag*.[2] Fortunately, he writes more about his family in the 'preface' (*dkar-chags*) to the manuscript. He praises his nephews *Sri-dar rnam-rgyal*, *Rin-chen*, and *ḥKhro-ba*, and especially his elder brother *Yaṅ-ston Tshul-khrims rnam-rgyal*, who consecrated the finished manuscript. Thus despite the difference in name, these relationships identify him firmly with Lama *Rin-chen rgyal-mtshan*, who is referred to in the genealogy of the lamas of Samling as a great producer of books. *gZi-brjid* is specifically mentioned. 'It was the measure of an arrow (in size), and as a sign of (this lama's) phenomenal powers each time the pen was dipped in the inkpot a whole string of words was written.'[3] Unfortunately, the scanty references to dates in this genealogy leave the period uncertain. It is, however, possible to calculate that this *Rin-chen rgyal-mtshan* belonged to the ninth generation from *Yaṅ-ston rGyal-mtshan rin-chen*, the founder-lama of Samling, who must have lived in the thirteenth century.[4] Thus, our manuscript is

[1] It was brought to England by Geshey Sangye Tenzin Jongdong in 1961. Concerning Samling see my *Himalayan Pilgrimage*, Oxford, 1961, pp. 110 ff. I made a second visit in 1961.

[2] *Klu-brag* is the name of a monastery and village which is situated up a steep side-valley of the Kāli Gandaki just south of Kāgbeni. It is marked as 'Lubra' on the Survey of India maps of the region (ref. 83° 48′ E., 28° 45′ N.). Since Samling was founded from *Klu-brag*, it remained the main source for their texts.

[3] Folio 39a of the genealogy of the lamas of Samling, entitled *rGyal-gśen Ya-ṅal gyi bkaḥ-brgyud kyi gduṅs-rabs* 'Genealogy of the religious line of the noble priests of *Ya-ṅal*'.

[4] The lamas of Samling, like the lamas of *Klu-brag*, are an hereditary line of the *Ya-ṅal* family. The title *Yaṅ-ston*, which they are frequently given, is presumably an abbreviation of *Ya-ṅal ston-pa* '*Ya-ṅal* Teacher'. Some of them have been married men, but some have been celibate. Thus the line has passed sometimes from father to son, and sometimes from uncle to nephew. Although so far I have no firm confirmation of this, *Klu-brag* Monastery was probably founded by a certain *bKra-śis rgyal-mtshan*, who is usually referred to as 'The Man of *Klu-brag* Protector of Sentient Beings' (*ḥGro-mgon Klu-brag-pa*). He was the son of a renowned *bonpo* lama *Yaṅ-ston chen-po Śes-rab rgyal-mtshan*. Brief biographies are given in the *rnam-thar* section of the *Źaṅ-źuṅ sñan-rgyud*, of *Śes-rab rgyal-mtshan*, of two of his sons, *ḥBum-rje* and *Klu-brag-pa*, and of a grandson *rTog-ldan dbon-po kun-bzaṅ* (of whom more below). No dates of any kind are given, but

probably about 400 years old. It was copied from an existing manuscript at *Klu-brag* and then brought to Samling.

gZi-brjid is an enormous work, totalling in our manuscript 2,791 folios. There are twelve volumes numbered *ka* to *da* with a final volume *a*. The text is arranged in sixty-one chapters, and a list of these chapters will give some idea of the scope of this composite work:

Volume	Chapter		
ka	1	'The Teacher descends from the gods of Pure Light' (*ston-pa ḥod-gsal-lha las bab paḥi leḥu daṅ-po*)	ff. 1b–104b
	2	'The Teacher turns the Wheel of *Bon* for the non-gods' (*ston-pa lha-min la bon-ḥkhor bskor baḥi leḥu*)	–144b
	3	'The *sūtra* of the coming of the doctrine of the buddhas' (*saṅs-rgyas bstan-pa chag phebs paḥi mdo*)	–189a
	4	'The *sūtra* of *gŚen-rab*'s taking birth' (*gśen-rab kyi skye-ba bźes paḥi mdo*)	–256b
kha	5	'The *sūtra* of the young prince's playful sport' (*rgyal-bu gźon-nu rol-rtsed kyi mdo*)	ff. 1b–86a
	6	'The *sūtra* of the prince's enthronement' (*rgyal-bu rgyal-sar phyuṅ baḥi mdo*)	–137a
	7	'The *sūtra* of the prince's law-giving' (*rgyal-bus bkaḥ-khrims stsal baḥi mdo*)	–189b
	8	'The *sūtra* of the IInd Way of the Shen of the Visual World' (*theg-pa gñis-pa snaṅ-gśen gyi mdo*)	–212b
	9	'The *sūtra* of the IIIrd Way of the Shen of Illusion' (*theg-pa gsum-pa ḥphrul-gśen gyi mdo*)	–235a
ga	10	'The *sūtra* explaining the Way of the Shen of Existence' *srid-gśen theg-pa gtan la phab paḥi mdo*)	ff. 1b–47a
	11	'The *sūtra* that teaches the meaning of the *maṇḍala* of the five universal (buddha-)bodies' (*kun-dbyiṅs sku lṅa dkyil-ḥkhor gyi don bstan paḥi mdo*)	–136a

we are told that *Klu-brag-pa* studied in *gTsaṅ*, where he received vows and consecrations from two well-known *bonpo* lamas, *Ye-śes blo-gros* and *sMan-goṅ-pa*, for both of whom dates are given in the *bstan-rtsis* of *Ñi-ma bstan-ḥdzin* (see p. 3, n. 2). According to this *Ye-śes blo-gros* founded the Academy (*gtsug-lag-khaṅ*) of *Dar-ldiṅ-gser-sgo* in A.D. 1173, and *sMan-goṅ-pa* was born in A.D. 1123. Thus we may safely deduce that *Klu-brag-pa* was studying as a young man in *gTsaṅ* in the mid-twelfth century. It is upon this calculation that all my subsequent calculations depend.

The eldest son of *Klu-brag-pa* was known as the 'Tantric Lama' (*bla-ma sṅags-pa*) and he was the first of the line to go to *Bi-cher* in Dolpo. (This place is variously spelt as *Bi-cher* or *Byi-byer*. It appears on the Survey of India maps as Phijorgaon. See my *Himalayan Pilgrimage*, p. 129.) This 'Tantric Lama' had three children, two sons and a daughter. The elder son died young. The younger son became a monk. The daughter left and married elsewhere. Being anxious to establish a line of illustrious lamas at *Bi-cher*, the 'Tantric Lama' invited from *sTag-rtse* in Upper *gTsaṅ* a boy of eight who belonged to a parallel branch of the family. This boy was *rGyal-mtshan rin-chen*, who founded Samling Monastery near *Bi-cher*. He himself remained celibate, and the line of Samling lamas descended from his younger brother. *rGyal-mtshan rin-chen*'s teacher was *rTog-ldan dbon-po kun-bzaṅ*, who was the pupil and nephew of the 'Man of *Klu-brag*', for whom we have approximate dates. Thus the son of the 'Man of *Klu-brag*' brought *rGyal-mtshan rin-chen* to *Bi-cher*, and the nephew of this same 'Man of *Klu-brag*' was his teacher. Therefore he must have been active at *Bi-cher* and Samling during the first half of the thirteenth century.

Volume	Chapter		
ga	12	'The *sūtra* explaining the Way of the Virtuous Adherers' (*dge-bsñen theg-pa gtan la phab-paḥi mdo*)	–219b
	13	'The *sūtra* explaining the Way of the Great Ascetics' (*draṅ sroṅ theg-pa gtan la phab-paḥi mdo*)	–260a
ṅa	14	'The *sūtra* of the VIIth Way of Pure Sound' (*theg-pa bdun-pa a-dkar gyi mdo*)	ff. 1b–50b
	15	'The *sūtra* of the VIIIth Way of the Primaeval Shen' (*theg-pa brgyad-pa ye-gśen gyi mdo*)	–79b
	16	'The *sūtra* of the IXth and Supreme Way' (*theg-pa dgu-pa bla-med kyi mdo*)	–103b
	17	'The *sūtra* explaining the *bon* of the various translations' (*skad-ḥgyur so-soḥi bon bstan paḥi mdo*)	–137a
	18	'The *sūtra* of spreading the doctrine by converting those who are hard to convert' (*gdul dkaḥ btul nas bstan pa spel baḥi mdo*)	–175b
	19	'The *sūtra* of the *maṇḍala* of the Loving Conqueror' (*byams-ldan rgyal baḥi dkyil-ḥkhor gyi mdo*)	–194b
	20	'The *sūtra* of the very firm and precious doctrine' (*bstan-pa rin-chen rab-tu brtan paḥi mdo*)	–230a
ca	21	'The *sūtra* of the three tenets taught by the Teacher' (*ston-pas peḥu-tse rnam-pa gsum bstan-paḥi mdo*)	ff. 1b–37a
	22	'The *sūtra* of the spreading rays that convert sentient beings' (*ḥgro ḥdul ḥod-zer spro-baḥi mdo*)	–109a
	23	'The *sūtra* explaining cause and effect' (*rgyu ḥbras rnam-par ḥbyed paḥi mdo*)	–166a
	24	'The *sūtra* of the Teacher drawing beings to salvation' (*ston-pas ḥgro-ba thar-bar draṅ-baḥi mdo*)	–224a
cha	25	'The *sūtra* of the light of the Blessed All-Knowing' (*bde-bar gśegs-pa kun-rig sgron-maḥi mdo*)	ff. 1b–93a
	26	'The liturgy of the All-Good the Ocean of Victory' (*kun-tu bzaṅ-po rgyal-ba rgya-mtshoḥi cho-ga*)	–145a
	27	'The *sūtra* of the washing away of the sins of King *Gu-wer*' (*gu-wer rgyal-poḥi sgrib-pa sbyaṅs paḥi mdo*)	–169b
	28	'The *sūtra* of the Teacher's taking the most glorious of wives' (*ston-pas khab-kyi dpal-ḥbar bźes-paḥi mdo*)	–247b
ja	29	'The *sūtra* of the Teacher's producing the offspring of Method and Wisdom' (*ston-pas thabs daṅ śes-rab kyi sras sprul baḥi mdo*)	ff. 1b–23b
	30	'The *sūtra* of the Teacher's assumption of royal power' (*ston-pas chab-srid ḥdzin-paḥi mdo*)	–57a
	31	'The *sūtra* of the producing of offspring who convert sentient beings' (*ḥgro ḥdul sras sprul-baḥi mdo*)	–94b
	32	'The *sūtra* of the Teacher teaching *bon* to the gods' (*ston-pas lha la bon ston-paḥi mdo*)	–124a
	33	'The spell of the Fierce Destroyer' (*khro-ba rnam-par ḥjoms-paḥi gzuṅs*)	–161a
	34	'*Maṇḍala* of the liturgy of the God of Medicine' (*sman-lhaḥi cho-gaḥi dkyil-ḥkhor*)	–209b

Volume	Chapter		
	35	'The *sūtra* of the pure prayer of good conduct' (*legs-spyod smon-lam rnam-par dag-paḥi mdo*)	–246a
ña	36	'The *sūtra* of the Teacher teaching *bon* to the serpents' (*ston-pas klu la bon ston-paḥi mdo*)	ff. 1b–42a
	37	'The *sūtra* of *Māra*'s magical display to the Teacher' (*ston-pa la bdud kyis cho-ḥphrul bstan-paḥi mdo*)	–77b
	38	'The secret spell the Destroyer of *Māra*' (*bdud-ḥjoms gsaṅ-baḥi gzuṅs*)	–92b
	39	'The *sūtra* of the Teacher establishing the realm of *Māra* in salvation' (*ston-pas bdud-khams thar-bar bkod-paḥi mdo*)	–156a
	40	'The *sūtra* of removing obstructions and subduing *Māra*' (*bdud btul bar-chod bsal-baḥi mdo*)	–186a
	41	'The *sūtra* of producing offspring for continuing the family-line of royal sway' (*mi-rje srid-pa gduṅ-ḥdzin gyi sras sprul-baḥi mdo*)	–201a
	42	'The *sūtra* for establishing the teaching of the IXth Way' (*theg dgu bstan-pa rjes-bżag gi mdo*)	–228a
	43	'The *sūtra* for establishing the teaching about relics' (*sku-gduṅ bstan-pa rjes-bżag gi mdo*)	–274a
ta	44	'The *sūtra* of the acquisition of the way of salvation of the supreme order' (*bla-med go-ḥphaṅ thar-lam sgrub-thabs kyi mdo*)	ff. 1b–23b
	45	'The Mother *Sūtra* the Great Way of the Word of the Perfection of Wisdom' (*bkaḥ śes-rab kyi pha-rol tu phyin-pa theg-pa chen-po yum gyi mdo*)	–205a
tha	46	'The *sūtra* of the *maṇḍala* of the Great Way of the Mother' (*theg-pa chen-po yum gyi dkyil-ḥkhor gyi mdo*)	ff. 1b–66b
	47	'The spell of the Sacred Light of *Vaiḍūrya*' (*be-du-rgya ḥod dam-paḥi gzuṅs*)	–128b
	48	'The liturgy of the basic *maṇḍala* of (the goddess) Loving Kindness' (*byams-ma rtsa-baḥi dkyil-ḥkhor gyi mdo*)	–183a
da	49	'The *sūtra* in praise of the twenty-one forms of (the goddess) Loving Kindness' (*byams-ma ñi-śu-rtsa-gcig gi bstod paḥi mdo*)	ff. 1b–51b
	50	'The *sūtra* establishing the three forms of the doctrine' (*bstan-pa rnam gsum rjes-su bżag-paḥi mdo*)	–111a
	51	'The *sūtra* of the Teacher leaving his home and becoming a religious wanderer' (*ston-pas khyim spaṅs rab-tu byuṅ baḥi mdo*)	–145a
	52	'The *sūtra* of the perfecting of austerities, the actions of a Shen' (*gśen gyi mdzad-spyod dkaḥ-thub mthar-phyin gyi mdo*)	–176b
	53	'The *sūtra* of the manifestation of the four-spoked Wheel of *Bon*' (*bon gyi ḥkhor-lo tshig-bżi bstan-paḥi mdo*)	–199a
	54	'The *sūtra* of pure disciplinary rules' (*ḥdul-khrims gtsaṅ-maḥi mdo*)	–223a
a	55	'The basic *sūtra* of the pure regulations of the Shen' (*gśen gyi bsruṅ-khrims rnam-par dag-pa rtsa-baḥi mdo*)	ff. 1b–34b

Volume	Chapter		
a	56	'The *sūtra* of the sections of the regulations of the Shen' (*gśen gyi bsruṅ-khrims yan-lag gi mdo*)	–88b
	57	'The *sūtra* of the pure virtuous conduct of the Shen' (*gśen gyi dge-spyod rnam-par dag-paḥi mdo*)	–114a
	58	'The *sūtra* of removing the hellish evils of King *Koṅ*' (*koṅ rgyal-po na-rag sgrib-pa sbyaṅs-baḥi mdo*)	–127a
	59	'The *sūtra* of the Teacher leaving his entourage and practising in solitude' (*ston-pas ḥkhor spaṅs dgon-pa mdzad-paḥi mdo*)	–150b
	60	'The *sūtra* explaining the meanings of the names, marks and qualities of the buddhas' (*saṅs-rgyas kyi mtshan dpe yon-tan gyi don bstan-paḥi mdo*)	–191b
	61	'The *sūtra* of the Teacher handing the *Bon* doctrine over into the care (of others)' (*ston-pas bstan-pa bon gyi gtad-gñer mdzad paḥi mdo*)	–208a

The titles of these chapters will indicate at once to any (non-Tibetan) Buddhist scholar the dependence of this work upon Buddhist material. Although the study of *gZer-mig* remains incomplete, there has never been any doubt that the inspiration and the framework for the legend of *gŚen-rab* have been derived from the life of *Śākyamuni*. Yet this framework has been filled with indigenous Tibetan legendary material which still awaits serious study.

In this present work we have made a very restricted use of *gZi-brjid*, extracting excerpts relevant to the *bonpo* doctrines of the 'Nine Ways'. The Tibetan term *theg-pa*, as all Buddhist scholars of Tibetan will know, simply represents the Sanskrit Buddhist term *yāna*, and I translate it sometimes as 'Way' and sometimes as 'Vehicle'. However, there are very few Tibetans, however well educated, who know the original meaning of *theg-pa* (as connected with the verb *ḥdegs-pa* and its various roots, meaning 'raise' or 'sustain'), and who thus understand it in the meaning of 'vehicle'. No Tibetan Buddhist would think of accusing the *bonpos* of having appropriated terms that were originally Buddhist. To all Tibetans, whether Buddhist or *bonpo*, their religious vocabulary is just part of their own language to be used as they please. But the non-Tibetan Buddhist scholar readily recognizes those terms which were once specially coined as the Tibetan equivalents of Indian Buddhist technical terms. He is thus able to pass judgement on *bonpo* material in a way which no Tibetan has yet thought of doing.

The brief extracts here edited have been taken from Chapters 7, 8, 9, 10, 12, 13, 14, 15, and 16.

In editing we have not hesitated to emend the text as seemed desirable. The original manuscript spellings are shown in the case of all 'main word' (*miṅ*) changes, but we have not recorded every 'particle' (*tshig-phrad*) emendment. Connecting particles (*kyi*, *gyi*, etc.) are often written instead of the corresponding instrumental particles (*kyis*, *gyis*, etc.) and vice versa. The particles *te*, *ste*, *de* are sometimes used incorrectly (e.g. *yin-ste* instead of *yin-te*), and *la* is written for *las* and vice versa. It would be tedious and misleading for any student to follow the text from the translation if such corrections were not made.

The text is written in *dbu-med* and abbreviated compounds are quite frequent. Numerals are normally written in figures and not in letters, and since I have spelt out the numerals in every case, it will no longer be obvious how for example 'eight' may be safely corrected to 'two'. Written as numerals, only the top hook distinguishes Tibetan 2 from 8. After final vowels (not only after *a*) *ḥ* is regularly added, as in *gtoḥ*, *dbyeḥ*, etc. In conformity with later Tibetan practice, I have omitted *ḥ* except after final *a*.

Generally, the manuscript is clear and remarkably accurate. Some 'mistakes' tend to be regular. For example *gñan* 'a fury' is regularly written as *gñen*; *kluṅ-rta* (= *rluṅ-rta*, see note 10 of the text) is regularly written as *sruṅs-rta*. Certain spellings, which may appear unusual to other scholars, we have, however, preserved, for example, *sgra-bla* for *dgra-lha* (see note 20 of the text).

From the mistakes he makes, the scribe was clearly far less sure of himself when dealing with the material of the first two 'Vehicles', and this bears out what was said above concerning the unfamiliarity of later generations of *bonpos* with the really early material.

I present the translation in the hope that interested readers will assist me in identifying the associations that may be apparent to them in much of the material, for I do not pretend to have solved all the problems. A brief survey of the 'Nine Ways' may assist comprehension.

I. THE WAY OF THE SHEN OF THE PREDICTION (*phyva-gśen theg-pa*)

This describes fairly coherently four methods of prediction:

(*a*) sortilege (*mo*)
(*b*) astrological calculation (*rtsis*)
(*c*) ritual (*gto*)
(*d*) medical diagnosis (*dpyad*).

II. THE WAY OF THE SHEN OF THE VISUAL WORLD (*snaṅ-gśen theg-pa*)

This is the longest and most difficult section of our work. It is concerned with overpowering or placating the gods and demons of this world, but I suspect that even the original compiler of the work was already unfamiliar with many of the divinities and rites to which he refers. Thus the account is not really coherent, but it makes quite sufficient sense. The various practices are arranged into four parts:

1. The lore of exorcism (employing) the 'great exposition' of existence. (I have written on 'exposition' *smraṅ* in note 9 of the text. The manner of the rite is clearly described on pp. 49–51.) The text then goes on to describe various types of divinities, the *thug-khar*, the *wer-ma*, and others. Some are described in great detail, and some, such as the *caṅ-seṅ* and *śug-mgon*, scarcely mentioned except by name. Finally, we are told the 'lore of the stream of existence' (*srid-paḥi rgyud gźuṅ*). This is presumably all part of the 'exposition' (*smraṅ*) of the officiating priest.

2. This deals with demons (*ḥdre*) and vampires (*sri*), their origin, nature, and the ways of suppressing them.

3. This deals with ransoms of all kinds. Their extraordinary variety testifies to their importance in early Tibetan religion. Tenzin Namdak can identify very few of them, and I doubt if any other living Tibetan can do much better. My translations of the many unfamiliar terms are as literal as possible, but they do not pretend to be explanatory.

4. This deals with fates (*phyva*) and furies (*gñan*) and local divinities generally (*sa-bdag*, *gtod*, *lha*, *dbal*, etc.), and the offerings due to them.

III. THE WAY OF THE SHEN OF ILLUSION (*ḥphrul-gśen theg-pa*)

This is concerned with rites for disposing of enemies of all kinds. The rites described here are to be found in the *bon* tantras, e.g. those of *dBal-gsas* and the *khro-baḥi rgyud drug*, which we have on microfilms. Similar practices are referred to in Buddhist tantras, e.g. *Hevajra-Tantra*, I. xi.

IV. THE WAY OF THE SHEN OF EXISTENCE (*srid-gśen theg-pa*)

This deals with beings in the 'Intermediate State' (*bar-do*) between death and rebirth, and ways of leading them towards salvation.

V. THE WAY OF THE VIRTUOUS ADHERERS (*dge-bsñen theg-pa*)

dge-bsñen is the normal Tibetan term for *upāsaka* which in India referred to the Buddhist layman. Similarly, here it refers to those who follow the practice of the ten virtues and the ten perfections, and who build and worship stūpas.

VI. THE WAY OF THE GREAT ASCETICS (*draṅ-sroṅ theg-pa*)

draṅ-sroṅ translates *ṛṣi* which in India refers to the great seers of the past. *draṅ-sroṅ* is used by *bonpos* to refer to fully qualified monks, corresponding to the Buddhist term *dge-sloṅ* (= *bhikṣu*). This is the way of strict ascetic discipline. The whole inspiration is Buddhist, but many of the arguments and even the substance of some of the rules are manifestly not Buddhist.

VII. THE WAY OF PURE SOUND (*A-dkar theg-pa*)

This deals with higher tantric practice. It gives a very good account of the tantric theory of 'transformation' through the *maṇḍala*. (I have already summarized these ideas in my introduction to the *Hevajra-Tantra*, pp. 29 ff.) It then goes on to refer briefly to the union of Method and Wisdom as realized by the practiser and his feminine partner. This anticipates VIII. The section ends with concise lists of nine 'reliances', eighteen 'performances', and nine 'acts'. The 'reliances' comprise a list of primary needs, the 'performances' resume the whole process of ritual of the *maṇḍala*, and the 'acts' represent the total power that accrues to one from mastering all the Nine Vehicles.

VIII. THE WAY OF THE PRIMEVAL SHEN (*ye-gśen theg-pa*)

This deals with the need for a suitable master, a suitable partner, and a suitable site. The preparation of the *maṇḍala* is then described in detail together with important admonitions not to forget the local divinities (*sa-bdag*). The process of meditation (known as the 'Process of Emanation'—in Sanskrit *utpattikrama*) is recounted.[1]

The last part of this section describes the 'Process of Realization' (Sanskrit *niṣpannakrama*), which is the 'super-rational' state of the perfected sage. His behaviour might often be mistaken for that of a madman.

IX. THE SUPREME WAY (*bla-med theg-pa*)

This describes the absolute, referred to as the 'basis' (*gźi* corresponding to Sanskrit *ālaya*), from which 'release' and 'delusion' are both derived. 'Release' is interpreted as the state of fivefold buddhahood, and 'delusion' as the false conceptions of erring beings in the 'Intermediate State' (*bar-do*). The 'Way' is then described as mind in its absolute state, as the pure 'Thought of Enlightenment'. The 'Fruit' or final effect is then finally described in terms of the special powers of the perfected sage. The whole subject-matter is then resumed under the four conventional headings of insight, contemplation, practice, and achievement.

The categories and ideas elaborated in this IXth Vehicle are usually referred to as the teachings of the 'Great Perfection' (*rdzogs-chen*).

What is remarkable about these 'Nine Ways of BON' is the succinct manner in which they resume the whole range of Tibetan religious practices: methods of prediction, to which Tibetans of all religious orders and

[1] This whole passage from pp. 102–7 describes at the same time the normal course of worship of the great beings as it is performed in any Tibetan temple of any religious order, *bon* or Buddhist. See my comments on the relationship between ritual and meditation in *Buddhist Himālaya*, Cassirer, Oxford, 1957, p. 234.

of all ranks of society are addicted; placating and repelling local divinities of all kinds of whose existence all Tibetans, lay and religious, are equally convinced; destroying enemies by fierce tantric rites, practices in which Buddhists and *bonpos* are equally interested; guiding the consciousness through the 'Intermediate State', powers claimed equally by the older orders of Tibetan Buddhism and by the *bonpos*; moral discipline of devout believers and strict discipline of monastic orders, ways that have followers in all orders of Tibetan religion; tantric theory and ritual, fundamental to the iconography and the worship of all Tibetan religious communities; tales of perfected wonder-working sages, typical again of the older orders of Tibetan Buddhism as well as *bonpos*. All that is missed out of this list is the religious life of academic learning which is now typical of educated monks of the *dGe-lugs-pa* ('Yellow Hat') order. This is only omitted because when the list of 'Nine Ways' was elaborated, the *dGe-lugs-pa* way had not yet come into existence. But nowadays the *bonpos* have this, too, with their scholars of philosophy and logic and their academic honours and titles. Nor are they just dressed in others' plumes. They really have developed the practices of all these diverse ways over the last thirteen centuries or so, and they have produced a very large literature of their own in support of all the various ways of their practice. Much of this literature, e.g. some of their *sūtras* and especially the 'Perfection of Wisdom' teachings, has been copied quite shamelessly from the Buddhists, but by far the greater part would seem to have been absorbed through learning and then retold, and this is not just plagiarism.

In classing the four lower ways as 'BON of cause' and the five higher ways as 'BON of effect', they were trying sincerely to relate the old ways of magic ritual to the new ways of morality and meditation. If one practises even the rites of the Ist Way intent on the 'Thought of Enlightenment', benefit will come to all living beings (see p. 29). Likewise the IInd Way 'is something for delighting living beings with benefits and happiness, but it is important to have as basis the raising of one's thoughts (to enlightenment)' (p. 97). The IIIrd Way, if practised properly, reaches out towards the VIIIth Way, achieving the effect where Method and Wisdom are indivisible (p. 113). The practiser of the IVth Way, concerned as he is with rescuing others who wander in the 'Intermediate State', is effectively preparing himself for buddhahood. Conversely, the rites of the lower ways are still indispensable even when one has reached the higher ones. 'Fertile fields and good harvests, extent of royal power and spread of dominion, although some half (of such effects) is ordained by previous actions (viz. karmic effect), the other half comes from the powerful "lords of the soil"—so you must attend to the "lords of the soil", the serpents and the furies' (p. 199). Now every Tibetan, whatever his religious order, believes this, but—to my knowledge—only the *bonpos* have formulated this belief as doctrine.

Buddhist ideas certainly pervade BON throughout: the definition of truth as absolute and relative (this was a useful idea for the *bonpos* as it could provide a justification for the lower ways of magic ritual, e.g. see p. 27 and p. 101); the realization of the 'Thought of Enlightenment' as the coalescence of Method and Wisdom; the whole conception of living beings revolving through the six spheres of existence; the notion of buddhahood as five-fold and the whole gamut of tantric theory and practice. Some might be tempted—when there is still so much else of interest in Tibetan civilization that awaits investigation—to neglect this developed and elaborate BON as mere second-hand Buddhism. But there have been also serious scholars who conversely would regard Buddhism in Tibet as little more than demonological priestcraft. Waddell's remarkable book, *Lamaism*, which contains so much precise information about Tibetan Buddhist practices of all kinds, provides evidence enough that BON and Buddhism in Tibet are in their theories and practices one and the same.[1] What Waddell perhaps failed to appreciate is that Tibetan Buddhism—and for that matter *bon* too—is often sincerely practised by Tibetans as a moral and spiritual discipline.

We are thus concerned not only with pre-Buddhist Tibetan religion, but with Tibetan religion regarded as one single cultural complex. The *bonpos* merely pose the problem nicely for us by having arranged all types of Tibetan religious practice within the framework of their 'Nine Ways'. Regarded in this way, BON might indeed claim to be the true religion of Tibet. Accepting everything, refusing nothing through the centuries, it is the one all-embracing form of Tibetan religion. Its few remaining educated representatives seem to be still motivated by its spirit. Western scholars of Tibetan well know how difficult it is to persuade an indigenous Tibetan scholar to take any interest in forms of Tibetan literature that lie outside his particular school. Normally a *dGe-lugs-pa* ('Yellow Hat') scholar would be ashamed at the idea of reading a work of any other Tibetan Buddhist order, let alone a *bonpo* work. Yet educated *bonpo* monks clearly have no such inhibitions. They will learn wherever they can, and given time they will absorb and readapt what they have learned.

Regarded in this way BON is a strange phenomenon, and what we really want to know is how it began to develop in its early stages. The *bonpos* themselves concede that their religion as practised in Tibet consisted in the

[1] In a recent book *Religious Observances in Tibet*, which is concerned with Tibetan religion as it is practised nowadays, Robert B. Ekvall makes the most misleading statements about BON and its relationship to Buddhism. He writes nothing of the 'higher ways' of BON and nothing of the 'lower ways' of Buddhism.

first place of little more than ritual magic, and they believed that *gŚen-rab* himself established these practices there. A clear account is given of the story in Chapter XII of *gZer-mig*, which recounts how the demon *Khyab-pa lag-riṅ* sends his followers who steal the seven horses of *gŚen-rab* from the sacred city of *ḥol-mo luṅ-riṅ*. In the previous chapter it was related how this demon had carried off *gŚen-rab*'s daughter *gŚen-bzaḥ ne-chuṅ* and forcibly married her. Their two children were then abducted by *gŚen-rab* and concealed at *ḥol-mo luṅ-riṅ*. At the beginning of Chapter XII the demon sends his followers to see where the children are. They cannot be found, so he gives orders for the theft of the horses as a form of reprisal. Rather than keep the horses in his own realm (*bdud-yul mun-paḥi gliṅ*), he plans to keep them in *rKoṅ-po*, and he sends messengers to make arrangements with the two rulers of *rKoṅ-po*, named *rKoṅ-rje dkar-po* and *rKoṅ-rje dmar-po*. *gŚen-rab* himself together with four followers comes after them, not (as he explains) in order to get the horses only, but because the time has come to spread the doctrine in *Źaṅ-źuṅ* and Tibet. The demons block his way with snow, then fire, then water, and then sand, but he disperses them and reaches *Źaṅ-źuṅ*.

* *gŚen-rab* gave to the *bonpos* of *Źaṅ-źuṅ* as *bon* (doctrine) the 'inspired teaching' (*luṅ*) about bombs[1] and spells, and as ritual items he instructed them in the 'Divine Countenance of the Celestial Ray'[2] and in black and white 'thread-crosses'.[3] Then he went on to *Bye-ma lu-ma dgu-gyes* ('The Ninefold Spreading of the Desert Spring') in *gTsaṅ*, where he pronounced this prayer: 'Now it is not the occasion for establishing the doctrine among all the *bonpos* of Tibet, but may "*Bon* of the Nine Stage Way" spread and be practised there some time!' As he said this, a group of demons was subjected to him. *gŚen-rab* gave to the *bonpos* of Tibet as *bon* (doctrine) the 'inspired teaching' concerning prayers to the gods and the expelling of demons, and as ritual items he showed them various small aromatic shrubs, the use of barley as a sacrificial item[4] and libations of *chang*. Nowadays the *bonpos* of Tibet, summoning all gods and demons by means of *bon*, get their protection, and by worshipping them send them about their

* gśen rab kyis źaṅ źuṅ gi bon po la bon du btso[1] daṅ sṅags kyi luṅ phog / yas stags su mu zer lha źal[2] daṅ / nam mkaḥ[3] dkar nag bstan / de nas *gtsaṅ bye ma lu ma dgu gyes* su byon nas / źal nas smon lam btab pa / bod kyi bon po thams cad la bstan pa bźag paḥi da ruṅ gnas med pas / nam źig theg pa rim dguḥi bon dar nas spyod par śog gsuṅs nas / bdud kyi ḥkhor bcom / gśen rab kyis bod kyi bon po la bon du lha gsol ba daṅ / ḥdre bkar ba gñis kyi luṅ phog / yas stags su rtsi śiṅ ban bun daṅ / źug śaṅ[4] daṅ / gser skyems bstan / da lta bod kyi bon pos lha ḥdre thams cad kun / bon gyis bos na ḥgon la / mchod na ḥgro źiṅ brduṅs na thub pa / ston paḥi źal mthoṅ baḥi dus su dbaṅ du bsdus paḥi rtags yin /

[1] Concerning *btso* 'bomb' see note 5 to the text.

[2] This refers to the patterning of the threads to correspond to the countenance of the divinity.

[3] Concerning *nam-mkaḥ* and not *mdos* as the primary term for 'thread-cross' see note 11 to the text.

[4] A mixture of lightly roasted and black roasted barley grains, used as an offering. According to Tenzin Namdak it makes the same as *śel-tshigs* (Chos-kyi-grags-pa's Dictionary, p. 885).

tasks, and by striking them prevail over them. This is the proof of *gŚen-rab*'s having subdued them when they beheld his countenance.

In historical terms this account simply means that before Indian religious ways spread to Tibet, Tibetan religion consisted of magical rituals (of the kind enumerated in the Second Way of BON) performed by priests known as *bon* and as *gśen*.[1] The full doctrine (referred to as the 'BON of the Nine Stage Way') came later and—except for the rituals that were already practised in Tibet—through translations. The *bonpos* were certainly impressed by the need for translations. Thus BON teachings, they claim, were translated into 360 languages and taught throughout the known world, which for them consisted of India generally, the states of north-west India in particular, Central Asian states and peoples, Nepal, and China.[2] Lastly, it reached Tibet, again from the west through translations from the language of *Źaṅ-źuṅ*.

This BON that spread west and south and north of Tibet was of course Buddhism, and it is quite conceivable that the Tibetans of western Tibet, whose ancestors first made contact with the forms of Buddhism popularly practised in Jālandhara (*za-hor*) and Kashmir (*kha-che*), in *Uḍḍiyāna* (*o-rgyan*) and Gilgit (*bru-śa*), were unaware of its direct connexion with the Buddhism officially introduced into Tibet in the eighth century by King *Khri-sroṅ-lde-btsan*. The *bonpos* are insistent that their teachings came from the west, and there are good reasons for believing that Buddhist yogins and hermits, and probably Hindu ascetics as well, had already familiarized the villagers of western Tibet with Indian teachings and practices before Buddhism was formally introduced by the Tibetan religious kings. Moreover, these 'informal' contacts continued over several centuries. Perhaps the main original difference between *bonpos* and *rñiṅ-ma-pas* (Tibetan Buddhists of the 'Old Order') consists in the fact that the *rñiṅ-ma-pas* acknowledged that their doctrines, despite their earlier promulgation, were nevertheless Buddhist, and that the *bonpos* never would make this admission. Fundamental to an elucidation of this interesting problem is a comparative study of the tantras and the *rDzogs-chen* ('Great Perfection') literature of these two oldest 'Tibetan Buddhist' groups.

[1] It is generally agreed that the story of *gŚen-rab*'s life is a deliberate fabrication, for which the inspiration was the life of *Śākyamuni*. *gŚen-rab* just means 'Best of *gŚen*'. But a study of the local traditions and legendary material from which the story has been pieced together would be a worth-while literary task. The story of the 'religious hero' *gŚen-rab* is in effect another great Tibetan epic, comparable in importance with the great epic of Gesar, which thanks to the intensive studies of R. A. Stein, is now far better known. Yet *gŚen-rab*'s legend is supported by a whole complex system of religious practices, altogether an extraordinary phenomenon.

[2] The countries given in the *srid pa rgyud kyi kha byaṅ chen mo* (Richardson's MS., f. 7a[5] onwards) are: *źaṅ-źuṅ*, *stag-gzigs*, *phrom*, *rgya-gar*, *rgya-nag*, *kha-che*, *za-hor*, *o-rgyan*, *ḥdan-ma*, *bal-yul*, *sum-paḥi yul*, *a-źaḥi yul*, *bskor-yul*, *ḥjaṅ*, *li-yul*, and *me-ñag*.

The organizing of their religious practices into 'Nine Ways' must have come somewhat later, perhaps by the tenth century. The *rñiṅ-ma-pa* set of nine begins with the three 'ways' of conventional Indian Buddhism, the *śrāvakayāna*, the *pratyekabuddhayāna*, and the *bodhisattvayāna*. The other six 'ways' are ever higher stages of tantric practice, viz. *kriyātantra*, *upāyatantra*, and *yogatantra*, and finally, the *mahāyogatantra*, *anuyogatantra*, and *atiyogatantra*. Thus the *rñiṅ-ma-pas*, recognizing their connexions with the newly established official religion, were content to organize themselves as tantric adepts of Buddhism. The *bonpos*, despite their ever increasing cultural and literary contacts with the official religion, persisted in claiming that this religion had really been theirs from the start. Driven very early, certainly already in the eighth century,[1] into a position of opposition, they set to work to organize a full-scale religion of their own, using all their own remembered indigenous resources and all they could acquire from their opponents. The magnitude of the task was really astounding, if judged only by the vast bulk of literature which they so speedily accumulated. The 'Nine Ways of BON' is a mere summary of their achievements.

The *bonpos* often refer to their full complement of doctrines and practices not only as the 'BON of the Nine Stage Way', but also as the BON of the 'Four BON Portals and the Treasury as Fifth':

bon sgo bźi mdzod lṅa daṅ theg pa rim dguḥi bon.

This term *sgo bźi mdzod lṅa* has no easy explanation. The four 'portals' are *dpon-gsas*, *chab-nag*, *chab-dkar*, and *ḥphan-yul*. The first, *dpon-gsas*, may be safely translated as 'Master Sage'. It is the term used for the hermit sages of the *źaṅ-źuṅ sñan-rgyud*. As one of the four 'portals' of *bon* it refers to their teachings of the 'Great Perfection' (*rdzogs-chen*). As for *chab-dkar* and *chab-nag*, *chab* remains uncertain in meaning. Tenzin Namdak accepts these names as technical terms without any proper meaning, and so, while he and other educated *bonpos* know what the terms refer to, they remain quite uninterested in the origin of the terms themselves. *Chab* has two different meanings: (i) royal sway or power and (ii) the honorific term for water. The compound *chab-sgo* means an 'imperial portal' and perhaps this might encourage us to choose the first meaning. The 'White Sway' and the 'Black Sway' would make quite good translations. But in our selected texts (p. 42, line 33 onwards) *chab* is clearly

[1] Perhaps the oldest version of the story of how *Khri-sroṅ lde-btsan* arranged for the assassination of *Lig-mi-rgya*, king of *Żaṅ-źuṅ*, occurs in the *Żaṅ-źuṅ sñan-rgyud*, chapter entitled *bstan pa dar nub kyi lo-rgyus*. The story is retold from this source in the *rGyal-rabs bon gyi ḥbyuṅ-gnas* edited (abominably) by Sarat Chandra Das, Calcutta, 1915, p. 58. The story of *Khri-sroṅ-lde-btsan*'s persecution of the *bonpos* is also told in the *srid-pa rgyud kyi kha byaṅ chen-mo*, Chapter 5 (Richardson's MS., ff. 29b ff.).

interpreted as though it meant 'water'. I have therefore taken the term provisionally in this meaning. The term is used only as a label in any case. The 'White Waters' refer to higher tantric practice and the 'Black Waters' to magic rites of all kinds. European writers have often referred to 'White *Bon*' and 'Black *Bon*', but clearly without any intended reference to *chab-dkar* and *chab-nag*.

ḥPhan-yul is a well-known place-name in Central Tibet, but once again my *bonpo* helpers insist that this term which refers to their 'Perfection of Wisdom' teachings, has nothing to do with the *ḥPhan-yul* Valley. But I think they are mistaken. The name *ḥPhan-yul* often occurs in *bonpo* texts both as a place-name[1] and as a term referring to particular doctrines. Before the 'Teacher *gŚen-rab*' spread the teachings in the world of men he is supposed to have taught *ḥPhan-yul* texts in the realms of the serpents (*klu*), furies (*gñan*), mountain-gods (*sa-bdag*), and rock-gods (*gtod*).[2] One wonders if there is some connexion here with the well-known story of *Nāgārjuna*'s visit to the *nāgas* (= Tibetan *klu*) to obtain his 'Perfection of Wisdom' teachings. There is no doubt that in *bonpo* usage *ḥPhan-yul* means 'Perfection of Wisdom' texts, and therefore it might have seemed suitable to give this name to texts which *gŚen-rab* was supposed to teach to serpents and others. I mention this possibility merely since I suspect that it is just such a haphazard association of ideas that often accounts for the use of many terms in *bonpo* material, and we may well be wasting our time looking for more scholarly associations. As for the special meaning that the *bonpos* gave to *ḥPhan-yul*, perhaps it was here in this place, which was certainly important in the early spread of Buddhism in Tibet, that they first learned and studied 'Perfection of Wisdom' literature. It is perhaps fair to add that Tenzin Namdak discounts such an idea altogether. As for the special *bonpo* meanings of these terms, he has kindly drawn my attention to some very good definitions occurring in *gZer-mig*:

The 'Master Sage' belongs to the BON of precepts and inspired teachings. It purifies the stream of knowledge, avoids words and concentrates on the meaning.[3]

The 'Black Waters' belong to the BON of the stream of existence. It purifies the stream of knowledge. By means of the many verbal accounts which arise there, much is accumulated for the good of living beings under three (headings):

[1] In the *rGyal-rabs bon gyi ḥbyuṅ-gnas* it is listed as one of the thirteen centres of *bon* in Central Tibet, *viz*. Das, p. 37: *ḥphan yul chab* (Das writes *grab*) *dkar bon gyi gnas*. In the *srid-pa rgyud kyi kha byaṅ chen-mo* it is clearly referred to as *yul ḥphan-yul* (p. 28a³). In this context it refers to a group of three sets of teachings, *ḥphan-yul rgyas-pa*, *dpon gsas gsaṅ-ba*, and *a-bo gsaṅ-ba*. Is *a-bo* connected with Sanskrit *āpaḥ* 'waters', thus corresponding to Tibetan *chab* in *chab-dkar* and *chab-nag*?

[2] *srid-pa rgyud kyi kha-byaṅ chen-mo*, Richardson's MS., f. 7ᵃ.

[3] *gZer-mig*, vol. *kha*, f. 97a⁴ onwards: dpon gsas man ṅag gi bon du gtogs pa ni / śes rab rgyud sbyaṅs tshig bor don la sgom paḥo /

the outer stream of death rites and funeral rites, the inner stream of sickness rites and ransom rites, and the middle stream of diagnosis rites and rituals.[1]

The vast *ḥPhan-yul* belongs to the BON of the Hundred Thousand (Verse Text) in the *Sūtras*. It purifies the stream of knowledge. It tells of monastic discipline and vows. This BON has two aspects, as a series (Skr. *parivarta*) and as recitation. Again the series has two aspects, the series of the phenomenal world and the series of passing from sorrow (Skr. *nirvāṇa*). The recitation is of two kinds again, recitation that enunciates and originates in the words of enunciation, and enunciation that is consecrated to the good of living beings and serves for ceremonies. Being read and recited, it accumulates much (merit) for living beings, and it should be used for ceremonies.[2]

The 'White Waters' belong to the BON of potent precepts and spells. It purifies the deep stream of knowledge. It embraces the profound 'reliance' and 'performance'. As for this BON, when one has been consecrated, one becomes of the self-nature of fivefold buddhahood. As effect one has in the Body the five symbolic gestures of the self-nature (of buddhahood): as effect in the Speech one recites spells continuously: as effect in the Mind one practises the profound meditation of the 'Process of Emanation' and the 'Process of Realization'. As effect in one's Accomplishments one accumulates and delights in ritual items. As effect in one's Acts one praises the buddha-names in recitation.[3]

Defined in this way, the 'Four Portals' cover all the types of religious practice included in the 'Nine Ways'.

The 'Master Sage' Portal represents the Ninth Way.
The 'Black Waters' Portal represents the First, Second, and Fourth Ways.
The *ḥPhan-yul* Portal represents the Fifth and Sixth Ways.
The 'White Waters' Portal represents the Seventh and Eighth Ways. It also includes the Third Way in so far as this is directed towards the '*Bon* of Effect'.

Thus these 'Four Portals' seem to represent an earlier and quite coherent attempt by the *bonpos* to arrange their accumulated religious materials into four groups:

1. Precepts and teachings of sages and hermits, e.g. *źaṅ-źuṅ sñan-rgyud* and other *rdzogs-chen* literature.
2. Ways of prediction, death ceremonies, and magical rites of all kinds (viz. the 'original' *bonpo* material).

[1] chab nag srid pa rgyud kyi bon du gtogs pa ni / śes rab rgyud sbyaṅs tshig gi lo rgyus maṅ po skyes pas phyi rgyud śi thabs ḥdur thabs daṅ / naṅ rgyud na thabs glud thabs daṅ / bar rgyud dpyad thabs gto thabs gsum / sems can don du maṅ po tshogs par sgyur /

[2] ḥphan yul rgyas pa mdo khuṅs ḥbum gyi bon du gtogs pa ni / śes rab rgyud sbyaṅs ḥdul khrims sdom pa gsuṅ baḥo / bon ni ḥgres daṅ tshig bśad gñis / ḥgres la rnam pa gñis / ḥkhor baḥi ḥgres daṅ / mya ṅan las ḥdas paḥi ḥgres / tshig bśad la yaṅ rnam pa gñis / ḥdon tshig ḥbyuṅ khuṅs ḥdon paḥi tshig bśad daṅ / mchod sbyin sems can don du bsṅo baḥi tshig bśad gñis / sems can don du maṅ po ḥtshogs sar bklag daṅ bsgrag ciṅ mchod sbyin gtaṅ /

[3] chab dkar man ṅag drag po sṅags kyi bon du gtogs pa ni / śes rab zab moḥi rgyud sbyaṅs bsñen sgrub zab mo daṅ du blaṅ baḥo / bon ni byin gyis brlabs nas bdag ñid bder gśegs lṅaḥi raṅ bźin ni lus kyi las su raṅ bźin phyag rgya lṅa / ṅag gi las su ḥdzab graṅs ma chad par bgraṅ / yid kyi las su tiṅ ḥdzin bskyed rdzogs bsgom / yon tan las su yo byad bsag bsod bya / ḥphrin las kyi las su tshig bśad mtshan bstod do /

3. Texts and practices connected with monastic religion. (One may observe that the reading of 'Perfection of Wisdom' literature as a meritorious rite was as popular then as now.)
4. Texts and practices of the tantras.

As for the 'Treasury which makes the fifth', this is the 'Pure Summit' (*gtsaṅ mtho thog*), which once again is best defined by a quotation from *gZer-mig*:

As for the 'Pure Summit', it goes everywhere. As insight it belongs to the BON which is a universal cutting off. It purifies the stream of knowledge in all the 'Four Portals'. It simply involves that insight into the non-substantiality of appearances. It understands the deluding nature of the 'outer vessel' as relative truth. It knows, too, the empty atomic nature of the 'inner essences'. In terms of absolute truth non-substance, too, is an absurdity.[1]

Thus 'BON of the Nine Stage Way' and the 'Four BON Portals with the Treasury as Fifth' are simply two different ways of grouping the different types of BON practice. It has already been observed (p. 13 above) that the practices and doctrines described in these groups might with very little change serve equally well as a description of Tibetan Buddhism. BON and Buddhism have pervaded one another completely, yet each persists in denying the debt it owes to the other. The *dGe-lugs-pas* ('Yellow Hats') would be most offended if one suggested that the Great Oracle of *gNas-chuṅ*, to whom the Dalai Lama and the Tibetan Cabinet would so often resort, really belonged as a religious practice to BON Way I, the 'Way of the Shen of Prediction'. The writer of the *rGyal-rabs bon gyi ḥbyuṅ-gnas* observes that as a result of *Khri-sroṅ-lde-btsan*'s persecution of the *bonpos* 'some agreed to be Buddhist monks, but in their mind they reflected on BON, and in word and act they performed CHOS (*dharma*)'.[2] But even this has proved an understatement, for most Tibetans are still *bonpos* at heart and they have recourse to BON of all kinds, not only in their minds, but in words and acts as well.

It is noteworthy that so far as their activities are concerned, the *bonpos* have seemingly preserved little of the 'original BON' which has not also been incorporated by other Tibetan Buddhists in the many rites and ceremonies and strange practices which form part of Tibetan social and religious life. But in their texts they have preserved quantities of early legendary material and of ritual utterances. They still hold to the legends,

[1] gtsaṅ mtho thog spyir rgyug lta ba spyi gcod bon du gtogs pa ni / sgo bźi la śes paḥi rgyud sbyaṅs / snaṅ la raṅ bźin med paḥi lta ba gcig tu ḥjog paḥo / kun rdzob bden par phyi snod sgyu maḥi raṅ bźin du rtogs / naṅ bcud ñid kyaṅ stoṅ paḥi raṅ bźin ḥphra rab rdul du go / don dam bden par dṅos med cir yaṅ ma yin paḥo / (*gZer-mig*, vol. *kha*, f. 98b[2] onwards).

[2] kha cig ban deḥi chad byed ciṅ / yid la bon bsam źiṅ / kha daṅ lus ni chos la spyod / (Das, p. 50).

certainly those that have been associated with the life of *gŚen-rab*, but the ritual utterances would seem to have little significance to the *bonpos* of today. These ritual utterances were proclaimed originally as an 'exposition' (*smraṅ*) of the 'archetype' (*dpe-srol*), and it was this exposition which gave validity to the rite (see page 50, line 6). The Gurungs of Nepal, a people of early Tibetan origin, still practise these kinds of rites, as we now know from the interesting oral material collected by the late Bernard Pignède.[1] Their recitations of the 'archetype' are known as *pé*, pronounced like the Tibetan word *dpe*, still used in the meaning of 'example'. Some 'original BON' survived in oral traditions, and it was just such ancient oral traditions that *bonpo* scholars of ten centuries ago were incorporating into their new composite works.

Although BON has often been understood by Western scholars as referring primarily to certain (never clearly specified) pre-Buddhist religious practices of the Tibetans, vaguely described sometimes as animism or shamanism, the term BON is in fact never used in early Tibetan works with any such meaning. The *bon* were just one class of priests among others, whose practices and beliefs are covered by the general term of *lha-chos*, which may be translated perhaps as 'sacred conventions'.[2] The term BON, as referring to a whole set of religious practices, would seem to have come into use at a latter stage in deliberate opposition to the new use of CHOS which now had the meaning of Sanskrit *dharma* limited specifically to the religion of *Śākyamuni*.[3] Thus there is probably no such thing as pre-Buddhist BON, for from the start the followers of BON were anxious to accept and readapt religious teachings and practices of all kinds, whether indigenous or foreign. It was not Buddhist teachings that they objected to, but rather the claim that all these teachings had first been taught by the Indian Sage *Śākyamuni*. Nor were they entirely wrong, as we know well now, for the Buddhism that reached Tibet more than a thousand years after the death of its founder comprised a whole range of teachings and practices that he would have found very strange indeed. If one understands the term BON as the *bonpos* understand it, one will not be surprised or

[1] See his work, *Les Gurungs, une population himalayenne du Népal*, Mouton, The Hague (École Pratique des Hautes Études), 1966, especially pp. 323–4, 363–5.

[2] I would not hesitate to connect *bon* in the sense of 'priest' with the verb *ḥbod-pa* 'to invoke' (see p. 1 fn. 1). Such a *bon* ('invoker') would have been competent in the all-important ritual of the 'exposition of the archetype' (see p. 256). BON in the sense of 'Tibetan religion' is probably connected with *Bod* (even occasionally written *Bon* in early texts) meaning 'Tibet', and possibly with *bon* as in *sa-bon* 'seed'. The original meaning may be 'autochthonous', and so was used for the 'people of the homeland' in much the same way that the Germans refer to themselves as 'Deutsch', a term which simply means originally 'the people (of the homeland)'. See also Marcelle Lalou, 'Tibétain Ancien BOD/BON', *Journal Asiatique*, 1953, pp. 275–6.

[3] The term *chos* I would connect with the verb *ḥchaḥ-ba*/*bcas*, etc. 'make or construct' and with such cognate terms as *chas* 'things or requisites', and *bcos-pa* 'modified or affected'.

disappointed to discover that *bon* literature includes a very large amount of material that is normally regarded as Buddhist.

Western scholars have been misled to some extent by the non-*bonpo* Buddhists of Tibet (the *chos-pa*), who have identified the BON which they knew as their only serious rival in later centuries as the same rival against which the first Buddhists had to fight in Tibet, while the (later) *bonpos* have merely added to the confusion by assuming that they were not only the original rivals of the *chos-pa*, but that they already possessed in the earlier period all the developed (Buddhist) teachings which they had in fact only gradually incorporated in the course of the eighth to thirteenth centuries. *Bon* (meaning 'priest who invokes') is one thing, and *bonpo* meaning 'follower of BON ("Tibetan religion")' is another. The early Buddhists certainly came into conflict with the *Bon* ('priests who invoke') who were active in Tibet long before Buddhist doctrines were introduced, but their real long-term rivals were the *bonpos* who were busy constituting their BON ('Tibetan religion') while the Buddhists (*chos-pa*) were busy constituting their CHOS (*Dharma*). The development of BON and CHOS were parallel processes, and both *bonpos* and *chos-pas* were using the same literary language within the same cultural surroundings. It would be naïve to expect *bonpo* literature to be totally different from Buddhist literature. On the contrary, it is rather remarkable that *bonpo* texts contain so much comprehensible pre-Buddhist material, and it is not surprising that *bonpo* composers of texts (even perhaps as early as the eighth or ninth century) were already uncertain of the meanings of many names and terms of the indigenous (entirely oral) tradition. Some indigenous material, especially the beliefs and practices associated with the early kings, may be better preserved by the Buddhists than the *bonpos*, for the Buddhists were able to claim in retrospect the whole line of historical kings, except *Glang-dar-ma*, as Buddhist. But for information concerning the whole range of pre-Buddhist Tibetan religion, it is better to investigate *bonpo* literature rather than Buddhist, for even when Buddhist writers are not trying deliberately to denigrate their rivals, their accounts are slipshod and often unintelligible.[1]

[1] As an example of this see the brief survey of BON teachings in the *Blon-po bkaḥi thaṅ-yig*, edited and translated by Hoffmann in his *Quellen zur Geschichte der tibetischen Bon-Religion*, pp. 249 ff. and 348 ff. On the other hand the *rGyal-po bkaḥi thaṅ-yig* contains an interesting chapter (ff. 39a–40b) describing the attendance at the royal tomb of *Sroṅ-btsan-sgam-po*. This clearly belongs to the same context as the 'Rituel Bon-po des funérailles royales' as presented by Mlle Marcelle Lalou in the *Journal asiatique*, 1952, pp. 339–61.

TEXT AND TRANSLATION

I. PHYA GŚEN THEG PA

[extract from vol. *kha*, f. 184a[5] onwards]

mo rtsis gto dpyad bźi po la ||
spyi ru bśad daṅ sgos kyi bśad ||
spyi ru rnam graṅs bstan pa daṅ ||
sgos su ḥdus so ḥdzin pa gñis ||
thog mar spyiḥi rnam graṅs la ||
pra ltas mo yi mtshan ñid la ||
mo pra sum brgya drug cu mchis ||
rno[a] mthoṅ rtsis kyi mtshan ñid la ||
gab rtse sum brgya drug cu mchis ||
na gso gto yi mtshan ñid la
gto thabs sum brgya drug cu mchis ||
ḥchi bslu dpyad kyi mtshan ñid la ||
dpyad thabs ñi khri gcig stoṅ mchis ||
spyi ru bstan paḥi rnam graṅs ṅes ||
sgos su bsdus paḥi ḥdus so la ||
mo la rnam pa bźi yin te ||
ye srid ḥphrul gyi ju thig daṅ ||
ye mkhyen sgra blaḥi mṅon śes daṅ ||
ye rje [184b] smon paḥi rmi lam daṅ ||
ye dbaṅ lha yi bkaḥ bab daṅ ||
rnam pa bźi ru śes paı bya ||
rtsis la rnam pa bźi yin te ||
gab rtse ḥphrul gyi me loṅ daṅ ||
spar kha sme ba gliṅ skor daṅ ||
ḥbyuṅ ba[b] dus kyi ḥkhor lo daṅ ||
ju źag rten ḥbrel las rtsis daṅ ||
rnam pa bźi ru śes par bya ||
gto la rnam pa bźi yin te ||
ḥbyuṅ ba ḥkhrugs paḥi yo gto daṅ ||
mdos cha rten ḥbrel brdeg gto daṅ ||
bag ñan zlog paḥi thun gto daṅ ||
mñam gñis bsor baḥi brje gto daṅ ||
rnam pa bźi ru śes par bya ||
dpyad la rnam pa bźi yin te ||
rgyu rkyen mthoṅ la dpyad pa daṅ ||

[a] snaṅ [b] baḥi

THE WAY OF THE SHEN OF PREDICTION

FOR the four subjects of (i) sortilege, (ii) astrological calculation, (iii) ritual, and (iv) diagnosis, there are explanations in general and in particular—an explanation of general lists and a concentration on particulars. These are the two matters of consideration.

First we deal with general lists:

In characterizing sortilege, which is the divining of prognostics, there are 360 sortilege prognostics.

In characterizing astrological calculation, which perceives so sharply, there are 360 horoscopes.

In characterizing rites of curing illness, there are 360 methods.

In characterizing diagnosis, which provides ransoms[1] for death, there are 21,000 methods of diagnosis.

Such indeed are the lists explained in general.

As for concentrating on particulars,
there are four kinds of sortilege:
(*a*) the knot-sortilege[2] of *Ye-srid-ḥphrul*,
(*b*) the clairvoyance of *Ye-mkhyen sgra-bla*,
(*c*) the dream of *Ye-rje smon-pa*
(*d*) the soothsaying of *Ye-dbaṅ-lha.*
So they are to be known as of four kinds.

There are four kinds of astrological calculation:
(*a*) the mirror of mysterious horoscopes,[3]
(*b*) the *sPar-kha* and *sMe-ba* circle,
(*c*) the Time Wheel of the Elements,
(*d*) calculations of combinations and effects by (the method known as) *ju-źag.*[4]
Thus they are known as of four kinds.

There are four kinds of ritual:
(*a*) the 'Awry' Rite for the elements in disorder,
(*b*) the 'Striking' Rite using a combination of devices,
(*c*) the 'Harrying'[5] Rite for overcoming evil influences,
(*d*) the 'Exchange' Rite of transposing two equal things.
Thus they are known as four kinds.

There are four kinds of diagnosis:
(*a*) Diagnosis by seeing the chief and subsidiary causes,

ṅos ḥdzin rtsa la dpyad pa daṅ ||
phan gnod chu la dpyad pa daṅ ||
ḥchi sos khams la dpyad pa daṅ ||
rnam pa bźi ru śes par bya ||
mo rtsis gto dpyad bźi bo las ||
kun gyi thog mar mo yi sṅa ||
ye srid ḥphrul gyi rgyal po daṅ ||
kun śes ḥphrul gyi draṅ mkhan gñis ||
mṅon śes phyaḥu g·yaṅ dkar gsum ||
srid paḥi pra ltas gtan la phabs ||

bden brdzun las kyi draṅ śan phyes ||
mthoṅ daṅ mi mthoṅ brtag tshad dbab ||
de la dpyad ciṅ chag la gźal ||
chag la gźal ciṅ rtsis la gdab[a] ||
sṅa phyi da ltaḥi yin tshul daṅ ||
skyon yon tshe tshad gtan la dbab ||
bzaṅ ṅan phan gnod graṅs su gzuṅ[b] ||
graṅs su bzuṅ źiṅ rtsis la gdab[c] ||
mo daṅ rtsis la bla bzuṅ nas ||
bar du gso rkyen gto yis byed ||
med la yod daṅ stoṅ la gaṅ ||
ḥgrib la ḥphel daṅ ḥjig la chag ||
dbul la phyug daṅ ḥchi ba sos ||
gnod la phan daṅ mkho la rtsis ||
skye ḥgro de yis [185a] gso bar byed ||
tha mar las mthaḥ dpyad kyis sdud ||
mi bde tha mar bde bar sdud ||
na ba tha mar sos par sdud ||
gnod paḥi tha mar phan par sdud ||
ḥchi baḥi tha mar bslaṅ bar sdud ||
dug gi[d] tha mar rtsi ru sdud ||
las kyis chad na[e] ḥbrel bar sdud ||
kun rdzob thabs la[f] brten pa tsam ||
phya gśen thugs kyi dkyil du źog || ces gsuṅs so /
yaṅ ston pas bkaḥ stsal pa /
ñon cig legs rgyal thaṅ po ñon ||
de rnams graṅs kyi rim paḥo ||
da gñis pa ḥjug daṅ spyod pa ni ||
thog mar ḥjug paḥi rim pa la ||
sems skyed sñiṅ rjeḥi gźi bzuṅ nas ||
ḥgro la phan paḥi sems ldan źiṅ ||

[a] btabs [b] bzuṅ [c] btab [d] gis [e] las kyi ḥchad nas [f] las

(*b*) Identification by examination of the connecting channels,
(*c*) Diagnosis of the urine (to discover) what will be of use and what is causing harm,
(*d*) Diagnosis of (the patient's) appearance (to discover) whether he will die or be cured.

Thus they are known as four kinds.
Of these four, sortilege, calculation, ritual, and diagnosis, sortilege comes first as the foremost.

The three (gods) *Ye-srid-ḥphrul-gyi rgyal-po*, *Kun-śes-ḥphrul-gyi draṅ-mkhan*, and *mNon-śes phyaḥu g·yaṅ-dkar* arranged this divination of prognostics for the phenomenal world, making a straight-forward distinction of true and false effects.

Make an examination from what is seen and what is not seen.
On the basis of this diagnosis, make an estimate.
Having made an estimate, fix your calculations,
take stock of (the patient's) former, future, and present state, his disadvantages and his advantages.
Count up the good and bad points, the beneficial and the harmful ones.
Having counted them up, fix your calculations.
Relying on your sortilege and calculation,
you next act by means of the rite the conditions (necessary) for the cure.
Being for non-being, filling where there was emptiness,
increase for decrease, production for destruction,
wealth for poverty, recovery instead of death,
benefit instead of harm, by thus accounting (to him)
whatever is required, by these means you cure the person concerned.
Finally as the end of the effects he is integrated by means of the diagnosis.
As the end of unhappiness he is integrated in happiness.
As the end of sickness he is integrated in recovery.
As the end of harm he is integrated with what benefits.
As the end of death he is integrated in being raised up.
As the end of poison he is integrated with elixir.
If anything is broken by his karmic effects, it is now integrated by being brought into union.
(All this) is just reliance on methods which refer to relative truth.
Phya-gśen, keep it in your mind!

Again the Teacher (Shen-rab) said:

Listen, *Legs-rgyal Thaṅ-po*, listen!
Those items have been ordered in lists.
Now secondly as for setting to work and practising,
at the start of the process of setting to work
raise your Thought towards Enlightenment and keep compassion as your basis,
and with your mind intent on benefiting living beings,

mo rtsis gto dpyad gaṅ bslab kyaṅ ||
mkhas par bya la śes par bslab[a] ||
mkhas pas gnod la gñen par bya ||
brñas par byuṅ na gyoṅ por sdod ||
ḥdun par byuṅ na ran tshod ḥdzin ||
gus par byuṅ[b] na legs par bslab ||
rgol ba byuṅ na phyi śul gcod ||
rtsod pa byuṅ na ṅaṅ thag bsriṅ[c] ||
ḥgran[d] par byuṅ na ṅaṅ gis gźag[e] ||
phan par byuṅ yaṅ ṅa bo spaṅ[f] ||
gnod par byuṅ yaṅ źom par gźil ||
ḥthad par byuṅ yaṅ raṅ sor gźag[g] ||
mi ḥthad byuṅ yaṅ thabs kyis spaṅ[h] ||
khro gtum can la bźin mi bzlog ||
g·yo sgyu can la ḥdzum mi ston ||
bslu brid can la mtshar mi bźad ||
log khrid can la kha mi ya ||
draṅ por smra la ṅag mi bskuṅ ||
g·yo can tshig la mchid ma byin ||
rdzun chen gtam gyi rjes mi ḥbreṅ ||
mtho sar phyin kyaṅ dmaḥ mo bskyaṅ ||
chen po red kyaṅ dmaḥ mo bskyaṅ ||
mkhas par byuṅ yaṅ mi śes khrid ||
goms par yod kyaṅ tshod la brtag ||
[185b] ḥbul tshogs che yaṅ śed mi bskyed[i] ||
chuṅ yaṅ sems bskyed rim par bya ||
gaṅ du mi bzod de daṅ bstun ||
raṅ daṅ tshod kha thabs daṅ sbyor ||
mod par mi bya dkon par ḥtshaṅs ||
dkon par mi bya bden par bkrol ||
spyir ni rgyu ḥbras bon rnams la ||
sems bskyed gźi ma med pa na ||
gaṅ yaṅ rgyu yi ḥbras mi ḥtshol ||
don dam rñed pa[j] ga la ḥgyur ||
rgyu yi bon la gtogs lags kyaṅ ||
byaṅ chub sems kyis ṅaṅ thag bsriṅ ||
de nas ḥgro la phan thog ḥbyuṅ ||
lag len med paḥi tshod mdaḥ spaṅ[k] ||
śes so bsam paḥi che ba spaṅ[k] ||
mkhas so bsam paḥi dregs pa spaṅ[k] ||

[a] bslabs [b] ḥbyuṅ [c] bsriṅs [d] ḥgren [e] ḥgren [f] spaṅs [g] bźag
[h] kyi spaṅs [i] skyed [j] par [k] spaṅs

whatever you learn of sortilege, calculation, rites, and diagnosis,
be clever and learn so as to know it!
A clever man should turn harmful things to good use.
If others would contemn you, stay stern.
If people agree with you, take a right measure in their regard.
If some show devotion, instruct them well.
If some oppose you, cut off future trace of them.
If there are arguments, be long-suffering.
If others would vie with you, be indifferent to them.
Although you benefit others, avoid pride.
Although you cause harm, get rid of despondency.
If things turn out well, accept them as they are.
If things turn out ill, find a method to avoid them.
Do not turn your face away from an angry man.
Do not show a smiling countenance to one who comes with deceiving words.
Do not laugh in wonderment at a man who deceives.
Do not reply to one who tempts you.
Do not conceal your words from a man who speaks honestly.
Do not give reply to deceiving words.
Do not follow after false rumours.
Although you reach a high position, protect lowly people.
Although you are great, protect lowly people.
Although you are clever, guide those who do not know.
Although you are experienced, watch your own measure.
Although large offerings are made to you, do not act the big man.
Although they are small, raise your Thought towards Enlightenment in the proper way.
Where no one is patient[6] continue to act kindly.
Apply yourself suitably in due measure and with skill.
Do not do too much. Treat (your learning) as precious.
But do not do too little. Explain things truly.
If as a general rule both in the *Bon* of Cause and the *Bon* of Effect, you do not raise your Thought towards Enlightenment as your basic intent, you will not gain anywhere the (higher) effects of the (worldly) causes.[7] So how should one obtain the highest truth?
Although one is concerned here with the *Bon* of Cause, keep going all the time with the Thought of Enlightenment.
Thence benefit will come to living beings.
Avoid unskilful precipitancy.
Avoid the self-esteem of thinking one knows.
Avoid the pride of thinking one is clever.

gźan la ḥdzug paḥi tsher ma spaṅ[a] ||
raṅ la bstod paḥi ḥphyar g·yeṅ spaṅ[a] ||
mi śes pa yi pho rgo spaṅ[a] ||
mi mthun pa yi bya ba spaṅ[a] ||
mi ḥgro ba yi yas stags spaṅ[a] ||
ma mthoṅ ba yi rdzun bu spaṅ[a] ||
ma rig pa yi dom chol spaṅ[a] ||
mi śes pa yi kha bo spaṅ[a] ||
ma phyin pa yi lo rgyus spaṅ[a] ||
ma myoṅ ba yi lag len spaṅ[a] ||
mi ḥdra ba yi las spyod spaṅ[a] ||
mi ldan pa yi ḥdod bźed spaṅ[a] ||
spyir yaṅ g·yo daṅ sgyu med ciṅ ||
blun poḥi gseb du mkhas pa rmoṅs ||
mi śes pa la phal daṅ ḥdra ||
ma rig pa ⟨la⟩ gser yaṅ rdo ||
de phyir mkhas pa mkhas gral btsun ||
mo rtsis gto dpyad gaṅ spyod kyaṅ ||
ḥjug daṅ bslab rim spaṅ[b] daṅ blaṅ ||
dgos paḥi rim pa de ltar bya ||
de nas mkhas śiṅ goms pa daṅ ||
ḥdris śiṅ rgyud la brten pa des ||
thabs mkhas lag len ldan pa de ||
mkhas par yoṅs su bkur gnas ḥbyuṅ ||
gaṅ źig de las de spros paḥi ||
[186a] phya gśen theg paḥi hgro ba ḥdren ||
snaṅ srid dgaḥ bde bskyed pa yis[c] ||
dpag med rgya cher ḥphel bar ḥgyur || ces gsuṅs so /
yaṅ gsuṅs pa /
ñon cig legs rgyal thaṅ po ñon ||
thog mar ḥjug tshul de ltar la ||
bar du spyod paḥi rim pa ni ||
mo rtsis gto dpyad bźi po la ||
daṅ po mo pra brtag pa yaṅ ||
gźi ma liṅ phyiṅ dkar po la[c] ||
sṅon mo nas kyi sbran ma blug ||
mtsho ro g·yu yi sgron ma btag ||
li mar mdaḥ yi srog mkhar btsug ||
bdud rtsiḥi śiṅ gi dud par sbreṅ ||
dri źim spos kyi gśegs śul mtshon ||
phye mar ḥol kon phud kyis mchod ||

[a] spaṅs [b] las [c] paḥi

Avoid pricking thorns into others.
Avoid the relaxation of being pleased with yourself.
Avoid the insolence of one who does not know.
Avoid acts which do not fit the occasion.
Avoid ritual items which are unsuitable.
Avoid untruths of things unseen.
Avoid ignorant gossip.
Avoid ignorant 'big talk'.
Avoid news of where you have not been.
Avoid techniques in which you are inexperienced.
Avoid unsuitable activities.
Avoid desiring what you do not possess.
In all things be free from deceit.
In the company of fools a clever man (appears) foolish.
To those who do not know he seems quite ordinary.
To the ignorant gold may seem as stone.
Therefore it is good for a clever man to be among clever men.

Sortilege, calculation, ritual, diagnosis, whichever of these you do, you must follow the required order,
avoiding or accepting (as occasion demands) in starting (this work) and in the order of instruction.
Thus by being skilled and accomplished,
experienced and self-reliant, clever in method and skilful,
such a man will be honoured for his skill.
As for what spreads forth from this, he acts thereby as guide in the Way of the Shen of Prediction, producing happiness in the phenomenal world and causing it to spread wide and boundless.

Again he said:

Listen, *Legs-rgyal Thaṅ-po*, listen!
The way of setting about this work is as above.
Now next we deal with the order of operation.
Of sortilege, calculation, ritual and diagnosis,
first we consider the prognostics of sortilege.
On a piece of white felt which serves as the basis
one places the 'sprinklings' of green barley,
and one sets up the 'symbol of life', the bronze-tipped arrow, to which is attached a turquoise ornament.
There are wafts of smoke from the incense-wood,
marking the way taken by the sweet-smelling incense.
Worship with an offering of the sacrificial heap of barley-flour and butter.

g·yu ḥbraṅ bdud rtsi skyems kyis gsol ||
sgrub gśen dbal bon smraṅ gis[a] bkrol ||
lha chen phu wer dkar po mchod ||
ye srid ḥphrul gyi ju thig bdar ||
ye mkhyen sgra blaḥi mṅon śes bsgrub[b] ||
ye rje smon paḥi rmi lam brtag ||
ye bdaṅ lha yi bkaḥ dbab[c] bya ||
sṅa staṅs[d] thams cad miṅ nas bzuṅ ||
phyi staṅs[e] thams cad thig la btab ||
skyon yon tshe tshad yi ger bris ||
bzaṅ ṅan legs ñes draṅ śan phyes ||
bden rdzun srid paḥi gzu bor[f] bya ||
gaṅ la gaṅ dgos ci bźin du ||
phan gdab rim pa de ltar bya ||

gñis pa gab rtse brtsi ba la ||
za ḥog ber gyi gdan steṅ du ||
rtsis kyi śo[g] gźi khra bo bkod ||
rtsis kyi śo[h] rdo dkar nag bkram ||
ye srid lha dbaṅ rgyal po mchod ||
ḥbyuṅ ba dus kyi lha mo bṙṅan ||
dbaṅ chen bdag por mṅaḥ yaṅ gsol ||
de nas chag la gźal te brtsi ||
gab rtse ḥphrul gyi me loṅ blta[i] ||
spar kha[j] sme ba gliṅ skor bya ||
ḥbyuṅ ba dus kyi ḥkhor lo brtsi ||
[186b] ju źag srid paḥi rten ḥbrel brtag ||
brtag ciṅ rig pas dpyad ciṅ dbye ||
sṅa phyi da ltaḥi yin tshul daṅ ||
rgyu daṅ rkyen las srid tshul daṅ ||
las daṅ smon lam mthun tshul daṅ ||
bskal srid ḥbyuṅ baḥi ḥgyur[k] tshul daṅ ||
rten ḥbrel sṅon la dbaṅ tshul daṅ ||
nam zla[l] dus bźiḥi ḥgyur tshul daṅ ||
lha bdud kluṅ[m] rtaḥi dar rgud daṅ ||
skyon yon las kyi ḥphen len daṅ ||
dge sdig tshe tshad chag tshad daṅ ||
lo zla źag graṅs dus tshod daṅ ||
ḥphel daṅ ḥgrib paḥi mtshan ñid rnams ||
mkhas par byas la dal bar rtsi ||

[a] gi [b] bsgrubs [c] bab [d] staṅ [e] ltaṅ [f] gzuḥo [g] śog
[h] śod [i] lta [j] par kham [k] gyur [l] sla [m] sruṅs

Worship with the sacrificial offering of consecrated *chang*.
The officiating priest[8] should recite the exposition.[9]
Worship the great god *Phu-wer dkar-po*.
Invoke the knot-sortilege of *Ye-srid-ḥphrul*.
Produce (within yourself) the clairvoyance of *Ye-mkhyen sgra-bla*.
Reflect upon the dream of *Ye-rje smon-pa*.
Effect the soothsaying of *Ye-dbaṅ-lha*.
Name everything that has happened in the past (of your client).
Set in order everything referring to the future.
Write down evils and benefits (to come) and the length of his life.
Distinguish in a straightforward way the good and the bad, the fair and the foul.
Truth and falsehood there may be, but make true distinction.
Such is the way of benefiting people,
according as each may require.

Secondly for calculating the horoscopes,
on a cloth (made) of a piece of brocade silk
one must set the squared calculating board,
arrange the white and black pieces.
Worship *Ye-srid lha-dbaṅ rgyal-po*.
Requite the goddesses of the Elements and Time-Periods.
Pray to *dBan-chen bdag-po*.
Then make an estimate and calculate.
Look in the mystic mirror of the horoscope.
Work the *sPar-kha sMe-ba* Circle.
Calculate the cycles of the Elements and the Time Periods.
Examine the combinations occurring by (the method) *ju-źag*.
Examining them, identify and distinguish them knowledgeably:
the former, past and present state,
the way it comes about from major and minor causes,
the way events and prayers have corresponded,
ways of change in Time, Existence and the Elements,
the way these influence former combinations,
ways of change in the Four Seasons,
Strength and weakness of gods, demons and *kluṅ-rta*,[10]
avoiding and accepting the effects of evils and benefits,
an estimate of good and bad and of length of life,
the characteristics of increase and decrease
of the years, the months, the days, the hours,
a wise man must do this and calculate it quietly.

gaṅ du gnod pa ṅos kyis bzuṅ ||
gaṅ la ḥphan pa brda yis sprad ||
gaṅ daṅ mthun paḥi rten ḥbrel bsgrig ||
gaṅ du ḥbyuṅ ba yi ger btab ||
sems can ḥgro la phan gdag bya ||

gsum pa gto yis gso ba la[a] ||
ḥgro ba ma rig sems can rnams ||
spar kha[b] lo skor sme ba gliṅ ||
ḥbyuṅ ba dgra gśed ḥkhrugs pa daṅ ||
stoṅ gsum ḥkhrugs paḥi yo gto bya ||
gtsaṅ maḥi sa las ma ḥdal daṅ ||
sa tshon sna lṅas dal du bris ||
rtsi śiṅ bal tshon dar sna lṅa ||
ḥbru snaḥi bśos gtsaṅ dkar mṅar phud ||
ḥbyuṅ ba dus kyi lha mo mchod ||
rgyal baḥi[c] bden pa smraṅ gis bkrol ||
ḥbyuṅ ba sñiṅ phur ḥkhrugs[d] pa bsal ||
ḥkhrugs[e] pa gnas su mñam par bźag ||

sems can mi rnams dbul ḥphoṅs pa[f] ||
tshe dpal bsod nams bskyed paḥi phyir ||
mdos cha rten ḥbrel brdeg gto bya ||
gźi ma gtsaṅ maḥi steṅ du ni ||
ḥbru yis g·yuṅ druṅ ḥkhyil ba bris ||
mdos cha phya rten g·yaṅ rten bśams ||
gser skyems brṅan cha[g] g·yu ḥbraṅ phud ||
phya g·yaṅ dpal gyi lha brgyad mchod ||
[187a] bon rnams thams cad rten ciṅ ḥbrel ||
rten ciṅ ḥbrel baḥi ya ka brjod ||
ḥgro la phan bdes[h] gso bar bya ||

ḥgro drug sems can thams cad ni ||
kag la bab ciṅ ḥchi bar ñen ||
kag las thar daṅ ñes bzlog phyir ||
pra mtshan rig pas bsnun paḥi[i] gto ||
bdud btsan ma mo gśin rje daṅ ||
tshe bdud kag sri srog bdud la ||
tshe bslu srog gtaḥ[j] srog mkhar gzugs ||
tshe skyin srog glud lan chags ḥjal ||
tshe dpal skyob paḥi lha brgyad mchod ||
bab ñen bzlog ciṅ kag las[k] thar ||

[a] las [b] par kha [c] ba [d] khrug [e] ḥkhrug [f] ḥphon bas
[g] mṅon cha [h] bde [i] pa [j] gtam [k] la

He must identify harm wherever it is,
and explain benefits wherever they are,
and arrange whatever combinations can be brought into accord.
He must write down whatever will happen,
and so bring benefit to living beings.

Thirdly as for making cures by means of rites
for living beings, ignorant creatures,
when *sPar-kha*, Year-Cycle, the *sMe-ba* sphere,
and antagonistic elements are in disarray,
one must perform the 'Awry' Rite for the Universe in disarray.
Draw a magic circle with clean sand,
a circle drawn with sand of five colours.
(Set up) twigs with coloured wools and silk of five colours.

Make a first offering of a pure sacrificial cake made from different grains, and of the three milk and the three sweet substances.
Worship the goddesses of the Elements and the Time-Periods.
Recite as a prayer some true expositions of the Conqueror.
Thus the completely disarrayed elements will be quietened,
And everything disarrayed will be put in place.

In order to produce long life, happiness and good fortune for those creatures wretched men,
Perform the 'Striking' Rite, combining use of ritual devices.
On some clean place as working-base draw a swastika in grain.
Prepare the devices for the rite, the implements and talismans.
Offer libations, gifts and consecrated *chang*.
Worship the eight gods of Prediction and Good Fortune
And bring all phenomenal elements into interrelation.
Pronounce the blessing of interrelationship,
and beings will be cured with benefits and happiness.

When beings of the Six Spheres
Are struck with an impediment and come near to death,
in order to save them from impediments and reverse this evil, (use) the 'Stinging' Rite which works by knowledge of prognostic signs.
For devils, fiends, she-demons, spirits of death,
devils which attack man's length of days, sprites which cause impediments, and devils which attack the life-force,
(against these) establish life-ransoms, life-pledges and amulets.
Pay debts of evil with life-ransoms as payment for life.
Worship the eight gods who preserve life and happiness. Reverse the troubles that befall men and save them from their impediments.

ḥchi ba bslus śiṅ srog mkhar ḥtshugs ||
ḥgro la phan bde dgaḥ ba bskyed ||
ḥgro ba sems can thams cad la ||
lha srin za kha sdaṅ ba daṅ ||
sde brgyad byol kha bab pa daṅ ||
mñam gñis bsor baḥi brje gto bya ||
mdos daṅ yas stags rdzas rnams bsag ||
sku glud riṅ tshad ṅar mi daṅ ||
nam rgyaṅ mdaḥ ḥphaṅ śiṅ ris daṅ ||
pho thoṅ mo thoṅ mtshe ñuṅ daṅ ||
mi nor yul mkhar ḥdod yon daṅ ||
mñam gñis brjes na glud re bzaṅ ||
mtshuṅs gñis bsor na skyin re ḥdam[a] ||
rgyal ba ḥphags paḥi tshogs rnams la ||
phyag ḥtshal mchod ḥbul skyabs ḥgro bya ||
glud yas bden pas bkrol te ḥbul ||
tshe zad dus la bab gyur yaṅ ||
lo gsum bar du bźol bar ḥgyur ||
ḥgro la phan phyir gto yis gso ||
ḥbul ba yon gyis mñes par bya ||
gto yi phan thabs bstan paḥo ||

bźi pa dpyad kyis ḥtsho ba la ||
ḥgro drug sems can ma rig pa ||
ñon moṅs nad kyis gduṅ ba la ||
nad la dpyad kyis phan paḥi phyir ||
sman pa byaṅ chub sems [187b] ldan gyis ||
tshad med bźi yi sems bskyed nas ||
rgyal baḥi tshogs la skyabs su ḥgro ||
drin len mchod pa ma ḥdal ḥbul ||
saṅs rgyas sman lha mched brgyad daṅ ||
be du rgya ḥod rgyal po mchod ||
mkhas khyad lag len ldan pa yis ||
rgyu rkyen thams cad mthoṅ la dpyad ||
nad ṅos ḥdzin pa rtsa la dpyad ||
phan gnod thams cad chu la dpyad ||
ḥchi sos thams cad khams la dpyad ||
de ltar nad ṅos ḥdzin pa daṅ ||
tsha graṅs bad mkhris ḥdus pa las ||
bsil drod[b] sñoms paḥi sman sbyar nas ||
phye ma ri lu ḥde[c] gu daṅ ||

[a] bdam [b] gros [c] rde

Thus he is ransomed from death and fixed up with an amulet,
and so you produce benefits, joy and happiness for living beings.
For all living beings,
afflicted with attacks by the eight kinds of sprite,
by hating and consuming gods and demons,
you must perform the 'Exchange' Rite of transposing two equal things.
Prepare the ritual devices[11] and ritual items,
the right sized figurine as ransom for the (patient's) body,
the sky symbol, the tree symbol, the arrow, distaff, and the ritual stakes,
the male figure, the female figure, the rock-plant *mtshe*, and mustard-seed,
(a model of) the house and its wealth, the things one desires.
If they are exchanged as equal things, the ransom will be good.
If they are transposed as equivalents, they will be chosen as payment.
To the hosts of noble buddhas
make salutation, offerings and prayer for refuge.
Then offer the items of ransom, explaining them truly.
Although (your patient) is about to die,
you can delay his death for the space of three years.
In order to benefit beings, profit them by means of these rites.
They will make you happy with offerings and fees.
So the benefits of ritual have now been explained.

Fourthly in caring (for others) by means of diagnosis,
when the ignorant beings of the Six Spheres
suffer from diseases (arising from) molestations (*kleśa*),
in order to benefit them in their illness by diagnosis,
the physician with his Thought set on Enlightenment,
should raise his thought to the four immeasurable virtues,
take refuge in the hosts of buddhas,
and offer a *maṇḍala* in thanksgiving and worship.
He should worship the King *Be-du-rgya-'od* (*Vaiḍūrya*) and his eight fellow buddhas, gods of medicine.
Then he should diagnose the major and minor causes in all that can be seen,
and identify the disease by diagnosis of the connecting channels.
Diagnose from the urine what is of benefit and what is of harm.
Diagnose from the appearance all signs of death and signs of cure.
Thus identifying the disease,
Heat or cold, phlegm or bile, or some combination,
the medicine is then applied, cooling, warming, equalizing,
powder, pills, or syrup,

thaṅ daṅ byug daṅ sman mar daṅ ||
gaṅ la gaṅ sman [ḥgro ba] nad daṅ sbyar ||
tsha ba thams cad bsil gyis[a] ḥdul ||
graṅ ba thams cad drod kyis[b] ḥdul ||
bad kan thams cad gsiṅ gis dbye ||
mkhris pa can rnams bsdud kyis[c] byin ||
ḥdu ba ḥkhrugs na sñoms kyis[d] ḥdul ||

ḥdu ba ñi khri chig stoṅ la ||
ñi khri chig stoṅ sman sbyor gyis ||
ma rig ñon moṅs druṅs[e] nas ḥbyin ||
ḥtsho ba rnam pa bźi yin te ||
bdud rtsi sman gyis ḥtsho ba daṅ ||
lus gso sman gyis ḥtsho ba daṅ ||
thabs daṅ spyod lam ḥtsho ba daṅ ||
luṅ ma bstan gyis ḥtsho ba ḥo[f] ||

bcos la rnam pa bźi yin te ||
sman daṅ gtar daṅ me btsaḥ daṅ ||
thabs daṅ sṅags kyis[g] źi byed pa ||
gaṅ dgos nad kyi ṅo daṅ sbyar ||
[sman pa] ro daṅ nus pa źu baḥi rjes ||
ro yi drod daṅ nus pas drag ||
źu rjes ḥjam la des paḥo ||
nad la skyug daṅ bśal daṅ rjes ||
skyug gis ḥdren daṅ bśal bas[h] sbyaṅs ||
rjes śul źi daṅ bde baḥo ||
kha zas ḥbyor daṅ gnod daṅ sñoms ||
ḥbyor ba brten la gnod pa spaṅ[i] ||
sñoms kyi cha mñam ran tshod bzuṅ ||

dpyad la rtsa daṅ chu daṅ khams ||
rtsa la lta źiṅ chu la [188a] brtags ||
khams la dpyad ciṅ thig par bya ||
ṅes par ḥchi baḥi ltas mthoṅ na[j] ||
dkar po dge baḥi las la ḥbad ||
las kyis chad na gto dpyad rdug ||
nan tar[k] ḥchi baḥi dus byuṅ na ||
lus gso zas kyaṅ srog gi[l] bdud ||
de ltar ma lags[m] ḥphral rkyen daṅ ||
glo bur nad kyis gduṅ ba la ||
ḥtsho ba sman gyis[n] slus par ḥgyur ||

[a] gyi [b] gros kyi [c] kyi [d] sñom gyi [e] druṅ daṅ [g] kyi
[h] daṅ [i] paṅs [j] nas [k] tad [l] gis [m] lag [n] gyi

potion, ointment, or butter-mould.
Medicine for every man must fit with the disease.
All feverish conditions are counteracted by the cooling kind,
all cold conditions by the warming kind,
all phlegmatic conditions by the dispersing kind,
conditions of bile by the uniting kind,
combination disturbances by the equalizing kind.

For the 21,000 types of combinations
one applies 21,000 types of medicine,
and so expels the afflicted conditions of ignorance.

Treatment is of four main kinds:
treatment with medicine of elixir,
treatment with medicine for bodily cure,
treatment with method and practice,
treatment in unprescribed ways.

Curing is of four main kinds:
medicine, bleeding and branding,
tranquillizing with method and spells.

Whatever is required must accord with the type of disease.

After absorbing (the medicine) come taste and effect,
pleasance of taste and force of effect.
After absorption it is gentle and pleasant.
For the disease vomiting and excretion are the after-effects,
drawing it forth by vomiting and purifying by excretion,
and the after-state is tranquil and pleasant.
Food may be suitable, harmful, or indifferent.
Keep to what is suitable and avoid what is harmful,
taking the right measure of the part that is indifferent.

In diagnosis we have the connecting channels, the urine and the general appearance.
Watch the channels, examine the urine,
and diagnosing from the general appearance, let the result coincide.

If you are sure you see signs of death,
urge him to the practice of virtue.
If he is cut off by karmic effects, ritual and diagnosis are useless.

If it is certain his time of death has come,
Even food which should nourish the body may be his life's enemy.
But if it is not such a case, and he suffers from an accident or a sudden disease,
you will save him by treatment and medicine.

gal te thabs mkhas lag len daṅ ||
goms ḥdris ga dar ma soṅ na ||
sman du mi ḥgro dug du ḥgro ||
nad pa mi sos ḥchi yun thuṅ[a] ||
de phyir thabs mkhas lag len gces ||
de ltar mo rtsis dpyad gto[b] bźi ||
spyod daṅ ḥjug daṅ rtogs pa yis ||
sems can ḥgro la phan par bya ||
phya gśen legs rgyal thugs la źog ||
ces gsuṅs so /

[a] ḥthuṅ [b] daṅ

If your skill and cleverness of method
have not been perfected by practice,
you will not produce medicine, but poison.
You will not cure the sick man and he will die before long.
So skill and cleverness of method are very important.

So by practising, setting about and understanding these four, sortilege, astrological calculation, ritual and diagnosis,
living beings must be benefited.

Keep this in mind, O *Phya-gśen Legs-rgyal.*

This is what he said.

II. SNAṄ GŚEN GYI THEG PA

[vol. *kha*, f. 197a^5 onwards]

de la ston pas bkaḥ stsal pa /
ñon cig snaṅ gśen gtsug phud ñon /
snaṅ gśen theg paḥi bon sgo la ||
spyi ru rnam pa bźi yin te ||
chab nag chu bo sel gyi sgo ||
chab dkar ḥdre daṅ sri yi sgo ||
ḥphan yul mñam brje glud kyi sgo ||
dpon gsas phyva gñan gto yi sgo ||
de ltar gyer sgo bźi las su ||
gcoṅ brgyad skad kyis brda sprad nas ||
tshul daṅ lugs bźin spyod pa na ||
snaṅ ni snaṅ źiṅ srid pa snaṅ ||
gśen ni de dag ḥdul bas gśen ||
snaṅ gśen theg paḥi [197b] bon sgo yis ||
ḥgro ba[a] kha lo bsgyur baḥo ||
snaṅ gśen gtsug phud thugs la źog ||
ces gsuṅs so / de la yaṅ gsol pa /
thams cad mkhyen paḥi ston pa lags ||
de ltar snaṅ gśen theg pa las ||
gyer sgo bźi ru gsuṅs pa yi ||
de yi dbye ba ci ltar lags ||
de la gcoṅ brgyad skad sbyar nas ||
skad kyi rnam graṅs ci ltar lags ||
bdag cag rig paḥi blo rtsal źan ||
źib tu dbye nas bkaḥ bstsal ḥtshal ||
źes gsol to / de la rgyal bus bkaḥ stsal pa /
ñon cig snaṅ gśen gtsug phud daṅ /
ḥdus paḥi ḥkhor rnams thams cad kun ||
ma yeṅs dbaṅ po brtan par ñon ||
snaṅ gśen theg paḥi sgo bźi la ||
thog mar chab nag sel gyi sgo ||
de la rnam pa bźi yin te ||
chab nag chu bo gźuṅ chen las ||
smraṅ rgyud chu bźi gyes pa de ||
zad pa med paḥi rgya mtsho ḥdra ||
rgyun chad med pa chu bo ḥdra ||

[a] baḥi

II. THE WAY OF THE SHEN OF THE VISUAL WORLD

At that the Teacher said:

Listen, *sNaṅ-gśen gTsug-phud*, listen!
As for the *Bon* Portal of the Way of the Shen of the Visual World,
there are in general four types:[12]

(1) the 'Black Waters', the river, the portal of exorcism,
(2) the 'White Waters', the portal of demons and vampires,
(3) *ḥPhan-yul*, the portal of ransom by equal exchange,
(4) the 'Master Sage', the portal of Ritual for fates and furies.

Thus in this matter of the four portals of incantation,
indicating the terms with the sound of the eight ululations,
and performing according to form and to pattern,
the Visual World is so called because it is visible and existing,
and the Shen is referred to as Shen because he overcomes it.
By this means one guides living beings,
sNaṅ-gśen gTsug-phud, keep that in mind.

So he spoke. He was questioned again:

O Teacher, who know everything!
Thus in the Shen Way of the Visual World
There are four doors of incantation, you have told us.
What is the difference between them?
Then with reference to the sounds of the eight ululations,
What is the list of these sounds.
We are weak in intellectual understanding.
We beg you to tell us by explaining carefully.

Thus they asked him, and the Prince replied:

Listen, *sNaṅ-gśen gTsug-phud*
and all you who have gathered as his entourage.
Listen with senses unwavering and fixed.
Among the four portals of the Shen Way of the Visual World,
(1) first (we take) the Black Waters, the portal of exorcism.
This has four parts.
From the great lore of the Black Waters
four rivers separate themselves as streams of exposition.
It is like the inexhaustible ocean.
It is like a continuously flowing river.

ḥgro la phan pa char pa ḥdra ||
gar bsgyur bde ba chu phran ḥdra ||
skye ḥgro gso ba lu ma ḥdra ||
ḥphel kha chu bo ḥbrug pa ḥdra ||
yag pa lo tog legs[a] pa ḥdra ||

srid pa smraṅ chen sel gyi gźuṅ ||
thug khar gñan[b] po lhaḥi gźuṅ ||
sgra bla wer ma dpaḥ khrom gźuṅ ||
srid pa miḥu rgyud kyi gźuṅ ||
de chab nag chu bo gźuṅ bźi yin ||

de la so sor gyes pa las ||
sel la rnam pa bcu gñis te ||
rtsa dkar ḥphel baḥi yar sel bźi[c] ||
rtsa nag ḥgrib paḥi mar sel [daṅ] bźi ||
mñam ñid bsor[d] baḥi bar sel bźi ||
rtsa dkar ḥphel baḥi [198a] yar sel la ||
gaṅ la gaṅ ḥdul bon yin pas ||
sems can blo ṅos gsum daṅ sbyar ||
smaṅ la ḥphen par ḥdod pa la ||
g·yuṅ druṅ srid pa ḥphel sel bya ||
dbul la phyug par ḥdod pa la ||
srid pa ba gar gyen sel bya ||
khas ñan btsan por ḥdod pa la ||
kluṅ[e] rta dar baḥi gar sel bya ||
chuṅ la che bar ḥdod pa la ||
rgyal gyi khri ḥphaṅ goṅ sel bya ||
rtsa nag ḥgrib paḥi mar sel la ||
rmaṅ ste chad la khad pa la ||
ḥdre dgu sri[f] bcuḥi thur sel bya ||
dbul te ltog la khad pa la ||
srid paḥi sa bdag thur sel bya ||
rlag ste ñes la khad pa la ||
byur daṅ mi laḥi chu sel bya ||
dmaḥ ste lhuṅ la khad pa la ||
mtho ru mi ster ñen sel bya ||
mñam ñid bsor baḥi bar sel la ||
lha klu gñan[b] daṅ ḥgras pa na ||
lha mi bar gyi dbyen sel bya ||

[a] lag   [b] gñen   [c] daṅ   [d] gsal   [e] sruṅs   srid

It is like rain which benefits living beings.
It is like a stream which may be easily directed anywhere.
It is like a spring that succours living beings.
It is like a rising flood that gushes forth.
It is like a fine and good harvest.

(1A) The lore of exorcism—the great exposition of existence,
(1B) the lore of the gods—of the *Thug-khar* Furies,
(1C) the lore of the genies—of the hero-gathering of the *Wer-ma* Genies
(1D) the lore of the original human stream of existence,
these are the four river-like lores of the Black Waters.

(1A) Separating from each other,
there are twelve kinds of exorcism:
the four upward exorcisms of increase of the white channel,
the four downward exorcisms of decrease of the black channel,
the four intermediate exorcisms of transposing equivalents.
As for the upward exorcisms of increase of the white channel, they are the *bon* that overcomes whatsoever (opposes) anything, and they should be fitted to the three dispositions of beings.
If it is a matter of prospering the feeble,
perform the increase exorcism of swastika being.
If it is a matter of bringing wealth to replace poverty,
perform the upward exorcism of existence in the 'universal womb'.[13]
If you want strength instead of weakness,
perform the strong exorcism of the potent *kluṅ-rta*.
If you want greatness instead of being small,
perform the top exorcism of the royal throne.
As for the downward exorcisms of decrease of the black channel:
if being feeble, one is near one's end,
perform the downward exorcism of the nine demons and the ten vampires.
If being poor, one is near to hunger,
perform the downward exorcism of the local gods of the phenomenal world.
If being lost, one is near to harm,
perform the water exorcism of *byur* and *mi-la*.[14]
If being down, one is near to falling,
perform the exorcism of the calamity which does not let you go higher.
As for the four intermediate exorcisms by transposing equivalents:
if one is at enmity with gods, serpents and furies,
perform the exorcism of this dissension of gods, men and intermediate beings.

śin tu gag ñen rtsub pa la ||
bya dmar[a] mtshal buḥi gag sel bya ||
sme mnol mi gtsaṅ ḥbag pa la ||
dme mug nal gyi btsog sel bya ||
mi mthun pra ltas ṅan pa la ||
ltas ṅen bzlog paḥi than sel bya ||

de ltar gźuṅ chen bcu gñis la ||
sṅon srid pa gaṅ gis dar ba yiḥi ||
re re la yaṅ bcu re ste ||
srid paḥi dpe srol re daṅ sbyar ||
dpe srol re la sel sgo re ||
de la srid pa smraṅ gźuṅ re ||
sel sgo brgya daṅ ñi śu [re] dbye ||
de la skad kyi gcaṅ brgyad sbyar ||
daṅ po srid pa gsum po las ||
gtsaṅ sme blaṅ dor bźen ḥdebs pa ||
stag mo ṅar baḥi gcoṅ las draṅ[b] ||
de nas sel gyi smraṅ gyer baḥi ||
[198b] bya khyi rta yi gcoṅ[c] las draṅ[b] ||
bya skad sna tshogs ḥgyur ba yin ||
khyi skad zug daṅ ṅur[d] ba yin ||
rta skad ḥtsher daṅ sñan pa yin ||
gcoṅ gi sñan[e] ṅag legs[f] par bya ||

spyir yaṅ ḥgro drug sems can rnams ||
sdug bsṅal ñon moṅs gduṅ ba la ||
ñon moṅs nad rnams sel ba daṅ ||
bde baḥi don daṅ ldan pa daṅ ||
thabs daṅ thugs rje mi ḥgag phyir ||
gaṅ la bon sgo gaṅ ḥdul bstan ||
skyon yon legs ñes ma śes daṅ ||
gtsaṅ sme blaṅ dor ma phyed pas[g] ||
mi dge ñes paḥi gźi ma byuṅ ||

dme daṅ mug daṅ nal daṅ btsog ||
than daṅ ltas ṅan byur yug ḥbag ||
thab daṅ mkhon daṅ dbar la sogs ||
de dag lha yi spyan la phog ||
gtsaṅ ris lha la mnol phog pas ||
gźi gnas mṅa dbaṅ yul sa mnol ||
de yi grib chags kha rlaṅs rnams ||
ḥgro ba mi yi tshogs la phog ||

[a] mar   [b] draṅs   [c] smraṅ   [d] mdur   [e] bsñan   [f] leg   [g] daṅ

In the case of severe danger from an impediment,
perform the exorcism of the impediment of the Red Bird Vermilion.[15]
In the case of defilement from murder, adultery or other impurity,
perform the exorcism of this filth of murder, of fatherless child or of incest.
In the case of bad signs from unfavourable prognostics,
perform the exorcism of evil for the overpowering of evil signs.

Likewise for the twelve great lores
which spread forth originally,
for each of them there are ten again,
with an original archetype associated with each one,
and a way of exorcism for each archetype.
So for each original lore of exposition
there is subdivision into 120 ways of exorcism,
and with these are associated the eight ululations of sound.
First in the case of the three originals
for urging the acceptance of purity and rejection of defilement,
effect the ululation of the growling tigress.
Then for the incantation of the exposition of exorcism,
effect the ululation of bird and dog and horse.
There are various variable sounds of birds.
The sound of the dog is barking or growling.
The sound of the horse is neighing and pleasant.
The utterance of ululations must be done well.

In general when beings of the Six Spheres
are tormented with the afflictions of suffering,
in order to exorcise the diseases of their afflictions,
and to provide them with the substance of happiness,
and so that there should be no end of method and compassion,
show to whomever it is the *bon* way that quells whatsoever it is.

If one does not know harm from benefit and good from evil,
or distinguish purity from defilement and acceptance from rejection,
a basis for non-virtue and evil will result.
The impurities of murder, fatherless child, incest,
evils, bad signs, and defiling misfortunes,
defilement of the hearth, of animosity, anger and the rest,
they strike the eyes of the gods.
If defilement touches the gods of the Pure Abode,
the domains of the Lords of the Soil are defiled.
The vapours of their defilement
strikes upon the company of human beings,

ḥjig rten źiṅ hdir dbul ḥphoṅs daṅ ||
nad daṅ mu ge ḥkhrugs pa daṅ ||
mi bde sdug bsṅal sna tshogs ḥbyuṅ ||
de dag bsaṅ źiṅ[a] dag pa daṅ ||
ḥgro ba ma lus gso baḥi phyir ||
chab nag srid pa rgyud khog la ||
sel sgo śiṅ lo ḥdab rgyas byuṅ ||
dkar nag bsal bas sel źes bya ||
gtsaṅ sme bsal bas sel źes bya ||
sme mnol bsal bas sel źes bya ||
dme mug bsal bas sel źes bya ||
dbul ḥphoṅs bsal bas sel źes bya ||
ḥgag pa bsal bas sel źes bya ||
kag ñes bsal bas [199a] sel źes bya ||

de la bya thabs ḥdi lta ste ||
gnas daṅ rdzas daṅ bcaḥ gźi daṅ ||
gyer daṅ tha ma rjes bźiḥo ||
gnas ni mdo daṅ mdud la gtad ||
ḥgyiṅ daṅ ḥkhyil daṅ dpal daṅ mdud ||
ḥgyiṅ la rgyab gtad ḥkhyil par[b] bcaḥ ||
dpal la goṅ bstod mdud la ḥbor ||
rdzas ni bzaṅ źiṅ sna tshogs daṅ ||
bya spu bal tshon śel tshigs daṅ ||
ḥdod ḥjoḥi ba daṅ ḥdab chags bya ||
sprel dkar kloṅ grum ba dkar daṅ ||
bya ma byel bu la sogs bsag[c] ||
gźan yaṅ ḥbru snaḥi mchod pa daṅ ||
dkar mṅar śa khrag ḥdod yon rdzas ||
phun sum tshogs paḥi yo byad bsag ||
srid paḥi sel ra gñen por bskos ||
yar la yod kyi ral chen gsum ||
mar la med paḥi luṅ chen gsum ||
bar na lha mi ḥtshog paḥi gnas ||
lha gźi dkar poḥi steṅ du ni ||
sṅon mo nas kyi sbran ma[d] blug ||
lha mdaḥ sgro dkar rten la gzugs ||
sel bsal mchod paḥi yo byad bśams ||
srid paḥi sel bon smra chen gyis ||
dbu la ḥgyiṅ baḥi thod kyaṅ bciṅ ||

[a] ciṅ [b] pas [c] bsog [d] smran ma

and in this world region poverty, disease, famine, disturbances, unhappiness and sufferings of all kinds arise.

In order to cleanse them and clear them away
and in order to cure all beings,
inside this original stream of the Black Waters
there emerged the ways of exorcism spreading as branches, leaves and petals.
They are known as exorcisms (viz. cleansers) because they cleanse the white and the black.
They are known as exorcisms because they cleanse the pure from the foul.
They are known as exorcisms, because they cleanse filth and impurity.
They are known as exorcisms, because they cleanse the defilement of murder and of the fatherless child,
They are known as exorcisms, because they remove poverty.
They are known as exorcisms, because they remove obstructions.
They are known as exorcisms, because they remove impediments and evils.

Now the method of operation is like this:
(i) the place, (ii) the items and their arrangement,
(iii) the incantation, and (iv) lastly the final part.

As for the place, one must face towards the lower part of a valley and a cross-roads.
(There must be) a lofty mountain, an amphitheatre (formed by surroundin cliffs), some good ground and some cross-roads.
Turn your back to the lofty mountain and make preparations in the amphitheatre.
As good ground a raised place is commendable, and at the cross-roads you must leave (your ransom-offerings).

The items should be good ones and various:
birds' feathers, coloured wool, sacrificial barley,
a wish-granting cow and feathery fowl,
a white monkey, a badger, and a white cow,
a bat, and other such things should be gathered together.

Furthermore an offering of green barley,
the three milk-products, the three sweet offerings, flesh and blood, and other desirable offerings,
these are the excellent necessaries to be gathered together.

Set up as an aid the original exorcizing ring.
Above the three great high vales of being,
below the three great low vales of non-being,
in between the place where gods and men may come together,
(here) on the white sacred mat
place the 'sprinklings' of green barley.
Set up as symbol the divine arrow with the white feather.
Prepare the necessaries for offering to the pure divinities of the exorcizing rite.
The great speaker of the original exorcizing *bon*
binds the turban on his head.

źal na skyem paḥi skyems yaṅ gsol ||
phyag na ḥbul baḥi yon kyaṅ ḥbul ||
źal nas gcoṅ gis smraṅ kyaṅ gyer ||
mi ḥgro yas stags spaṅ bar bya ||
smraṅ ni źib la rgyas par bya ||
chab nag nus pa smraṅ la ḥbyuṅ ||
chab dkar nus pa sṅags la ḥbyuṅ ||
dpon gsas nus pa rin chen yin ||
de phyir chab nag smraṅ gis gtso ||
rjes kyi bya ba yag [199b] ka brjod ||
sems can ḥgro la sman par mdzod ||
ḥgro ba gaṅ la gaṅ phan gyis ||
sems bskyed gźi ma ldan par gces ||
snaṅ gśen gtsug phud thugs la źog ||
ces gsuṅs so /

ñon cig snaṅ gśen gtsug phud ñon ||
gñis pa thug khar lha gźuṅ la ||
ḥgro drug sems can thams cad ni ||
mi bde sdug bsṅal gduṅ ba la ||
thug khar lha yi dmag tshogs brṅan[a] ||
de la[b] rnam pa bźi yin te ||
ye srid lha gźuṅ dkar po daṅ ||
ye dbaṅ gñan[c] gźuṅ khra bo daṅ ||
ye ḥdul dmag gźuṅ nag po gsum ||
thog mar lha gźuṅ dkar po la ||
lha ḥkor gsum brgya drug cu yod ||
bar pa gñan[c] gźuṅ khra bo la ||
lha ḥkhor gñis brgya lṅa bcu yod ||
tha ma dmag gźuṅ nag po la ||
lha ḥkhor brgya daṅ rtsa brgyad yod ||
de gsum gcig tu dril ba yi ||
thug khar dgu khri gliṅ mkhar yin ||
dgu khri gliṅ mkhar nam mkhaḥi rdzoṅ ||
nam mkhaḥ yaṅs paḥi gsas mthoṅ na ||
raṅ grub rin chen sprul paḥi mkhar ||
rmeṅ gźi rin chen gser la byas ||
logs bźi lo phrom bse la byas ||
zur bźi sṅo mñen[c] lcags la byas ||
sgo gźi ba le duṅ la byas ||

[a] sman [b] las [c] gñen

In his mouth he receives the draught that is to be drunk.
In his hand he offers the thing that is to be offered.
With his voice he intones the exposition using ululations.
Unsuitable ritual items must be avoided.
The exposition must be done carefully in full.
The potency of the 'Black Waters' emerges in the exposition.[16]
The potency of the 'White Waters' emerges in the spells.
The potency of the Master-Sages is a gem.
So for the 'Black Waters' exposition is the most important thing.

As the final part recite the blessing.
Do good to living beings.
Do whatever is of benefit to them.
It is essential to raise your Thought towards Enlightenment as the basis (of your action).
sNaṅ-gśen gTsug-phud, keep this in mind.

This is what he said.

Listen, *sNaṅ-gśen gTsug-phud*, listen!
(1B) Secondly as for the sacred lore of *Thug-khar*,[17]
all the beings of the Six Spheres,
when afflicted with unhappiness and suffering,
should requite the army of the *Thug-khar* gods.
Of these there are four [*sic*] kinds:
the White Lore of the Gods of eternal existence,
the Dappled Lore of the Furies of eternal power,
the Black Lore of the Armies of eternal subjugation, these are the three.
First in the White Lore of the Gods
there is an entourage of 360 gods.
Secondly in the Dappled Lore of the Furies
there is an entourage of 250 gods.
Lastly in the Black Lore of the Armies
there is an entourage of 108 gods.
These three (sets) gathered together
are the *Thug-khar* 'Island Citadel of the 90,000'.
The 'Island Citadel of the 90,000' is a sky-fort.
In the divine vault of the spacious sky
is a self-produced magic citadel of gems.
Its four foundation-supports are made of gems and gold.
Its four walls are made of burnished copper.
Its four corners are made of supple steel.
Its four doors are made of *ba-le*[18] shells.

kha bad mtsho ro g·yu la byas ||
rdo rje bźin gyi brtan cig yod ||
ri bo bźin gyi brjid cig yod ||
nam mkhaḥ bźin gyi gsal cig yod[a] ||
bar snaṅ bźin gyi yaṅ cig yod[a] ||
ñi ma bźin gyi dro cig yod ||
zla ba bźin gyi bsil [200a] cig yod ||
lho sprin bźin gyi phon[b] cig yod ||
rgyu[c] skar bźin gyi bkrag cig yod ||
yod pa ye yod mtshams na[d] yod ||
bzuṅ ba thug khar lha yis[e] bzuṅ ||

mkhar de srid pa phyin cad nas ||
da lta diṅ saṅs phan chad la ||
g·yuṅ druṅ bstan pa ñams ma myoṅ ||
lha miḥi dbu ḥphaṅ dmaḥ ma myoṅ ||
sdaṅ baḥi dgra bos brgol ma myoṅ ||
gnod paḥi bgegs kyis tshugs mi srid ||

thug khar bu dgu yab daṅ bcu ||
dguṅ sman mched bdun yum daṅ brgyad ||
dgu khri dgu ḥbum dmag daṅ bcas ||
ḥphel chen yag ka[f] brjod na dgos ||
śas chen dmag la chas na dgos ||
rgyug chen bya rdaṅ bkyag na dgos ||
lha dmag dgra la bśig na dgos ||
rgyal po rgyal sa gnon na dgos ||
btsun mo rtsa dkar ḥphel na dgos ||
blon po dar sa ḥdzin na dgos ||
yo ma ḥphel kha rtsi na dgos ||
de dgos paḥi do gal che brgyad yin ||

snaṅ gśen srid paḥi bon po yis ||
rgyud las ḥbyuṅ baḥi bon spyod ciṅ ||
rigs su mchod paḥi lha bdar nas ||
sems can ḥgro la phan gdag[g] nas ||
thug khar lha rabs gźuṅ bźi las ||
gyer daṅ bsgrub daṅ mchod brṅan bkyag ||
gaṅ du byed paḥi las ño loṅ ||
dben daṅ gtsaṅ maḥi gnas ñid du ||
sme daṅ mnol ba ma phog par ||
gtsaṅ maḥi sa la dkyil ḥkhor bźeṅs ||
mchod paḥi rdzas daṅ yo byad bśam ||

[a] dgos [b] phan [c] sgyun [d] ḥtshams nas [e] yi [f] ya ga [g] bdag

Its protruding eaves are made of turquoise.
It is firm as a powerbolt (*vajra*).
It is magnificent as a mountain.
It is translucent as the sky.
It is spacious as the atmosphere.
It is glowing as the sun.
It is cool as the moon.
It is dense as a cloud from the south.
It is brilliant as the constellations.
As for its existence, it exists at the limit of eternal existence.

As for those who hold it, it is held by the *Thug-khar* gods.
From the time that that citadel came into being
up until the present time,
the swastika doctrine has experienced no weakening,
the dignity of gods and men has experienced no abasement,
there has been no opposition from hateful enemies,
there has been no attack from harmful demons.

The nine *Thug-khar* sons—with their father totalling ten,
the seven celestial goddesses of medicine—with their mother totalling eight,
together with their army 99,000 strong,
when reciting a blessing for prosperity, we need them.
Especially when going to war, we need them.
When presenting the 'bird-rack'[19] of the Great Runner, we need them.
When the royal army would destroy the enemy, we need them.
When the king would subdue the kingdom, we need them.
When the queen would induce pregnancy, we need them.
When the minister would gain influence, we need them.
When we reckon prosperity by mares, we need them.
These are the eight important times when we need them.

The *bonpos* of the original (way of the) Shen of the Visual World
should perform the *bon* which comes by tradition,
invoking the gods who are to be worshipped in such cases,
and benefiting living beings.
According to the fourfold lore of the divine *Thug-khar* lineage,
they intone, they bring the divinity to their presence, and they make offerings of requital.
Undertake the rite wherever it is to be done,
in a lonely and clean place.
Avoiding filth and impurity,
lay out the magic circle on clean ground.
Arrange the ritual items and necessaries.

ltag śa sñiṅ khrag dam rdzas bsag ||
mdaḥ dar me loṅ rin chen daṅ ||
bla bre[a] ḥphan gdugs rgyal mtshan daṅ ||
zur gsum bśos gtsaṅ [200b] phud kyis mchod ||
rṅa gśaṅ duṅ gliṅ skad kyis[b] ḥbod ||
dri źim ṅad ldan śul gyis[c] mtshon ||
tshig bśad gtaṅ rag dbyaṅs kyis[b] bkrol ||
thugs kyi[d] sñiṅ po ḥdzab nas bgraṅ[e] ||
sku gsuṅ yon tan sgo nas bstod ||
ḥphrin las rnam bźi drag tu bcol ||
g·yuṅ druṅ bstan pa dar bar bcol ||
gśen rab dbu ḥphaṅ mtho bar bcol ||
snaṅ srid bskos la ḥdebs par bcol ||
ḥbyuṅ ba cha la ḥbebs[f] par bcol ||
kha drag dar la che[g] bar bcol ||
bdud srin log pa ḥdul bar bcol ||
ḥdre srin cham la ḥbebs par bcol ||

de ltar bsgrub daṅ las la sbyor ||
gaṅ du byed paḥi las ka ni ||
bkaḥ daṅ[h] gźuṅ bźin spyod par bya ||

ma brtags ma gzab[i] tho co daṅ ||
mthoṅ mthoṅ yas daṅ thos thos bon ||
dran dran glu ru len mi bya ||
lar yaṅ thug khar lha gźuṅ la ||
gtsaṅ sme ma ḥdres dag par bya ||
ḥjig rten lha tshog gtsaṅ la dgaḥ ||
gtsaṅ la dgaḥ źiṅ sme la ḥjigs ||

de ltar gtsaṅ sme ma ḥdres pa ||
luṅ nas ḥbyuṅ bźin spyad pa na ||
bstan pa chags paḥi dar so la ||
med la yod par srid pa daṅ[j] ||
de yaṅ thug khar lha yi drin ||
stoṅ la gaṅ bar ḥphel ba daṅ ||
de yaṅ thug khar lha yi drin ||
ḥjig[k] la chags par srid pa daṅ[j] ||
de yaṅ thug khar lha yi drin ||
dman[l] la mtho bar ḥgro ba daṅ[j] ||
de yaṅ thug khar lha yi drin ||
dbul la phyug par srid pa daṅ[j] ||
de yaṅ thug khar lha yi drin ||

[a] bla re [b] kyi [c] gyi [d] kyis [e] draṅs [f] ḥpheb [g] phye
[h] bkaḥ pa [i] zab [j] yaṅ [k] ḥjigs [l] dmen

Accumulate flesh from the nape of the neck, blood from the heart, the sacred items,
the arrow with silk band, mirror and gem (all attached),
the canopy, the ceremonial umbrella, the banner of victory,
and make a first offering with the three-cornered sacrificial cake.
Call with the sound of drum, flat bell, conch and shawm.
Show the way with the passage of sweet-smelling incense.
Intone the verses according to the chant of the ceremony.
Repeat according to number the essential spell (that relates to the divinity's) Mind.
Praise him according to his Body, his Speech and his Qualities.
Urge him strongly to fourfold Action.
Urge him to spread the Swastika doctrine.
Urge him to raise the dignity of the best of Shen.
Urge him to bring order into the phenomenal world.
Urge him to bring the elements into a proper balance.
Urge him to increase and to spread our might.
Urge him to quell perverse demons.
Urge him to bring devils to subjection.

Thus summoning him and setting him to work,
wherever any rite is to be performed,
it must be done according to tradition and lore.

Thoughtless and careless capriciousness,
items just as one sees them, *bon* just as one hears it,
chants just as one remembers them, such must not be made use of.

But in this sacred lore of *Thug-khar*
do not mingle impurity with purity. Be clean.
The gods of this world rejoice in purity.
Rejoicing in purity, they fear impurity.

Thus if you do not mingle impurity with purity
and perform the rite as it is prescribed,
where the doctrine spreads in the place of its arising,
this coming into being where there was nothing before,
this too is by favour of the *Thug-khar* gods.
Prosperity which turns emptiness into fullness,
this too is by favour of the *Thug-khar* gods.
Destruction which is turned into production,
this too is by favour of the *Thug-khar* gods.
Baseness which is turned into high rank,
this too is by favour of the *Thug-khar* gods.
Poverty which is turned into wealth,
this too is by favour of the *Thug-khar* gods.

rmaṅ la ḥphan par srid pa daṅ[a] ||
de yaṅ thug khar lha yi drin ||
khas ñan[b] dpaḥ bar ḥgro ba daṅ[a] ||
rgyal khams mṅaḥ ris dar ba daṅ[a] ||
de yaṅ thug khar lha yi drin ||
nad yams ḥkhrugs [201a] pa źi ba daṅ[a] ||
de yaṅ thug khar lha yi drin ||
bkra śis dge rtags ḥphel ba daṅ[a] ||
de yaṅ thug khar lha yi drin ||
snaṅ srid dge la mos pa daṅ[a] ||
de yaṅ thug khar lha yi drin ||

de phyir thug khar gñen par brtsi ||
kun rdzob mtshan ma dṅos por bden ||
sems can ḥgro la sman par ḥgyur ||
snaṅ srid dgaḥ bde ḥphel bar ḥgyur ||

don dam stoṅ pa ñid du bden ||
ḥgro ba thar lam ḥbyed par ḥgyur ||
mthar yaṅ don dam bden pa daṅ ||
kun rdzob mtshan maḥi bden pa daṅ ||
bden pa gñis po dor mñam nas ||
so so ma yin tha mi dad ||
gñis su med ciṅ byar med de ||
mñam pa ñid kyi don rtogs na ||
bdag kyaṅ mkhaḥ la rtse ru chib ||
gźan yaṅ dbyiṅs su lhun gyis grub ||
snaṅ gśen gtsug phud thugs la źog ||
sems can ḥgro la smin par mdzod || ces gsuṅs so /

yaṅ ston pas bkaḥ stsal pa /
ñon cig snaṅ gśen gtsug phud ñon ||
gsum[c] pa sgra blaḥi dpaḥ khrom la ||
ḥgro drug sems can thams cad ni ||
sdug bsṅal ñon moṅs gduṅ ba daṅ ||
kag ñen[d] ḥphrag dog rtsub pa daṅ ||
bstan pa dar rgyas chuṅ ba daṅ ||
pha rol dgra ru laṅ ba daṅ ||
kluṅ[e] rta dbaṅ thaṅ rgud pa daṅ ||
g·yul so tshur la laṅ ba na[f] ||
sgra bla wer maḥi dpaḥ khrom bkyag ||

[a] yaṅ [b] ñes [c] gñis [d] ñan [e] sruṅs [f] daṅ

Feebleness which is turned into prosperity,
this too is by favour of the *Thug-khar* gods.
Weakness which is turned into heroism,
this too is by favour of the *Thug-khar* gods.
Extension of the spheres of influence of the kingdom,
this too is by favour of the *Thug-khar* gods.
The stilling of epidemics and disturbances,
this too is by favour of the *Thug-khar* gods.
Increase of blessings and signs for the good,
this too is by favour of the *Thug-khar* gods.
That the everyday world should take delight in good,
this too is by favour of the *Thug-khar* gods.

Therefore you should reckon the *Thug-khar* as your aid.
The outward signs (of the phenomenal world which belong to the sphere)
of relative truth are true (in so far) as (they are) things,
and these will be of benefit to living beings.
They increase the joy and happiness of everyday existence.

Absolute truth is true (in so far) as (it refers to) the Void.
It opens the way of salvation for living beings.

In the final analysis absolute truth
and the truth of relative outward signs,
when both truths are paired together,
they are not separate and there is no difference.
They are not two and must not be made (into two).
If one understands the meaning of Sameness,
one reaches the top oneself,
and others in the whole sphere are spontaneously perfected.
sNaṅ-gśen gTsug-phud, keep this in mind,
and bring all beings to a state of ripeness.

Again the Teacher said:
Listen, *sNaṅ-gśen gTsug-phud*, listen.
(1c) Thirdly, as for the hero-gathering of the Genies,[20]
all living beings of the Six Spheres,
when they are tormented with the afflictions of suffering,
or troubled with impediments and jealousies,
when the spread of the doctrine diminishes,
and outsiders rise up as enemies,
when well-being and influence are in decline,
and the battle-ground comes back upon one,
then one must make offering to the hero-gathering of the *Wer-ma* Genies.

mgon po bya rdaṅ sruṅ ma bsten ||
caṅ seṅ śug mgon gñan[a] po brṅan ||
kun rdzob bden pa yin pas gtso ||

de yaṅ rnam pa bźi yin te ||
sgra bla gñan[a] daṅ wer ma rje ||
caṅ[b] seṅ gñan[a] daṅ śug mgon rdzi ||
gźun chen bźi[c] ru śes par bya ||
de yaṅ daṅ po sgra bla la ||
ye srid ḥphrul gyi sgra bla daṅ ||
ye rje smon paḥi sgra bla daṅ ||
ye dbaṅ mthu yi [201b] sgra bla gsum ||
daṅ po ye srid sgra bla la ||
sgra bla khyuṅ nag ral chen byuṅ ||
sgra bla khyuṅ nag ral chen la ||
ye mkhyen sgra blaḥi dmag tshogs grol ||
spyi gtsug nor bu rin chen la ||
sgra bla yid bźin lha dbaṅ srid ||
khyuṅ ru g·yas daṅ g·yon pa la ||
sgra bla lha gsas dar ma srid ||
rna ba g·yas daṅ g·yon pa la ||
sgra bla ṅar chen g·yu ḥbrug srid ||
spyan mig g·yas daṅ g·yon pa la ||
sgra bla yod khams kun gsal srid ||
khyuṅ mchu[d] thur du bgrad pa la ||
sgra bla khyuṅ nag śa zan srid ||
sgro chen sum brgya drug cu la ||
sgra bla sum brgya drug cu srid ||
thel śog gser gyi ḥdab ma la ||
sgra bla ñi khri dgu ḥbum srid ||
khyuṅ sder sa la ḥjum[e] pa la ||
sgra bla klu ḥdul khyuṅ chen srid ||
sṅon srid pa chags paḥi ru ma la ||
ye nas srid pa chags paḥi sgra bla yin ||

de ḥog ye rje smon pa la ||
srid pa[f] chags paḥi gźi ma daṅ ||
mi rgyud grol baḥi ru ma ru ||
g·yas kyi gser ri g·yu luṅ daṅ ||
g·yon gyi duṅ ri mchoṅ luṅ daṅ ||
thad kyi śel brag ḥod mtsho las ||
sgra bla smon paḥi seṅ gsum srid ||

[a] gñen [b] gcaṅ [c] gźi [d] chu [e] ḥdzum [f] paḥi

One must trust in the Defender 'Bird-Rack' as one's guardian,
and one must requite the *Caṅ-seṅ* and the *Śug-mgon* Furies.

As it concerns relative truth, these are very important.

These too are of four kinds:
(i) the Genie-Furies, (ii) the *Wer-ma* Lords,
(iii) the *Caṅ-seṅ* Furies, (iv) the *Śug-mgon* Leaders.
They are thus to be known as four great lores.

(i) So first as for the Genies, they are of three kinds:
  (*a*) the *Ye-srid-ḥphrul* Genies,
  (*b*) the *Ye-rje-smon-pa* Genies,
  (*c*) the *Ye-dbaṅ-mthu* Genies.

Firstly as for (*a*) the *Ye-srid-ḥphrul* Genies,
there appeared the Genie 'Black *Khyuṅ* Great Mane'.
From 'Black *Khyuṅ* Great Mane'
there came the army of *Ye-mkhyen sgra-bla.*
From the precious gem of the top (of the *Khyuṅ*'s head)
came the Genie *Yid-bźin-lha-dbaṅ* (Wish-granting-divine-power).
From the right and left horns of the *Khyuṅ*
came the Genie *Lha-gsas-dar-ma* (Divine-manhood).
From its right and left ears
came the Genie *Ṅar-chen g·yu-ḥbrug* (Great-strength-turquoise-dragon).
From its right and left eyes
came the Genie *Yod-khams-kun-gsal* (Quite-purifying-existence).
From the *Khyuṅ*'s beak which gaped wide downwards
came the Genie *Khyuṅ-nag-śa-zan* (Black *Khyuṅ* Flesh-Eater).
From its 360 great feathers came 360 Genies.
From the small feathers of its golden down came 29,000 Genies.
From the *Khyuṅ*'s claws contracted earthwards
came the Genie *Klu-ḥdul-khyuṅ-chen* (Great *Khyuṅ* Serpent-Subduer).

These are the Genies who appeared originally from the beginning
at the source of the appearance of existence.

Next as for (*b*) the *Ye-rje-smon-pa* Genies:
at the foundation of the appearance of existence
and at the source of the coming of the lineage of men,
from the Turquoise Vale by the Golden Mountain on the right
and the Chalcedony Vale by the Conch-coloured Mountain on the left,
and the Lake of Light by the Crystal Crag straight ahead
there came the three lions of the *sMon-pa* Genies.

de la srid ciṅ grol ba yi ||
mi rgyud de la sgra bla re ||
sgra bla re la lha dmag re ||
lha dmag re la kha ḥdzin re ||
kha ḥdzin re la rdzi bu re ||
de ye rje smon paḥi sgra bla yin ||

de ḥog ye gśen dbaṅ rdzogs kyis ||
srid pa rgyud kyi lha bdar źiṅ ||
duṅ duṅ mchod mchod bsten bsten[a] nas ||
ṅar ṅar dgra la rbad[b] pa yi ||
sgra bla dra ma gźuṅ chen bźi ||
raṅ bźin [202a] sprul pa ḥphrul gyi gźuṅ ||
raṅ grub rin chen mkhar gyi gźuṅ ||
rin chen sme ba[c] gliṅ gi gźuṅ ||
raṅ ḥbyuṅ dra ma ñag gcig gźuṅ ||
de sgra bla dra ma gźuṅ bźi yin ||
dra ma mched dguḥi dmag daṅ chas ||
ye dbaṅ mthuḥi sgra bla yin ||

wer maḥi dpaḥ khrom gźuṅ bźi yod ||
sṅon lha gsas dbal gsum rdzu ḥphrul las ||
nam mkhaḥ stoṅ paḥi dbyiṅs rum nas ||
rin chen sna lṅaḥi sgo ṅa cig ||
raṅ bźin śugs kyis brdol ba las ||
sgoṅ śun skyob paḥi go ru srid ||
bdar śa sruṅ baḥi mtshon du srid[d] ||
sgoṅ chu dpaḥ baḥi ṅar chur srid ||
sgoṅ pri ḥkhra baḥi mkhar du srid[d] ||
khro chu dmu rdzoṅ mun gyi mkhar ||
gsal ba ñi maḥi kha ḥod ḥphrog ||
sgo ṅa naṅ gi sñiṅ po las ||
rdzu ḥphrul mi pho gcig du srid ||
seṅ geḥi mgo[e] la dbyi yi rna ||
ḥkhro baḥi[f] gdoṅ la glaṅ chen sna ||
chu srin źal la rgya stag mche ||
ral griḥi rkaṅ la chu gri gśog ||
bya khyuṅ dar maḥi rva dbal la[g] ||
yid bźin nor buḥi dbu brgyan can[h] ||

[a] bstan bstan [b] sbad [c] rme ba [d] bsrid [e] gho [f] ba [g] las
[h] brñen can

As they came forth into existence,
there was a Genie for each lineage of men,
and for each Genie there was a divine army,
and for each army there was an overseer,
and for each overseer a leader.
These are the *Ye-rje-smon-pa* Genies.

Next (*c*) *Ye-gśen-dbaṅ-rdzogs*,
invoking the gods of the original tradition,
persistently making offerings and giving instructions,
fiercely he sets them upon the enemy,
the *Dra-ma* Genies according to their four great lores:
the lore of the Magic of 'Personal Manifestation',
the lore of the Citadel of 'Self-Manifesting Gems',
the lore of the Region of the Precious *sMe-ba*,
the single lore of the 'Self-Originating *Dra-ma*'.
The nine *Dra-ma* brothers together with their armies
are the *Ye-dbaṅ-mthu* Genies.

(ii) There are four lores of the hero-gathering of *Wer-ma*.
Formerly by the magical powers of the Gods, the *gSas* and the *dBal*
from the celestial womb of the empty sky
an egg (formed) of the five precious gems
burst open by its own innate force.
From it the shell became protecting armour,
the tegument became defending weapons,
the white became a strength-potion for heroes,
the inner skin became a citadel for them to dwell in.
The dark citadel *Khro-chu-dmu-rdzoṅ*
so bright was it, it stole the sun's light.

From the very inner part of the egg
there came a man of magical powers.
He had the head of a lion and the ears of a lynx,
a fierce face and an elephant's nose,
a crocodile's mouth and a tiger's fangs,
feet like swords, and feathers like sabres,
and between the horns of the vigorous bird *Khyuṅ*,
he had as his head-adornment a wish-granting gem.

de la miṅ ḥdogs miṅ med pa ||
ye gśen dbaṅ rdzogs mthu yis bsgrubs ||
dpaḥ chen wer ma ñi ña źes ||
mthu ldan yoṅs kyi thu bo po[a] ||
bon daṅ gśen gyi bstan pa bsruṅ ||
dgra daṅ bgegs kyi dpuṅ tshogs gźom ||
dkar daṅ dge baḥi sdoṅ grogs mdzad[b] ||
de la wer ma gźuṅ bźi grol ||
wer ma lha daṅ bsdebs pa las[c] ||
lha yi wer ma bdud ḥdul srid ||
wer ma gñan[d] daṅ bsdebs pa la ||
gñen gyi wer ma dgra ḥdul [202b] grol ||
wer ma khyuṅ daṅ bsdebs pa la ||
khyuṅ gi[e] wer ma klu ḥdul grol ||
wer ma seṅ daṅ bsdebs[f] pa la ||
dpaḥ ḥdul wer ma mched gsum grol ||
wer ma dpaḥ baḥi dpaḥ khrom grol ||
dmag tshogs dgu khri dgu ḥbum grol ||
lha la grol źiṅ gsas la chad ||
dbal[g] la ḥdra źiṅ bdud la ḥtshig ||
gaṅ la yaṅ ni ḥphrag[h] dog ciṅ ||
kun thub gaṅ yaṅ ḥjigs pa med ||
tsha dbal ḥjoms śiṅ graṅ dbal len ||
gaṅ gis mi śig nam mkhaḥi mkhar ||
kun gyis mi ḥjigs wer maḥi sku ||
g·yuṅ druṅ bon gyi bstan paḥi[i] srog ||
dgra bgegs ḥdul baḥi gñen por byuṅ ||
de wer ma dpaḥ baḥi gźuṅ bźi yin ||

caṅ seṅ gñan[j] la gźuṅ bźi yod ||
byes thub dpaḥ bo spun drug yod ||
gźis[k] sruṅ khra mo rdzoṅ drug yod ||
caṅ seṅ ḥgron yag[l] bcu gsum yod ||
lam lha gñan[j] po mched brgyad yod ||

śugs mgon rdzi bu[m] bcu gsum ste ||
kha drag srid paḥi śugs mgon la ||
śug mgon brgya daṅ rtsa brgyad grol ||

de yaṅ srid paḥi dpe srol la ||

[a] thu ba po [b] mdzod [c] la [d] gñen [e] gis [f] bsdeb [g] dpal
[h] ḥphraṅ [i] pas [j] gñen [k] gźi [l] mgron g·yag [m] sdziḥo

No name was given him, so he had no name,
but *Ye-gśen-dbaṅ-rdzogs* conjured him with magical force,
and gave him the name 'Great Hero *Wer-ma Ñi-ña*'.

He is the foremost of all the powerful ones,
protecting the doctrines of *Bon* and of Shen,
overcoming the hordes of foes and opponents,
acting as friends of goodness and virtue.

From him are derived *Wer-ma* according to four lores.
The *Wer-ma* united with gods,
and so the God-*Wer-ma*, subduers of demons, were produced.
The *Wer-ma* united with Furies,
and so the Fury-*Wer-ma*, subduers of foes, were produced.
The *Wer-ma* united with *Khyuṅ*,
and so the *Khyuṅ-Wer-ma*, subduers of serpents, were produced.
The *Wer-ma* united with lions,
and so the Three Brothers, the *Wer-ma* hero-subduers, were produced.
There was produced the hero-gathering of *Wer-ma* heroes.
There was produced the army 99,000 strong.

Produced from gods, born from *gSas*,
equal to *dBal*, destroyers of demons,
envious of everyone,
able to do everything, fearing no one,
destroying the Extreme (*dBal*) of Heat, seizing the Extreme (*dBal*) of Cold.
Their Sky-Citadel, no one can destroy,
they fear nothing, these *Wer-ma* forms.
They are the life of the doctrine of Swastika *Bon*,
and have come as aids for the subjugation of foes and obstructions.
These are the four lores of the *Wer-ma* Heroes.

(iii) There are four lores of the *Caṅ-seṅ*[21] Furies:
the six brother-heroes capable of travel,
the six 'chequered' castles which protect the estate,
the thirteen *Caṅ-seṅ* who are good at wayfaring,
and the eight brother-furies who are gods of the road.

(iv) There are thirteen *Śug-mgon* Leaders,
and from these *Śug-mgon* of the 'generations of might'
there were produced 108 *Śug-mgon*.

As for the archetypes of the generations,

srid pa re la śug mgon re ||
de la smraṅ daṅ cho rabs re ||

de ltar sgra bla wer maḥi dmag ||
caṅ seṅ gñan[a] daṅ śug mgon rdzi ||
mgon po bya rdaṅ sruṅ ma ste ||
bsten[b] ni dkar gsum phud kyis bsten[b] ||
gsol ni dmar gsum don gyis gsol ||
mchod ni bdud rtsi sman gyis mchod ||
dgra sdaṅ ḥdul baḥi gñen por mchod ||
bstan pa sruṅ baḥi sruṅ mar mchod ||
mdaḥ mduṅ ral gri rten du ḥdzugs ||
[203a] gser g·yu rin chen rten du ḥdzugs ||
sgra bla dpaḥ yi mṅaḥ yaṅ gsol ||
bya bon bcu gsum ḥphrin yaṅ bskyol ||
srid paḥi bon pos smraṅ yaṅ bkrol ||
rgyug chen mgon poḥi bya rdaṅ bkyag ||
rin chen sna lṅaḥi gsas mkhar brdzeg ||
de ltar dpaḥ khrom dmag gi gźuṅ ||
ḥjig rten bde la bkod pa daṅ ||
snaṅ srid kha yo[c] bsñom paḥi phyir ||
kun rdzob bden paḥi don du phob ||
de yaṅ bstan paḥi cha las su ||
rgyu yi theg pa zur ḥdegs tsam ||
raṅ bas gźan don gtsor byed ciṅ ||
sems can ḥgro la smin pa daṅ ||
bstan paḥi don du ched[d] bsam nas ||
don la mi gol ḥjug sgoḥi lam ||
ḥjig rten źiṅ khams bde skyid daṅ ||
bsod nams dge ba śugs kyis ḥphel ||
snaṅ gśen gtsug phud thugs la źog ||
sems can ḥgro la sman par mdzod ||
ces gsuṅs so /

yaṅ rgyal bus bkaḥ stsal pa /
ñon cig snaṅ gśen gtsug phud ñon ||
bźi[e] pa srid paḥi rgyud gźuṅ la ||
ḥgro drug sems can thams cad ḥdi ||
daṅ por phyi snod chags pa nas ||
srid pa ci ltar srid pa daṅ ||
bskos pa ci ltar bskos pa daṅ ||

[a] gñen [b] bstan [c] kha lo [d] mched [e] gsum

to each generation there was a *Śug-mgon*,
and for each there was an exposition and a parental lineage.

Thus we have (i) the Genies, (ii) the army of *Wer-ma*,
(iii) the *Caṅ-seṅ* Furies, and (iv) the *Śug-mgon* Leaders,
and this Defender 'Bird-Rack', who is our guardian.
They must be attended with offerings of the three milk-products.
They must be made offerings with the substance of the three red products.
They must be worshipped with elixir and medicament.
They must be worshipped as an aid for subduing hateful foes.
They must be worshipped as guardians who will guard the doctrine.
One sets up as symbols the arrow, the spear and the sword.
One sets up as symbols gold and turquoise and precious stones.
One beseeches the Genie-Heroes.
One despatches the message by the Thirteen Birds of *Bon*.[23]
The original *bonpos* intone the exposition.
One presents the 'bird-rack' of the Defender Great Runner.
One builds a shrine of the five kinds of gems.
Such is the lore of the hero-gathering-army.
Arranging for happiness in this world and for smoothing what is awry in phenomenal existence, you turn to affairs of relative truth.
As supplementary to the doctrine, the Vehicle of Cause is just a supporting help.
But if you place more importance on others' affairs than your own,
and give your thoughts to perfecting living beings and advancing the doctrine,
there will be no conflict in the matter, and it will be a way in,
so that happiness, merit and goodness will increase automatically in the realm of this world.
sNaṅ-gśen gTsug-phud, keep this in mind!
Do good to living beings!
This is what he said.

Again the Prince* said:
Listen, *sNaṅ-gśen gTsug-phud*, listen!
(ID) Fourthly, as for the lore of the stream of existence,
(I speak of) all these sentient beings of the Six Spheres,
how they originated in their origins
when once the outer vessel (of the world) had appeared,
how their ordering was ordered,

* The Teacher Shen-rab is referred to as 'Prince' in deference to his royal lineage. He is presented in all things as the peer of *Śākyamuni*.

mi rgyud gaṅ ltar grol ba daṅ ||
sṅon gyi cho rabs bśad pa daṅ ||
bden paḥi smraṅ gis bkrol pa ste ||
sems can ḥgro la sman pa yi ||
thabs kyi mtshan ñid rim pa rnams ||
mi śes rmoṅs pa bsal phyir bstan ||

phyir yaṅ thos bsam thams cad la ||
daṅ po ñan ciṅ thos par gces ||
bar du thos śiṅ go bar gces ||
tha ma brtag ciṅ dpyad[a] par gces ||
de nas grub paḥi ḥbras bu ḥbyuṅ ||

de phyir ḥjug sgoḥi yan lag la ||
naṅ srid skye ḥgro srog dbugs bsdus ||
nam mkhaḥi khyab tshad ḥgro ba ḥdi ||
[203b] daṅ po ci ltar srid pa daṅ ||
bar du ci ltar gnas pa daṅ ||
tha ma ci ltar ḥgyur ba yi ||
mtshan ñid bye brag thams cad ḥdi ||
śes par byed na[b] blo kha ḥbyed ||
blo sgrom[c] lde mig thos pas ḥbyed[d] ||
mi śes lkugs pa yi ges[e] smra ||
ma rig mun la rig pas[f] gsal ||

de phyir thos śiṅ dpyad pa[g] ⟨ni⟩ ||
srid paḥi grol phug ḥdi dag la ||
daṅ po ma bsrid srid pa daṅ ||
rgyu mthun srid la ḥbyuṅ srid daṅ ||
ḥod gsal lha la grol ba daṅ ||
lha la mi ru chad pa daṅ ||
mi la spyi sgos byed brag ste ||
ye smon rgyal poḥi cho rabs las ||
bskal srid chags paḥi gźuṅ chen daṅ ||
smon lam mkhar gyi gliṅ bźi daṅ ||
srid pa miḥuḥi rgyud ḥbum daṅ ||
mtshon mgon sgra blaḥi gźuṅ chen bźi ||

de yaṅ srid[h] pa rgyud kyi bon ||
de srid bon la mi srid med ||
de phyir ḥgro la mi sman med ||
mi sman med pas mi ḥphan med ||
mi ḥphan med pas mi dge med ||

[a] spyad [b] nas [c] sgram [d] byed [e] geḥi [f] pa [g] spyad paḥi
[h] bsrid

how the human species was derived.
With the telling of their first parental lineage
and an explanation with the True Exposition of things,
these duly ordered characteristics of methods
are taught so that the obscurity of ignorance may be removed.

Again in all learning,
first listening and attending is important;
then attending and understanding is important;
finally examining and diagnosing is important;
then the intended effect is produced.

As for the parts of the introduction,
these living beings of the phenomenal world,
composite beings with life and with breath,
equal in measure with the all-pervading sky,
first how they originated,
next how they remained constant,
finally how they changed,
if one knows all these different characteristics,
one's mind will be opened.
Attentive listening is the key that opens the casket of the intellect.
Words produce understanding where once there were ignorance and folly.
Knowledge brings clarity where there was dark incomprehension.

So we listen and we diagnose.
At these uttermost limits of the emanation of existence
first the non-existent came into existence,
and things emerged according to their species.
They emerged from the gods of the Clear Light,
as men they were born from gods.

Regarding men, there are differences of a general and special kind.
From the parental lineage of *Ye-smon-rgyal-po* came
(i) the great lore of the birth of time-period and existence,
(ii) the Four Continents of the 'prayer-citadels',
(iii) the 100,000 species of human kind,
(iv) the great lore of the genies, the armed guardians,
four great lores in all.

Furthermore as for this *bon* of the stream of existence,
for this original *bon* there is nothing which is not possible.
Thus there is nothing which does not benefit living beings.
As there is nothing that does not benefit, there is nothing that does not further their interests.
As there is nothing that does not further their interests, there is nothing that is not good.

de phyir dge ba ma lus pa ||
phan daṅ bsod paḥi rgyu la ḥbyuṅ ||
byaṅ chub sems la bag yod na[a] ||
sems can rnams la phan yon yod ||
sems can rnams la phan yod pas ||
de la grub paḥi mthaḥ yod do ||
chab nag srid pa rgyud kyi bon ||
chu bo gźuṅ chen sde bźi las ||
chu bran ñi śu rtsa bźir gyes ||
de las so sor gyes pa ste ||
zad pa med ciṅ ḥphel ba med ||
ḥphel ba med ciṅ ḥgrib pa med ||
rtsi śiṅ nags tshal graṅs tsam gyes ||
ḥgro drug sems can thams cad kun ||
chab nag chu bo rgyun gyis gso ||
snaṅ gśen gtsug phud thugs la źog ||
sems can ḥgro la sman par mdzod ||

[204a] ces gsuṅs so / de nas yaṅ rgyal bus bkaḥ stsal pa /

ñon cig snaṅ gśen gtsug phud daṅ ||
ḥdus paḥi ḥkhor rnams thams cas kun ||
ma yeṅs dbaṅ po brtan par ñon ||
chab nag gyer gyi sgo bźi las ||
gñis pa chab dkar srid paḥi sgo ||
ḥgro drug sems can thams cad kun ||
skad cig bde ba mi ster ba ||
ḥdre dgu sri bcu sdaṅ ba la ||
ḥdre dgu skyas kyi ḥdebs pa daṅ ||
sri bcu thur du gnon pa la ||
de yaṅ rnam pa gñis yin te ||
thabs daṅ thugs rje gñis suḥo ||
thog mar thabs la rnam pa gñis ||
thabs kyis ṅo nas bzuṅ ba daṅ ||
thabs kyis rdzoṅ ḥdebs bskyal baḥo ||
thabs kyis ṅo nas ḥdzin pa ni ||
pra ltas gsal baḥi me loṅ thabs ||
raṅ gi[b] śes rgyud druṅ sbyar nas ||
gñis su med par bltas[c] pa na ||
pha rol ḥgro la gnod pa yi ||
srid rtse na rag yan chad kyi ||
ci srid gnod ciṅ ḥtshe ba rnams ||
miṅ daṅ mtshan ma ṅos kyis zin ||

[a] nas [b] gis [c] ltas

Thus unmitigated good arises from this beneficial and felicitous cause.

If one takes heed of the Thought of Enlightenment,
there will be true benefit for living beings.
By benefiting living beings the end in view is gained.

This 'Black Waters' *bon* of the stream of existence
has four main river courses
which separate themselves into twenty-four rivulets.
They cannot be exhausted and they do not increase.
They do not increase, nor do they decrease.
They spread as numerous as a forest of aromatic shrubs,
and all beings of the Six Spheres
are revitalized by the river-flow of the 'Black Waters'.
sNaṅ-gśen gTsug-phud, keep this in mind,
and do good to living beings.

This is what he said. Then he spoke again.

Listen, *sNaṅ-gśen gTsug-phud* together with your whole entourage which is gathered together,
listen with unwavering attention.
(2) Of the four portals of incantation of the 'Black Waters',[23]
the second is the original portal of the 'White Waters'.

Those who would not allow one moment's happiness to all the living beings of the Six Spheres,
the nine hateful demons and ten hateful vampires,
for dispatching these nine demons
and suppressing these ten vampires,
there are two parts in the matter,
namely Method and Compassion.

Firstly Method has two parts,
recognizing methodically,
and dispatching methodically.

As for recognizing methodically,
one must combine one's own experience
with the method of the Mirror of Clear Prognostics,
and then if you gaze one-pointedly,
you can recognize the names and characteristics
of those who harm other beings,
whoever these may be who harm and torment
from the peak of existence right down to hell.

de yaṅ srid paḥi ḥdre dgu ni ||
sṅon srid [pa] ltaṅ dbyal rnam pa gñis ||
dbu btud śaṅs ma lhan[a] pa ru ||
nam phyed dus su ḥtshos pa la ||
yod med dge sdig rgyu ḥbras daṅ ||
snaṅ mun las kyi ḥdu byed kyis ||
lha bdud dkar nag srid paḥi phyir ||
skya bo bkrag med sgoṅ gcig srid ||
sgo ṅa de ñid[b] brdol pa las ||
sgo ṅa phyi yi śun pa la ||
gdon daṅ dri zaḥi rgyal khams srid ||
sgo ṅa bar gyi bdar śa la ||
ltas ṅan brgyad cu[c] rtsa gcig daṅ ||
ye ḥbrog sum brgya drug cu srid ||
sgoṅ chu sa la bo ba la ||
nad rigs bźi brgya rtsa bźi srid ||
sgo ṅa de yi sñiṅ po la ||
gdon rigs sum brgya drug cu daṅ ||
rlaṅs pa [204b] bar du ḥkhyil ba la ||
rkyen rigs ñi khri chig stoṅ srid ||
sñigs ma sa la phog pa la ||
bgegs rigs stoṅ phrag drug cu srid ||
gzeg ma[d] kun du ḥthor ba la ||

srid paḥi ḥdre dgu sri bcu srid ||
de rnams gaṅ la gaṅ ḥdul gyi ||
thabs la mkhas paḥi skyes bu yis ||
ḥgro ba yoṅs la phan gdag phyir ||
nad rnams thams cad dpyad kyis gso ||
rkyen rnams thams cad gto yis sel ||
ltas ṅan ye ḥbrog mthu yis bzlog ||
gdon rigs brgyad bcu stobs kyis ḥdul ||
bgegs rigs stoṅ phrag glud kyis ḥjal ||
ḥdre dgu sri bcu bskyas kyis ḥdebs ||

de yaṅ ḥdre dgu sri bcu ste ||
gnas pa sa gźiḥi kloṅ du gnas ||
rgyu ba phyogs ḥtshams brgyad du rgyu ||
bsdoṅ ba ma bla chud daṅ sdoṅ ||
gtoṅ ba glo bur ye ḥbrog gtoṅ ||
mtho ru mi ster dmaḥ baḥi ḥdre ||

[a] rlan [b] dag [c] brgya bcu [d] zer ma

As for these nine original demons,
in the first place they had two original parents.
They bowed their heads together, but did not rub noses,
and at midnight the offspring was born.
By the combined effect of acts of right and wrong, good and evil, cause
and effect, light and darkness,
for the producing of gods and demons, whites and blacks,
a greyish lustreless egg was produced.
The egg burst open and the outer shell
became the realms of evil spirits and parasites (*gandharvas*).
The inner tegument of the egg
became the eighty-one evil portents
and the three hundred and sixty injuries.
The white of the egg spilled on the ground
and became the 404 kinds of disease.
The centre of the egg
became the 360 classes of evil spirits.
The vapour that rose up in the air
became the 21,000 accidental circumstances.
The residue that fell on the ground
became the 60,000 classes of obstructions.
Small particles sprinkling everywhere
became the nine original demons and ten vampires.

The man who is clever in methods
of subduing any of them wherever they may be,
in order to benefit all living beings,
cures by diagnosing all illnesses,
exorcises by ritual all accidental circumstances,
reverses by magical force evil portents and injuries,
subdues by force the 80 classes of evil spirits,
pays with ransoms the thousands of obstructions,
dispatches the nine demons and ten vampires.

Now as for these nine demons and ten vampires,
for dwelling place, they dwell on the face of the earth.
For moving, they move in all eight directions.
As associates, they associate with *Ma-bla-chud*.
As for what they send, they send sudden injuries.
There are demons of depression who do not allow one to rise,

yod du mi ster med paḥi ḥdre ||
phyug du mi ster dbul baḥi ḥdre ||
ḥphan du mi ster rmaṅ baḥi ḥdre ||
gaṅ du mi ster stoṅ baḥi ḥdre ||
chags su mi ster ḥjig paḥi ḥdre ||
yag du mi ster ñes paḥi ḥdre ||
skyid du mi ster sdug[a] gi ḥdre ||
ḥphel du mi ster ḥgrib kyi ḥdre ||
srid pa chags nas srid pa yis[b] ||
srid paḥi ḥdre dgu bya ba ste ||
de las mas kyi sri ldaṅ ba ||
pho sri ral chen gri[c] bdud rje ||
mo sri dar ma gźon bdud rje ||
pho mo staṅ dbyal ḥtshos pa la ||
che sri chuṅ sri dar sri daṅ ||
rgan sri gźon sri dar sri daṅ ||
bye sri byur sri la sogs te ||
ḥdre dgu sri bcu dmag daṅ chas ||
snaṅ srid ḥjig rten khams su ḥphyo ||
rgyal khams[d] mi bde ḥkhrugs par byed ||
stoṅ khams mi bde nad yams gtoṅ ||
[205a] sems can thams cad sdug ciṅ bsṅal ||
ḥgro ba mi la bdud du ḥbebs ||
byol soṅ phyugs la gnod ciṅ ḥtshe ||
de dag thabs la brten te gzuṅ ||
miṅ daṅ mtshan ma śes par bya ||
thabs kyis[e] ṅos nas gzuṅ baḥo ||

thabs kyis[e] rdzoṅ ḥdebs bskyal ba ni ||
chab nag srid paḥi bon po yis[f] ||
lha gźiḥi goṅ du sbran ma[g] blug ||
sbran maḥi[h] steṅ du sgron me bkyag ||
lha ni gar gsas btsan po bsgom ||
srid paḥi smraṅ gis gzu dpaṅ[i] gsol ||
gar gsas btsan po mṅon spyan draṅs ||
gser g·yu rin chen spyan gzigs ḥbul ||
g·yu ḥbraṅ bdud rtsi phud kyis mchod ||
de la skad kyi gcoṅ gñis sbyar ||
snaṅ źiṅ srid paḥi ḥjig rten na ||
gnas paḥi skye ḥgro ma lus rnams ||
srid pa gsas kyis bźen ḥdebs pa ||

[a] dug [b] paḥi [c] dri [d] ḥkhams [e] kyi [f] pohi [g] sman ma
[h] sman maḥi [i] gzuḥ dpuṅ

demons of wrong who do not allow one to be right,
demons of poverty who do not allow one to be rich,
demons of feebleness who do not allow one to prosper,
demons of emptiness who do not allow repletion,
demons of destruction who do not allow production,
demons of evil who do not allow good,
demons of suffering who do not allow happiness,
demons of diminution who do not allow increase.
Because they came into existence when the existing world was produced,
they are called the nine original (viz. existing) demons.
Then there arose the vampires of the lower regions,
the father vampire is the Lord Murder-Devil of the Great Mane,
the mother vampire the Lady Youth-Devil of Life's Prime.
From these parents, male and female, were produced
Great Vampires, Small Vampires, (Medium) Vampires,
Old Vampires, Young Vampires, Prime-of-Life Vampires,
Divorcing Vampires, Malicious Vampires, and all the rest,
together with the Ten Devil Nine Vampire Army.
They meander about the regions of the phenomenal world.
They cause unhappiness and disputes in all lands.
Everywhere they send unhappiness and plagues.
All living beings are in suffering.
Upon men they descend as devils.
Upon animals and cattle they bring harm and torment.
Lay hold of them by relying on right methods
and know their names and characteristics.
This is what is meant by methodical recognition.

Now as for dispatching them methodically,
The *bonpo* of the original 'Black Waters'[24]
scatters libations on the sacred mat,
presents lights over the libations,
meditates on the god *Gar-gsas-btsan-po*,
begs him to be mediator, using (the words of) the original exposition,
invites *Gar-gsas-btsan-po* to be present,
offers before him gold, turquoise and gems,
worships him with an offering of consecrated *chang*.
For this one uses two vocal ululations:
when the Original *gSas* (viz. *Gar-gsas-btsan-po*) exhorts all the living beings who dwell in the existing world,

bya rgyal khyuṅ gi gcoṅ la[a] draṅs ||
ḥdre dgu sri bcu bźen ḥdebs pa[b] ||
skad sñan ne tsoḥi gcoṅ la draṅs ||
gsal dag smraṅ gis go bar bya ||
ḥdod paḥi glu daṅ yas stags bsṅo ||
sna tshogs rdzas kyis rdzoṅ[c] la ḥdebs ||
ḥdod dgu re baḥi[d] skya yas rdzoṅ ||
glu yas gnas su thiṅ par bsṅo ||
ḥdre dgu bskyal baḥi smraṅ gto bya ||
sri bcu gnon paḥi sri gto bya ||
kag ñen bzlog paḥi ñen gto bya ||
rten ḥbrel srid paḥi rtsis gto bya ||
de ltar gto thabs gźuṅ bźi las ||
gaṅ ḥdul bye brag so sor dbye ||
de ni thabs kyis ḥdul baḥo ||

gñis pa thugs rjes[e] ḥdul ba la ||
thugs rje las kyis[f] ḥdul ba daṅ ||
thugs rje thabs kyis ḥdul baḥo ||
thugs rje las kyis ḥdul ba la ||
sṅon nas las kyi ḥphro can gyis ||
[205b] sbyaṅs pa sṅon soṅ nus pa yis ||
da lta skyes lus mṅon[g] byuṅ la[h] ||
tiṅ ṅe ḥdzin gyi[i] ḥod zer daṅ ||
las kyi ḥphro mthun nus pa yi ||
sṅon sbyaṅs śugs kyis ḥdul baḥo ||
thugs rje thabs kyis ḥdul ba la[j] ||
ḥdi ru thabs la[j] brten nas su ||
bsñen daṅ sgrub paḥi sgo ru ḥjug ||
thabs kyi[k] lag len ldan pa yis[l] ||
thabs kyi man ṅag bslab par bya ||
thabs kyi man ṅag ldan pa yis[l] ||
thabs kyi rgyun la ḥjug par bya ||
thabs kyi rgyun la ḥjug pa yis[l] ||
thabs kyi[k] drod tshad ldan par bya ||
yi dam lha yi mṅon rtogs[m] bsgom ||
snaṅ źiṅ srid pa bskos la ḥdebs ||
lha srin sde brgyad bźen ḥdebs bya[n] ||
ḥdre dgu sri bcu thur du gnon ||
gar gsas dbal gyi sku ru bskyed ||

[a] khyuṅ la gcoṅ las [b] ḥdebs paḥi [c] rdzoṅs [d] bas [e] gñis pa thabs kyis [f] kyi [g] sṅon [h] las [i] gyis [j] las [k] kyis [l] yi [m] rtog [n] bye

he invites them with the ululation of the royal bird *Khyuṅ*;
when he exhorts the nine demons and ten vampires,
he invites them with the well-sounding ululation of the parrot.

By means of a clearly given exposition all will be understood.
Pleasing songs and ritual items must be consecrated as gifts,
and one dispatches them with various offerings and dismisses them with the desirable presents for which they hoped.
One must consecrate the songs and the offerings so that they reach the intended object.
For removing the nine demons one must do the Exposition Ritual.
For suppressing the ten vampires one must do the Vampire Ritual.
For rebutting impediments one must do the Ritual against Troubles.
For happenings in dependent relationship do the Calculation Ritual.

Thus according to the four lores of ritual methods,
distinguish differences wherever you do the subduing.
This is subduing by Method.

Secondly as for subduing by means of Compassion,
there is a way of subduing by means of compassionate karmic effects,
and a way of subduing by means of compassionate methods.

As for subduing by means of compassionate karmic effects,
one who has a continuance of karmic effects from previous births,
by capabilities practised in former times,
in the body which he now really has,
subdues with a force derived from former practice,
(a force) of which the effectiveness corresponds with the continuance of karmic effects and with the rays of his profound meditation.

As for subduing by means of compassionate methods,
in this case relying upon method,
one begins by way of invocation and conjuration.
One who has the techniques of method
must learn the art of method.
One who has the art of method
must embark upon the process of method.
He who has embarked upon the process of method
must acquire the 'advance-grades' of method.
He must meditate upon the delineation of the tutelary divinity.
He must bring (mentally) the phenomenal world into order.
He must set the eight kinds of sprites, demons and the rest, to their tasks.
He must suppress the nine demons and ten vampires.
He must invoke *Gar-gsas-dbal* in bodily form,

gdug pa ḥdul mdzad drag poḥi dbal ||
dgu khri dgu ḥbum dbal gyi tshogs ||
bye ba sa ya gtso daṅ ḥkhor ||
ma rig log par gol ba yi ||
ṅa rgyal dreg paḥi ri bo gźom ||
źi nas snaṅ srid dgaḥ bde bskyed ||
stoṅ gsum ḥkhrugs pa gto yis[a] bcos ||
ḥkhros nas khams gsum dbaṅ du bsdu ||
snaṅ źiṅ srid pa dbaṅ la ḥdebs ||
gar gsas btsan po dbaṅ gi lha ||
thabs daṅ thugs rje zuṅ ḥbrel gyis ||
e ma ṅo mtshar che baḥi bon ||
snaṅ gśen gtsug phu thugs la źog ||
sems bskyed gźi ma ldan par gyis ||
sems can ḥgro la sman par mdzod ||

ces gsuṅs so / de nas yaṅ rgyal bus bkaḥ stsal pa /

ñon cig snaṅ gśen gtsug phud daṅ /
ḥdus paḥi ḥkhor rnams thams cad kun ||
ma yeṅs dbaṅ po brtan par ñon ||
chab nag gyer gyi sgo bźi la ||
gsum pa ḥphan yul glud gyi sgo ||
ḥgro [206a] drug sems can thams cad daṅ ||
snaṅ źiṅ srid pa thams cad la[b] ||
phan daṅ gnod par byed nas su ||
glud daṅ yas su sñeg pa la ||
chab nag srid paḥi bon po yis ||
sems can ḥgro la phan gdag phyir ||
mñam gñis brje la glud re bzaṅ ||
mñam gñis brje baḥi mtshuṅs[c] gto bya ||
de la rnam pa gsum yin te ||
pho glud mo glud chuṅ glud gsum ||
pho glud dag[d] la rnam pa bcu ||
dbus nas lha min ḥkhrugs mdos daṅ ||
steṅ nas tshaṅs paḥi lha mdos daṅ ||
śar nas rgyal poḥi skyoṅ mdos daṅ ||
byaṅ nas btsan gyi skoṅ mdos daṅ ||
nub nas bdud kyi khram mdos daṅ ||
lho nas gśin rjeḥi zlog mdos daṅ ||

[a] gtoḥi [b] pa [c] mtshuṅ [d] bdag

the mighty *dBal* who subjugates evil,
the host of *dBal* 99,000 strong,
the chief and his entourage, a million times ten million strong.
He must overcome the mountain of arrogance and pride, ignorantly and falsely erring.
Having brought tranquillity, he must bring joy and happiness to phenomenal life,
and by means of the ritual he must cure the world's disturbances.

In his wrath he shall bring all the world in his power.
He shall subdue to his power all phenomenal existence,
this *Gar-gsas-btsan-po*, god of power.

Since it unites as a pair Method and Compassion,
O how wonderful is the great *Bon*!

sNaṅ-gśen gTsud-phud, keep this in mind.
Having raised your Thought (towards Enlightenment) have this as your basis of action,
and bring benefit to living beings.

This is what he said. Then again the Prince said:

Listen, *sNaṅ-gśen gTsug-phud* and all your entourage which is gathered here.
Listen attentively with senses alert.

(3) Of the four portals of incantation of the 'Black Waters'
the third is *ḥPhan-yul*, the portal of ransom.

Doing both good and harm
to all the beings of the Six Spheres
and to the whole of phenomenal existence,
(gods and demons) hasten for ransoms and ritual offerings.
So the *bonpo* of the original 'Black Waters',
in order to benefit living beings,
exchanges two equal things and so (gives) a good ransom,
performing the Rite of Equivalence, the exchange of two equal things.

This rite is of three kinds,
male ransom, female ransom and child ransom.

The male ransom is of ten kinds:
from the centre the 'confusion' quittance of the non-gods,
from above the quittance of the pure gods,
from the east the 'protecting' quittance of the kings,
from the north the 'atoning' quittance of the fiends,
from the west the 'tally-stick' quittance of the demons,
from the south the 'averting' quittance of the spirits of death,

lho śar dmu yi gcun[a] mdos daṅ ||
byaṅ śar btsan gyi dal mdos daṅ ||
byaṅ nub klu dbaṅ gtad mdos daṅ ||
lho nub srin poḥi mkhar mdos bcu ||
pho glud dag tu śes par bya ||
mo glud dag la rnam pa bcu ||

chud kyi rgyal moḥi[b] g·yaṅ mdos daṅ ||
steṅ phyogs ma moḥi skoṅ[c] mdos daṅ ||
ma yam rgyal moḥi zlog[d] mdos daṅ ||
snaṅ srid ma moḥi ḥkhrugs mdos daṅ ||
brtan ma[e] dmag gi khram mdos daṅ ||
skyoṅ ma khram gyi gzi mdos daṅ ||
kha la gaṅs dkar sman mdos daṅ ||
sman mo gzed kyi tshaṅ mdos daṅ ||
ma bdud rgyal moḥi brtan[f] mdos daṅ ||
ma yam btsun[g] moḥi gnad mdos bcu ||
mo glud dag tu śes par bya ||

chuṅ glud dag la rnam pa bcu ||
ḥdre dgu sri bcu tshaṅ mdos daṅ ||
tshe bdud nag poḥi zlog mdos daṅ ||
skyes bu brgyad kyi dpuṅ mdos daṅ ||
dbaṅ ldan bgegs kyi glud mdos daṅ ||
sa bdag gtod kyi spur mdos daṅ ||
gtsaṅ sme ḥdres paḥi skyom [206b] mdos daṅ ||
mtshuṅs gñis gsor baḥi skyon mdos daṅ ||
mñam gñis brje baḥi glud mdos daṅ ||
rtsa dkar ḥphel baḥi gag mdos bcu ||
chuṅ glud dag tu śes par bya ||

de rnams dag la gyes pa yi ||
g·yen sde sum cu rtsa gsum la ||
rgyan mdos sum cu rtsa gsum yod ||
de ltar drug cu rtsa gsum las ||
mdos rigs sum brgya drug cu gyes ||
pho glud thams cad brjid daṅ bcas ||
mo glud thams cad bkrag daṅ bcas ||
chuṅ glud thams cad blta[h] na sdug ||
spyir ni ḥtshogs paḥi yo byad ni ||
snaṅ gśen glud yas smraṅ gi brug[i] ||
rgyal ba ḥphags paḥi bden pas bkrol ||

[a] bcun [b] dal mdos [c] bskaṅs [d] zlogs [e] brten ma [f] bstan [g] bcun
[h] bltas [i] drug

from the south-east the 'subduing' quittance of the *dMu*,
from the north-east the 'disease' quittance of the fiends,
from the north-west the 'imprecation' quittance of the serpents,
from the south-west the 'citadel' quittance of the monsters.
These are to be known as the male ransoms.

The female ransom is of ten kinds:
the 'blessing' quittance of the queen of the *Chud*,
the 'atoning' quittance of the mother-goddesses of the upper regions,
the 'averting' quittance of the queen *Ma-yam*,
the 'confusion' quittance of the mother-goddesses of phenomenal existence,
the 'tally-stick' quittance of the army of *brTan-ma*.
the 'banded agate' quittance of *sKyoṅ-ma-khram*,
the 'medicament' quittance of *Kha-la-gaṅs-dkar*,
the 'complete' quittance of *sMan-mo-gzed*,
the 'firm' quittance of queen *Ma-bdud*,
the 'vital' quittance of lady *Ma-yam*.
These ten are to be known as the female ransoms.

The child ransom is of ten kinds:
the 'complete' quittance of the nine demons and ten vampires,
the 'averting' quittance of the black life-demons,
the 'host' quittance of the eight children,
the 'ransom' quittance of the powerful obstructors,
the 'corpse' quittance of the local gods of the soil and the rocks,
the 'shaking' quittance of mingled purity and impurity,
the 'fault' quittance of the transposing of two equivalent things,
the 'ransom' quittance of the exchanging of two equal things,
the 'impediment' quittance for producing a child.
These ten are to be known as the child ransoms.

So these are clearly separated,
but for the thirty-three divisions of non-gods
there are thirty-three 'adornment' quittances.
Then from the total of sixty-three
there come 360 kinds of quittance.

All the male ransoms have brilliance.
All the female ransoms have lustre.
All the child ransoms are fair to behold.

Generally considered the ritual necessaries which have been brought together,
the *sNaṅ-gśen* ransoms and ritual items are explained
by the flow of the exposition which is the true word of the noble conquerors.

stoṅ gsum stoṅ gi ḥjig rten na[a] ||
tshaṅ rgyuṅ ri bdun rol mtsho bcas ||
lcags ri khyud mo ḥkhor moḥi gliṅ ||
gliṅ bźir gliṅ phran ñi zlaḥi ḥod ||
dpag bsam ljon pa[b] zil gnon khyuṅ ||
mtho ste srid paḥi rtse mo man chad daṅ ||
dmaḥ ste na rag yan chad la[c] ||
ma tshaṅ mi tshaṅ med pas su ||
glud daṅ yas su bstan[d] pa ni ||
stoṅ gsum stoṅ la ci yod pa ||
mi lus dag la de yod pas ||
glud kyaṅ[e] de bźin ḥdod paḥo ||
ḥbyuṅ po mi min[f] dri zaḥi tshogs ||
ḥgro ba mi la dpyad tsam na ||
stoṅ gsum tshaṅ rgyuṅ ḥjig rten na[g] ||
ḥdod yon sna tshogs ra ba na[g] ||
pho rnams staṅ daṅ mo rnams dbyal ||
yid du ḥoṅ daṅ ḥdod dgu ldan ||
de dag gnas daṅ ḥkhra[h] sar ḥdod ||
de phyir skye ḥgro gzugs su źugs ||
de la rol rtsed ltad mo daṅ ||
zas skom bcud la rol par snaṅ ||
ḥgro ba ma rig rtog[i] tshogs sbyoṅ[j] ||
rig paḥi ye śes mthoṅ med ciṅ ||
ma rig mun paḥi smag gnas kyaṅ[k] ||
de la tshor myoṅ dran par [207a] ḥgyus ||
mi bde sdug bsṅal byuṅ tshor bas ||
ma rig pa la nad du bslaṅ[l] ||
ma rtogs gol baḥi rkyen du bslad ||
de las[m] gzuṅ ḥdzin ñon moṅs skyes ||
raṅ gi ma rig pa las[n] byuṅ ||
gźan gyi ma rtogs pa la rkyen ||
don du raṅ gźan gñis kaḥi lan[o] ||
tshor myoṅ der ḥdzin ḥdu ba ḥkhrugs ||
yul la ma rmoṅs gces ḥdzin dran ||
sems la byuṅ tshor ḥjigs skrag byed ||
ri dvags rgya ru chud pa ḥdra ||
ma go ma rig ma rtogs pas ||
mo gto dpyad kyis[p] phan par ḥdod ||

[a] nas [b] paḥi [c] pa [d] bnan [e] yaṅ men [g] nas
[h] ḥkhras [i] rtogs [j] sbyaṅ [k] kyaṅs [l] lhaṅ [m] de la [n] la
[o] kas len [p] kyi

In the 1,000 times 3,000 world-complex,[25]
the Universe with its seven (surrounding) mountain ranges and seven sprightly oceans,
a circular land-mass with a ring of iron-mountains,
with four continents, and lesser continents, and light of sun and moon,
with the tree of paradise surmounted by the Bird *Khyuṅ*,
from its summit, the highest point of existence,
down to its depths in the hells,
there is nothing whatsoever incomplete,
and all this is shown as ransom and items of ritual.
Whatever there is in the 1,000 times 3,000 world-complex,
since it exists for human bodies,
they want the ransom to be like that.
The hosts of spirits, non-human beings and parasites,
when they look at human beings,
in this world of the 3,000-fold universe,
in this enclosure of so various desirable things,
they want as their abode and their dwelling place
the males the husbands, the females the wives,
with their pleasing and desirable things.
So they enter the bodies of living beings.
They play there delightedly and seem to take pleasure in what they see and in the goodness of food and drink.
In their ignorance living beings are inured to a host of doubts.
Lacking the insight of understanding knowledge,
they remain in the dark blackness of ignorance.
But they feel it and they dart here and there in their thoughts.
They feel that unhappiness and suffering have come,
and to them in their ignorance it is turned into sickness.
It is corrupted into an occasion of erring incomprehension
and from this there arise the afflictions which affect self and others.[26]
This happens because of their own ignorance
and its occasion is the incomprehension of others.[27]
In effect both self and others are to blame.
They cling to what they feel and the balance of the humours is disturbed.
They think of worldly things with unimpaired attachment.
They feel something has happened to their mind and they are frightened.
They are like a deer which has run into a trap.
Lacking understanding, comprehension and knowledge,
they want to be helped by sortilege, ritual and diagnosis.

smre źiṅ sdug bsṅal mchi ma ḥbyuṅ ||
sdug bsṅal ñon moṅs sbyoṅ ba las ||
de la rgyal baḥi thugs rje yis ||
nad la dpyad daṅ bgegs la gto ||
gaṅ la gaṅ dgos rim pa yi ||
gaṅ ḥdul der ston thabs mchog bstan ||
ma rig pa la rig pa bstan ||
ma rtogs pa la go bas[a] bkrol ||
brda daṅ thabs kyis[b] don bstan pa ||
sems can ñon moṅs raṅ sar źi ||
kun rdzob mtshan bcas dṅos por bden ||
g·yuṅ druṅ bon la yid kha brod ||
gśen poḥi tshig la gñan par[c] brtsi ||
dkar poḥi dge la spro ba bskyed ||
bstan paḥi bon la mos pa yi ||
dad pa goṅ du ḥphel ba daṅ ||
gśen poḥi smraṅ la[d] gñan[e] pa yis ||
phyis kyaṅ bkaḥ gñan[f] btsan par ḥgyur ||
deḥi phyir lha la yon phul ciṅ ||
nag po bdud la glud gtoṅ ba ||
ḥjug sgo thabs kyi yan lag yin ||
lar yaṅ ḥgro ba ḥdul ba la ||
thabs daṅ thugs rje zuṅ ḥbrel nas ||
yun du mi thog ḥphral la ḥgrub ||
rgyu ḥbras theg paḥi rim pa yaṅ ||
rgyu yi [207b] theg pa thabs yin źiṅ ||
ḥbras buḥi theg pa thugs rjeḥo ||
de gñis zuṅ du ḥbrel ba na ||
bla na med paḥi theg pa ste ||
rgyu ḥbras gñis su med paḥi don ||
ma brtsal lhun gyis grub paḥo ||

deḥi phyir bgegs kyi bar chod las ||
bgegs la glud phan gto ru bya ||
gto la rnam graṅs maṅ yod kyaṅ ||
ḥdi ni mñam gñis brje ba daṅ ||
mtshuṅs gñis gsor baḥi skyin gto ste ||
srid pa rgyud kyi bon po yis[g] ||
sems can ḥgro la phan ḥdogs na ||
chab nag rgyud las byuṅ ba ltar ||
mdos kyaṅ glud kyi yo byad bsag[h] ||

[a] baḥi [b] kyi [c] bsñen pa [d] ba [e] bñen [f] gñen [g] yi [h] bsags

They lament and shed tears in their suffering.
For them the Conqueror's compassion, removing evils and afflictions,
(gives) diagnosis for illness and ritual against demons.
Whatever is required by anyone, all in good order,
for whatever is to be subdued the Teacher has taught an excellent method.
He has taught knowledge to the ignorant.
To the incomprehending he has explained things through the understanding.
By signs and methods he demonstrates the matter
and the afflictions of living beings are properly calmed.
The characteristics of relative truth are true in relation to things,
(and if you help people with these things) their minds will take pleasure in Swastika *Bon.*
They will take solemn account of the word of the priest.
They will delight in virtuous deeds,
and with devotion to doctrinal *bon*
their faith will be on the increase.
By listening to the exposition of the priest,
the coercion will be potent afterwards.
Therefore making offerings to the gods
and giving ransoms to black demons
are methodical ways for entering (the doctrine).
Moreover in converting living beings,
one unites Method and Compassion,
so it does not take long—the work is effected in no time.
The whole order of the Ways of Cause and Effect
relates method to the (four) Ways of Cause
and compassion to the (five) Ways of Effect.
These two united are the highest of all ways,
for that which does not distinguish cause and effect
is effortlessly and spontaneously produced.

So when obstructing demons give trouble,
perform the ritual which benefits by giving ransom to these demons.
Although there are long lists of rituals,
this (we are concerned with) is the 'pledge ritual', the exchanging of two equal things, the transposing of two equivalent things.
The *bonpo* of the original tradition,
when he thus benefits living beings,
must assemble the quittance[28] and items of ransom,
as manifested in the tradition of the 'Black Waters'.

raṅ bas gźan don gtso che źiṅ ||
raṅ la ḥdod paḥi lhad med par ||
rgyu ḥbras mi brtsi thob rdzob spaṅ[a] ||
snaṅ gśen ḥbras bu draṅ sroṅ bsñag ||
deḥi phyir spyod lam dal bar bya ||
mi ḥgroḥi yas sogs spaṅ bar bya ||
mkho mthun rdzas cha bsgrub par bya ||

mdos la rnam pa gsum yin ste ||
phyi mdos naṅ mdos gsaṅ mdos gsum ||
phyi mdos sog khrig lag len rdzas ||
naṅ mdos glud yas gyer daṅ smraṅ ||
gsaṅ mdos tiṅ ḥdzin dgoṅs paḥi rdzas ||
gsum ka zuṅ ḥbrel ḥgro ba skyob ||
daṅ por phyi mdos sog khrig lag len la ||
rgyas ḥbriṅ bsdus gsum skabs daṅ sbyar ||
rgyas pa dag la khri ḥgyur ḥbum ||
ḥbriṅ po dag la stoṅ ḥgyur bcu ||
tha ma dag la brgya ḥgyur bcu ||
yaṅ mthaḥ dag la bcu ḥgyur bcu ||

de yaṅ so soḥi dbaṅ ris[b] la ||
stoṅ gsum sgron me khri ḥgyur ḥbum ||
ḥkhor lo bsgyur rgyal stoṅ ḥgyur khri ||
de ḥog gśen po brgya ḥgyur stoṅ ||
rgyal phran dag la lṅa brgyaḥo ||
btsun [208a] mo sum brgya drug cu ste ||
blon po ded dpon brgya bcu drug ||
btsun pa brgya daṅ rtsa brgyad de ||
khyim pha drug cu rtsa gcig go ||
gźi ḥdzin btsun mo lṅa bcu gcig ||
khyeḥu bu mo ñi śu lṅa ||
bran daṅ pho ña bcu gsum la ||
dman pa dag la lṅa re sogs ||
ji bźin rim pa mtho ba bźin ||
rkyen kyaṅ de bźin gñan[c] por sloṅ ||
ji bźin ḥkhor lo bsgyur ba bźin ||
bdud kyaṅ[d] de bźin źiṅ khams g·yo ||
deḥi phyir goṅ ḥphel sog daṅ sbyor ||

[a] spaṅs [b] ri [c] gñen [d] kyi

Making others' interests more important than his own,
without the impurity of selfish motives,
he must avoid the false ambition which takes no account of the fact that effects must follow from causes.
The Way of the Shen of the Phenomenal World seeks after as effect the Way of the Great Ascetics,
so perform your practice carefully.
Avoid unsuitable items, and prepare things as fitting.

The quittance is of three kinds,
the external quittance, the internal quittance and the secret quittance.
The outer quittance consists of the set of implements, the technical items.
The internal quittance consists of the item of ransom, the incantation and the exposition.
The secret quittance consists of meditation and the things of thought.
Uniting all three, one protects living beings.
First, as for the outer quittance, the technical matter of the set of implements,
in accordance with the occasion (these are done) in extended manner, in medium manner and in a compressed manner.
For the extended manner 10,000 times 100,000 (sets are prepared),
for the medium manner 10 times 1,000,
for the inferior manner 10 times 100,
and for a very inferior manner 10 times 10.

Thus according to the importance of each case:
for a Light of the Universe (i.e. a Buddha) 10,000 times 100,000,
for a universal monarch 1,000 times 10,000,
for a priest 100 times 1,000
for a petty king 500,
for a queen 360,
for a minister or general 116,
for a man of religion, 108,
for a householder 61,
for a woman of property 51,
for a youth or a maiden 25,
for a servant or a messenger 13,
for their inferiors 5 each.
According to the elevation of rank,
circumstances are more seriously excited.
In so far as one is a universal monarch,
demons may wander throughout all one's realms.
So the sets of implements must accord with such increase.

mdos gźi tshaṅ rgyuṅ ḥjig rten nas ||
dpe blaṅ de bźin skye ḥgroḥi gzugs ||
ji ltar tshogs bźin de bźin śes ||
srid paḥi rtse mo man chad nas ||
na rag gdar so yan chad la ||
srid pa ḥgreṅ[a] daṅ ḥphred ñal sbub ||
gnam la ḥphur daṅ sa la ḥdzul ||
bar na ḥgrim dguḥi gzugs brñan bya ||
pho mo skye mched spu mtshan gzugs ||
mi bas glud bzaṅ lhems se lhem ||
bya bas ḥdab bzaṅ spu ru ru ||
sgam bas mchid smra śa ra ra ||
rgyal bas brjid ḥgyiṅ lam se lam ||
blon bas che btsun ḥjol lo lo ||
rta rgyug mdaḥ ḥphen gźu brduṅ cog ||
glu len bal bkal phyar ra phyor ||
rtsed ḥjo[b] gar stabs ldem ma ldem ||

snaṅ gśen phan gnod gñis su[c] blta ||
sems can yoṅs la phan sems bsgom ||
gar gsas btsan po lha ru bdar ||
gśen rab bden paḥi smraṅ gis[d] bkrol ||
gto yas gnas su thiṅ bar bya ||
snaṅ srid lha ḥdre skoṅ gis[d] bskaṅ ||
tshe skyin srog glud dam pa daṅ ||
gsaṅ mdos ṅar mi rgyan ldan daṅ ||
ḥbul ba raṅ gis mi [208b] nor la ||
bźes pa gdon gyis mi nor bar ||
tiṅ ḥdzin smraṅ gis brda sprad bya ||
de la skad kyi gcoṅ gñis sbyar ||
glud gsas lha yi bźen ḥdebs la ||
seṅ ge ṅa roḥi gcoṅ la draṅ[e] ||
lha srin bskod la bźen ḥdebs pa ||
lcog gaḥi ḥgyur skad gcoṅ la draṅ[e] ||
de ltar ḥphan yul glud kyi sgo ||
sems can ḥgro la sman par ḥgyur ||
snaṅ gśen gtsug phud thugs la źog ||
ḥgro baḥi sdug bsṅal źi bar mdzod ||
ces gsuṅs so /

[a] ḥgriṅ [b] ḥjol [c] gñis bas [d] gi [e] draṅs

For the substance of your quittance take as model the Universe,
and the shapes of living beings, as many as are gathered there, you must pay regard to them too.
From the peak of existence down to the very bottom of hell,
beings that go upright, athwart and bowed down,
those that fly in the sky and creep in the earth,
those that wander through space, make effigies of all.
Give males and females their sense-organs, their hair and characteristic marks.
The ransom must be better than a human being.
Feathers must be better than those of real birds.
The words must be better than those of the (proverbial) bat.
The glory must be greater than that of a king.
The nobility must exceed that of a minister.
Racing horses, firing arrows, drawing bows,
singing songs, spinning wool, all so busy
playing games and dancing, all so gay.

According to the Way of the Shen of the Phenomenal World, one must see benefit and harm as two distinct things.
One must concentrate the mind on benefiting all beings.
One must invoke *Gar-gsas-btsan-po* as presiding divinity.
One must give explanation with the exposition which is the true word of the Best of Shen.
By means of the ritual one must strike the mark.
By ceremony of atonement one must satisfy the gods and demons of the phenomenal world.
With regard to the sacred ransom and pledge of life,
and the secret quittance with its outer adornment of figurines,
the offerer himself must make no mistake.
So that the demons who receive the items do not make mistakes,
the intention of the profound meditation must be explained by means of the exposition.
Two kinds of ululation are used for the words.
For coercing the presiding divinity of the ransom,
draw him with the ululation of a roaring lion.
For coercing gods and monsters to their appointed tasks,
draw them with the ululation of a lark's warbling note.
Thus the *ḥPhan-yul* way of ransoms
will bring benefit to living beings.
sNaṅ-gśen gTsug-phud, keep this in mind.
Quieten the sufferings of living beings.

This is what he said.

de nas yaṅ rgyal bus bkaḥ stsal pa /
ñon cig snaṅ gśen gtsug phud ñon[a] ||
raṅ che gyoṅ kheṅs ṅa rgyal spyad ||
ma saṅs gñan[b] la kha che źiṅ ||
sa bdag gtod la lag riṅ nas ||
dbyiṅs na bźugs paḥi lha mi mchod ||
mkhaḥ la gnas paḥi dbal mi bskaṅ ||
kloṅ na[c] dam can tshogs mi bsten ||
deḥi phyir ma saṅs gñan daṅ ḥgras ||
sa bdag gtod kyi tshogs daṅ mkhon ||
dbyiṅs na[c] bźugs paḥi lha mi mñes ||
mkhaḥ la gnas paḥi dbal mi bskaṅ ||
kloṅ du dam can tshogs kyis bkyon ||
de bźin sa bdag klu gñan daṅ ||
bdud btsan ma mo gśin rje daṅ ||
brtan ma[d] skyoṅ maḥi tshogs daṅ ḥgal ||
lha sruṅ dam can rnams daṅ ḥgal ||
de yi bkaḥ chad ñes skyon gyis ||
ḥgro ba mi la bdud du bab ||
tshe srog dbaṅ po dpal kha ñams ||
kluṅ[e] rta dbaṅ thaṅ bsod nams rgud ||
ḥgro ba mi bde sdug bsṅal sbyoṅ ||
de la rgyal baḥi thugs rje yis[f] ||
thabs daṅ thugs rje ma ḥgag phyir ||
ḥgro baḥi sdug bsṅal sel ba la ||
dpon gsas phyag gñen gto yi sgo ||
ḥdi la rnam pa bźi yin te ||
dbyiṅs kyi lha tshogs tshogs kyis mchod ||
mkhaḥ yi dbal mo skoṅ gis bskaṅ[g] ||
[209a] kloṅ gi dam can rten gyis brten ||
sa bdag klu gñan gto yis bcos ||

thog mar lha tshogs mchod pa la ||
srid pa rgyud kyi bon po yis ||
tshogs chen mchod paḥi yo byad gdeg ||
[stobs chen gar gyi dbal tshogs la ||]
gźi ma gtsaṅ maḥi steṅ du ni ||
ḥbru yi tshom bu dgod par bya ||
de steṅ dbal gyi bśos bu la ||
śa khrag dkar mṅar ḥdod yon tshogs ||

[a] daṅ [b] gñen [c] nas [d] brten ma [e] sruṅs [f] yi
[g] skaṅs gi bskaṅs

Then again the Prince spoke:

(4) Listen, *sNaṅ-gśen gTsug-phud*, listen.
Acting with self-esteem, arrogance and pride,
to be overweening with the *Ma-saṅs* Furies,
to be mean with the lords of the soil and the rocks,
failing to worship the gods who dwell in the celestial sphere,
failing to satisfy the *dBal* who live in the sky,
not trusting in the host of our divine guarantors throughout space,
results in the ill-will of the *Ma-saṅs* Furies,
in the animosity of the lords of the soil and the rocks,
in the displeasure of the gods who dwell in the celestial spheres,
in the dissatisfaction of the *dBal* who live in the sky,
in the spite of our divine guarantors throughout space.
In this way the lords of the soil, the serpents and furies,
the demons, the fiends, the mother-goddesses, the spirits of death,
the *brTan-ma* and the hosts of protectors will oppose us,
the protecting gods and divine guarantors will oppose us.
Punishment from them which is evil and harm brings demonish assaults upon human beings.
The lustre of life and of sense-powers will be weakened,
Well-being, influence and merit will decline.
One eliminates the unhappiness and suffering of beings, for due to the compassion of the Conqueror,
So that Method and Compassion may not be limited
and for removing the sufferings of living beings
(we have) this portal of ritual, the 'office' of the Master-Sages.
It is of four kinds:
worshipping with general offerings the hosts of gods in the heavens,
satisfying with atonement the *dBal-mo* of the skies,
trusting with trust the divine guardians of space,
remedying with ritual the lords of the soil, the serpents and the furies.

First, for worshipping the hosts of gods.
the *bonpo* of the original tradition
should set up the items for worshipping with the great mass of offerings.
On a clean place (which serves as) the basis
he should place heaps of grain,
and then the point-shaped sacrificial cake,
flesh and blood, the milk-offering, sweet-offerings and the general offerings of all desirable things,

yu ti źal zas loṅs spyod tshogs ||
du sam maṅ thun baṅ ṅe bśos ||
gzugs sgra dri ro reg byaḥi tshogs ||
ḥdod yon mchod pa dpag med bśam ||
tiṅ ḥdzin dgoṅs pas[a] dag[b] par spel ||
stoṅ gsum gtos daṅ nam mkhaḥi rgya ||
ḥdod yon zad med rgya mtshoḥi kloṅ ||
snaṅ srid rin chen gter gyis bkaṅ ||
dmigs med mchod pa nam mkhaḥi sprin ||
lha gsas dbal la mchod pa ḥbul ||
thugs dam rgyud mñes chag ñams bskaṅ ||
gar gsas dbal gyi dṅos grub źu ||
des ni ḥgro baḥi bar chod sel ||

gñis pa dbal[c] moḥi ⟨ma⟩ tshogs la ||
snaṅ źin srid pa mkhaḥ la bskaṅ ||
bskaṅ baḥi gnas der bskaṅ bas bkyag ||
srid paḥi dpe blaṅs ri rab gliṅ ||
lcags ri khyud mo ri bdun mtsho ||
dpag bsam ljon pa zil gnon khyuṅ ||
rnam rgyal khaṅ pa blta na sdug[d] ||
śiṅ rta rtsub ḥgyur dgaḥ ba ḥdres ||
ud ḥbar me tog skyed moḥi tshal ||
mtshal ri lha ḥdun ar moḥi rdo ||
ñi ma zla ba gsal baḥi sgron ||
bkra śis rdzas brgyad phun sum tshogs ||
rin chen nor bdun gram khrod gter ||
lhab lhub lda ldi chun ḥphyaṅ ḥphrul ||
ye śes gźal yas nam khaḥi rgya ||
śiṅ ris rgyan rdzas loṅs spyod dkor ||
rgyaṅ ḥphan bal tshon bla re gur ||
mdaḥ [209b] bkra ḥphaṅ bkra thabs śes rtags ||
ḥdab chags ri dvags g·yuṅ dvags dkor ||
ris bkra ⟨gcan gzan⟩ spu sdug mdzes ||
mi nor yul mkhar ḥdod yon rdzas ||
pho toṅ mo toṅ lan chags glud ||
rta rgyug mdaḥ ḥphen rtsed ḥjo[e] stabs ||
mkho mthun yo byad phun sum tshogs ||

[a] paḥi [b] bdag [c] dpal [d] lta na sdugs [e] ḥjol

chang, food-offerings, and the general offerings of all enjoyable things,
drink-offerings, sweetened sacrificial cakes, meat, ordinary sacrificial cakes,
offerings (symbolizing) form, sound, smell, taste and touch,
innumerable items of worship are set up in the form of all desirable things.
By concentration of meditation he increases the offering in all purity.
The vastness of the Universe, the expanse of the sky, the space of the ocean,
is filled with an infinite number of desirable things,
with all the treasures of phenomenal existence.
These unconfined offerings like clouds in the sky
are offered in worship to the gods, *gSas* and *dBal.*
All this delights them in accordance with their thoughtful purpose,
and atones for all wrong-doings.
It calls down the special powers of *Gar-gsas-dbal*,
and he removes the difficulties of living beings.

Secondly for the feminine host of the *dBal-mo*
one must make an atonement offering (to them) in the sky of the whole of phenomenal existence.
In that place of atonement one must offer up as atonement
the land-mass of the Best of Mountains taken as a model of existence,[29]
with the tree of paradise surmounted by the Bird *Khyung*,
the encircling iron mountains and the seven circles of mountains and seas,
the 'Palace of Victory' so fair to behold,
with the Park for Riding, the Park of Fierceness, the Park of Pleasure and the Park of Intermingling,
the Park of Blue Lotuses,
the Park of the Red Mountains where the gods assemble, and the Park of Fine Stone (pavements),
with sun and moon (to serve as) bright lights,
with the eight auspicious symbols, all excellently done,
and the treasure of sparkling heaps of the seven kinds of gems.
(Adornments hang) in folds and pleats and interwoven loops.
The Palace of Wisdom (made from) nets of crossed threads,
ritual stakes, decorations and a wealth of pleasing things,
the tree-symbol made of coloured wools and the canopy,
the fine arrow and distaff, symbols of Method and Wisdom.
a wealth of feathered fowl, wild animals and domestic animals,
fierce beasts of wonderful form with coats of fine hues,
the substance of men's wealth, their houses and the things they value,
male effigies, female effigies, ransoms for debts of evil,
horses running, men shooting arrows, others in the act of play,
the necessary items, all excellently done.

raṅ mthun gtor ma rgyan daṅ ldan ||
gser g·yu dar stag lhab lhub rgyan ||
g·yu ḥbran bdud rtsi skyems paḥi phud ||
rṅa gśaṅ duṅ gliṅ sñan paḥi sgra ||
bden paḥi smraṅ daṅ smra baḥi tshig ||
go baḥi brda sbyar srid paḥi gźuṅ ||
sṅon gyi dpe srol cho rabs bśad ||
srid paḥi lugs nas ḥbyuṅ bźin du ||
dbal mo ma tshogs mkhaḥ la bskaṅ ||
dam can rgya mtsho kloṅ mñes ||
srid pa gsum po zil gyis gnon ||
snaṅ źin srid paḥi kha yo[a] sñoms ||
ḥgro ba sdug bsṅal ñon moṅs źi ||
des ni bar chod rkyen rnams bzlog ||
snaṅ srid źi bde cha la sñoms ||
deḥi phyir dbal mo skoṅ gis bcos ||
mkhaḥ kloṅ rab ḥbyams dbyiṅs sy bskaṅ ||
chab dkar sṅags kyi gźun la ḥgres[b] ||

gsum pa kloṅ gi dam can la ||
raṅ mthun rten gyi[c] dam rdzas bśam ||
ḥdod yon loṅs spyod mṅon cha ḥbul ||
śa khrag dkar mṅar g·yu ḥbraṅ phud ||
ḥban tshogs lha yi gtor mas mchod ||
thugs dam gnad bskul ḥphrin las bcol ||
dgyes mdzad dam paḥi dṅos grub źu ||
ḥgro baḥi tshe dpal dmu thag[d] skyob ||
dam can sruṅ ma ṅaṅ gis ḥdu ||
gar gsas dbal gyi pho ña la ||
dmigs paḥi rten ḥdzug ḥphrin las bcol ||

bźi pa sa bdag klu gñan la ||
snaṅ srid gto yis bcos pa [210a] la ||
stoṅ gsum ḥkhrugs paḥi yo bcos daṅ ||
ḥbyuṅ ba ḥkhrugs paḥi ḥgram bcos daṅ ||
ye ṅam ḥkhrugs paḥi bsdum bcos daṅ ||
sa bdag sme baḥi gliṅ bcos daṅ ||
klu gñan gtod kyi ḥgram bcos daṅ ||
snaṅ srid kha bskaṅ źi bcos daṅ ||
rnam pa bdun du śes par bya ||

[a] kha lo [b] ḥdres [c] bstan paḥi [d] dmu dag

Sacrificial cakes suitable for each (divinity) and well-adorned,
gold, turquoise, silk, tiger-skin, decorations hanging in folds,
offerings of consecrated *chang* as libations,
drums, flat bells, conch-shells, shawms, all well-sounding,
the exposition of truth, words that produce understanding,
the original lore which is the explanation of (the priest) who understands.
He explains the earliest archetype and the lineage
As it appears according to the original pattern,
one must make atonement to the feminine host of the *dBal-mo* in the sky.
The ocean-like host of divine guarantors will be gratified.
The three spheres of beings will be subjected.
The crookedness of phenomenal existence will be smoothed flat.
The sufferings and afflictions of living beings will be assuaged.
By such means opposing circumstances will be reversed.
Phenomenal existence will be smoothed into a state of peace and happiness.
So attend to the *dBal-mo* with the ceremony of atonement,
performing it through the celestial spheres of the vast space of the sky.
This is continued in the Lore of Spells of the White Waters.

Thirdly for the divine guarantors in space
prepare the sacred items serving as symbols fitting to each one.
Offer the gifts of desirable and pleasing things,
flesh and blood, the milk-offerings, the sweet offerings, and the libations of *chang*,
and worship them with the general offerings and the sacred cakes of the gods.
Urge their purposes to essential things and set them to work.
Cause them to rejoice, and request the sacred special powers.
They will defend the life-lustre and the 'heavenly cord' of living beings.
The guarantor-defenders will gather around of their own accord.
Set up the symbols intended for the functionaries of *Gar-gsas-dbal* and set them to work.

Fourthly for the lords of the soil, the serpents and the furies,
for remedying phenomenal existence by means of ritual,
it should be known that there are seven types:[30]
'remedy for crookedness of the Universe in disorder',
'remedy for harm of the great elements in disorder',
'reconciling remedy for gods and demons in disorder',
'remedy of the *sMe-ba* region for lords of the soil',
'remedy for harm of serpents, furies and lords of the rocks',
'tranquillizing remedy of atoning for phenomenal existence'.

ḥgro ba sems can don ched du ||
srid pa rgyud kyi bon po yis[a] ||
gtsaṅ maḥi sa la ma ḥdal bya ||
sa tshon sna lṅas gźal yas bris ||
sa bdag klu gñan gtod kyi tshogs ||
spar kha lo skor sme ba[b] gliṅ ||
gźi gnas mṅaḥ dbaṅ ḥkhor daṅ bcas ||
ḥbru snaḥi gzugs daṅ bśos gtsaṅ daṅ ||
ḥdab chags ri dbags g·yuṅ dvags daṅ ||
gcan gzan mi nor yul mkhar daṅ ||
skye ḥgroḥi gzugs daṅ chu gnas daṅ ||
sna tshogs spu mtshan tshaṅ ba daṅ ||
śiṅ rtsi bal bu bya spu mtshon ||
gser g·yu dar zab sna tshogs brgyan ||
ḥdod yon mchod pa dpag med bśam ||
tiṅ ḥdzin dgoṅs paḥi sṅags kyis spel ||
gar gsas btsan po lha ru bdar ||
rṅa gśaṅ duṅ gliṅ skad kyis ḥbod ||
ba dan ru mtshon brda yis g·yab ||
gser skyems g·yu mṅon brṅan cha ḥbul ||
rgyal ba bden paḥi smraṅ gis[c] bkrol ||
de la skad kyi gcoṅ gñis sbyar ||
dpon gsas phyag gñen bskos ḥdebs śiṅ ||
snaṅ źin srid pa kha gnon pa ||
sgra rgyal ḥbrug gi gcoṅ la draṅ[d] ||
gto yas glud kyi ṅo bsṅo źiṅ ||
phyag gñen gnas su bstim pa ni[e] ||
gsuṅ sñan khu byug gcoṅ la draṅ[f] ||
snaṅ źiṅ srid pa thams cad la[g] ||
glud yas gtor ma gnas su thiṅ ||
stoṅ khams re ba bskaṅ bar bya ||
snaṅ srid źi bde źi bar bya ||
[210b] sa bdag klu gñan bsdum par bya ||
thams cad ḥkhrugs pa źi ba daṅ ||
snaṅ srid dgaḥ bde bskyed par bya ||
de nas ḥgro la phan bde bsod ||
snaṅ źiṅ srid pa cha la ḥbebs ||
źiṅ khams dge baḥi gźi mar ḥgyur ||

[a] yiḥi [b] rme ba [c] gi [d] las draṅs [e] paḥi [f] draṅs [g] las

For the sake of living beings
the *bonpo* of the original tradition
must make the mystic circle on a clean place.
He draws the divine palace with the five different colours.
(This is for) the lords of the soil, the furies and lords of the rocks in their hosts,
the circle of *sPar-kha* and the region of *sMe-ba*,
the local divinities with their powerful entourage.

Effigies (made from) the different kinds of grain and pure sacrificial cakes,
feathered fowl, wild animals and domestic animals,
fierce beasts, the subtance of men's wealth, their houses,
the forms of living beings and those who live in water,
with fur and marks of different kinds, all (shown) complete,
aromatic shrubs, woollen strands stuck with birds' feathers,
all adorned with gold and turquoise and different kinds of silks.
Thus one must prepare limitless worship of desirable things.
One increases it by means of the spells of concentrated meditation.
One invokes *Gar-gsas-btsan-po* as presiding divinity.
One calls him with drums, flat bells, conches and shawms.
One waves as signals flags and pennants.
One offers gifts and a libation of consecrated *chang*.
One explains by means of the exposition which is the truth of the Conqueror.
For the voice one uses two ululations.
For ordering the 'office' of the Master-Sages
and for subduing phenomenal existence
one uses the ululation of the dragon, the king of sound.
For consecrating the ransoms, the items of ritual,
and for directing the 'office' to its objective,
one uses the ululation of the sweet-sounding cuckoo.

In the whole of phenomenal existence the sacrificial cakes (which serve as) items of ransom attain their objective.
The thousand regions will have their hopes fulfilled.
Phenomenal existence will be tranquillized in peace and happiness.
The lords of the soil, the serpents and the furies will be reconciled.
All disturbances will be tranquillized and joy and happiness will be produced throughout phenomenal existence.
Thus living beings will enjoy benefits and happiness.
Phenomenal existence is put into order,
and these regions become a foundation for virtue.

snaṅ gśen gtsug phud sprul paḥi gśen ||
spyir yaṅ snaṅ gśen theg paḥi bon ||
ḥgro la phan bde bsod paḥi cha ||
snaṅ srid dge ba ḥphel baḥi thabs ||
sems bskyed bźi ma ldan par gces ||
sems bskyed gźi ma mi ldan źiṅ ||
log par gol baḥi tshogs rnams kyaṅ ||
bkaḥ luṅ tshul bźin spyad byas pas ||
mthar ni don daṅ yon tan yaṅ ||
khams gsum sa dgu yar brgal nas ||
snaṅ gśen grub ste mos par spyod ||
g·yuṅ druṅ sa bcu rim par bgrod ||
g·yuṅ druṅ sa bcu rim bgrod nas ||
bcu gcig kun snaṅ ḥod la gnas ||
de ru mṅon par saṅs rgyas thob ||
rgyu yi theg pas ḥbras bur bsñag ||
theg rim yar bgrod ltuṅ ba med ||
don la mi gol rtsis mi ḥphyug[a] ||
bon sgo rim pas spyod tshul lo ||
snaṅ gśen gtsug phud sprul paḥi gśen ||
snaṅ gśen bon gyi gyer sgo bźi ||
gcoṅ brgyad skad kyis gtaṅ rag sbyar ||
snaṅ gśen theg pa rgyu yi bon ||
snaṅ gśen gtsug phud thugs la źog ||
sems can ḥgro la sman par mdzod ||
sems bskyed gźi ma ldan par mdzod ||
ma rig dom chol spaṅ bar mdzod ||
bkaḥ luṅ tshul bźiṅ spyod par mdzod ||
khri smon rgyal bźad bdag tu bsko ||
snaṅ gśen bon gyi ḥkhor lo bskor ||
bdag gi bstan paḥi gñer zuṅ źig ||

źes bkaḥ stsal nas / theg pa gñis pa snaṅ [211a] gśen gyi bon rnams gtan la phab ste gsuṅs paḥo ||

[a] ḥchug

sNaṅ-gśen gTsug-phud, Shen who manifest yourself as you will!
In general the *bon* of the Shen Way of the Visual World is something for delighting living beings with benefits and happiness.
It is a method for increasing the good of phenomenal existence.
But it is important to have as basis the raising of one's Thought (to Enlightenment).

Although they may not have as basis this raising of Thought,
even these hosts of mistaken (beings),
by acting in accordance with these teachings,
in the end (gain) objective and qualities,
and having traversed the threefold world and nine stages,
they perfect the Shen Way of the Visual World and practise it with devotion.
Then they traverse in due order the ten Swastika stages,
Having traversed in due order the ten Swastika stages
they abide in the eleventh stage of 'Universal Shining Light'.
There they gain perfect buddhahood.
The Vehicles of Cause follow on to those of Effect.
As one traverses upwards through the vehicles, there is no falling back.
There is no mistaking the objective and no error in calculation.
This is the way of practising in due order the Portals of *Bon*.

sNaṅ-gśen gTsug-phud, Shen who manifest yourself at will!
These are the Four Portals of Incantation of the *Bon* of the Shen of the Visual World,
and the ceremonies accord with the sounds of eight ululations.
This traditional *bon* of the Way of the Shen of the Visual World,
sNaṅ-gśen gTsug-phud, keep it in mind!
Bring benefit to living beings.
Act with the raising of Thought (towards Enlightenment) as your basis.
Avoid ignorant gossiping.
Practise in accordance with the teachings.
Take charge of the *Khri-smon-rgyal-bźad* Palace.
Turn the wheel of the *bon* of the Shen of the Visual World,
and watch over the doctrine I have taught.
This is what he said, thus setting forth the teachings of the Second Way of the Shen of the Visual World.

III. ḤPHRUL GŚEN THEG PA

[vol. *kha*, f. 221b^4 onwards]

de nas rgyal bus bkaḥ stsal pa /
ñon cig ḥphrul gśen gtsug phud ñon ||
da ltaḥi dus daṅ gnas skabs ḥdi dag tu ||
theg pa gsum pa ḥphrul gśen ḥchad par byed ||
ḥphrul ni snaṅ źiṅ srid pa ḥphrul bas ḥphrul ||
gśen ni de dag ḥdul bar byon pas gśen ||
ma rig sems can rkyen gyis gol ba rnams[a] ||
bar chod bgegs[b] kyi rkyen las thar ba daṅ ||
ḥjig rten dregs pa dbaṅ du bsdu ba daṅ ||
dgra bgegs log lta tshar thag gcad[c] pa daṅ ||
bstan pa bśig pa gnas su bgral baḥi phyir ||
dben paḥi gnas gzuṅ brten[d] paḥi rdzas kyaṅ bsag ||
rdzu ḥphrul lha bsgom drag poḥi sṅags kyaṅ bzlaḥ ||
phyi naṅ mtshams gcad yeṅ med bsñen daṅ bsgrub ||
brnag paḥi las rnams mthaḥ ru dbyuṅ bar bya ||
ḥgro baḥi rkyen bsal mi mthun bar chod bzlog ||
bstan paḥi so gzugs log lta cham la dbab ||
bstan paḥi cha daṅ ⟨ḥgro ba⟩ spyiḥi phyir du ||
yid la brnag paḥi źe sdaṅ [222a] mi dgos daṅ ||
gsad gcad dbab daṅ bsgral baḥi las byas kyaṅ ||
don la mi gol ḥjug sgoḥi yan lag yin ||
ḥgro baḥi źiṅ khams de yis bde bar ḥgyur ||
ḥphrul gśen gtsug phud thugs kyi dkyil du źog ||
ces bkaḥ stsal to / de la yaṅ gsol pa /
rgyal bu ston pa gśen rab lags ||
g·yuṅ druṅ bon la rgya che graṅs maṅ yaṅ ||
mdor bsdus theg pa rim dgur gsuṅs pa yi ||
theg pa gsum pa ḥphrul gśen bon sgo la ||
spyi yi sde daṅ sgos kyi bye brag gi ||
rnam graṅs ṅes par brjod du mchis lags sam ||
spyod daṅ ḥjug paḥi mtshan ñid ci ltar lags ||
tha ma don daṅ yon tan ci ltar thob ||
bdag la ṅes paḥi bkaḥ gnaṅ mdzad du gsol ||
ces gsol to /

[a] rgol ba la [b] brgeg [c] bcad [d] bstan

III. THE WAY OF THE SHEN OF ILLUSION

Then the Prince said:

Listen, *ḥPhrul-gśen gtsug-phud*, listen.
At this present time and on this present occasion
I will explain the third vehicle, the Shen of Illusion.
It is called 'Illusion' because the phenomenal world is illusive with illusions.
It is called 'Shen', because the Shen come to overcome the illusions.
For rescuing ignorant beings in erring circumstances from such impeding and obstructing circumstances,
for reducing to subjection the proud ones of this world,
for finally destroying the false view of foes and impeders,
for removing wreckers of the doctrine to their proper place,
you should betake yourself to a quiet place and gather there the things on which the rite depends.
Meditate on the Gods of Illusion. Mutter powerful spells.
Fix the boundary of the profane (outside) and the sacred (inside), and undistractedly practise invocation and conjuration.
Evil effects must be expelled.
The circumstances of living beings must be purified and opposing obstructions overcome.
Establish the doctrine and suppress false views.
For the sake of religion and for living beings in general
one does not want the sort of wrath which perverts the mind,
and although one uses the rites of slaughter and of 'enforced release',[31]
they do not conflict with the true intention, for they are an entrance-way.
By such means the realm of living beings will become happy.
ḥPhrul-gśen gTsug-phud, keep this in mind!

This is what he said. Then they asked him again:

Princely Teacher, Best of Shen,
Although the ways of Swastika *Bon* are vast and numberless,
you have said that they are compressed into a set of Nine Vehicles.
Now as for the third vehicle, the *Bon* Way of the Shen of Illusion,
will you explain to us clearly the contents of the general divisions and special sections.
What are the characteristics of the practice and of starting the practice,
and finally what result and what special qualities are gained?
We beg you to tell us clearly.

de la yaṅ ston pas bkaḥ stsal pa /
ñon cig ḥphrul gśen gtsug phud ñon ||
ḥphrul gśen theg paḥi bon sgo la ||
spyi ru rnam pa gsum yin te ||
bsñen daṅ bsgrub daṅ las sbyor ro ||
bsñen ni dpon gsas lha la bsñen ||
mtshan ñid ldan paḥi bla ma ni ||
gśen rnams kun gyi rab tu ste ||
ri boḥi sku daṅ rgya mtshoḥi gsuṅ ||
nam mkhaḥi thugs can mkhyen daṅ brtse ||
mthu dbaṅ byin rlabs phun sum tshogs ||
mos ḥdun gsum gyi sgo nas btsal[a] ||
skad cig ḥbral mi phod pa yis ||
ma phyir bu ḥbreṅ lta bur btsal[a] ||
ḥjigs paḥi tshogs la g·yaṅ zaḥi phyir ||
lam ḥjigs skyel ma lta bur btsal[a] ||
raṅ mos gźan la dran med paḥi ||
mdzaḥ mthun sñog pa lta bur btsal[a] ||
btsal[e] nas rñed paḥi bsten tshul ni ||
lus ṅag yid daṅ gsum duḥo ||
lus kyi phyag daṅ gus pas bsten ||
ṅag gi bstod tshig gduṅ bas bsten ||
yid kyi dad daṅ ḥdun [222b] pas bsten ||
de yaṅ źu tshul rnam pa gsum ||
lus kyi lus srog rgyan la sogs ||
gaṅ du ḥbyor lcog gaṅ yod pa ||
chags med blo yis ḥbul la źu ||
ṅag gi spro dgaḥ dbyaṅs skyed ciṅ ||
mchod brjod gduṅ tshig sñan pas źu ||
yid kyi dad daṅ mos pa daṅ ||
dad pa phyir mi ldog pas źu ||
de la bsñen tshul rnam pa gsum ||
lus bskyed drin can pha ma daṅ ||
sems bskyed rdo rje slob dpon daṅ ||
mthun paḥi grogs bskyed lha sras lcam ||
khoṅ paḥi sñiṅ daṅ dpral baḥi mig ||
lus kyi gtso bo mgo ltar bsñen ||
de las ḥbyuṅ[b] tshul rnam pa gsum ||
bdag la phan paḥi thugs rje ḥbyuṅ ||
gźan la phan paḥi thabs mchog ḥbyuṅ ||
de gñis zuṅ ḥbrel mthar phyin ḥbyuṅ ||

[a] brtsal [b] byuṅ

Then the Teacher said:

Listen *ḥPhrul-gśen gTsug-phud*, listen.
In the *Bon* Way of the Vehicle of the Shen of Illusion
there are three general sections,
veneration, conjuration and application.
For veneration, one venerates the divine Master-Sages
as teachers possessing the right characteristics and as the Best of all Shen.
(We liken) their body to a fair mountain,
their voice to the ocean, their mind to the sky.
In knowledge and love, in strength and grace, they are excellent.
One should seek them with three kinds of devotion.
One should seek them as a child runs after its mother, not bearing a moment's separation.
One should seek them like an escort on a fearful path, as before an abyss where there is a host of fears.
One should seek them as one pursues a loving friend, who is devoted to oneself alone and gives no thought to others.
When one has sought out (such a one), the ways of cleaving to the one you have found
are threefold (as expressed) by body, speech and mind.
With the body you must cleave to him by serving and devotion.
With speech you must cleave to him with longing (as expressed) in words of praise.
With the mind you must cleave to him with faith and desire.
Then there are three ways of asking him (for guidance).
Ask him by offering him your body and life, your jewelry and so on, whatever you are able to obtain, whatever there is. Offer it with a mind free from attachment to these things.
Ask him with sweet-sounding words of longing and formulas of worship, which arouse melodies of joy.
Ask him with irreversible faith, with the faith and devotion of mind.
The way of veneration is of three kinds:
your kind parents who gave you your body,
your Powerbolt-Teacher who produced in you the Thought of Enlightenment,
the sacred companion, male or female, who gave rise to loving friendship,
all these should be venerated like the heart in your body, the eyes below your forehead, and your head which is the chief part of the body.
From this (veneration) there are three kinds of arising:
the arising of compassion which benefits oneself,
the arising of excellent methods which benefit others,
the arising of perfection which is a combination of both.

deḥi phyir dpon gsas lha la bsñen ||
lus ṅag gus pas źu ba dbul[a] ||
skad cig ḥbral med spyi bor bsgom ||
mos gus gduṅ ba gsol ba ḥdebs ||
sems bskyed dag pas gźan phan bsam ||
rgyud daṅ luṅ la gźig[b] ḥgrel gtoṅ ||
man ṅag goms ḥdris ga dar bslab ||
ḥbral med lhan cig ḥgrog par bya ||
dbaṅ gźi don daṅ ldan par bya ||
yid dam lha yi rdzoṅ la źen ||
sñiṅ po sṅags kyis brlab par bya ||
tiṅ ṅe ḥdzin gyi go cha bgo ||
thog mar bsñen paḥi rim paḥo ||

gñis pa bsgrub paḥi rim pa la ||
gnas daṅ rdzas daṅ bcaḥ gźi gsum ||
tiṅ ḥdzin sñiṅ po phyag rgya gsum ||
tshig bśad ḥphrin las rjes byaḥo ||
gnas ni ri brag ḥjigs su ruṅ ||
yaṅ na dur khrod ḥjigs pa ste ||
rigs kyi sruṅ daṅ rtags kyis brgyan ||
rdzas ni gaṅ la gaṅ dgos kyi ||
[223a] dkyil ḥkhor lha rdzas mchod pa daṅ ||
brten[c] paḥi dam rdzas bsgrub rdzas daṅ ||
mkho baḥi phyag cha mthun rdzas daṅ ||
gaṅ lcog bsgrub la brtson ḥgrus bya ||
bcaḥ gźi dkyil ḥkhor lha stegs daṅ ||
bum pa gtor ma la sogs te ||
bla gur bla ri yol ba daṅ ||
gdugs daṅ rgyal mtshan la sogs dbub ||
phun sum tshogs paḥi yo byad bśam ||
gtsaṅ ma phud kyis phyi g·yen bskaṅ ||
śel dkar ḥod daṅ nam mkhaḥi snaṅ ||
ḥod dkar ḥdzin daṅ bon bdag la ||
sruṅ ba mtshams kyi ḥphrin las bcol ||
sgrub rten lha rdzas yid ḥoṅ dgram[d] ||
tiṅ ḥdzin rnam gsum rim par bsgom ||
de bźin ñid snaṅ rgyu yis bskyed ||
sñiṅ po rnam gsum yi ge ḥbru ||
lha sku thig le bźu ḥdu[e] bya ||
bcaḥ sgyur phyag rgya mkhaḥ la dgrol[f] ||

[a] ḥbul [b] ḥbrel [c] bstan [d] bkram [e] bdul [f] bkrol

So one must venerate the divine Master-Sages.
You must make your requests with devotion of body and speech.
You must meditate upon them as though they were enthroned above you and so as not to be separated from them for one moment.
You must make your supplications with devotion and longing.
Concentrate on benefiting others by raising pure Thought towards Enlightenment.
Give careful study to the traditions and inspired texts.
Learn thoroughly so as to perfect yourself in the teachings.
Keep the company (of your lama) without separating from him for a moment.
Be possessed of the effects of the four consecrations.
Long for the citadels of the tutelary divinities.
Learn through spells their very essence.
Wear the armour of profound meditation.
Firstly then this is the order of veneration.

Secondly as for the ordering of the conjuration,
(we distinguish) the place, the items and the preparation,
then meditation, essence and gesture,
the phases of the liturgy and the afterpart.
The place should be in fearful mountains or in a fearful cemetery,
and it should be adorned with the 'Family Defenders' and 'Family Signs'.[32]
The items are whatever may be required in whatever case,
the mystic circle, the sacred items of worship,
the symbolic articles, the articles for coercing (the divinity),
the necessary instruments and suitable articles.
You must strive to effect whatever you can.

For preparations you must set up the table for the mystic circle,
the vase, the sacrificial cakes and so on,
the canopy and the curtains,
umbrellas, banners of victory and so on.
You must prepare the very best of things.
With pure offerings make atonement to the outer regions of the non-gods,
and set the guardian divinities to their work in the (four) quarters, *Śel-dkar-ḥod* (in the east), *Nam-mkhaḥi-snaṅ* (in the north), *ḥo-dkar-ḥdzin* (in the west) and *Bon-bdag* (in the south).
One must arrange in a pleasing way the ritual articles and sacred items.
One must concentrate on meditation in three stages:
the very truth itself (*de-bźin-ñid*)
its universal manifestation (*kun-tu snaṅ-ba*)
its substantial manifestation (*rgyu*).
The essence is of three parts, the seed-syllables, the divine form and the dissolution into the central dot.
(The gesture consists of) the hands at rest, the turning of the hands, the forming of the gesture, the release of the gesture in space.

mkhaḥ la gsas dbab kloṅ du bstim ||
gñis su med par dam tshig bsre ||
mchod paḥi yo byad ḥdod yon rdzas ||
mṅon sprul nam mkhaḥi mthaḥ mñam dbul[a] ||
dgyes skoṅ[b] thugs dam rgyud nas bskul ||
tshig bśad gyer daṅ bskul baḥi brda ||
rṅa gśaṅ rol mos sñan gsan dbab ||
dbyiṅs nas ye śes mṅon spyan draṅ ||
dug lṅa raṅ grol khri gdan dbul[a] ||
sgo gsum phyag ḥtshal sdig pa bśag ||
mkhaḥ gsal ye śes mchod pas bskaṅ ||
bdud rtsi sman gyi rgyud la brten ||
thugs dam bdag daṅ bar mtshams sbrel ||
phyag rgya gar gyis snod bcud rol ||
sku bstod ḥphrin las dbyiṅs su bcol ||
bla med grub paḥi rtags su gsal ||
dkyil ḥkhor sgo dbye bdag źal blta ||
gñis su med par gtan dam bcaḥ ||
mchog daṅ thun moṅ dṅos grub gsol ||
dbaṅ bźi yoṅs rdzogs byin rlabs [223b] blaṅ ||
bcol paḥi ḥphrin las dbyiṅs su bsgrub ||
dbal moḥi za lam dgra la bstan ||
las kyi ḥphrin las dbyiṅs su bsdu ||
bdag med raṅ bźin mkhaḥ la bstim ||
bdag gźan don grub kloṅ du mñam ||
de rnams[c] sgrub paḥi rim paḥo ||

gsum la las la sbyor ba la ||
brnag pa rgyu ḥphrul dra ba la[d] ||
ḥgal daṅ ḥbrel ba zuṅ du ḥjug ||
ḥphrul gśen theg paḥi bon sgo la ||
spyod lam ḥgal źiṅ don la ḥbrel ||
drag poḥi sa gnas spyod la ḥgal ||
thams cad dbaṅ bsdus don la ḥbrel ||
brnag paḥi las ka spyod la ḥgal ||
bstan paḥi so ḥdzug don la ḥbrel ||

[a] ḥbul [b] bskaṅs [c] bsñen daṅ [d] daṅ

(There are gestures for) inviting the *gSas* from the skies, for their absorption into space, for uniting as one in the sacrament, for indicating items of worship and desirable things, which one offers in illusory form equalling in extent the limits of the sky, thus pleasing and satifying them, and urging them in accordance with their thoughtful purposes.

The liturgy consists of the incantations and the sounds for urging on (the gods),
drums, flat bells, with these sounds one calls them,
inviting the gods of knowledge down from the celestial spheres.
One must offer them the thrones of the 'Five Evils Self-Released',[33]
salute them with body, speech and mind, and confess ones faults.
One must make atonement to them with the worship known as 'Knowledge of the Clear Sky',
and make use of the traditional means of elixir and medicaments.
The tutelary divinity and oneself are brought together in the intervening space (which once separated them).
The world and its creatures sport in a gesturing dance.
One praises the forms (of the gods) and urges them to their tasks in the celestial spheres.
There is clarity in the (divine) signs so excellently effected.
(As for the afterpart) one opens the mystic circle and sees the face of the chief divinity,
and one makes the firm vow of never being two,
and begs for the special powers of both the extraordinary and the ordinary kind.
One receives the perfect grace (flowing from) the four ritual acts,
and one effects in the celestial spheres the tasks to which (the divinities) are committed.
The consuming way of the *dBal-mo* is turned upon one's enemies.
The phases of the rite are concentrated in the celestial spheres.
Selfless self-nature is absorbed into the heavens.
That which is effected for self and for others is resolved into the sameness of space.
Such is the order of the conjuration.

Thirdly as for the application,
in this magic net of ferocity
contradiction and coherence join in pairs.
In this *bon* way of the Vehicle of the Shen of Illusion
there is contradiction in the practice and coherence in the result.
Staying in a wild place contradicts normal practice,
but subduing all to one's power is coherent in result.
Ferocious actions contradict normal practice,
but to establish the doctrine is coherent in result.

śa khrag dmar mchod spyod la ḥgal ||
sbyor sgrol rol pa don la ḥbrel ||
dam rdzas lṅa po spyod la ḥgal ||
dug lṅa gnas dag don la ḥbrel ||
mtshan ldan gzuṅs ma spyod la ḥgal ||
thabs śes dbyer med don la ḥbrel ||
rtogs paḥi rgyaṅ mtshams[a] spyod la ḥgal ||
dben paḥi gnas brten don la ḥbrel ||
brnag paḥi źe sdaṅ spyod la ḥgal ||
raṅ bźin byams pa don la ḥbrel ||
dregs paḥi ṅa rgyal spyod la ḥgal ||
źiṅ khams źi bdeḥi don la ḥbrel ||
thabs kyi rdzu ḥphrul spyod la ḥgal ||
log rtog ḥdul ba don la ḥbrel ||
dgra la brnag pa spyod la ḥgal ||
bar chod dben pa don la ḥbrel ||
phan gnod ḥdzin pa spyod la ḥgal ||
ḥgro la phan bde don la ḥbrel ||
bzaṅ ṅan ñe riṅ spyod la ḥgal ||
bzaṅ po spyod pa don la ḥbrel ||
legs ñes ḥdzin pa spyod la ḥgal ||
legs paḥi bya ba don la ḥbrel ||
srog gi ḥkhor lo spyod la ḥgal ||
ma rig gnas spar don la [224a] ḥbrel ||
maṅ saḥi gtor ma spyod la ḥgal ||
gti mug raṅ grol don la ḥbrel ||
rak taḥi mchod pa spyod la ḥgal ||
ḥdod chags rtsad gcad don la ḥbrel ||
rus paḥi gram khrod spyod la ḥgal ||
źe sdaṅ dbyiṅs sgrol don la ḥbrel ||
źiṅ chen g·yaṅ gźi spyod la ḥgal ||
ḥphrag dog raṅ grol don la ḥbrel ||
srog dbugs mchod pa spyod la ḥgal ||
ṅa rgyal rtsad gcad don la ḥbrel ||
yu tiḥi mchod pa spyod la ḥgal ||
g·yu ḥbraṅ bdud rtsi don la ḥbrel[b] ||
bhāṇ ḍa[c] lcaṅ lo spyod la ḥgal ||
mtshan ldan yol chen don la ḥbrel ||
drag poḥi phur pa spyod la ḥgal ||
ḥkhor ba gtiṅ non don la ḥbrel ||

[a] ḥtsham [b] rol [c] bhan dha

Red offerings of flesh and blood contradict normal practice,
but the three practices of ritual union, ritual slaughter and magical manifestation are coherent in result.
The five sacred items contradict normal practice,
but to purify the Five Evils is coherent in result.
The special female partner contradicts normal practice,
but when Method and Wisdom are mutually indistinguishable this is coherent in result.
To cut oneself off far from learning contradicts normal practice,
but to keep to a desolate place is coherent in result.
Ferocious anger contradicts normal practice,
but a loving nature is coherent in result.
Arrogant pride contradicts normal practice,
but to reduce the world to peace and happiness is coherent in result.
Methodical magic contradicts normal practice,
but to suppress false considerations is coherent in result.
Ferocity with regard to enemies contradicts normal practice,
but to remove obstructions is coherent in result.
To cause benefits by causing harm contradicts normal practice,
but to bring (overall) benefits to living beings is coherent in result.
To practise good and evil near and far contradicts normal practice,
but the (overall) practice of good is coherent in result.
To cause both good and harm contradicts normal practice,
but when done for good it is coherent in result.
The *Circle-of-Life* Practice contradicts normal practice,
but to raise the position of the ignorant is coherent in result.[34]
The sacrificial offering of meat contradicts normal practice,
but to rescue the stupid is coherent in result.
The offering of blood contradicts normal practice,
but to root out desire is coherent in result.
The heap of bones contradicts normal practice,
but to dispose of wrath is coherent in result.
The use of human skins[35] contradicts normal practice,
but to dispose of envy is coherent in result.
To sacrifice the life (of creatures) contradicts normal practice,
but to root out pride is coherent in result.
To use *chang* for worship contradicts normal practice,
but the consecrated *chang* is coherent in result.
The use of hairy skulls contradicts normal practice,
but the special skull-shaped vessel is coherent in result.
The ferocious ritual dagger contradicts normal practice,
but to suppress the cycle of existence is coherent in result.

e kloṅ ḥbrub khuṅ spyod la ḥgal ||
bon ñid kloṅ yaṅs don la ḥbrel ||
rtsaṅ dmar mtshon cha spyod la ḥgal ||
srid paḥi dra ba don la ḥbrel ||
dmigs paḥi liṅ ga spyod la ḥgal ||
ma rtogs ḥdul ba don la ḥbrel ||
sreg ḥphaṅ mnan gsum spyod la ḥgal ||
bon ñid gnas spar don la ḥbrel ||
de ltar ḥgal ḥbrel cha mthun paḥi ||
brnag pa rgyu ḥphrul dra ba la ||
phyi rgyud naṅ rgyud gsaṅ rgyud gsum ||
phyi rgyud mkhaḥ ḥgyiṅ dbal gyi rgyud ||
naṅ rgyud dbal gsas drag poḥi rgyud ||
gsaṅ rgyud las kyi thig leḥi rgyud ||
phyi rgyud mkhaḥ ḥgyiṅ dbal tshogs la ||
dzo dbal thigs kyi sṅags byad daṅ ||
lha rgod ñi khriḥi dmod byad daṅ ||
ma mo thun gyi zor byad daṅ ||
nag po bdud kyi lda byad bźi ||
ḥphrin las bźi yi gźuṅ la ḥbrel[a] ||
dbal gsas drag poḥi brnag pa la ||
dbaṅ sdud las kyi brnag pa daṅ ||
drag po bzlog paḥi ḥkhor lo daṅ ||
drag po [224b] rdzu ḥphrul rgyud chen daṅ ||
zil gnon khyuṅ nag ral chen bźi ||
las bźi brnag paḥi rgyud bźi byuṅ ||
gsaṅ rgyud las kyi thig le la ||
dbal mo las kyi thig le daṅ ||
dbal mo srog gi thig le daṅ ||
dbal mo srog gi spu gri daṅ ||
dbal mo las kyi byaṅ bu bźi ||
sum cu rtsa gsum ḥbrel[b] nas byuṅ ||
de ltar rgyud chen bcu gñis la ||
las mkhan ḥjig rten dmod byad bcas ||
sṅags ḥgrel brgya daṅ rtsa brgyad byuṅ ||
de la yaṅ ḥgrel stoṅ rtsa gñis ||
bcas daṅ lag len ldan par bya ||

[a] ḥgrel [b] ḥdrel

The triangular smiting cavity contradicts normal practice,
but if *bon* itself extends through space, this is coherent in result.
Red stakes and weapons contradict normal practice,
but the net of existence is coherent in result.
The *Liṅga* Practice with (foes) envisaged contradicts normal practice,
but the subduing of ignorance is coherent in result.
To burn, to send flying, to hold down, these three acts contradict normal practice,
but to elevate *bon* is coherent in result.

In this magic net of ferocity where contradiction and coherence are related in pairs,
there are three tantric series, the outer, the inner and the secret.
The outer series is the tantra of *mKhaḥ-ḥgyiṅ-dbal.*
The inner series is the tantra of Fierce *dBal-gsas.*
The secret series is the tantra of the Essences of Acts (of the *dBal-mo*).
In the outer series, the group of *mKhaḥ-ḥgyiṅ-dbal*
there is the malevolence of spells of *Dzo-dbal-thigs*,
the malevolence of imprecations of the 20,000 wild gods,
the malevolence of the hurled offerings of the mother-goddesses,
the special malevolence of the black demons, making four in all.
They are connected with the basic tradition of the four ritual acts.
In the ferocious practice of Fierce *dBal-gsas*,
there is the ferocity of the subduing act,
the fierce circle of expulsion,
the great tantra of magic, the fierce one,
the subduer *Khyuṅ-nag ral-chen*, making four in all.
These four acts occur as the four ferocious tantras.

In the secret series, the Essences of Acts,
there are the essences of acts of the *dBal-mo*,
the essences of the life-force of the *dBal-mo*,
the razor of life-force of the *dBal-mo*,
the indications of actions of the *dBal-mo.*
They occur in connexion with the thirty-three.

Thus with these twelve tantras which include as expedients the malevolence of imprecations of the gods of the world,
there are 108 tantric commentaries, and furthermore 1,002 subsidiary commentaries.
Subsidiary technical matters are also to be included.

de ltar sgrub bsñen mthar bskyal nas ||
drag poḥi las la sbyor ba na ||
drag po ḥjigs paḥi gnas dag tu ||
e kloṅ drag poḥi thun khaṅ bcaḥ ||
gzaḥ skar pra ltas śis la ḥjug ||
lha ni dbal gsas rṅam pa bsgom ||
bdud ni mi mthun log lta ḥdul ||
srog gi ḥkhor lo gnad la bsnun ||
mi ldog srog yig them la blaṅ ||
gnad la bskor la gcun la ḥbor ||
brten[a] paḥi gtaḥ gzugs srog mkhar gzugs[b] ||
śa khrag dmar la dbal mo dbab ||
ḥjig rten lha rgod phud kyis mchod ||
mchod daṅ brten[a] paḥi las la brtson ||
dgra daṅ bgegs kyi miṅ byaṅ ḥbri[c] ||
dmigs paḥi ḥben la gsal bar bskyed ||
thun daṅ sna tshogs mtshon chas bsnun ||
dgug[d] daṅ bstim daṅ gsad daṅ bsgral[e] ||
bstab daṅ rol daṅ thugs dam bskaṅ ||
brnag paḥi las la sñiṅ rje med ||
las sbyor mthaḥ [225a] ru phyin par bya ||
sreg ḥphaṅ mnan gsum skabs daṅ sbyar ||
rjes śul bon ñid rgya yis gdab ||
ḥphrul gśen gtsug phud dbal gyi gśen ||
brnag paḥi las sbyor thugs la źog ||
sems can ḥgro la sman par mdzod ||

yaṅ rgyal bus bkaḥ stsal pa /

ñon cig ḥphrul gśen gtsug phud la sogs ||
ḥdus paḥi ḥkhor rnams thams cad kun ||
theg pa gsum pa ḥphrul gśen la ||
ḥjug ciṅ spyod paḥi gaṅ zag rnams ||
spyir yaṅ bon rnams thams cad la ||
sems bskyed gźi ma mi ldan na ||
źiṅ sa ṅan paḥi sa bon ḥdra ||
skam la bab na ḥbras bu ḥtshig ||
myu gu ḥkhruṅ bar ga la ḥgyur ||

[a] bstan [b] btsug [c] bris [d] ḥgug [e] sgrol

Having thus completed this account of conjuration and veneration,
(we come to) the practical application of ferocity.
In a wild and fearsome place
prepare the magic receptacle of the ferocious triangle,
and set to work when the stars and other prognostics are auspicious.
Meditate upon *dBal-gsas* the Fierce One as presiding divinity,
and suppress as demons antagonistic false views.
Pierce the *Circle-of-Life* to the heart.
Take the infallible *Life-Letter* as the symbol.
Encircle the heart and reduce it to subjection.
Set up the pledge-symbols of the attendant (divinities) and set up the 'life-force citadel'.
Call down the *dBal-mo* for the offerings of flesh and blood.
Worship with offerings the wild gods of this world.
Make effort in the worship and the actions of service.
Write the name-cards of foes and obstructors.
Produce a clear idea of the envisaged target.
Sting with the deterrents and various weapons.
(The whole process consists of) coercing (the enemy), dissolving (him into the *liṅga*), slaying (him) and disposing of him, then offering, rejoicing and atonement.
In these ferocious acts there is no compassion.
This practical application must be performed in its entirety.
To burn, to send flying, to hold down, these three acts must suit the occasion.
After all is over, set upon it the seal of *bon*.
ḥPhrul-gśen gTsug-phud, Shen of *dBal*.
Keep in mind this ferocious application, and do good to living beings.

Again the Prince spoke:
Listen *ḥPhrul-gśen gTsug-phud*
and all your entourage assembled here.
People who enter and practise this third vehicle of the Shen of Illusion,
if in regard to all *bon* in general they do not have as the basis (of their practice) the raising of their Thought to Enlightenment,
they are like seed which is thrown on bad ground.
For if it is thrown in a dry place, it shrivels up,
so how can the shoot come to birth?

deḥi phyir bon la spyod pa la ||
raṅ la phan paḥi dad pa dgos ||
gźan la phan paḥi sems bskyed dgos ||
sems bskyed rtsa ba sñiṅ rje yin ||
dad paḥi rtsa ba mi rtag yin ||
mi rtag rtsa ba stoṅ pa ñid ||
stoṅ pa sñiṅ rje zuṅ ḥbrel yin ||
ḥgro ba thar pa de yis ḥdroṅ ||
deḥi phyir sñiṅ rje bskyed par bya ||
sñiṅ rje bdag phyogs med par bskyed ||
bdag phyogs byuṅ na sñiṅ rje gol ||
khra spyaṅ sñiṅ rje bdag phyogs can ||
ḥgro la mi phan raṅ mthun gso ||
de la ḥbras bu chuṅ bar byed ||
ḥgro la ma ltar byams pa daṅ ||
kun la ñi ltar bsñam pa daṅ ||
sems bskyed gźi ma ldan par bya ||
bag yod bźin du spyad par bya ||
ḥgro ba gaṅ la gaṅ phan bya ||
sems bskyed ma gol gźan phan bya ||
ḥphrul gśen theg pa rgyu yi bon ||
luṅ daṅ tshul bźin spyad pa na ||
don la mi gol ḥjug sgoḥi lam ||
yan lag thabs kyi bon yin te ||
ḥbras buḥi theg [225b] pa a dkar bsñag[a] ||
don du a dkar sa la ṅes ||
thabs śes dbyer med ḥbras bu thob ||
deḥi phyir deḥi don la slobs ||
ḥdi yi don la ḥjug par gyis ||
ḥdi yi don la brtag par bya ||
ḥdi yi don la spyod par gyis ||
ḥdi yi don la bsgom par gyis ||
ḥdi yi don la bsgrub par gyis ||
ḥdi yi don la gnas par gyis ||
des na don daṅ yon tan ni ||
ḥdi la ḥjug daṅ rtogs pa yis ||
khams gsum ḥkhor baḥi sa bsgral nas ||
mos par spyod paḥi sa la gnas ||
mos spyod sa bźi yar brgal nas ||
g·yuṅ druṅ sa bcu rim par bgrod ||

[a] sñeg

Thus in the practice of *bon*
one must have the faith that will benefit oneself,
and one must raise one's Thought to Enlightenment as benefiting others.
The basis for thus raising Thought is compassion.
The basis of faith is impermanence.
The basis of impermanence is Voidness.
Voidness and Compassion go together as a pair.
By their means beings are led to salvation,
so one must exercise compassion.
But one must exercise compassion free of self-interest.
If self-interest arises, this contradicts compassion.
The hawk and the wolf have compassion of a self-interested kind.
It does not benefit others. It preserves one's own kind.
The fruits of this are very small.
Loving living beings like a mother,
practising the same towards everyone, as does the sun,
you must have as the basis (of your action) this raising of the Thought (towards Enlightenment).
You must act carefully.
You must do whatever benefits living beings in whatever case.
Do nothing to contradict this raising of one's Thought and act for others' benefit.

The Way of the Shen of Illusion is *Bon* of Cause.
But if it is practised according to the inspired teachings and according to custom,
it will not be contradictory in effect. Rather it will be an entrance-way.
It is *bon* of a methodical kind,
and it reaches out towards the Way of Effect of 'Pure Sound'.
In result it is sure (to reach) the stage of 'Pure Sound'.
It achieves the effect where Method and Wisdom are indistinguishable.
Therefore do your learning with this as the intended result.
Investigate towards this result.
Practise towards this result.
Meditate towards this result.
Perform conjurations towards this result.
Be resolute towards this result.
So as for the result and the accomplishments,
by starting on this Way and comprehending it,
one traverses the stages of this threefold world,
and abides in the stage of 'Devotional Practice'.
Having traversed the four stages of 'Devotional Practice',
one traverses in order the ten Swastika stages.

g·yuṅ druṅ sa bcu rim bgrod nas ||
kun snaṅ gliṅ du mṅon ḥtshaṅ rgya[a] ||
kun snaṅ gliṅ du saṅs rgyas nas ||
ḥgro ba sems can dpal du ḥgyur ||
mthar thug yon tan de ltar thob ||
gnas skabs yon tan bsam las ḥdas ||
ḥjig rten źiṅ ḥdir bde legs daṅ ||
saṅs rgyas bstan pa dar ba daṅ ||
g·yuṅ druṅ dbu ḥphaṅ mtho ba daṅ ||
źiṅ khams bde la dgod[b] pa yi ||
cha gcig ḥphrul gśen thabs la thug ||
stag lha me ḥbar sprul paḥi gśen ||
ḥphrul gśen gtsug phud ṅo mtshar can ||
ḥphrul gśen gtsug phud la gñer gtad ||
kho ma ne chuṅ bdag tu bsko[c] ||
groṅ khyer sgyu ḥphrul dgaḥ ba la ||
bon gyi ḥkhor lo bskor bar mdzod ||
ces bkaḥ stsal to /

[a] saṅs rgyas [b] bkod [c] bskos

Having traversed the ten swastika stages,
one gains buddhahood at the stage of Universal Shining Light.
Having gained buddhahood at this stage,
one becomes the glory of living beings.
One gains perfect accomplishments like these,
and one's accidental accomplishments surpass all thought.
For one thing the Way of the Shen of Illusion is concerned with a method
for happiness in this world,
for spreading the Buddhist doctrine,
for raising the Swastika dignity,
and for establishing the spheres of existence in bliss.

Of Shen of Illusion, *sTag-lha me-ḥbar*,
ḥPhrul-gśen gTsug-phud, most wonderful.
I give the responsibility to you *ḥPhrul-gśen gTsug-phud*.
You must take charge of the Palace *Kho-ma-ne-chuṅ*,
and turn the wheel of *bon* in the city of *sGyu-ḥphrul-dgaḥ-ba*.

This is what he said.

IV. SRID GŚEN THEG PA

theg pa bźi pa srid gśen ḥchad par byed ||
ḥkhor baḥi sems can ma rig ñon moṅs [*ga* 27b] rnams ||
raṅ rig ma rtogs ma rig ḥkhrul ḥkhor ḥkhyam ||
skye śi kha brgyud śa yi gdos pa can ||
ma rig pa la ñon moṅs nad du ldaṅ ||
bźi brgya rtsa bźi nad kyi sdug bsṅal gduṅ ||
ma rtogs pa la don gyi khu ḥphrig ldaṅ ||
stoṅ phrag drug cu gdon gyi lan chags bsñag ||
ḥchi sa ma ṅes ḥchi baḥi gnas ma ṅes ||
ḥchi rkyen ma ṅes ḥchi baḥi dus ma ṅes ||
rgas daṅ gźon daṅ byis pa[a] skyes ma thag ||
gri daṅ ḥkhrugs pa nad daṅ yams la sogs ||
glo bur ye ḥbrog sdug bsṅal sbyaṅ daṅ ḥchi ||
ma rig ma rtogs ḥkhrul paḥi las dbaṅ gis ||
bla yid sems gsum dum bu gsum du mthoṅ ||
bdag med stoṅ paḥi ṅo bo ma rtogs pas ||
rig pa bdag med bdag po gñis su ḥdzin ||
gcig ni lhan cig skyes paḥi lha ru ḥdod ||
gcig ni lhan cig skyes paḥi ḥdre ru ḥdod ||
lha yis phan ciṅ ḥdre yis gnod pa daṅ ||
dbugs len srog gcod bdud phyir ḥbreṅ ba daṅ ||
gnas daṅ yul daṅ ḥdug sa ḥtshol ba daṅ ||
dge sdig rgyu ḥbras dkar nag mthoṅ ba daṅ ||
ḥchi bdag gśin rjeḥi sdug bsṅal sbyaṅ ba daṅ ||
de ltar gcig la du mar ḥdzin pa yis ||
bde baḥi skabs med ḥchi khaḥi nad pa ḥdra ||
dbaṅ po kun tshaṅ tshu rol gnas daṅ ḥdra ||
thogs pa med pa bar snaṅ rluṅ daṅ ḥdra ||
ḥjigs skrag bred pa ri dvags rgyar chud ḥdra ||
yid kha rmoṅ ba sa mthaḥi ku hraṅ ḥdra ||
thar du mi re mun khaṅ btson doṅ ḥdra ||
ḥdug sa ḥtshol ba byeḥu phrug [28a] tshaṅ yar ḥdra ||
skyabs gnas med pa dva phrug mas[b] bor ḥdra ||
bkres śiṅ skom pa yi dvags dbul ḥphoṅs ḥdra ||
yid la mi bde zil bsgyur ḥdres bded ḥdra ||
raṅ dbaṅ med pa la khaḥi bya sgro ḥdra ||
gźan dbaṅ bsgyur ba khrims kyi mṅaḥ ḥog ḥdra ||

[a] sba [b] ma

IV. THE WAY OF THE SHEN OF EXISTENCE

I shall explain the fourth vehicle, the Shen of Existence.
The living beings of *samsāra*, ignorant and afflicted,
not understanding self-knowledge, ignorantly wander in a circle of illusion.
Things of flesh, linked in a series of birth and death,
in their ignorance their afflictions take the form of disease.
They are distressed with the sufferings of the 404 types of disease.
Erroneous views of things are aroused in the case of the ignorant,
and they are pursued by the 60,000 demonish retributions.
The place of death is uncertain and the condition of death is uncertain.
The circumstances of death and the time of death are uncertain.
The old, the young, the children and those just born,
by murder, riot, sickness, plague and the rest,
experiencing sudden injuries and miseries, they die.
By force of deluded karmic effects, with no knowledge and no understanding,
they regard spirit, thought and mind as three separate parts.[36]
Not understanding the void nature of the non-self,
the knowledge, which is non-self, they conceive as two selves.
One they assert to be the innate divinity.
One they assert to be the innate demon.[37]
Gods are of help to them and demons do harm.
Their breath is withdrawn, they are killed and they run after devils,
seeking a place and a country and somewhere to stay.
Good and evil, cause and effect, white and black are seen,
and they experience the sufferings of the master of death, the Lord of the Dead.
Thus they conceive of one as many.
There is no occasion of happiness. It resembles the sickness of the time of one's death.
Their sense powers (after death) are complete like those that remain on this side,
but unobstructed they pass through space like the wind.
They are frightened and fearful like a deer which has entered a trap.
Their thoughts are confused like the wild ass of the frontier regions.
They have no hope of release, as though emprisoned in a dungeon.
They search for their resting place, like a young bird for its nest.
They have no place of refuge, like an orphan child, or one abandoned by its mother.
They are hungry and thirsty like poor tormented spirits.
Their thoughts are unhappy and frenzied, as though pursued by demons.
They have no power of their own, like a feather on the top of a pass.
They are like those who have fallen into another's power and remain under punishment.

sdug bsṅal ñon moṅs de yi gduṅ ba la ||
rgyal baḥi thabs daṅ thugs rjes ma ḥgag phyir ||
srid gśen bon gyi thabs daṅ brda sbyor la ||
śi thabs rgan gźon dar rgyas byis paḥi[a] tshogs ||
śi rkyen nad daṅ dug mtshon gdon la sogs ||
gaṅ du ma ṅes rkyen gyis śi ba la ||
ḥdur thabs de daṅ mthun par gaṅ ḥdul gyis ||
gson gśin brda sprod sdug bsṅal thaṅ la dbyuṅ ||
bla yid sems gsum lus sems gcig tu sdus ||
bar sa de la gnas paḥi gnas su źog ||
sṅon gyi bag chags rjes dran bon sgo ston ||
bde baḥi gnas sñog bon ñid sa la khod ||
srid gśen gtsug phud thugs kyi dkyil du źog ||

[vol. *ga*, f. 29a[2]]

de ltar kun rdzob mtshan ma la[b] ||
mtshan ma dṅos po bden dgos pas ||
srid pa rgyud kyi bon po yis ||
thog mar rtsis kyis gtan la dbab[c] ||
rtsis kyis gtan la ma phab na ||
gaṅ la gaṅ dgos śan mi phyed[d] ||
deḥi phyir skye ba sṅa phyi daṅ ||
da ltaḥi tshe tshad riṅ thuṅ daṅ ||
rgyu rkyen śi rabs yin tshul daṅ ||
rjes śul bkrag daṅ mi bkrag daṅ ||
de la phan daṅ mi phan daṅ ||
don rtags gtan la dbab par bya[e] ||

gñis pa gto gñan gtad bcol la ||
rin chen gser gyi sa gźi la ||
dbaṅ chen bdag po mṅaḥ dbaṅ che ||
de las gźi bslaṅ ḥdur dgos pas ||
rgyal poḥi sa daṅ blon paḥi sa ||
btsun mo ded dpon bran khol daṅ ||
goṅ na gñan pa la sogs pa ||
gaṅ du śi ba brtag par bya ||
de la gźi bslaṅ cho gas bcos ||
srid pa śi rabs lo rgyus las ||
sṅon gyi srid pa chags pa nas ||
srid pa dpe blaṅ da ltaḥi bar ||
srid paḥi lugs su bon smraṅ gyer ||

[a] sbaḥi [b] las [c] phab [d] ched [e] pheb par bya

In order not to check the Conqueror's Method and Compassion in the case of those tormented with such sufferings and afflictions,
there is this method and instruction of the *bon* of the Shen of Existence.
The many ways of death (affecting) old and young, the mature and the children,
the circumstances of death, sickness, poison, weapons, demons and so on,
in the case of such uncertainties of place and circumstance,
do whatever in the way of death rites accords with the way of death.
The living must explain to the deceased and get rid of his suffering.
Spirit, thought and mind must be united as a single unity of body and mind.
Take stock of the place where he is in the Intermediate State.
Remind him of adverse influences from former births, and show him the door of *bon*.
Lead him on to a place of happiness and place him in the realm of true *bon*.
Srid-gśen gTsug-phud, keep this in mind.

Thus the characteristics of relative truth (viz. the phenomenal world),
are acceptable as true with regard to the things themselves.
So the *bonpo* of the original tradition
must first get matters in order by means of calculation.
If he does not order things by means of calculation,
he cannot decide what is required in each case.
So he must get into order all the indications of the affair:
former and future births,
the measure and length of the present life,
the cause, circumstances and manner of death,
the prosperity or absence of prosperity of those left behind,
and what will be of benefit and not of benefit in the case.
Secondly he must perform the rite for coercing the furies (viz. the Lords of the Soil).
In this earthly domain with its gems and gold
the powerful Lords (of the Soil) are strong in their power.
So you must ask a site from them and consecrate it.
A site for a king, or a site for a minister,
for a queen, for a military commander, for a servant,
those who are important by rank and so on,
you must examine where the dead man (should rest).
Then ask for the site and prepare it ceremonially.
From the stories about the original ordering of death,
how it originally arose in the first place,
taking the original archetype up to the present time,
chant the *bon* exposition in its original form.[38]

gdos pa thag chod chags pa bsal ||
ḥkhor baḥi gag sel źen pa skyur ||
[29b] dpe don śi rabs lo rgyus bśad ||
bla yid sems gsum ḥthor ba sdud ||
legs kyaṅ g·yeṅ[a] khams byiṅ ba gsiṅ ||
thar pa bde baḥi lam la bkod ||
kun rdzob mtshan mar dṅos po bden ||
mthar ni don dam kloṅ du sdud ||
srid ni thams cad srid pas srid ||
gśen ni de dag ḥdul baḥi gśen ||
lta ba bla yid sems daṅ gsum ||
sdud ciṅ thar pa ḥdren par lta ||
sgom pa bdag gźan gñis med do ||
btaṅ sñoms chen poḥi tiṅ ḥdzin bsgom ||
spyod pa ḥgro ba thams cad la ||
byams daṅ brtse baḥi tshul du bya ||
ḥbras bu ye gśen theg pa bsñag ||
lha ni ḥdur gsas rma bo bsgom ||
srid gśen gtsug phud thugs la źog ||
kun rdzob mtshan maḥi ḥdur boṅ no ||
don dam bden paḥi ḥdur ba ni ||
gśen rab lta dgoṅs rtsal ldan gyis ||
ḥgro ba ñams thag sems can la ||
sñiṅ rje dpaḥ med bskyed nas su ||
tshad med bźi daṅ ldan pa yis ||
raṅ bas gźan don gtsor byed ciṅ ||
mtshan maḥi rdzas la lus sems gzuṅ ||
duṅ śog dkar la g·yu ris bri ||
dri ma skye mched tshaṅ bar bya ||
ṅan soṅ gnas sbyaṅ sa bon dgod[b] ||
bar chod bgegs bskrad gśed daṅ phral ||
bla yid sems gsum gcig tu sprad ||
bde bar gśegs pa mchod pa ḥbul ||
ris drug bgegs la sbyin pa gtaṅ[c] ||

[a] yaṅ dbyen [b] bkod [c] btoṅ

Fix the material elements. Clarify their arising.
Remove the impediment of the phenomenal circle, and get rid of consuming desire.
Thus tell the story of the ordering of death (according to) the meaning of the archetype.
Bring together those three, spirit, thought and mind, which are scattered.
Although happy, he is inattentive. Disperse the indolence of his disposition.[39]
Establish him in the way of salvation and bliss.
Take these things as true in terms of the characteristics of phenomenal truth.
Finally one is united in the space of absolute truth.
Existence means the coming of all things into existence.
The Shen are so called because they subdue those things.
Their theory concerns spirit, thought and mind, these three,
and they regard the uniting of these as (the means of) leading (beings) to salvation.
In their meditation self and other are one and not two,
And they meditate with profound concentration in great equanimity.
As for their practice, with regard to all beings
they must act in the ways of kindness and love.
As fruit (of their practice) they strive towards the Vehicle of the Primeval Shen.
As presiding divinity, they meditate upon *ḥDur-gsas rma-bo.*
Srid-gśen gTsug-phud, keep this in mind. This is the *Bon* of Death Rites[40] and has the characteristics of relative truth.
As for death ritual (in terms of) absolute truth,
the Best of Shen who is expert in meditation
and who has aroused feelings of immeasurable compassion towards feeble living beings,
and who possesses the four measureless virtues,
puts the good of others before himself
and grasps body and mind (as one) in the things that characterize (the deceased).
He must draw the design in blue on pure white paper.[41]
He must make (the image) complete with sense-organs and with (characteristic) smell (viz. used garments).
He must put there the seed-syllables which will remove (risk of rebirth in) the places of evil rebirth.
He must expel obstructing demons and get rid of the minions of hell.
He must unite spirit, thought and mind, these three into one.
He must make offerings to the Blessed Ones,
and present gifts to the demons who inhabit the six regions.

ḥbyuṅ pa yi dvags glud kyis bskaṅ ||
ṅan soṅ gnas sbyaṅ rim par draṅ ||
dri ma mtshan byaṅ rdzas la bstim ||
bar sa de la g·yaṅ sar [30a] dbyuṅ ||
ḥjigs paḥi ḥphraṅ bsgral bde bar dgod[a] ||
sṅon gyi bag chags rjes dran bśad ||
lha daṅ slob dpon bdag źal sprad ||
dus drug ḥtsho ba spyan gzigs bteg ||
ḥdod yon zad med gter daṅ sprad ||
ḥjig rten ḥkhor baḥi las spyod la ||
mi[b] chags mi len mi źen par ||
źen pa bzlog paḥi bon sgo bśad ||
khams gsum sa dguḥi ñes dmigs bstan ||
yaṅ dag thar lam bcu gñis daṅ ||
g·yuṅ druṅ theg paḥi sa bcu daṅ ||
mthar phyin sa gsum brod kha btiṅ ||
bde baḥi gnas spar dbyiṅs su dgod[a] ||
phyir mi ldog daṅ phyir mi ḥoṅ ||
lan gcig phyir ḥoṅ rgyun du źugs ||
dgra bcom ḥbras thob smon lam gdab ||
lta dgoṅs nam mkhaḥ lta bu yi ||
gśen rab rig paḥi rtsal ldan gyi ||
sems can don nus ma gtogs pa ||
phal daṅ phal gyi spyod yul min ||
gñis phuṅ ṅan soṅ brgyud ñen che ||
sṅon nas sbyaṅ paḥi ḥphro can gyis ||
tshad med bźi yi rgyun źugs nas ||
sems can ḥgro la sman par ḥbyuṅ ||
raṅ bas gźan don gtsor byed ciṅ ||
ḥgro la phan sems rtse gcig tu ||
byams daṅ sñiṅ rjeḥi gźi ldan na ||
srid gśen theg pa ḥgro baḥi don ||
don la mi gol ḥjug sgoḥi lam ||
mthar yaṅ don daṅ ḥbras bu ni ||
khams gsum sa dgu yar brgal nas ||
mos par spyod paḥi sa la gnas ||
mos spyod sa [30b] bźi yar brgal nas ||
g·yuṅ druṅ sa bcu rim bgrod ciṅ ||
thar par mṅon par ḥtshaṅ rgyaḥo[c] ||
ces gsuṅs so /

[a] ḥkhod [b] ma [c] saṅs rgyas so

He must satisfy with items of ransom the sprites and tormented spirits.
He must lead (the deceased), removing one by one (the risks of rebirth in) the unhappy regions.
He must then dissolve (the deceased) into the clothes and characterizing items,
and bring him out from the Intermediate State into Blessedness.
He must take him through the path of fear and establish him in happiness.
He must speak to him, reminding him of former adverse influences.
Bring him face to face with his tutelary divinity and his lama.
Set up a display of sustenance for the six (daily) periods.
Let him see treasure of limitless desirable things,
and explain the *bon* door which disposes of desire,
so that one does not yearn for, does not seize at,
does not desire the activities of worldly existence.
Show the disadvantages of the nine stages of the threefold world,
and display the joys of the twelve ways of salvation, of the ten stages of the Swastika Way and of the three final stages.
Establish him in the sphere where he is raised up to the place of bliss.
Pray that he may gain the fruits of a non-returner, of a once-returner, of one who enters the stream, of an *arhat*.
Except for the Best of Shen, expert in knowledge and whose meditation is (vast) like the heavens,
this ability in the affairs of living beings is no sphere of activity for ordinary people.
Both (the officiator and the deceased) will fail, and there is great danger of connecting up with evil rebirths.
One who has been continuously purified from previous times
and who has entered the stream of the four measureless virtues,
is able to benefit living beings.
Making other's concern more important than his own,
if his mind is one-pointedly directed towards benefitting beings, and is established in kindness and compassion,
there will be benefit in following the Way of the Shen of Existence.
There will be no error in the intention. This is the entrance-way.
Then finally as the result and the effect,
one will traverse the nine stages of the threefold world,
and rest in the Stage of Devotional Practice.
Then having traversed the four stages of Devotional Practice,
one will traverse the ten Swastika Stages
and become a perfect buddha in the state of salvation.

This is what he said.

V. DGE BSÑEN THEG PA

[vol. *ga*, f. 164a⁶ onwards]

thams cad mkhyen paḥi ston pa lags ||
ston pas theg paḥi rim pa las ||
rgyu daṅ ḥbras bu gñis su gsuṅs ||
rgyu yi theg paḥi rim pa sogs ||
bskos paḥi gśen la gñer du gtad ||
da lta ḥbras buḥi theg pa la ||
theg [164b] pa lṅa pa dge bsñen bon ||
bdag la gñer du gtad gsuṅs pa ||
dge źes bya ba ci ltar dge ||
bsñen na ci ltar bsñen pa lags ||
rtsa baḥi ḥbyuṅ khuṅs gaṅ la gtogs ||
bdag cag ḥkhor la bstan du gsol ||

de la ston pas bkaḥ stsal pa /
ñon cig tshaṅs pa gtsug phud ñon ||
dge bsñen theg paḥi bon sgo ni ||
dge źes bya ba sdig pa med ||
lus ṅag yid gsum dge bar bkol ||
daṅ du blaṅ bas dge ba źes ||
bsñen źes bya ba yaṅ dag don ||
phyin ci ma log bsñen pas bsñen ||
dge la bsñen ciṅ tshul la gnas ||
yaṅ dag don la ḥjug spyod do ||
rtsa baḥi ḥbyuṅ khuṅs mdo las byuṅ ||
bon la rgya che graṅs maṅ yaṅ ||
tshur bsdus rnam pa bźi ru ḥdus ||
mdo ḥbum gzuṅs gsum man ṅag bźi ||
man ṅag dpon gsas luṅ gi bon ||
gzuṅs ni chab dkar nag po sṅags ||
ḥbum ni rgyas pa spyir spro ba ||
mdo ni rgyu ḥbras gźal bya ste ||
theg pa thams cad rtsa ba ni ||
mdo sde dag las byuṅ baḥo ||
rgyu ḥbras gźal źes bya ba ni ||
sṅon du btaṅ ba rgyu ru ste ||
phyis su ḥbyuṅ ba ḥbras buḥo ||
gźal bya dag ni dkaḥ sla gñis ||

V. THE WAY OF THE VIRTUOUS ADHERERS

(*Tshaṅs-pa gTsug-phud* said:)

All-knowing teacher!
You have told us that the series of vehicles are divided into those of cause and effect.
The series of the vehicles of cause have been committed to the Shen responsible.
Now as for the vehicles of effect,
you have said that you will commit to my keeping the fifth vehicle, that of the Virtuous Adherers.
What does 'Virtuous' mean in this context?
and what does 'Adherer' mean?
Where does the basic origin belong?
I beg you to inform me and my entourage.

Then the Teacher said:

Listen, *Tshaṅs-pa gTsug-phud*, listen!
As for the way of *bon*, the vehicle of Virtuous Adherers,
'Virtuous' means free from evil,
committed to virtue in Body, Speech and Mind,
and because one must comply with this, we use the term 'virtue'.
'Adherer' implies adhering infallibly to this perfect matter,
and so we use the term 'adherer'.
Adhering to virtue and keeping to the pattern,
one enters upon this perfect matter.

The basic origin comes from the *sūtras*.
Although *bon* is vast and beyond number,
Compressing it, we bring it together in four kinds,
(i) *sūtras*, (ii) the 'Perfection of Wisdom',[42]
(iii) spells, and (iv) wise lore.
Wise lore is the inspired *bon* of the Master-Sages.
Spells are the *mantras* of the White Waters and the Black.
The 'Perfection of Wisdom' is the composition of ten thousand verses which spreads everywhere in its full form.
The *sūtras* are cause and effect and the appraisal.
The basis of all vehicles has come from the *sūtras*.[43]
As for the cause, the effect and the appraisal,
that which is put first is the cause
and that which appears afterwards is the effect,
while the appraisal comprises easy and difficult couples.

de yaṅ thog mar rgyu ḥbras la ||
źiṅ pa dag daṅ so nam ḥdra ||
sa bon sṅon du btab pa na ||
ḥbras bu ljaṅ pa rjes su ḥbyuṅ ||
ljaṅ pa dag la brten pa yi ||
lo ḥbras me tog bcud du smin ||
ḥgro ba sems can gsos su ḥgyur ||
dpe don de yi mtshon nas su ||
dad pa sṅon du btaṅ ba na ||
brtson ḥgrus rjes su ḥbyuṅ bar ḥgyur ||
dad pa bskyed [165a] na brtson ḥgrus myur ||
le lo med pa phyir mi ldog ||
btson ḥgrus sṅon du btaṅ ba na ||
śes rab rnam gsum ḥbras bu ḥbyuṅ ||
thos daṅ bsam daṅ sgom pa yis ||
gzuṅ so gdag sgo go lam phyed ||
śes rab sṅon du soṅ ba na ||
ḥbras bu dge bcu rjes su ḥbyuṅ ||
dge bcu spyad na thar pa thob ||
mi dge spyad na ṅan soṅ brgyud ||
dge bcu sṅon du btaṅ ba na ||
ḥbras bu pha rol phyin bcu thob ||
sbyin pa brtson ḥgrus dkaḥ thub źi ||
bzod daṅ bsam gtan spyod yul dag ||
stobs daṅ sñiṅ rje smon lam mchog ||
thabs daṅ śes rab rgyud ḥbyaṅ ṅo ||
pha rol phyin pa bcu spyad na ||
g·yuṅ druṅ sa bcu rim gyis non ||
sa lam rim bgrod ḥkhrul pa med ||
g·yuṅ druṅ theg paḥi sar ḥdzegs nas ||
saṅs rgyas sa la ḥkhod par ḥgyur ||
saṅs rgyas sa la gnas la kyaṅ ||
ḥgro ba sems can dpal du ste ||
rgyu daṅ ḥbras buḥi mtshan ñid do ||

gźal bya dkaḥ daṅ sla ba ste ||
yig rtsis rgyud la ḥjug dkaḥ yaṅ ||
mthun paḥi[a] grogs kyis brid pa sla ||
sems bskyed ma bźi skye dkaḥ yaṅ ||
raṅ la dpe blaṅ sñiṅ rje sla ||
sbyin pa phyogs med gtoṅ dkaḥ yaṅ ||
rkyen gyis bslaṅ na grol ba sla ||

[a] ḥdun paḥi

Now first as for cause and effect,
it is like the farmer and work on the fields.
First the seed is planted and the shoots appear afterwards as the fruit (or effect).
Following upon the shoots the leaves, flowers and grains ripen into the sustenance, which sustains living beings.

As is shown by this metaphor,
if faith is put first, zeal will come afterwards.
If faith is produced, zeal comes quickly, and there is no reverting to laziness.
Then if zeal is put first,
the three aspects of wisdom will come as effect,
and by learning, reflecting and meditating,
the field of study, the terminology and the course of understanding are characterized.
If wisdom goes first,
the ten virtues come afterwards as the effect.
If one practises the ten virtues, one achieves release.
If one practises evil, one continues in a series of evil rebirths.
If one puts the ten virtues first, one gains as effect the ten perfections, generosity, zeal, gentleness in adversity, forbearance, mental repose (which gives) purity in one's sphere of action, strength, compassion, excellent prayer, method and wisdom. These purify the spirit.
If one practises the ten perfections,
one treads in due order the ten Swastika stages,
and there is no delusion traversing this order of stages.
Having ascended the stage of the Swastika Vehicle,
One is established in the stage of buddhahood.
Abiding in the stage of buddhahood,
One becomes the glory of living beings.
Such are the indications of cause and effect.

As for the appraisal of easy and difficult things,
although it is difficult to fix writing and calculation in the mind,
it is easy to impose it with suitable help,
Although it is difficult to produce the four kinds of Thought-raising towards Enlightenment,[44]
compassion is easy if one uses oneself as example.
Although it is difficult to give gifts indiscriminately,
it is easy to part with them if one arouses the desire as occasion arises.

tshul khrims ḥchal med bsruṅ dkaḥ yaṅ ||
khrims kyis bcad na thub pa sla ||
bzod pa sran bcas bsgom dkaḥ yaṅ ||
sgyu ma bslab na thob pa sla ||
brtson ḥgrus drag po bskyed dkaḥ yaṅ ||
bde sdug gźal na brtson pa sla ||
bsam gtan mñam par gnas dkaḥ yaṅ ||
ṅaṅ thag bsriṅ na brtan pa sla ||
dge baḥi stobs la gźug dkaḥ yaṅ ||
sems rgya bskyed na ḥgrub pa sla ||
[165b] sñiṅ rje dpag med bskyed dkaḥ yaṅ ||
raṅ rgyud gźal na skye ba sla ||
smon lam re dogs med dkaḥ yaṅ ||
phyogs med bsten na mthar phyin sla ||
thabs mchog rmoṅs pa med dkaḥ yaṅ ||
bkri draṅ[a] bgyid na ḥdul ba sla ||
śes rab ḥkhrul pa med dkaḥ yaṅ ||
rnam gsum rgyud sbyaṅ mthar phyin sla ||
gźal bya dkaḥ slaḥi mtshan ñid do ||

[f. 166a[5], onwards]

de la yaṅ tshaṅs pa gtsug phud kyis gsol pa /
rnam pa thams cad mkhyen pa yi ||
cir yaṅ sprul paḥi sku mchog lags ||
mdo sde dag las byuṅ ba yi ||
theg pa lṅa pa dge bsñen bon ||
ma nor don la ḥjug pa nas ||
mi ḥkhyar don la bsgrub pa na ||
rgyu ḥbras rtsa ba ci ltar bsruṅ ||
spyod tshul rim pa ci ltar lags ||

[166b] de la ston pas bkaḥ stsal pa /
ñon cig tshaṅs pa gtsug phud ḥkhor ||
rgyu ḥbras rtsa ba ḥdi lta ste ||
ḥkhor baḥi las la blo ldog ciṅ ||
thar paḥi don la spro bskyed nas ||
rtse gcig byaṅ chub bsgrub pa na ||
sdig bcu mi dge rgyab tu bor ||
dge bcu rnam dag daṅ du blaṅ ||

[a] bkrid graṅs

Although it is difficult to keep rules of morality intact,
it is easy to do so, if discipline is exercised.
Although it is difficult to practise patient forbearance,
it is easy to do so, if one has learned about illusion,
Although it is difficult to arouse strong zeal,
effort is easy, if one makes an appraisal of happiness and suffering.
Although it is difficult to remain in a state of repose,
it is easy to be constant, if one perseveres.
Although it is difficult to embark upon virtuous power,
it is easy to effect it, if one widens one's mind.
Although it is difficult to arouse immeasurable compassion,
it is easy to arouse it, if one appraises one's own soul-series.
Although prayer is difficult free from hopes and fears,
it is easy to perfect it, if one keeps impartial.
Although perfect method free from folly is difficult,
it is easy to convert, if one guides and leads.
Although wisdom free from delusion is difficult,
it is easy to perfect it, if one purifies the three aspects of it in one's own soul-series.
Such are the indications of what is difficult and easy in the matter of appraisals.

Then again *Tshaṅs-pa gTsug-phud* asked:
O All-knowing One,
whose excellent form may be made manifest in any way soever!
As for this fifth vehicle, the *bon* of Virtuous Adherers,
which originates from the *sūtras*,
if one is to embark upon it free of error
and practise this matter unerringly,
how is the basis of cause and effect to be maintained,
and what is the sequence of the practice?

To this the Teacher replied:
Listen, *Tshaṅs-pa gTsug-phud* together with your entourage.
The basis of cause and effect is like this.
Turning your mind from the affairs of the world and arousing feelings of joy in this matter of salvation,
when you aim one-pointedly at enlightenment,
you must abandon completely the ten evil actions and comply with the ten virtuous actions.

de yaṅ goṅ du bstan pa ltar ||
sdig pa mi dge bcu po ni ||
lus kyi gsum daṅ ṅag gi gsum ||
yid kyi bźi las sogs paḥo ||
rtsa ba de las byuṅ ba yi ||
mtshams med lṅa daṅ ñe ba lṅa ||
lji ba bźi daṅ log pa brgyad ||
ḥkhrul pa dgu daṅ mi dge bcu ||
ḥkhrul rtog bcu ste ḥkhor baḥi las ||
bgyid daṅ bgyi ru rtsal ba daṅ ||
rjes su yi raṅ spaṅ bar bgyi ||
ḥkhor bar ltuṅ baḥi rgyu yin pas ||
rtsa baḥi dug lṅaḥi las spyod ni ||
śin tu dam par sruṅ ba gces ||
dge ba rnam dag bcu bo ni ||
de las so soḥi gñen po ste ||
lus kyi gsum daṅ ṅag gi gsum ||
yid kyi bźi las sogs pa daṅ ||
rtsa ba de las gyes pa yi ||
byams chen lṅa daṅ ltos pa lṅa ||
gus pa bźi daṅ ḥdun pa brgyad ||
ṅes pa dgu daṅ dge ba bcu ||
gźol ba bcu ste thar paḥi las ||
bgyid daṅ bgyi ru rtsal ba daṅ ||
rjes su yi raṅ blaṅ bar bya ||
thar par bgrod paḥi rgyu yin pas ||
rtsa baḥi ye śes lṅa po ni ||
śin tu ṅes par blaṅ ba gces ||
tshaṅs pa gtsug phud sprul paḥi gśen ||
rgyu ḥbras spaṅ blaṅ rtsa baḥo ||

spyod tshul rim pa ḥdi lta tes ||
dge bsñen gtan spyod rnam pa lṅa ||
dag pa khrus kyi spyod pa daṅ ||
phyag skor mos ḥdun spyod pa daṅ ||
sku gduṅ tsha tshaḥi [167a] spyod pa daṅ||
rnam dag mchod gtor spyod pa daṅ ||
tshogs rdzogs go chaḥi spyod paḥo ||
dge bsñen gtan khrims sna lṅa las ||
dge bsñen spyod tshul rnam pa lṅa ||
phyi tshul naṅ khrims zuṅ ḥbrel na ||
sgrib sbyaṅ tshogs gñis rdzogs par ḥgyur ||

źes bkaḥ stsal to /

As has been taught before, there are ten evil actions,
three of body, three of speech, four of mind and so on.
From this basis arise
the five immeasurable sins and the five related to them,
the four grave offences and the eight reversals,
the nine delusions and the ten evils,
the ten misapprehensions.
You must abandon doing these things, trying to get them done and taking pleasure in them.
They are the cause of sin in the world, so it is very important to avoid the practice of these five basic evils.
As for the ten pure virtues,
they are the antidotes of each type of action,
three of the body, three of speech, four of the mind and so on.
Derived from the basic ones
are the five great acts of love and the five related to them,
the four acts of respect and the eight aspirations,
the nine certainties and the ten virtues,
the ten diligent applications,
You must apply yourself to doing them, trying to get them done and taking pleasure in them.
They are the cause of advance towards salvation, so it is very important to practise decidedly these five basic wisdoms.

Tshaṅs-pa gTsug-phud, O Shen who is manifest at will!
Even such are the basic matters to be avoided and to be practised, and such are their causes and effects.

Now the sequence of practice is like this:
there are five kinds of fixed practice for Virtuous Adherers,
the practice of pure ablutions,
the practice of salutations, circumambulations and devotions,
the practice of shrines and *tsha-tsha*,[45]
the practice of the pure offering of water in worship,
the practice of the armour of the perfected accumulations (of knowledge and merit).
From the five kinds of fixed rules of Virtuous Adherers
come the five kinds of practice of Virtuous Adherers
When the outer form and the inner law are united
defilements are removed and the two accumulations are perfected.

So he spoke.

de la tshaṅs pa gtsug phud kyis gsol pa /
rnam pa thams cad mkhyen pa yi ||
ḥgro baḥi mgon gyur gśen rab lags ||
dge bsñen theg paḥi bon sgo las ||
phyi yi tshul daṅ naṅ gi khrims ||
naṅ khrims goṅ du gsuṅs lags kyaṅ ||
phyi yi spyod tshul rim pa la ||
lag len go rim ci ltar lags ||
bdag cag rig paḥi blo rtsal źan ||
thams cad mkhyen pas bśad du gsol ||

źes gsol to / de la ston pas bkaḥ stsal pa /

tshaṅs pa gtsug phud la sogs ḥdus paḥi ḥkhor / dus ḥdir tshogs pa rnams kyaṅ / sgrib gñis byaṅ źiṅ tshogs gñis rdzogs pa daṅ / phyi rabs rnams la dper bstan paḥi phyir du / rgyu dge baḥi rtsa ba las / bsod nams kyi tshogs rdzogs śiṅ sgrib pa sbyaṅ dgos pa yin pas / phyag skor mos gus daṅ mchod paḥi rten la / gśen gyi pho braṅ źig bźeṅs su ḥtshal gyis / rma lo daṅ g·yu lo daṅ / tshaṅs pa gtsug phud daṅ / spaṅ la nam gśen daṅ / gto rgyal khri śes daṅ / g·yu druṅ sems dpaḥ khyed rnams kyis / yo byad daṅ rdzas cha maṅ po sog cig / rje rigs kyi rgyal po ḥkhor lo ḥod gsal ḥkhor daṅ bcas pas / tshogs sbyor rgyuḥi yon bdag gyis [167b] śig / ces gsuṅs nas / ḥkhor rnams la bkaḥ stsal pa /

rje rigs kyi rgyal po ḥkhor lo ḥod gsal daṅ / rgyal poḥi khab dgaḥ ba can gyi mi rnams daṅ / g·yuṅ druṅ sems dpaḥ rnams kyis / phun sum tshogs paḥi yo byad maṅ po bsags te / bzo rgyal gar ma li śo la bkaḥ stsal nas / bźeṅs su gsol te / de yaṅ lcags ri pho ḥdom bźi rgyaḥi naṅ du / rmiṅ gźi khri ḥphaṅs rim lṅa brtsigs pa / deḥi steṅ du logs bźi rdzu ḥphrul dra ba la / g·yuṅ druṅ gi pa tras gtam pa / phyi log la pho ḥdom brgya ñi śus ḥkhor ba / deḥi naṅ du gser gyi ka ba daṅ / g·yuḥi gduṅ ma daṅ / ñi zlaḥi ka źu daṅ / pad maḥi ka gdan daṅ / gźaḥ tshon gyi dpyam gduṅ daṅ / ḥkhor loḥi dpyam bar daṅ / nor buḥi dpyam gduṅ daṅ / gźaḥ sprin gyi pa tra daṅ nam khaḥi ya gad daṅ / rgyu skar gyi za ra tshags daṅ / gźaḥ tshon gyi dar bu khad rlob pa /

deḥi steṅ du rta dbab rim pa lṅa ni / dkar ljaṅ dmar sṅo gser mdog daṅ lṅa la / ḥbyuṅ lṅaḥi pa tras spras pa / deḥi steṅ du bum pa śel gur dkar po la / rin po cheḥi ḥgur chu daṅ / za ra tshags gis brgyan pa / deḥi steṅ bre srog ḥkhor lo char khebs ldan pa / de la tog daṅ bya ru dar chun gyi

At that *Tshaṅs-pa gTsug-phud* replied:

O All-Knowing Guardian of living beings, Best of Shen!
As for the *bon* way of the Vehicle of Virtuous Adherers, its outer form and its inner law,
although you have explained the inner law above,
what is the order of techniques in the outward form of practice?
Our intellectual understanding is weak.
We beg you, All-Knowing One, to tell us.

Thus they asked him, and the Teacher replied:

Tshaṅs-pa gTsug-phud and the rest of the assembled company who are gathered here at this time! In order to instruct future generations, since in accordance with the basic virtues which are the cause (of all advance), we must perfect the accumulating of merit and remove our defilements, we should found a Shen Palace as a basis for our salutations, circumambulations, devotions and worship. Therefore O *rMa-lo*, *gYu-lo*, *Tshaṅs-pa gTsug-phud*, *sPaṅ-la nam-gśen*, *gTo-rgyal khri-śes*, all you Swastika Beings,[46] gather together implements and materials. And you, O King *ḥKhor-lo ḥod-gsal* of royal lineage, together with your entourage, be benefactor of the required materials.

Having thus addressed the company, King *ḥKhor-lo ḥod-gsal* of royal lineage, the people of the royal city *dGaḥ-ba-can*, together with the Swastika Beings, gathered together many necessary things of excellent quality, and they asked the Royal Artisan *Gar-ma-li-śo* to build. Then inside a surrounding wall 400 fathoms in circumference, he built foundations in five ascending steps, and on these he built four walls of a criss-cross pattern and decorated with swastika designs. The outer walls were 120 fathoms in circumference. Inside there were golden pillars and blue cross-beams. On the pillar capitals were designs of the sun and moon and the bases were designed as lotuses. The laths were coloured like the rainbow. There were wheel-patterns between the laths and jewel-patterns on the ends of the (protruding) laths. There were rainbow and cloud designs and sky-coloured decorative eaves, and it was hung with looped patterns of the lunar mansions and pleated hangings of rainbow colours.

Above there was a platform rising in five steps, white, green, red, blue and yellow, and decorated with the symbols of the five elements. On top of this (he built) the great vase, white as crystal, decorated with garlands of gems and decorative devices. Above this was a square support, and then the 'core of life', the rings and the umbrella. Above this was the top-piece

brgyan pa / sgo bźi phyogs bźiḥi kha dog la / gźaḥ tshon gyi sgo khyud daṅ / gser gyi sgo ḥgram daṅ / bye ruḥi sgo skyes btsug pa / de lta buḥi gźal yas khaṅ ñams dgaḥ ba yid du ḥoṅ ba / blta na sdug pa / spa źiṅ brjid pa / gzi źiṅ mtho ba / rab tu brtan pa / bar ḥkhyams ḥdod yon gyi ra ba daṅ [168a] bcas pa / phyi sgo la rgyal chen bźiḥi pho braṅ bcas pa / de lta buḥi gśen gyi pho braṅ chen po ni / lha daṅ klu daṅ mi la sogs pa / dge ba la ḥdun pa rnams kyis bźeṅs pas / guṅ źag bco lṅaḥi dus la grub bo /

de la ston pas bde bar gśegs paḥi sku gduṅ rnam dag gi rgyud las / mu tra lhaḥi dkyil ḥkhor źal phyes nas / mṅaḥ dbul daṅ rab gnas rgya chen por mdzad de / mtshan yaṅ g·yuṅ druṅ bkod legs kyi mchod rten źes bya ba gsol to / de la yaṅ steṅ gi lha daṅ / ḥog gi klu daṅ / bar gyi mi rnams kyaṅ śin tu spro ba skyes nas thams cad kun gyis mṅon par bstod do /

de la yaṅ ston pas / dge bsñen theg paḥi spyod tshul gtan la phab ste stsal pa / tshaṅs pa gtsug phud gaṅ źig rigs kyi bu daṅ rigs kyi bu mo dag / sdig pa mi dge baḥi las spaṅs nas / dge baḥi las daṅ du blaṅ bar ḥdod na / tshul daṅ khrims kyi las la źugs nas / yaṅ dag mthar phyin paḥi don daṅ ldan paḥi skyes bu / ḥgro ba ḥdul ba / kha lo bsgyur ba / rig pa gsal ba / stobs daṅ ldan pa / rmid du byuṅ ba / don mi bsñel baḥi gzuṅs thob pa / rnam par dag paḥi dge ba la ḥdun źiṅ / maṅ po ḥtshogs paḥi rgya mtsho gnon pa / gśen gyi mkhan slob daṅ dpaṅ po / de lta buḥi mdun du ḥkhod nas / dge bsñen gyi khrims nod par bya ste / phyiḥi tshul gos lṅa daṅ / naṅ gi gtan khrims lṅa daṅ / bar gyi spyod lam lṅa mthun par bya źiṅ / theg pa la [168b] ḥjug ste / daṅ po phyiḥi tshul gos lṅa ni / stod gos daṅ / smad śams daṅ / chag non daṅ / rmad ḥog daṅ / rmad gos phyar bu daṅ lṅaḥo / naṅ gi khrims lṅa ni / źe sdaṅ gi dbaṅ gis srog gcod pa daṅ / ḥdod chags gi dbaṅ gis ma byin pa len pa daṅ / gti mug gi dbaṅ gis rgyu ḥbras mi rtsi thob rdzobs su spyod pa daṅ / ṅa rgyal gyi dbaṅ gis dreg paḥi las bgyid ba daṅ / ḥphra dog gi dbaṅ gis tshig rtsub mo daṅ / ṅag ḥkhyal ba daṅ / rdzun daṅ ḥphra ma smra ba daṅ lṅa spaṅ baḥo /

blaṅ ba ni de las bzlog ste / yon tan gyi tshogs dpag tu med paḥo / bar gyi spyod tshul lṅa ni / dag pa khrus bgyid pa daṅ / phyag skor mos ḥdun spyod pa daṅ / sku gduṅ gi tsha tsha ḥdebs pa daṅ / rnam dag gi mchod gtor gtoṅ ba daṅ / tshogs bsags paḥi yan lag las / mchod pa ḥbul ba daṅ lṅaḥo /

with the (two) horns hung with garlands. As for the colours of the four sides, the walls around the doors were of rainbow colours, the edge of the doorway was gold and the doors themselves he made coral red.

Such was the pleasing and delightful palace, beautiful to behold, gloriously adorned, splendid and lofty, well and truly firm, and provided with a surrounding veranda with the necessary offerings, which was established by the gods, the serpents, by men and by all who delighted in virtue, and it was completed in fifteen days.

Then, in accordance with the ritual entitled 'Pure Reliquary of the Blessed Ones', the Teacher made manifest the mystic circle of the *Mu-tra* Gods, and performed a great ceremony of dedication and consecration, and he gave it the name of the 'Well-Established Swastika Stūpa'. Then the gods from above, the serpents from below, and human beings of the middle regions were all very joyful and all sang praises.

Then again the Teacher set forth the manner of practice of the Vehicle of Virtuous Adherers, saying:

O *Tshaṅs-pa gTsug-phud* and whichever sons of the lineage and daughters of the lineage are desirous of abandoning evil and applying themselves honestly to virtuous actions, they must enter this way and this law and (come) to the presence of a perfected sage, who converts living beings and guides them, whose intellect is clear, who is strong and wonderful, a sure (not forgetting the meaning) master of spells, who is zealous for the purest virtue, controlling a great company (of religious). They must come to the presence of such a Shen abbot, such a Shen teacher and such a Shen witness, and they must receive the law of Virtuous Adherers, and act in conformity with the outward manner (of the law) relating to the five articles of apparel, the five firm inner laws, and the five intermediate practices. When one enters this vehicle, first there is the outward manner relating to the five articles of apparel, the upper garment, the lower garment, the sandals, the ordinary cloak and the special cloak. As for the five inner laws, one must avoid killing in anger, stealing through covetousness, acting ambitiously without taking account of causes and effects as through ignorance, acting brazenly through pride, and quarrelling, talking nonsense and telling lies and slanders, all as through envy. One must apply oneself to the opposite of these, and then the accumulation of good qualities will be without measure. As for the five intermediate practices, they are the performance of ablutions, the practice of salutations, circumambulations and devotions, the attendance on shrines and *tsha-tsha*, the practice of the pure offering of water in worship, and from the items that produce an accumulation of merit the one of ceremonial worship.

VI. DRAṄ SROṄ THEG PA

[vol. *ga*, f. 242b[6] onwards]

yaṅ ston pas bkaḥ stsal pa /
ñon cig rnam [243a] dag gtsug phud ñon ||
sruṅ baḥi tshul la rnam pa gñis ||
thabs la brten te sruṅ tshul daṅ ||
raṅ bźin spyod paḥi ḥdra tshul lo ||
thabs la brten te sruṅ tshul ni ||
rnam pa gñis su ḥbyuṅ ba ste ||
blaṅ daṅ dbog pa gñis su ste ||
blaṅ ba dag la rnam pa gsum ||
mkhan daṅ slob dpon dpaṅ po rnams ||
mkhan po gser gyi mchod rten ḥdra ||
dpaṅ po ḥgyur med ri bo ḥdra ||
slob dpon dri med śel sgoṅ ḥdra ||
de la ma ñams rnam pa gsum ||
gser gyi mchod rten mdaṅs ma ñams ||
ḥgyur med ri bo dpaṅs ma ñams ||
dri med śel sgoṅ ḥod ma ñams ||
ñams pa med ciṅ gol ba med ||
rnam gsum blo daṅ ldan pa yis ||
sgo gsum g·yeṅ baḥi tshogs spaṅs nas ||
lus ṅag yid gsum gus pa yis ||
mkhan slob dpaṅ[a] poḥi mdun druṅ du ||
dgaḥ daṅ dad daṅ gus pas blaṅ ||
dug gsum bag chags bdar thag gcad ||
sku gsum ye śes ḥbras thob ḥgyur ||
dpaṅ poḥi druṅ du khas blaṅs pa ||
khas blaṅs ma yin dam bcaḥ yin ||
dam la ḥgal na ḥbras bu ḥtshig ||
skye ba lṅa brgyar ṅan soṅ brgyud ||
gar skyes slu ba rgyun tu ḥoṅ ||

byams daṅ sñiṅ rje btaṅ sñoms gsum ||
thabs daṅ tshul daṅ spyod lam gsum ||
rnam par dag paḥi sgo nas blaṅ ||

[a] rnam gsum dbaṅ

VI. THE WAY OF THE GREAT ASCETICS

Again the Teacher said:

Listen, *rNam-dag gTsug-phud*, listen!

The manner of keeping (to this vehicle) is twofold, keeping to it by adhering to methodical instructions,

and by all manner of examples for one's personal practice.

As for keeping to it by adhering to methodical instructions, this appears in two aspects: as receiving and as bestowing.[47]

The process of receiving has three aspects, (connected with) the abbot, the teacher, and the witness.

The abbot is likened to a golden shrine.

The witness is likened to a firm mountain.

The teacher is likened to an immaculate crystal ball.

Their freedom from defect is of three kinds.

There is no defect in the lustre of a golden shrine.

There is no defect in the height of a firm mountain.

There is no defect in the light of an immaculate crystal ball.

They are free from defects and free from error.

With one's threefold mind (viz. trained in learning [*thos*], thought [*bsam*] and meditation [*sgom*]),

avoiding the heaps of distractions of Body, Speech and Mind,

with the devotion of all three,

One should receive (initiation) with joy, faith and devotion in the presence of the abbot, the teacher and witness.

One must cut off completely the pervasive influences of the Three Evils,[48]

and one will gain the fruit of knowledge of the Three Buddha Bodies.

What you promise in the presence of the witness is not (just) a promise. It is a vow.

If you break an oath, the (good) effects are destroyed.

For 500 rebirths you will pass through the realms of wretchedness.

Wherever you are born, there will always be ensnarements.

Love, compassion, equanimity, these three,

method, manner, practice, these three,

must be taken up with a completely pure disposition.

dbog pa dag la rnam pa gsum ||
rtsa ba yan lag ñiṅ lag gsum ||
srog gcod pa daṅ ma byin blaṅ ||
mi gtsaṅ spyod daṅ che dregs bdud ||
gñis brgya lṅa bcu rdzogs par dbog ||
deḥi yan lag sde bźi las ||
kha zas sde daṅ gon paḥi sde ||
khri stan sde daṅ grogs [243b] kyi sde ||

de la so sor dbye ba ni ||
thog mar kha zas sde bźi las ||
maṅ thun śa daṅ yu ti chaṅ ||
ag tsoṅ dag daṅ rnam pa gsum ||
dus ma yin gyi kha zas bźi ||
śa la rnam pa bźi yin te ||
ltuṅ daṅ ñes daṅ ñams pa daṅ ||
sbyaṅ du btub[a] daṅ rnam pa bźi ||
spyir yaṅ śa yi ñes pa ni ||
tshe rabs thog ma med pa nas ||
da ltaḥi lus blaṅs yan chad du ||
srid pa ci ltar srid pa na ||
srog dbugs bsdus paḥi sems can rnams ||
pha mar ma gyur gcig kyaṅ med ||
deḥi phyir skye ḥgroḥi sems can ḥdi ||
dkar dmar thig leḥi rgyu las grub ||
de ni srid paḥi sñiṅ po ste ||
sred daṅ len paḥi sa bon las ||
ḥbyuṅ ba bźi yi gzugs su grub ||
phyi snod ḥbyuṅ ba rnam bźi la ||
naṅ bcud gnas pa ci bźin du ||
bźi bsdud gzugs kyi phuṅ po la ||
srin buḥi groṅ khyer sum brgya drug ||
phyi snod naṅ bcud bźin du chags ||
srin buḥi khroṅ khyer re re la ||
ḥphra moḥi sems can khri phrag re ||
de las de ḥgyur rtsis las ḥdas ||
sems can re reḥi srog bcad na ||
ḥphra moḥi sems can graṅs med gum ||
sems can re re bkol spyad na ||
ḥpha moḥi sems can graṅs med bsñal ||

[a] sbyar daṅ btul

The process of bestowing is of three kinds,
the roots, the limbs, the branches.
(The rules concerning) taking life and stealing,
impure behaviour and the demon of arrogance,
these are given in the full form of 250 items.
As for the four sections which are their 'limbs',
there is the section on food, on dress,
on couches and on friends.

Taking them each separately,
as for the section on food,
(we discuss) meat and *chang*,
onions as the third item,
and meals at improper times as the fourth.
(Eating of) meat may be considered in a fourfold way,
as sinful, as harmful, as debilitating,
and fourthly as (a sin) capable of being washed away.
Now as for the harm of meat-eating in general,
from the beginningless series of living states
to the receiving of this present body,
however they originated in their origins,
of all living beings who draw breath,
there is no one who has not been parent of any other.
In this way these living beings are produced from the white and red drops which are their cause.
This is the essence of existence,
and from this seed (characterized by) desiring and taking,
they are produced as bodies formed of the four elements.
Just as living beings who are the essence
abide in the outer world of the four elements which is their vessel,
likewise in the personal body formed of the four elements there are 360 communities of worms.
Just as the internal essences are manifest in the outer vessel,
so in each community of worms
there are ten of thousands of minute beings,
and the ones that are produced from them surpass all calculation.
For every being that is killed numberless minute beings die.
For every being that you set to work numberless minute beings suffer.

sems can re reḥi mṅal spyad na ||
ḥphra moḥi sems can graṅs med brgyal ||
deḥi phyir ḥdi yi ñes pa ni ||
srog bcad srin buḥi sdug bsṅal ni ||
nags tshal dag la me btaṅ ḥdra ||
khrag gi zegs ma me ru mthoṅ ||
bkol spyad srin buḥi sdug bsṅal ni ||
thar med brtson rar tshud pa ḥdra ||
lus srog bsdam paḥi śe maṅ ni ||
lcags kyi tha ram dam par mthoṅ ||
mṅal [244a] spyod srin buḥi sdug bsṅal ni ||
rgyal khams nad yams phyo ba ḥdra ||
lus zuṅs thig le dug tu mthoṅ ||
deḥi phyir srog spyod ma byin blaṅ ||
mi gtsaṅ spyod paḥi ñes pa yis ||
gtan du thar med ltuṅ ba yaṅ ||
bźi bsdus phuṅ poḥi rgyu las ḥbyuṅ ||
phuṅ poḥi bcud las śa ru byuṅ ||
deḥi phyir śa la spyod pa ni ||
srin po ñiṅ śa can daṅ ḥdra ||
ro mchog tshor ba brod pa la ||
źe ldaṅ me ltar ḥbar ba ḥbyuṅ ||
srog bcad bźin du srog la brod ||
gźan kyaṅ srog la rlom pa gdoṅ ||
glo bur bar chod hur pa daṅ ||
ñu le ḥjab bu de las byuṅ ||
gsad gcad rtsa ba śa la thug ||
nus pa bcud du smin pa las ||
ḥdod chags chu ltar khol ba ḥbyuṅ ||
mi gtsaṅ spyod bźin mi gtsaṅ ḥdod ||
tshims pa med ciṅ ṅoms pa med ||
gaṅ dag gzugs la rlom pa gtoṅ ||
ḥkhrig ciṅ sbyor bas sred len ḥphrod ||
ḥkhor baḥi skye ḥphel de las ḥbyuṅ ||
skye rga na ḥchi śa la thug ||
khu ba rtsa rgyud ḥgrim pa las ||
gti mug mun ltar ḥthib pa ḥbyuṅ ||
gñid log bźin du gñid la brod ||
byiṅ mug le lo che ba yis ||
tshe ḥdi gñid log rmi lam ḥdra ||
g·yeṅ skyon[a] le lo de las byuṅ ||

[a] skyoṅ

For every being whose womb is worked
countless small living beings feel faint.
Therefore as for its harmfulness,
this taking of life and the suffering of worms
is like setting fire to a forest,
for they see the drops of blood like fire.
As for setting animals to work and the suffering of worms,
they feel as though pressed into a dungeon where there is no escape.
As for the wretchedness of having their life-force in harness,
they see themselves as bound with iron fetters.
As for copulation and the suffering of worms then,
it is as though an epidemic pervaded their whole realm,
and they see the bodily element of seed as though it were poison.

Thus taking life and stealing
and the evil of impure behaviour
  are certainly mortal sins,
and they have as their cause the physical body formed of the four elements.
The essence of the physical body emerges as flesh.

So this addiction to flesh
  reminds one of demons who eat their own kind.
From relishing the sense of its excellent taste
  anger arises burning like fire.
Delighting in killing as he kills,
  a demon glories in taking the lives of others.
Sudden impediments and trickery
  and mean thieving all come from it.
The root cause of slaying is concerned with flesh.

Fleshly potency develops into an essence
  and desire arises like boiling water.
In the act of impurity one desires impurity.
There is no contenting and no satisfying.
Revelling transmits itself into all bodies there are.
Desiring and grasping are passed on through copulation.
From all this comes the birth-increase of this world.

Birth, old age, sickness and death are all concerned with flesh.
The seminal essence pervades the channels of the body,
and so there comes mental torpor like thickening darkness.
In the act of sleeping, one delights in sleep.
With such great drowsiness and indolence
this life becomes like a sleeping dream.
From all this come distraction and indolence.

mi lus chud zos śa la thug ||
daṅs ma kha dog mdaṅs la soṅ ||
laṅ tsho stobs śed rgyas pa las ||
ṅa rgyal rluṅ ltar ḥtshub pa ḥbyuṅ ||
ṅa rgyal bźin du dregs pa skye ||
chen po dag la ḥgran ya ṅa ||
gźan dag yul la rlom pa gtoṅ ||
bdag rgyal gźan [244b] pham de las ḥbyuṅ ||
ḥthab rtsod rtsa ba de la thug ||
rtsigs ma phuṅ poḥi gzugs la soṅ ||
phuṅ po yan lag rags pa las ||
ḥphra dog sa ltar skye ba ḥbyuṅ ||
ḥgraṅ[a] ba bźin du ḥgraṅ[a] mi khyag ||
mi khyag bźin du tshig la dgaḥ ||
rtsod pa tha sñad tshig las ḥbyuṅ ||
ru ṅa ḥphra dog de las ḥbyuṅ ||
bdag ḥdzin rtsa ba śa la thug ||
deḥi phyir dug lṅaḥi rtsa ba yaṅ ||
maṅ thun śa yi rgyu la thug ||
sa yi daṅs ma śa yin te ||
sa yis thams cad bskyed nas su ||
snaṅ srid gdos su gyur pa bźin ||
thams cad śa yi rgyus[b] bskyed pa ||
ñes pa thams cad rgyus[c] bskyed pas ||
ñes pa thams cad śa la thug ||
lhag par gti mug skyed paḥi rgyu ||
pha ma gñis kyi dkar dmar yin ||
gñen ḥbrel kun gyi ñiṅ śa yin ||
mig gis mthoṅ na skyi re ḥjigs ||
lag tu blaṅ na ya re ṅa ||
khoṅ du stim paḥi lugs ci yod ||
śa yi ñes pa de ltar che ||
de las mi bzaḥ spaṅ baḥi rigs ||

de la so sor dbye ba yis ||
ltuṅ baḥi śa la rnam pa lṅa ||
źe sdaṅ ḥdod chags gti mug daṅ ||
ṅa rgyal ḥphrag dog rnam pa lṅa ||
phuṅ po gzugs su grub paḥi śa ||
źe sdaṅ gcan chen srin poḥi śa ||
ḥdod chags byi la dar maḥi śa ||

[a] ḥdraṅ [b] śa yis thams cad rgyu [c] rgyu

The wasting of the human body is concerned with flesh.
Vitality passes into colour and complexion.
Strength of youth grows in force.
From this comes pride which rages like a storm,
and together with pride comes arrogance.
So contending against one's superiors,
acting boisterously in others' domains,
triumph for oneself and discomforture for others,
 this is the idea that results.
The root cause of quarrels is concerned with this.

The coarse elements (of meat) enter the physical body,
 and from the hardy physical limbs of the body
 envy arises coming into being like earth.
Although in a state of surfeit, it cannot bear the idea of surfeit,
and unable to bear it, it delights in words.
Argument arises from terms and words,
 and malice and envy come from that.
The root of selfishness is connected with flesh.
Thus the root of the Five Evils[48]
 is concerned with flesh as its cause.

The vital form of earth is flesh.
Everything is produced from earth
 and it is the basis of phenomenal existence.
So everything is produced with flesh as its cause,
and since all evils are causally produced,
all evils are concerned with flesh.
Especially is it the cause of the production of Ignorance (mental torpor),
It is the white and red essence of parents.
It is the 'flesh-essence' of all relations.
If one sees this, how frightening!
If one receives it, how terrible!
What is this idea of absorbing it in one's own person?
So great is the evil of flesh!
So let it not be eaten! It is good to avoid it.

When this matter is investigated in detail,
there are five kinds of sinful flesh.
This is the flesh of the five components (*skandha*)
 from which the body is made,
Wrath, Desire and Ignorance (mental torpor),
Pride and Envy, these are the five.
With Wrath (we associate) the flesh of the flesh-eating tiger.[49]
With Lust the flesh of the lustful tom-cat.

gti mug phag rgod rṅam paḥi śa ||
ṅa rgyal gyi liṅ nag paḥi śa ||
ḥphrag dog sprel rgod rṅam paḥi śa ||
de la ḥbag na ltuṅ bar byed ||
de bas ñes pa zur chuṅ ba ||
ñes paḥi śa la rnam pa brgyad ||
sprel daṅ byi la dom dred śa ||
gcan gzan ri mo can gyi śa ||
ḥdab chags ṅaṅ pa ṅur baḥi śa ||
khyu[a] mchog glaṅ daṅ boṅ drel daṅ ||
ñes pa che bas[b] [245a] spaṅ bar bya ||
de bas ñes pa zur chuṅ ba ||
ñams paḥi[c] śa la bcu drug ste ||
gyi liṅ rta daṅ bya waṅ[d] śa ||
ma he mdzo ḥgar rtol moḥi śa ||
ḥphar spyaṅ wa mo bya ma byel ||
dbyi gsaḥ grum[e] pa chu[f] sram śa ||
khyim bya de phoḥi śa la sogs ||
ñams pa che bas spaṅ bar bya ||

de las sbyaṅ du btub pa ni ||
śa rkyaṅ gtsod rgo ri dvags śa ||
g·yag lug ra gsum g·yuṅ dvags śa ||
sme bas ma ñams sbyaṅ du btub ||
de las sme bar gyur pa ni ||
ḥdul khrim phog pas ñes pa daṅ ||
skyes dman dag gis ñes pa daṅ ||
bar snaṅ gzaḥ yis ñes pa daṅ ||
zil bsgyur dag gis ñes pa bźi ||
sme bar gyur paḥi ñams pa spaṅ ||

spyir yaṅ śa yi ñes pa ni ||
ji bźin dug lṅa cha rags pa[g] ||
de bźin ñes pa che ba ste ||
spaṅ blaṅ de yi thabs daṅ bstun ||
sbyaṅ mi btub la gtan nas ḥdzem ||
sbyaṅ btub śa la gso sbyaṅ bya ||
g·yuṅ druṅ sems dpaḥi ltuṅ bśags daṅ ||
bde bar gśegs paḥi mtshan phyag ḥtshal ||
ṅan soṅ sbyoṅ baḥi sñiṅ po brjod ||
yan lag kha zas sde gcig go ||

[a] khyuṅ [b] ba [c] pa [d] bya bon [e] drum [f] khyur [g] pas

With Ignorance the flesh of the raging wild boar.
With Pride the flesh of the black *Gyi-liṅ* horse.
With Envy the flesh of the raging wild monkey.
If you defile yourself with these, you commit sin.
Slightly less harmful than these
there are eight kinds of harmful flesh:[50]
the flesh of monkey, cat, brown bear and yellow bear,
the flesh of the spotted tiger,
the flesh of goose and duck,
bell-wether, ox, donkey and mule.
Since the evil is great, they should be avoided.
Slightly less harmful than these,
There are sixteen kinds of debilitating flesh:
the *Gyi-liṅ* horse and the flesh of the bat,[51]
the flesh of buffalo, the dzo and her male and female crossbred offspring,[52]
the red wolf, the grey wolf, the fox and the bat,
the lynx, the snow-leopard, the badger and the otter,
the flesh of the domestic cock and so on,
these should be avoided because they are very harmful.

Then as for that which is capable of purification,
if the flesh of the wild ass, of antelope, of wild goat, and of deer,
and the flesh of the three domestic animals, yak, sheep and goat,
are not harmed by defilement, purification is possible.
As for defilements, these are:
 the harm that comes from the breaking of vows,
 the harm involved when a woman is the slayer,
 the harm involved (when the animal dies) from a nervous stroke,
 the harm involved when it dies of mad frenzy.
One must avoid being harmed by these defilements.

As for the harmfulness of flesh in general,
the more gross the Five Evils, the greater the harm.
Keep your practice in accordance with the method of avoiding (the evil) and accepting (the good).
You must carefully avoid it when purification is not possible,
and in the case of flesh where purification is possible, you must seek purification.
You must make the confession of Swastika Beings
and salute the Blessed Ones with invocations
And recite the essential prayer which saves from evil rebirths.
This is one 'limb' of the section on food.

rnam dag gtsug phud ḥdul baḥi gśen ||
chaṅ la rnam pa bźi yin te ||
ḥbru chaṅ sbyar[a] chaṅ ñiṅ khuḥi chaṅ ||
śiṅ ḥbras khu ba a mri ta ||
ḥbru chaṅ bdud rtsi phab kyis sbyar ||
sbyar chaṅ rtsi thog sñiṅ po sbyar ||
ñiṅ chaṅ ñiṅ nas ñiṅ du gtig ||
a mri ta ni śiṅ gi bcud ||
de yi ñams pa che chuṅ ni ||
ḥbru chaṅ dag gis ñes pa che ||
sbyar chaṅ dag gis ñams pa che ||
ñiṅ khu chaṅ gis srog la ñen ||
srog la ñen pas ltuṅ ba [245b] che ||
a mri ta ni bag yaṅ tsam ||
de yaṅ u dug ra ro daṅ ||
bag med spyod ḥchal ḥbyuṅ bar byed ||
spyir yaṅ chaṅ gi mtshan ñid ni ||
lha min mtshon cha sde bźi las ||
chaṅ ni chu yi mtshon cha ste ||
btuṅ bas ṅa rgyal che bar ḥgyur ||
des na raṅ srog ḥchad par byed ||
dug lṅa ñes paḥi rtsa ba yaṅ ||
rtsa ba sde gcib chaṅ las ḥbyuṅ ||
byams paḥi don la gnas tsam na ||
źe sdaṅ ñon moṅs skye ba yaṅ ||
chaṅ gi rgyu las ḥbyuṅ baḥo ||
sbyin paḥi don la gnas tsam na ||
ḥdod chags ñon moṅs skye ba yaṅ ||
chaṅ gi rgyu las ḥbyuṅ baḥo ||
ye śes don la gnas tsam na ||
gti mug gñid du ḥthib pa yaṅ ||
chaṅ gi rgyu las ḥbyuṅ baḥo ||
yaṅs paḥi don la gnas tsam na ||
ḥphrag dog ru ṅa skye ba yaṅ ||
chaṅ gi rgyu las ḥbyuṅ baḥo ||
mñam paḥi don la gnas tsam na ||
ṅa rgyal dregs pa skye ba yaṅ ||
chaṅ gi rgyu las ḥbyuṅ baḥo ||
bdag gźan mñam par bźag tsam na ||
bdag ḥdzin ru ṅa ldaṅ ba yaṅ ||
chaṅ gi rgyu las ḥbyuṅ baḥo ||

[a] sbyaṅ

rNam-dag gTsug-phud, O Shen who converts living beings,
there are four kinds of *chang*,
chang made from grain,
chang which is blended,
chang which is reduced to an essence,
chang made from fruit juice, referred to as 'ambrosia'.

Chang made from grain is an elixir prepared with yeast.
Blended *chang* is made from the essence of berries.
Concentrated *chang* is distilled to an ever stronger concentration.
Ambrosia is the essence of fruit-juice.

As for the degrees of harm they do:
chang made from grain causes great harm;
blended *chang* is very debilitating;
distilled *chang* endangers one's life,
and since it is dangerous to one's life, the sin is great;
in the case of ambrosia there is little concern.

Furthermore (*chang*) causes drunkenness and thoughtless bad behaviour.
As for the general characteristics of *chang*,
of the four weapons of the titans
chang is their liquid weapon.
By drinking it self-confidence increases,
and so one may cause one's own life to be cut off.
As for the harmful root-cause of the Five Evils,
one part of this cause comes from *chang*.
Even when one abides in a condition of love
stirrings of the molestations (*kleśa*) of anger
may arise with *chang* as their cause.
Even when one abides in a generous disposition
stirrings of the molestations of desire
may arise with *chang* as their cause.
Even when one abides in a state of knowledge,
a pervasion of mental torpor
may arise with *chang* as its cause.
Even when one abides in a state of broadmindedness,
the stirrings of envy and malice
may arise with *chang* as their cause.
Even when one abides in a state of equality,
the stirrings of pride and arrogance
may arise with *chang* as their cause.
Even when one equates oneself with others,
the stirrings of self-interest and malice
may arise with *chang* as their cause.[53]

[f. 247a^{2}, onwards]

chaṅ tshoṅ ba daṅ smad tshoṅ ba ||
sbraṅ tshoṅ ba daṅ rnam pa gsum ||
me lce ḥkhor lo ḥbar ba yi ||
naṅ gi sgrib pa can du sbyoṅ ||
gal te mtho ris gnas na yaṅ ||
sdug bsṅal dbul ḥphoṅs can du bskyed ||
deḥi phyir gdod nas spaṅ bar bya ||
ñes daṅ ñams daṅ ltuṅ ba la ||
bśags na saṅs rgyas sman gyi lha ||
be du rgya ḥod rgyal pos sel ||
de la ñes paḥi ltuṅ bśags daṅ ||
dag ciṅ tshaṅs paḥi cho ga bya ||
ḥgro la sman gyi sbyin pa ḥgyed ||
yan lag kha zas sde gcig go ||

rnam dag gtsug phud ḥdul baḥi gśen ||
gtsoṅ sgog rnam pa bźi yin te ||
sṅon med khams mun pa zer ldan gyis ||
dge sdig bstan pa rtsod pa yi ||
dri źim sman gyi tshal chen du ||
mṅan sems dri ma ḥthor ba la ||
kha dog sna bźiḥi rlaṅ du ḥphyur ||
de las mi źim ljon bźi skyes ||
gcig de ser po gser gyi mdog ||
gser gyi pad mo kha bye ḥdra ||
sa yi rgyu bskyed dri ma ṅan ||
gcig de sṅo ljaṅ g·yu ḥod ḥbar ||
me tog g·yu yi tshom bu ḥdra ||
rluṅ gi rgyu bskyed dri ma ṅan ||
gcig de dmar ljaṅ zaṅs ḥod chags ||
dmar[a] ljaṅ chun po gśib pa ḥdra ||
[247b] me yi rgyu bskyed dri ma ṅan ||
gcig de ne ljaṅ ud pal mdog[b] ||
rtsa ba duṅ po aṅ drag ḥdra ||
chu yi rgyu bskyed dri ma ṅan ||
de las so sor gyes pa yi ||
dug rigs sum brgya drug cu ste ||
rtsi daṅ dug gñis mñam par skyes ||
rtsi yis gsos śiṅ dug gis bskyed ||
sman gyis ḥjoms par byed paḥo ||

[a] g·yu [b] a par mdog

Purveyors of *chang* and prostitutes,
sellers of honey,[54] these three kinds of people,
experience the inner anguish of the 'Burning Circle of Tongues of Fire'.
Even if they abide in the (three) upper Spheres (viz. gods, titans or men)
they will be born in conditions of wretchedness and poverty.
So one must abandon (such things) altogether.
If one confesses this harm, debility and sin
the Buddha Lord of Medicine, *Vaidūrya* the King, will wash it away.
So confess this harmful sin to him and perform purificatory ceremonies,
and make gifts of medicaments to living beings.
This is (another) 'limb' of the section on food.

rNam-dag gTsug-phud, Shen who converts living beings,
there are four kinds of onion and garlic.
In earlier times *Mun-pa zer-ldan* of the Demon Realm,
there being a dispute about the teachings of good and evil,
scattered in the sweet-smelling grove of medicinal plants
the impurities of his cursed thoughts,
and they rose up as vapour of four different colours.
From them four unpleasant plants came into being.
One was yellow, the colour of gold.
It was like an open yellow lotus flower.
It was produced with earth as its cause. The smell was bad.
One was bluish-green, the colour of turquoise.
It was like a bunch of turquoise-coloured flowers.
It was produced with wind as its cause. The smell was bad.
One was reddish green, the colour of copper.
It was like a well-ordered posy of reddish-green flowers.
It was produced with fire as its cause. The smell was bad.
One was meadow-green, the colour of an *utpala* lotus flower.
Its root was white like conch.
It was produced with water as its cause. The smell was bad.
Separating from them came 360 evil kinds,
and both (beneficial) juice and poison were produced.
The juice cures (disease) and poison produces it.
Medicine overpowers it.

spyir yaṅ gtsoṅ sgog ñes pa ni ||
sgyu lus gzugs kyi phuṅ po ni ||
ḥbyuṅ ba rnam pa bźi las grub ||
srin buḥi groṅ khyer sum brgya gnas ||
sgog gtsoṅ kha zas zos pa na ||
la la na yin la la ḥchi ||
źiṅ der nad daṅ yams byuṅ mtshuṅs ||
sgog gtsoṅ ñes paḥi dri ma ni ||
gnas ris chen po bźi la tshor ||
saṅs rgyas źiṅ du mi gtsaṅ dri ||
dbyiṅs na bźugs paḥi lha daṅ ḥgal ||
dpag tshad lṅa brgya tshun chad la ||
gtsaṅ rigs mgon poḥi lha mi ḥkhor ||
nus pa bcud du smin pa la ||
rmug daṅ ḥthib daṅ byiṅ ba daṅ ||
tshor ba rags daṅ chags pa skye ||
sred che byi laḥi sde daṅ ḥdra ||
sdom pa ḥchal spyod dam tshig ñams ||
mgon skyob lha daṅ sruṅ ma bye ||
lus la srin buḥi groṅ khyer dmyal ||
chu la grub pas ltuṅ bar byed ||
me la grub pas ñes pa yin ||
rluṅ la grub pas ñams pa yin ||
sa la grub pas sbyaṅ btub tsam ||
ltuṅ baḥi gtsoṅ la ḥbags pa yis ||
ro myags ḥdam doṅ naṅ du sbyaṅ ||
ñes paḥi gtsoṅ la ḥbags pa yis ||
rnag khrag mtsho moḥi naṅ du sbyaṅ ||
ñams paḥi gtsoṅ la ḥbags pa yis ||
sdug bsṅal na tshaḥi lus su skye ||
sbyaṅ btub gtsoṅ la ma sbyaṅ na ||
lṅa brgyar bse dri can du skye ||
deḥi phyir śin tu spaṅ baḥi rigs ||
lag tu mi blaṅ khar mi bzaḥ ||
dri ma dag [248a] kyaṅ ḥdzem par bya ||
spyir yaṅ gtsoṅ gi ñes pa ni ||
dug lṅa nad sel sman gyi lha ||
be du rgya ḥod rgyal pos ḥbyoṅ ||
sman gyi mchod pa rgyun du ḥbul ||
sman gyi sbyin pa rgyun du gtoṅ ||
sman gyi cho gar brtson par bya ||
des na gtsoṅ gi ñes pa ḥbyoṅ ||

As for the general harm of onion and garlic,
in phenomenal bodies formed of the four elements
there are 300 communities of worms.
When you eat garlic and onion as your food,
some of them are ill and some of them die.
It is as though disease and epidemic had started in the place.
The harmful impurities of garlic and onion
are perceived in the four great realms.
(They produce) an unclean smell in the Buddha Fields.
They displease the gods who reside in space.
Protecting divinities of pure lineage
will not approach within a distance of 500 miles.
When the potentiality (of the evil of onion-eating) develops into a concentration,
sluggishness, dimness and languor,
insensitivity and passionate attachment result.
One is like the type of lecherous tom-cat.
Vows are reduced to loose practice and sacraments are broken.
Guardian divinities and protectors leave one
and the communities of worms in your body all suffer.
(The onion) produced from water causes sin,
The one produced from fire is harmful.
The one produced from wind is debilitating.
The one produced from earth is just capable of purification.

Defiled by the sinful onion,
one suffers in the mud-pit of the Hell of Putrefaction.
Defiled by the harmful onion,
one suffers in the Lake of Pus and Blood.
Defiled by the debilitating onion,
wretched disease appears on one's body.
If one does not seek purification in the case of the onion which is capable of it,
one is born with the stench of body-odour for 500 births.

So it is right to avoid them altogether.
They should not be picked up. They should not be eaten.
Even the impure smell is to be avoided.

As for the harmfulness of onions in general,
the Lord of Medicine, remover of the maladies of the Five Evils,
Vaidūrya the King, he purifies it.

Always make offerings of medicaments in worship.
Always give medicaments as gifts.
Exert yourself in medicinal ceremonies.
By such means the harm of onions is cleansed away.

ñes skyon rtsa ba mi śes pa ||
luṅ ma bstan du zos gyur yaṅ ||
gtsaṅ rigs lha sruṅ gñen mi ḥkhor ||
dbaṅ po ñams daṅ śes pa rmug ||
ñes skyon śes nas zos gyur yaṅ ||
ñams dan ñes ltuṅ ḥbyuṅ bar ḥgyur ||
yan lag kha zas sde gcig go ||

rnam dag gtsug phud ḥdul baḥi gśen ||
dus ma yin gyi kha zas bźi ||
srod daṅ tho raṅs dgoṅ mo daṅ ||
ñi ma dros daṅ bźi ru ste ||
khrims kyi kha zas dus ma yin ||
srod la śa za srin pos bzaḥ ||
ñi dros rgyal po gdan thog bzaḥ ||
dgoṅ mo mu steg phyin cis[a] bzaḥ ||
tho raṅs – – – – –[b]
dus kyi kha zas rnam pa gñis ||
ñi ma rtse śar khrus rtiṅ la ||
dag pa lha yis kha zas bzaḥ ||
ñi ma dguṅ gi dus tshod la ||
tshoṅ ḥdus g·yeṅ ba spaṅ nas su ||
rgyal pos khrims kyi kha zas bzaḥ ||
de min dus ma yin la gtogs ||
dus ma yin gyi kha zas ni ||
lus po śed che ḥdod chags skye ||
tshul daṅ mi ldan ṅo tsha bral ||
nad kyi rgyu rkyen ldaṅ bar byed ||
laṅ tsho stobs śed dar rgyas bskyed ||
de las g·yo daṅ ḥdzum pa daṅ ||
ḥphro daṅ rgod daṅ ldem gyaṅ[c] ḥbyuṅ ||
dus min kha zas spaṅ ba ni ||
bźi bsdus phuṅ po śed smad ciṅ ||
bag med spyod ḥchal [248b] mi ḥbyuṅ phyir ||
dus min kha zas spaṅ ba daṅ ||
dus kyi kha zas blaṅ bar ḥos ||
dus min kha zas bzaḥ ba ni ||
ḥdab chags ri dvags g·yuṅ dag daṅ ||
gcan gzan rṅam paḥi tshogs daṅ mtshuṅs ||

[a] cus [b] Five syllables missing in our MS. [c] ? *for* ldems kyaṅ

Even if in ignorance of the root-cause of the harm of onions,
you eat them in circumstances where nothing is asserted against them
(e.g. as a layman who has not taken vows),
the protecting divinities of pure lineage will not come around you.
Your sense-organs will be weakened and your understanding dimmed.
If you eat them in knowledge of their harmfulness,
debility, harm and sin will result.
This is (another) 'limb' of the section on food.

rNam-dag gTsug-phud, Shen who converts living beings,
there are four occasions of untimely food,
twilight, dawn, evening and in the morning (9–10 a.m.).
As for these times that are untimely according to rule,
at twilight flesh-eating demons eat,
in the morning enthroned rulers eat,
in the evening false heretics eat,
at dawn – – [*words missing*].

There are two proper times for eating:
after washing when the sun has risen
the pure gods take their food;
at noon-time kings eat their lawful food
away from the distractions of the market-place.
Except for these, other times are unlawful,
and as for the eating of untimely food,
the body becomes strong and desire increases,
one loses manners and sense of shame.
It produces the causes of diseases.
It produces the forcefulness and lustiness of youth.
From this comes playfulness and smiling,
inconstancy, wildness and excitability.

As for the avoiding of untimely food,
the strength of this body, compounded of the four elements, is reduced,
and thoughtless loose practice does not arise, so for this reason untimely
eating must be avoided,
and it is proper to eat at the right times.

As for eating at improper times,
birds, wild animals and domestic animals,
and fierce beasts of prey do the like.

dgra daṅ rkun bu ḥjab bu daṅ ||
ḥbyuṅ po ro laṅ tshogs rnams daṅ ||
dbye ba med par[a] śes pa ste ||
khrims la ḥgal bas ltuṅ ba phog ||
nad du ldaṅ bas ñes pa che ||
dbaṅ po rmug pas ñams par ḥgyur ||
deḥi phyir spaṅ baḥi rgyu ru śes ||
yan lag kha zas sde gcig go ||

gñis pa gon paḥi sde las su ||
rnam pa bźi ru śes pa ste ||
rgyal poḥi chas daṅ blon poḥi chas ||
btsun moḥi chas daṅ ded dpon chas ||
tshon chen sde daṅ ri mo can ||
ber daṅ ḥjol daṅ dpyaṅ ras sogs ||
rgyal poḥi cha lugs spaṅ baḥi rgyu ||
dbyi spyaṅ stag gzigs guṅ rgo[b] gsaḥ ||
ḥphar chen dom dred ldaṅ ḥgyu wa ||
chu[c] sram sprel daṅ grum[d] dkar ḥphyi[e] ||
spu mtshan thul pa za ḥog slag ||
blon poḥi cha lugs spaṅ baḥi rgyu ||
dkar ljaṅ dmar sṅo mthon ka ḥchol ||
sgeg daṅ phur daṅ ḥjol daṅ śam ||
btsun moḥi cha lugs spaṅ baḥi rgyu ||
ḥphar śam goṅ skor mu khyud spel ||
ska nan braṅ ṅa phu duṅ can ||
ded dpon cha lugs spaṅ baḥi rgyu ||
rgyal poḥi gon pas che ba skye ||
blon poḥi gon pas dregs pa skye ||
btsun moḥi gon pas chags pa skye ||
ded dpon gon pas rlom pa skye ||
lcags ri med daṅ luṅ ma bstan ||
g·yaṅ gźi lta bu srin poḥi gos ||
spaṅ baḥi rgyu ru bstan paḥo ||

blaṅ baḥi gos ni ḥdi lta ste ||
srin bal kha chu la sogs [249a] te ||
srog bcad spu bal ma yin pa ||
śi śon dag las byuṅ ba yi ||
dri med ras dkar gtsaṅ ma la ||
ṅur smrig rtsi yi kha dog sgyur ||

[a] paḥi [b] rgod [c] kyur [d] drum [e] phy

It is known that there is no difference in this
  from enemies, robbers and thieves, from demons and ghosts.
Contravening these rules, one falls into sin.
Illness is caused and the harm is great.
The sense-organs are affected with languor.
So know that this is something to avoid.
This is (another) 'limb' of the section on food.

The second section, that concerning dress,
  may be understood as fourfold:
  king's dress and minister's dress,
  lady's dress and officer's dress.
Those of a colourful kind and with patterns,
cloaks and trains and hanging garments,
being the dress of kings, should be avoided.
Lynx, grey wolf, tiger, leopard, caracal, wild goat, snow leopard,
red wolf, brown and yellow bear, – –* and fox,
otter, monkey, white badger and marmot,
such coats of fur and gowns of silk,
being the dress of ministers, should be avoided.
White, green, red, blue, sky-blue, gay,
coquettish and fluttering, flounces and fringes,
being the dress of women, should be avoided.
With trimmings and collar and edgings everywhere,
waisted, breasted and with fitted sleeves,
such being the dress of officers, this should be avoided.
Wearing king's things, one feels important.
Wearing minister's things, one feels arrogant.
Wearing women's things, one feels lustful.
Wearing officer's things, one feels boastful.
With no border and unauthorized,
animal skins and the like are the dress of flesh-eating beasts.
So things to be avoided have been explained.

The clothes one should wear are these,
those which are not of cloth made from the silk-worm's 'saliva',
  or from the fur and wool of slain animals,
but from the pure white cloth procured from cotton,
  which one dyes with saffron colour.

* Either two syllables are corrupt here or else *ldaṅ-ḥgyu* is the name of an unidentified animal.

pad lo ris drug gdiṅ ba bdun ||
g·yu mdaṅs sṅon poḥi mu khyud can ||
lcags ri ḥkhor yug mthaḥ goṅ med ||
lus kyi pags ltar gon par blaṅ ||
na bzaḥ pad lo ris drug ni ||
stod gos smad śams chag nan gsum ||
rmad gos rmad ḥog tshul gos gsum ||
pad źu pad lham pad gdan gsum ||
theg pa rim dguḥi tshogs daṅ sbyar ||
pad gdan pad lham smad śams gsum ||
chag nan rim bźi rgyu yi bon ||
stod gos rmad gos tshul gos gsum ||
rmad ḥog gliṅ snam ḥbras buḥi bon ||
pad źu rgyu ḥbras gñis med par ||
bla med theg pa chen poḥi tshul ||
thams cad kun la khyab par gnas ||
pad gdan gliṅ brgyad lte ba dgu ||
ḥkhor baḥi sa la mi gnas śiṅ ||
gaṅ la chags pa med paḥi tshul ||
pad lham pad brtsegs gñis sbyar te ||
rgyu drug ḥkhor baḥi lus blaṅs la ||
ḥdam gyis ma gos pad maḥi tshul ||
smad śams sul bu ñi śu lṅa ||
gliṅ chuṅ ñi śu rtsa lṅa dpag ||
dag paḥi gliṅ skyes dag paḥi lus ||
kun las rnam par ḥphags paḥi tshul ||
chag nan rim bźin chag goṅ can ||
tshul khrims bum pa sgeg pa daṅ ||
khrel daṅ ṅo tsha śes pa ste ||
tshad med bźi ldan byaṅ chub rgyun ||
rnam dag yid ḥoṅ sgeg paḥi tshul ||
stod gos ḥphrag dbyuṅ[a] goṅ bsnol med ||
ḥdab brgyad me tog kha byeḥi tshul ||
źe sdaṅ srin poḥi gos mi gon ||
byams pa ṅaṅ ldan źi baḥi tshul ||
[249b] tshul gos sul bu ñi śu lṅa ||
lcags ri mu khyud ḥkhor yug can ||
gliṅ bźi gru bźi gsal mthoṅs can ||
gtsaṅ khrims ñi śu rtsa lṅaḥi tshul ||
g·yas pa ḥog la g·yon pa steṅ ||
mdzes paḥi tshul gyis ḥphrag la gzar ||

[a] g·yas

These are the six kinds of 'lotus-leaf' garments
with a mat making seven in all.
(The mat) has a blue border, the colour of turquoise,
a surrounding border with no start or finish.
One should accept (the six items) as wearing apparel
as though they formed the skin of the body.
The six kinds of 'lotus-leaf' garments are these,
the upper garment, the lower garment and the sandals,
the special cloak, the ordinary cloak and the cope.
Then there are the lotus-hat, the lotus-boots and the mat.
These may be related to the ordered group of nine vehicles.
The lotus-mat, the lotus-boots and the lower garment,
and the sandals as fourth item (correspond with) the *bon* of Cause.
The upper garment, the special cloak and the cope,
the ordinary cloak and the patches (correspond with) the *bon* of Effect.
The lotus-hat without differentiation of cause and effect is of the type of the supreme vehicle, remaining associated with all the others.
The lotus mat with its eight sections and the centre as ninth, does not remain on terrestrial ground for it is of the type which is unattached anywhere.
The lotus-boots with their dual row of lotus designs have assumed a body (as it were) in the Six Spheres of the round of existence, but resembling the lotus in type they are unsoiled by the mud.
The twenty-five pleats of the lower garment, raised up as twenty-five little mounds, (represent) the supreme type of excellence of pure bodily form born in the pure isles.
The sandals with the four straps in order may be known as the beautiful vase of morality (characterized by) shame and modesty,
for they typify pure pleasing beauty, the flow of enlightenment with the four immeasurable virtues.
The upper garment, sleeveless and without overlapping collar is of the type of the opened eight-petalled flower.
Typifying loving peace, it is a garment not worn by wrathful monsters.
The cope with its twenty-five pleats and its surrounding border edging,
four sides, four corners and a hole in the middle, typifies the twenty-five rules of purity.
Below on the right and above on the left,
it hangs over the shoulders in a beautiful manner.

gtsaṅ ma gtsug phud khrims kyi gos ||
smad ḥog gliṅ snam ñi śu lṅa ||
ḥtsho ba byad len mu khyud med ||
gtsaṅ źiṅ dag par bya baḥi tshul ||
dge bsñen dge tshul khrims kyi gos ||
rmad ḥog gliṅ snam ñi śu lṅa ||
g·yas ḥog g·yon goṅ gru la gzar ||
khrus daṅ mchod paḥi g·yog byar mdzes ||
rmad gos gliṅ snam brgya daṅ brgyad ||
sprin daṅ me tog ldiṅ khaṅ na ||
dgra bcom saṅs rgyas brgya rtsa brgyad ||
ḥdul ba khrims kyi bon sgo la ||
ḥchad daṅ rtsod daṅ rtsom paḥi tshul ||
theg rim brgya daṅ rtsa brgyad la ||
grub paḥi ḥbras bu brgya rtsa brgyad ||
yaṅ dag mthar phyin rdzogs saṅs rgyas ||
rmad du byuṅ baḥi ḥdul gos so ||
pad źu sul bu rtsa lṅa la ||
ḥdab brgyad ge sar gźon nuḥi tshul ||
rnam par dag pa rin chen tshul ||
bslab pa mthar phyin dri ma med ||
rgyal mtshan mthon poḥi tog lta bu ||
dus gsum nub pa med pa ste ||
rnam par dag paḥi tshul ḥdzin no ||
de rnams kun gyi yan lag las ||
gźi bskur bcud ldan pad gyes daṅ ||
hos ru gsil ba sgra sñan daṅ ||
pad cha pad khug sṅon po daṅ ||
tshem khab dbal mo so leb daṅ ||
khrus bum pad gdan gtsaṅ ma daṅ ||
lcags kyi chan gri gñis sbyar daṅ ||
bkaḥ rgyud rin chen gleg bam daṅ ||
sgra sñan theb tse ḥkhrol mo daṅ ||
pad zaṅs [250a] gtsaṅ maḥi tshan snod daṅ ||
dri źim sman gyi sdoṅ po daṅ ||
khrims kyi gtsaṅ rdzas sde bcu ni ||
rgyun du dgos paḥi yo byad do ||
rnam dag gtsug phud ḥdul baḥi gśen ||
gon paḥi sde bźi spaṅ bar bya ||
pad lo ris drug blaṅ bar bya ||

It is the regulation garment of the 'top pure ones'.

The lower garment with its twenty-five patches is – – – – –[55] and has no border.

It typifies purity and cleanliness and is the lawful garment of Virtuous Adherers and novices.

The ordinary cloak with its twenty-five patches,

hangs over the arms below to the right and above to the left.

It is beautiful as one serves in ablutions and worship.

The special cloak with its 108 patches and 108 buddhas in squares of cloud and flower designs, typifies (the three functions of) expounding, confounding and propounding in the manner of *bon* moral teachings.

These are the 108 effects achieved in the 108 vehicles, and this is the wonderful monastic garment of a perfectly accomplished buddha.

The lotus-hat with its twenty-five pleats is like a young flower with eight petals (surmounted by) a pure gem.

It typifies the (three) perfect and immaculate teachings (*śīla*, *samādhi*, *prajñā*) and resembles the top of a tall banner of victory.

It is unfailing throughout past, present and future and takes the form of purity.

As 'limbs' (viz. implements) of all these:

the begging-bowl with its contents, and open like a lotus,
the jingling mendicant's staff,
the blue lotus-case for the lotus-items,
the needle with point and flat end,
the vase of ablution with its pure lotus-base,
the metal scissors,
the precious volume of traditional teachings,
the sweet-sounding dish with its ringing note,
the bowl of ablutions made of copper,
the sweet-smelling medicinal stick,

these ten lawful and pure items are things which are always required.

rNam-dag gTsug-phud, Shen who converts living beings,
The four kinds of (wrong) apparel are to be avoided.
The six 'lotus-leaf' garments are to be worn.

pad śun gdiṅ ba gdiṅ bar bya ||
pad lham pad źu mnab par bya ||
gtsaṅ rdzas sde bcu ḥtshag par bya ||
gos kyi spaṅ blaṅ bstan paḥo ||

gsum pa khri stan sde las su ||
rnam pa bźi ru śes pa ste ||
khri stan mthon po bya ba daṅ ||
khri stan chen po bya ba daṅ ||
khri stan bzaṅ po bya ba daṅ ||
khri stan drag po bya baḥo ||
mthon po gser dṅul śiṅ gi khri ||
rta daṅ glaṅ po ma he daṅ ||
boṅ drel la sogs rkaṅ ḥgros te ||
mthon po yin pas spaṅ bar bya ||
de la so sor dbye ba na ||
gser dṅul śiṅ khri chen poḥi khri ||
gnas paḥi yul la chags pa skye ||
rta daṅ glaṅ po ma heḥi khri ||
kheṅs sems dregs daṅ ṅa rgyal skye ||
mdzo daṅ boṅ drel dman paḥi khri ||
rabs chad ma niṅ u dug sgra ||
śin tu dman pas ñams pa che ||
chen po skyes dman za ma mo ||
ñams len yid ḥphrog snaṅ ba ḥkhrul ||
lha mo klu mo mi mo daṅ ||
bdud mo srin mo dman moḥi rigs ||
rnam pa drug tu phyed paḥo[a] ||
lha mo yid ḥphrog snaṅ ba ḥkhrul ||
klu mo mdzes ldan le lo g·yeṅ ||
mi mo ḥgro baḥi bag chags g·yo ||
bdud mo ge śan srog la rgol ||
srin mo za byed bla yid rku ||
dman mo groṅ rgyu[b] log par slu[c] ||
thar lam ḥgegs paḥi geg śiṅ byed ||
spyir yaṅ ñes [250b] paḥi mtshan ñid ni ||
rin chen sa ḥog sbas pa daṅ ||
śel sgoṅ ḥdam du bskyur ba daṅ ||
rtsi thog ba mos bcom[d] pa daṅ ||
me loṅ g·yaḥ yis bsgribs pa daṅ ||
ñi ma sprin gyis g·yogs pa daṅ ||
zla ba gzaḥ yis zin pa daṅ ||

[a] ched paḥo [b] rgyun [c] bslu [d] ḥjom

The mat of lotus-fibres is to be spread.
The lotus-boots and lotus-hat must be worn.
The ten pure items are to be assembled.
This is the section on avoiding and taking in the matter of dress.

Thirdly concerning couches,
These may be known as of four kinds.
high couches, large couches,
beautiful couches, fierce couches.

High couches are of gold, silver or wood.
They include riding animals, horses, elephants and buffaloes, donkeys, mules and so on.
Because they are high, they must be avoided.
If we distinguish the details,
great couches of gold and silver and wood
produce feelings of attachment to the place of your stay.
Horses, elephants and buffaloes, used as seats,
produce feelings of boastfulness, arrogance and pride.
Dzo, donkeys and mules are demeaning seats.
Animals that are impotent or neuter or make unpleasant sounds[56]
are very demeaning and this is very harmful.

As for large couches, women and feminine creatures
rob your learning and your thoughts and confuse all appearances.
Goddesses, mermaids, women,
demonesses, ogresses and prostitutes,
they are distinguished as six kinds.
Goddesses steal your thoughts and confuse appearances.
Mermaids are beautiful and distract you with indolence.
Women arouse latent impulses.
Demonesses are murderous and assail your life.
Ogresses are (flesh-)eaters and steal away your spirit and your thought.
Prostitutes go around the village and deceive you.
They act as blocks obstructing the way of salvation.
In general these are the signs of harm:
a jewel hidden under the ground,
a crystal ball thrown in the mud,
juicy fruit destroyed by hoar-frost,
a mirror disfigured by rust,
the sun obscured by clouds,
the moon seized by eclipse,

dar dkar dri mas bsgos[a] pa daṅ ||
sgron me ḥod mdaṅs ñams pa daṅ ||
dpag bsam sdoṅ po rul ba daṅ ||
me tog sad kyis khyer ba daṅ ||
rṅa gśaṅ sgra skad chag pa daṅ ||
ñams daṅ ñes daṅ ltuṅ ba che ||

bdud mo gdan du btiṅ ba na ||
ro myags ḥdam doṅ nag po ru ||
gtan tu thar med sdug bsṅal sbyaṅ ||
srin mo gdan du btiṅ ba na ||
me lce ḥkhor lo ḥbar ba ru ||
gdar tshan dmar poḥi sbub la sbyaṅ ||
dman mo gdan du btiṅ ba na ||
chu gliṅ mun paḥi rgya mtsho ru ||
klu srin pho moḥi lus blaṅ źiṅ[b] ||
ḥdod pa tshim med ñon moṅs skye ||
mi mo gdan du btiṅ ba na ||
mṅal gyi srin buḥi groṅ khyer na ||
sdug bsṅal thar med btson ra sbyaṅ ||
klu mo gdan du btiṅ ba na ||
gliṅ bar mun paḥi glin khrod[c] na ||
dbaṅ bo ma tshaṅs gya ñes sbyaṅ ||
lha mo gdan du btiṅ ba na ||
mthaḥ ḥkhob ma dag groṅ khyer du ||
sdug bsṅal na tshaḥi lus su sbyaṅ ||
spyi ru ñes pa de ltar che ||
sgos su ḥdul ba ḥdzin pa yi ||
bslab gsum ḥjug spyod gaṅ zag rnams[d] ||
lus kyis[e] spyad na ltuṅ ba che ||
ṅag gis spyad na ñes pa che ||
yid kyis bsam na ñams pa che ||
lus ṅag yid gsum log pa na ||
śin tu ñams pa chen po ste ||
rdza chag ḥphro bźin bskaṅ bar dkaḥ ||
de phyir chen poḥi khri stan spaṅ ||

bzaṅ [251a] po dar daṅ zab kyi gdan ||
srin daṅ za ḥog ḥbol gdan de ||
ri mo can daṅ mu khyud can ||
ñi zla ris daṅ nor bu ris ||

[a] gos [b] ciṅ [c] khrid [d] rnam [e] kyi

white silk soiled by a stain,
a lamp rendered feeble by daylight,
a tree of paradise turned rotten,
a flower destroyed by the frost,
a drum or a bell with a cracked sound.
They are debilitating, harmful and sinful.

If you have a demoness as your couch, you will experience suffering with no hope of salvation in the black mud pit of the Hell of Putrefaction.

If you have an ogress as your couch, you will experience the recess of red hot metal in the Hell of the Burning Circle of Tongues of Fire.

If you have a prostitute as your couch, (in your next birth) you will have the body of a male or female sea-monster in the ocean of the dark isles, and you will feel the molestations of unsated desire.

If you have a woman as your couch, you will experience the prison of suffering with no hope of salvation in the community of worms of the womb.

If you have a mermaid as your couch, you will experience the evil of deformity, (born) with limbs incomplete in the dark group of isles between the (great) continents.

If you have a goddess as your couch, you will experience a sick body of suffering in the impure barbarian country.

In general the harm is as great as this.
In particular those people who have started and are practising the threefold teaching which comprises monastic discipline,
are greatly in sin, if they so act with their body,
do very great harm, if they so act with their speech,
are much debilitated, if they so think with their mind.
If body, speech and mind are at fault, one is very much debilitated.
However long one continues, it is hard to fill a broken pot.
Therefore large couches must be avoided.

Beautiful ones are of fine or heavy silk,
mattresses of fine cloth and brocade,
finely patterned and bordered,
with designs of sun and moon and designs of gems,

g·yuṅ druṅ ḥkhor lo pad ma ris ||
me tog tshom bu pa tra ris ||
dpag bsam śiṅ lo gźaḥ sprin ris ||
dkar ljaṅ dmar sṅo mthiṅ nag ris ||
kha dog sna lṅa gźaḥ mtshon ris ||
ḥjam daṅ bde daṅ ḥbol ba ste ||
lus po bag yaṅs chags pa skye ||
btsun moḥi gdan yin spaṅ bar bya ||

drag po gcan gzan ris bkra ste ||
gtum chen dom daṅ rṅam chen dred ||
mi rgod rṅam paḥi pags pa gsum ||
gdan du btiṅ na ltuṅ ba phog ||
śa zan stag daṅ thig le gzigs ||
dpaḥ rtsal siṅ daṅ ṅar can gsaḥ ||
wal wol guṅ daṅ ḥphar spyaṅ dbyi ||
gdan du btiṅ na ñes par ḥgyur ||
rbad daṅ wa sbrel khyi daṅ grum ||
sme baḥi gdan yin ñams par ḥgyur ||
gdan khri ñams na khri ḥphaṅ gdeg[a] ||
khri ḥphaṅ dgu paḥi mchod rten bźeṅs ||
rin chen bkad[b] sa thaṅ la ñal ||
gdiṅ ba g·yu mdaṅs gdan du gdiṅ[c] ||
de min khri gdan spaṅ bar bya ||
rnam dag gtsug phud ḥdul baḥi gśen ||
mthon poḥi khri stan ñes par ḥgyur ||
chen poḥi khri[d] stan ltuṅ bar ḥgyur ||
bzaṅ poḥi khri stan chags[e] par ḥgyur ||
drag poḥi khri stan ñams[f] par ḥgyur ||
khri stan dag gi dbye baḥo ||

bźi pa grogs kyi sde las su ||
chags paḥi grogs daṅ ḥgal baḥi grogs ||
ñes paḥi grogs daṅ ñams paḥi grogs ||
rnam pa bźi ru śes par bya ||
gñen daṅ ñe du ḥbrel ba rnams ||
chags paḥi grogs yin rgyaṅ [251b] thag bsriṅ ||
bsño ḥbog rla rdol gdon gyis brlam ||
ḥgal baḥi grogs yin bar mtshams gcad ||
skyes dman bud med bslu brid can ||
ñes paḥi grogs yin rgyaṅ thag bsriṅ ||

[a] bteg [b] bkod [c] btiṅ [d] khriḥi [e] ñams [f] chags

designs of swastikas, wheels and lotuses,
flowers in clusters and criss-cross designs,
leaves of the tree of paradise, designs of rainbow and clouds,
white, green, red, blue, sky-blue and black in design,
colours of all five kinds, designs of rainbow hues,
soft, comfortable and springy,
the body is at ease and lust is aroused.
Such are the couches of women and must be avoided.

Fierce ones are adorned with wild animals,
the skins of the fierce brown bear, the raging yellow bear or the terrible
gorilla.
If these are laid down as mats, sin is committed.

The flesh-eating tiger and the spotted leopard,
the bold skilful lion and the powerful snow-leopard,
the restive caracal, the red wolf, the grey wolf and the lynx,
If these are laid down as mats, it is harmful.

The excitable[57] fox, the monkey, the dog and the badger,
These are mats that defile, and this is debilitating.
If you violate (the rules) in the matter of your couch, you must erect
nine steps,
you must build a *stūpa* with (a base of) nine steps.
Sleep on the ground in a precious (viz. religious) shelter.
You should put down as a mat a turquoise-coloured cloth.
Otherwise you should do without couch and mat.

O *rNam-dag gTsug-phud*, Shen who converts living beings!
High couches are harmful.
Large couches are sinful.
Beautiful couches are lustful.
Fierce couches are debilitating.
Such are the differences in the matter of couches.

Fourthly the section on friends.
There are clinging friends and erring friends,
harmful friends and debilitating friends.
Thus they are of four kinds.

Relatives and those who are closely connected
are clinging friends and must be kept at a distance.
Crazy, excitable people, those possessed of demons
make erring friends from whom one must cut oneself off.
Women who lead one into temptation
are harmful friends who must be kept at a distance.

dam tshig ñams dań sme mnol can ||
ñams paḥi grogs yin thabs kyis spań ||
spyir yań grogs kyi ñes pa ni ||
thar lam mi thob gag śiń byed ||
dge baḥi las la bar chod gtoń ||
phyin ci log gi bslu khar ḥgro ||
mi mthun rkyen g·yo sar[a] sna ḥkhrid ||
de bas thabs kyis spań bar bya ||
de las bzlog ste mthun paḥi grogs ||
tshańs par spyod dań mthun par ldan ||
dad dań brtse sems mos gus che ||
blo sems mi ḥgyur ḥgyur med sems ||
dad ldan zuń thub dam tshig can ||
rnam dag dkaḥ thub sruń khrims ldan ||
źi tshul ńań riń khoń ḥkhyul can ||
blań baḥi grogs su śes paḥo ||

rnam dag gtsug phud ḥdul baḥi gśen ||
chags paḥi grogs kyis ltuń bar byed ||
ḥgal baḥi grogs kyis ñes par byed ||
ñams paḥi grogs kyis ltuń bar byed ||
ñes paḥi grogs kyis sme bar byed ||
grogs kyi yan lag bstan paḥo ||

de ltar yan lag sde bźi las ||
kha zas sde dań gon paḥi sde ||
khri stan sde dań grogs kyi sde ||
thabs la brten te bsruń baḥi rgyu ||
yan lag kha zas sde bźi la ||
śin tu srog la ñes pas su ||
nad la sman du ḥgro ba dań ||
theg pa goń du spar bas su ||
de min gźan la dgag par śes ||
thabs la brten te bsruń baḥo ||

rań bźin gyis ni spyod tshul la ||
[252a] sgeg mos me loń phyi ba bźin ||
yań yań phyi źiń yań yań lta ||
ńań paḥi rgyal rigs khrus byed bźin ||
skad gcig mi yeń rtse gcig sruń ||

[a] zer

Those who have broken their vows and are defiled
are debilitating friends and must be methodically avoided.

In general then this evil of (bad) friends
acts as a block so that you miss the way of salvation.
They put obstructions in the way of virtuous acts.
You go the ways of false deceit
and they lead you into the crooked way of untoward events.
So they must be methodically avoided.

The opposite of these are those suitable friends,
who are pure in conduct and fitting persons,
faithful, loving and respectful,
constant and unchanging in mind,
faithful, understanding and true to their vows,
keeping to pure austere practices and obeying the rules,
gentle, forbearing and patient,
one knows these as the friends one should have.

rNam-dag gTsug-phud, Shen who converts living beings,
clinging friends cause sin,
erring friends cause harm,
debilitating friends cause sin,
harmful friends defile.
The 'limb' of friends has now been taught.

So in the matter of these four 'limbs',
the section on food and the section on dress,
the section on couches and the section on friends,
these are matters to observe and hold to methodically.
As for the four items in the section on food,
except when there is danger to your life
and they serve as medicine for illness,
and unless you transfer to a higher vehicle,
know that these items are otherwise forbidden.
These are matters to observe and to hold to methodically.

As for the manner of your own practice,
Be like the beautiful girl who wipes the mirror,
who wipes it continually and looks in it continually.
Be like the royal goose who when he is washing
does not wander for one moment but remains intent.

lha gñan śel sgoṅ btsaḥ ba ltar ||
skyon gyis ma gos ña ra gzab ||
rus sbel chu daṅ ḥo ḥbyed ltar ||
dge sdig rgyu ḥbras spaṅ blaṅ brtsi ||
stobs chen gyad kyis gźu brduṅ bźin ||
skad gcig thaṅ lhod med par bya ||
ri dvags tri sña śa ra ltar ||
byaṅ chub sems dpaḥ śes rgyud sbyaṅ ||
khrus daṅ gtsaṅ sbra dag par bya ||
phyi yi tshul daṅ naṅ gi khrims ||
gñis ka zuṅ ḥbrel mkhas par bslab ||
ḥjig rten ḥkhor baḥi las spyod la ||
skyi ḥjigs g·yaṅ za ṅo tsha śes ||
bag yod spyod pa śin tu gzab ||
rgyal po lta buḥi che ba daṅ ||
blon po lta buḥi g·yeṅs pa daṅ ||
tshoṅ dpon lta buḥi ḥdu ḥdzi daṅ ||
byis pa[a] lta buḥi spyod pa daṅ ||
spyod lam bźi po spaṅ bar bya ||
sgeg mo lta buḥi phyi bdar daṅ ||
ṅaṅ pa lta buḥi gtsaṅ sbra daṅ ||
loṅs sku lta buḥi cha lugs daṅ ||
byaṅ chub glaṅ poḥi spyod pa daṅ ||
spyod lam rnam bźi blaṅ bar bya ||
dgra la mi sdaṅ bźin mi bzlog ||
gñen la mi chags srid mi bskyaṅ ||
lus sems rtse gcig dal bar bya ||
phyi tshul wal wol g·yeṅ mi bya ||
naṅ khrims le lo g·yeṅ mi bya ||
rnam dag gtsug phud ḥdul baḥi gśen ||
phog paḥi khrims rnams yo thub na ||
skye ba gcig gis mṅon ḥtsaṅ rgya ||
raṅ bźin gyi ni spyod tshul lo ||

ces gsuṅs so /

[a] sba

Like the crystal egg which is born of gods and furies,
watch carefully that it is not defiled by a defect.
Like the tortoise who can distinguish water and milk,
work out what should be avoided and what should be done in the causes
and effects of good and evil.
Like the mighty champion drawing the bow,
do not relax for one moment.
Like the deer *Tṛṣṇaśara*
practise the *bodhisattva*'s flow of knowledge.
Make yourself clean by ablutions and purification.
Learn competently as a pair both
the outer practice and the inner rules.
With regard to the works of the phenomenal world,
be fearful, hesitant and modest.
Take care to be thoughtful in your practice
and avoid four kinds of action,
being great like a king,
being distracted like a minister,
being busy like a merchant,
and acting like a child.

Four kinds of action must be followed,
wiping (the mirror) like the girl,
purity like the goose,
in appearance like a god,
and acting like an elephant of enlightenment.

Do not hate enemies or turn your face away.
Be not attached to relatives and do not assume responsibilities.
Be single-minded and quiet in body and mind.
Do not act in a restive way in your outward manner.
Do not be lazy about the inner rules of conduct.

rNam-dag gtsug-phud, Shen who converts living beings.
If you are competent in all the rules that affect you,
in one lifetime you will gain buddhahood.
Such is the way of your own personal practice.

This is what he said.

VII. A DKAR THEG PA

[vol. *ṅa*, f. 19b² onwards]

de la yaṅ ston pas bkaḥ stsal pa /
legs so legs so rigs kyi bu ||
gsaṅ sṅags don ldan gsaṅ ba ḥdus ||
gsaṅ baḥi bdag po khyod legs so ||
khyod kyis źus paḥi don de dag ||
bdag gis yoṅs su bśad par bya ||
gsaṅ ba sṅags kyi theg pa la ||
spyi yi rnam graṅs de ltar na ||
don dam ñams su len pa la ||
phyi rabs rjes ḥjug gaṅ zag rnams ||
bon sgo theg pa gaṅ spyod pa ||
spaṅ bsgyur grol ba gsum du ḥjug ||
dge bsñen draṅ sroṅ rgyu ḥbras rtsi ||
dug lṅa spaṅs pas phar phyin ḥdod ||
ṅan spaṅ bzaṅ blaṅ chu yi gñer ||
zad pa med ciṅ ḥphri ba med ||
chu las chu ḥbyuṅ spaṅ mi ḥdzad ||
śiṅ las śiṅ skye bskam mi ḥgyur ||
me la śiṅ bsnan ga la ḥoṅ ||
spaṅ lam theg pa kor tshe ba[a] ||
theg pa chen poḥi don ma yin ||
theg chen bon daṅ rgyaṅ thag riṅ ||
a dkar ye gśen bsgyur lam pa ||
spaṅ du med ciṅ blaṅ du ḥdod ||
grogs su blaṅ źiṅ grogs su bsgyur ||
grogs su bsgyur pas gñis su med ||
dbyiṅs śes mkhaḥ kloṅ thabs śes sogs ||
gñis su med pas don mthar phyin ||
loṅs spyod rdzogs paḥi źiṅ du gsal ||
lha sku rigs stobs ye śes thob ||
theg pa chen poḥi don la sñeg ||
theg chen don la smon źiṅ ḥgrub ||
theg pa chen po grol baḥi lam ||
snaṅ srid ḥkhor ba myaṅ [20a] ḥdas bon ||
ñag gcig rig paḥi cho ḥphrul la ||
spaṅ daṅ bsgyur du ga la btub ||

[a] gor rtse ba

VII. THE WAY OF PURE SOUND

Then the Teacher said again:
Good, good, faithful son,
O *Guhyasamāja*, comprehender of secret spells,
Master of Secrets, you are good indeed.
The matters about which you ask,
I will explain in full.
In the vehicle of Secret Mantras
the general list of items is like that,
and as for realization of absolute truth,
people of future generations,
whatever vehicle of *bon* they practise,
they must embark upon (one of) the three ways,
Avoidance, Transformation, or Release.
Virtuous Adherers and Great Ascetics take account of cause and effect.
Avoiding the Five Evils, they desire perfection.
Avoiding evil, seeking good, (a process like) ripples on water!
It never ends, it never lessens.
Water rises from water. There is no end of avoidance.
Wood sprouts from wood. It never really dies.
Add wood to fire, and where does one get to?
The vehicles of the way of avoidance are self-centred.
They are not of the substance of the Great Vehicle.
They are remote from the *bon* of the Great Vehicle.[58]

The vehicles of Pure Sound and of Primeval Shen follow the way of Transformation.
Without avoiding, they seek to accept.
Taking (all) into companionship, they turn (all) into companions.
By turning (all) into companions, there is no duality left.
Celestial expanse and wisdom, sky and space, method and wisdom, and such pairs,
by loosing their duality, attain to perfection.
They shine in the realm of Perfect Enjoyment.
The five divinities, buddha-bodies, families, powers and wisdoms are gained.[59]
This follows the substance of the Great Vehicle,
And aspiring towards the substance of the Great Vehicle, it achieves it.
With regard to the way of Release of the Great Vehicle,
where the notions of phenomenal existence and its extinction are the magical play of undifferentiated knowledge,
what can be achieved with Avoidance and Transformation?[60]

ma bcos mñam paḥi ṅaṅ la bźag ||
ṅaṅ la bźag pas ṅaṅ du gnas ||
ṅaṅ la ṅaṅ ñid g·yo ba med ||
ṅaṅ las ṅaṅ ñid ḥdu ḥbral med ||
ṅaṅ ñid ṅo bo ñid du gsal ||
bla med śes rab pha rol phyin ||
zuṅ ḥjug rtogs paḥi phyag rgya thob ||
grol baḥi lam du bstan paḥo ||

de ltar spaṅ bsgyur grol gsum las ||
ḥdi ni bsgyur baḥi lam du ste ||
phyi naṅ snod bcud ḥkhor ḥdas bon ||
dug las ye śes rtsir bsgyur źiṅ ||
bdag ñid rol par ñams su len ||
phyi snod stoṅ gsum ḥjig rten daṅ ||
sa rdo ri brag gnas rten ḥkhras ||
loṅs spyod rdzogs skuḥi źiṅ du bsgyur ||
phyi snod lha yi gźal yas khaṅ ||
naṅ bcud skye ḥgro sems can ni ||
srog dbugs bsdus pa thams cad kun ||
lha daṅ lha moḥi sku ru bsgyur ||
naṅ bcud lha daṅ lha moḥi sku ||
ye nas rgyal ba rgya mtshoḥi źiṅ ||
gdod nas bon ñid loṅs spyod rdzogs ||
bon can mtshan ma cho ḥphrul gnas ||
phyi snod naṅ bcud de ltar la ||
spaṅ daṅ blaṅ ba ga la mchis ||
ma spaṅ rgyan śar ñams su blaṅ[a] ||
dug lṅa spaṅs paḥi pha rol na ||
ye śes bya ba ga la yod ||
dug daṅ ye śes gnas ḥgyur yin ||
sku daṅ źiṅ khams zuṅ ḥbrel yin ||
thabs daṅ śes rab sñoms ḥjug yin ||
dkar daṅ nag gñis mdaṅs ḥbyin yin ||
dge daṅ sdig pa brod skyed yin ||
bde daṅ sdug bsṅal sun ḥbyuṅ[b] yin ||

dug lṅa ye śes lṅa ru bsgyur ||
źe sdaṅ byams pa chen por bsgyur ||
mñam par gnas pa źi baḥi ṅaṅ ||
drag poḥi skur sprul khro boḥi sku ||

[a] len [b] dbyuṅ

Everything is placed in a condition of unaffected sameness.
Placed in this state, it remains in this state.
Being essentiality in essentiality, it cannot vary.
Essentiality cannot unite with or separate from essentiality.
Essentiality shines as essential essence.

This attaining of the supreme Perfection of Wisdom,
the Symbol of the knowledge of Two-in-One,
is taught as being the Way of Release.

Now of these three, Avoidance, Transformation and Release,
the one we are concerned with here is the way of Transformation.[61]
The notions of external and internal, of vessel and essence, of physical and metaphysical,
are transformed from the nature of the Five Evils into the essence of Wisdom,
and oneself is absorbed into the magical play.
The whole phenomenal world, earth, stones, mountains, rocks, villages, shrines and dwellings,
are transformed into the Body of Perfect Enjoyment.

The outer vessel of the world is transformed into a temple
and living beings who are the inner essence,
all those who draw breath,
are transformed into the form of gods and goddesses.

The forms of gods and goddesses who are the inner essence
become the Perfect Enjoyment of primeval *bon* itself,
the ocean realm of primeval buddhahood,
and all characterizable phenomenal elements exist as a magic play.
When the outer world and all that belongs inside it is regarded thus,
how can there be avoidance and acceptance?
Learn non-avoidance as your first principle,
for how can so-called wisdom exist
beyond (the state where) the Five Evils are avoided?
The (five) Evils and the (five) Wisdoms exchange place.
The divinities and their realms are related in pairs.
Method and Wisdom are adjusted together.
White and black temper one another.
Good and evil take pleasure in one another.
Happiness and misery refute one another.

The Five Evils are transformed into the five Wisdoms.
Wrath is transformed into great love,
a state of sameness and peace.
Transformed into a fierce divinity, of wrathful form,

mthiṅ nag bdud ḥjoms ḥod dpuṅ [20b] ḥbar ||
źe sdaṅ ḥkhor ba dbyiṅs su sgrol[a] ||
gñis su med pa bdag ñid ṅaṅ ||
ma spaṅ rgyan śar ñams su blaṅ[b] ||
bskyed daṅ rdzogs pa zuṅ du ḥjug ||
lha sku phyag rgya rigs stobs spyan ||
ñid la ñid du mṅon rol pa ||
bdag ñid chen po lhun gyis grub ||

gti mug ye śes chen por bsgyur ||
mñam par gnas pa źi baḥi ṅaṅ ||
drag poḥi skur sprul khro boḥi sku ||
gser mdog bdud ḥjoms ḥod dpuṅ ḥbar ||
gti mug ḥkhor ba dbyiṅs su sgrol[a] ||
gñis su med pa bdag ñid ṅaṅ ||
ma spaṅ rgyan śar ñams su blaṅ[b] ||
bskyed daṅ rdzogs pa zuṅ du ḥjug ||
lha sku phyag rgya rigs stobs spyan ||
ñid la ñid du mṅon rol pa ||
bdag ñid chen po lhun gyis grub ||

ṅa rgyal źi ba chen por bsgyur ||
mñam par gnas pa źi baḥi ṅaṅ ||
drag poḥi skur sprul khro boḥi sku ||
śel mdog bdud ḥjoms ḥod dpuṅ ḥbar ||
ṅa rgyal ḥkhor ba dbyiṅs su sgrol[a] ||
gñis su med pa bdag ñid ṅaṅ ||
ma spaṅ rgyan śar ñams su blaṅ[b] ||
bskyed daṅ rdzogs pa zuṅ du ḥjug ||
lha sku phyag rgya rigs stobs spyan ||
ñid la ñid du mṅon rol pa ||
bdag ñid chen po lhun gyis grub ||

ḥdod chags sbyin pa chen por bsgyur ||
mñam par gnas pa źi baḥi ṅaṅ ||
drag poḥi skur sprul khro boḥi sku ||
zaṅs mdog bdud ḥjoms ḥod dpuṅ ḥbar ||
ḥdod chags ḥkhor ba dbyiṅs su sgrol[a] ||
gñis su med pa bdag ñid ṅaṅ ||
ma spaṅ rgyan śar ñams su blaṅ[b] ||
bskyed daṅ rdzogs pa zuṅ du ḥjug ||

[a] bsgrol [b] len

it is dark blue, a destroyer of demons, blazing with light.
The cycle of wrath receives release in the celestial sphere,
free of duality and in a state of self-existence.
Learn non-avoidance as your first principle.
Unite the Process of Emanation and the Process of Realization.[62]
The (appropriate) divinity, buddha-body, symbol, family, power and eye
play together related together
and our great selfhood is spontaneously effected.

Mental Torpor is transformed into great knowledge,
a state of sameness and peace.
Transformed into a fierce divinity, of wrathful form,
it is yellow, a destroyer of demons, blazing with light.
The cycle of mental torpor receives release in the celestial sphere,
free of duality and in a state of self-existence.
Learn non-avoidance as your first principle.
Unite the Process of Emanation and the Process of Realization.
The (appropriate) divinity, buddha-body, symbol, family, power and eye
play together related together
and our great selfhood is spontaneously effected.

Pride is transformed into great peace,
a state of sameness and peace.
Transformed into a fierce divinity, of wrathful form,
it is crystal colour, a destroyer of demons, blazing with light.
The cycle of pride receives release in the celestial sphere,
free of duality and in a state of self-existence.
Learn non-avoidance as your first principle.
Unite the Process of Emanation and the Process of Realization.
The (appropriate) divinity, buddha-body, symbol, family, power and eye
play together related together
and our great selfhood is spontaneously effected.

Desire is transformed into great generosity,
a state of sameness and peace.
Transformed into a fierce divinity, of wrathful form,
it is copper-coloured, a destroyer of demons, blazing with light.
The cycle of desire receives release in the celestial sphere,
free of duality and in a state of self-existence.
Learn non-avoidance as your first principle.
Unite the Process of Emanation and the Process of Realization.

lha sku phyag rgya rigs stobs spyan ||
ñid la ñid du mṅon rol pa ||
bdag ñid chen po lhun gyis grub ||

ḥphrag dog yaṅs pa chen por bsgyur ||
mñam par gnas pa źi baḥi ṅaṅ ||
drag poḥi skur sprul khro boḥi sku ||
g·yu mdog bdud ḥjoms [21a] ḥod dpuṅ ḥbar ||
ḥphrag dog ḥkhor ba dbyiṅs su sgrol[a] ||
gñis su med pa bdag ñid ṅaṅ ||
ma spaṅ rgyan śar ñams su blaṅ[b] ||
bskyed daṅ rdzogs pa zuṅ du ḥjug ||
lha sku phyag rgya rigs stobs spyan ||
ñid la ñid du mṅon rol pa ||
bdag ñid chen po lhun gyis grub ||

tshogs brgyad rig pa chen por bsgyur ||
mñam par gnas pa źi baḥi ṅaṅ ||
drag poḥi skur sprul khro boḥi sku ||
sna tshogs bdud ḥjoms ḥod dpuṅ ḥbar ||
yul brgyad ḥkhor ba dbyiṅs su sgrol[a] ||
gñis su med pa bdag ñid ṅaṅ ||
ma spaṅ rgyan śar ñams su blaṅ[b] ||
bskyed daṅ rdzogs pa zuṅ du ḥjug ||
lha sku rigs stobs ye śes spyan ||
ñid la ñid du mṅon rol pa ||
bdag ñid chen po lhun gyis grub ||

rgyu bźi phuṅ po sku bźir bsgyur ||
mñam par gnas pa źi baḥi ṅaṅ ||
drag poḥi skur sprul khro boḥi sku ||
rigs bźi bdud ḥjoms ḥod dpuṅ ḥbar ||
skye bźi ḥkhor ba dbyiṅs su sgrol[a] ||
gñis su med pa bdag ñid ṅaṅ ||
ma spaṅ rgyan śar ñams su blaṅ[b] ||
bskyed daṅ rdzogs pa zuṅ du ḥjug ||
lha sku phyag rgya rigs stobs spyan ||
ñid la ñid du mṅon rol pa ||
bdag ñid chen po lhun gyis grub ||

dam rdzas lṅa po bdud rtsir bsgyur ||

[a] bsgrol [b] len

The (appropriate) divinity, buddha-body, symbol, family, power and eye
play together related together
and our great selfhood is spontaneously effected.

Envy is transformed into great openness,
a state of sameness and peace.
Transformed into a fierce divinity, of wrathful form,
it is turquoise-coloured, a destroyer of demons, blazing with light.
The cycle of envy receives release in the celestial sphere,
free of duality and in a state of self-existence.
Learn non-avoidance as your first principle.
Unite the Process of Emanation and the Process of Realization.
The (appropriate) divinity, buddha-body, symbol, family, power and eye
play together related together
and our great selfhood is spontaneously effected.

The eight perceptive groups are transformed into great knowledge,
a state of sameness and peace.
Transformed into a fierce divinity, of wrathful form,
they are variegated, destroyers of demons, blazing with light.
The cycle of the eight bases of perception receives release in the celestial sphere,
free of duality and in a state of self-existence.
Learn non-avoidance as your first principle.
Unite the Process of Emanation and the Process of Realization.
The (appropriate) divinity, buddha-body, symbol, family, power and eye
play together related together
and our great selfhood is spontaneously effected.

The four bodily elements are transformed into the four buddha-bodies,
a state of sameness and peace.
Transformed into a fierce divinity, of wrathful form,
the destroyer of demons of the four families, blazing with light.
The cycles of the four modes of birth receive release in the celestial sphere,
free of duality and in a state of self-existence.
Learn non-avoidance as your first principle.
Unite the Process of Emanation and the Process of Realization.
The (appropriate) divinity, buddha-body, symbol, family, power and eye
play together related together
and our great selfhood is spontaneously effected.

The five sacred items are transformed into elixir.

byaṅ sems gab pa sems kyi bdud ||
stoṅ ñid ye śes dag paḥi rtsi ||
źe sdaṅ ḥjoms pa sman gyi mchog ||
nam mkhaḥi lha mo bcud kyi dṅos ||
gtsaṅ sme blaṅ dor rtog pa ḥjoms ||
the tshom med par ñams su blaṅ ||
stoṅ ñid ye śes lhun gyis grub ||

gsaṅ śa gal chen gzugs kyi bdud ||
me loṅ ye śes dag paḥi rtsi ||
gti mug ḥjoms pa sman gyi mchog ||
sa yi lha mo bcud kyi dṅos ||
gtsaṅ sme blaṅ dor rtog pa ḥjoms ||
the tshom med par ñams su blaṅ ||
me loṅ ye śes lhun gyis grub ||

źim phod dri [21b] chen ḥdu byed bdud ||
mñam ñid ye śes dag paḥi rtsi ||
ṅa rgyal ḥjoms pa[a] sman gyi mchog ||
rluṅ[b] gi lha mo bcud kyi dṅos ||
gtsaṅ sme blaṅ dor rtog pa ḥjoms ||
the tshom med par ñams su blaṅ ||
mñam ñid ye śes lhun gyis grub ||

pad ma rak ta tshor baḥi bdud ||
sor rtogs ye śes dag paḥi rtsi ||
ḥdod chags ḥjoms pa sman gyi mchog ||
me yi lha mo bcud kyi dṅos ||
gtsaṅ sme blaṅ dor rtog pa ḥjoms ||
the tshom med par ñams su blaṅ ||
sor rtogs ye śes lhun gyis grub ||

mñam ñid dri chu ḥdu śes[c] bdud ||
bya grub ye śes dag paḥi rtsi ||
ḥphrag dog ḥjoms pa sman gyi mchog ||
chu yi lha mo bcud kyi dṅos ||
gtsaṅ sme blaṅ dor rtog pa ḥjoms ||
the tshom med par ñams su blaṅ ||
bya grub ye śes lhun gyis grub ||

dug gsum[d] sku gsuṅ thugs su bsgyur ||

[a] bźi brgya ḥjoms pa [b] kluṅ [c] ḥdu byed [d] dus gsum

The 'Thought of Enlightenment' in its secret meaning, which is the demon of Mind
(becomes) the essence of the pure *Wisdom of Voidness.*
The best of medicines, it is destructive of Wrath.
It is the essential nature of the goddesses of space.
It destroys the notions of the acceptance and rejection of purity and impurity.
Absorb it without hesitation
and the Wisdom of Voidness is spontaneously effected.

The indispensable 'secret flesh' is the demon of Body
(and becomes) the essence of the pure *Mirror-like Wisdom.*
The best of medicines, it is destructive of Mental Torpor.
It is the essential nature of the goddesses of earth.
It destroys the notions of the acceptance and rejection of purity and impurity.
Absorb it without hesitation
and the Mirror-like Wisdom is spontaneously effected.

The 'incense of great smell' is the demon of Impulses
(and becomes) the essence of the pure *Wisdom of Sameness.*
The best of medicines, it is destructive of Pride.
It is the essential nature of the goddesses of air.
It destroys the notions of the acceptance and rejection of purity and impurity.
Absorb it without hesitation
and the Wisdom of Sameness is spontaneously effected.

The 'lotus blood' is the demon of Feeling
(and becomes) the essence of pure *Discriminating Wisdom.*
The best of medicines, it is destructive of Lust.
It is the essential nature of the goddesses of fire.
It destroys the notions of the acceptance and rejection of purity and impurity.
Absorb it without hesitation
and Discriminating Wisdom is spontaneously effected.

The 'scent of sameness' is the demon of Perception
(and becomes) the essence of pure *Active Wisdom.*
The best of medicines, it is destructive of Envy.
It is the essential nature of the goddesses of water.
It destroys the notions of the acceptance and rejection of purity and impurity.
Absorb it without hesitation
and Active Wisdom is spontaneously effected.

The Three Evils[48] are transformed into Body, Speech and Mind.

źe sdaṅ ṅo bo stoṅ pa ñid ||
stoṅ źiṅ bdag med bon gyi sku ||
kha gtiṅ mtshan ma dpag tu med ||
yaṅs dog mthaḥ dbus ḥgyur ba med ||
ḥdi źes bzaḥ gtad spros ⟨mthaḥ⟩ bral ||
gdod nas ṅo bo ñid kyi dbyiṅs ||
bon ñid dkyil ḥkhor dbyiṅs na gnas ||
de bźin ñid kyi tiṅ ṅe ḥdzin ||
ma bcos spros bral ñams su blaṅ ||
bdag med stoṅ pa ye śes sku ||
ma bcos dri bral rnam par dag ||
ye saṅs rgyas paḥi ṅo bor gsal ||

gti mug ṅo bo rig pa ñid ||
raṅ bźin ḥod gsal rdzogs paḥi sku ||
sku daṅ źiṅ khams phyogs med rgyas ||
sgrib med ye śes ḥod zer ḥphro ||
mkhyen daṅ brtse baḥi bdag ñid can ||
gdod nas tshad med lhun la gnas ||
raṅ bźin dkyil ḥkhor mkhaḥ la rdzogs ||
kun tu snaṅ gi tiṅ ṅe ḥdzin ||
tshad med bźi ldan ñams su blaṅ ||
mi g·yo mñam gsal ye śes sku ||
mkhyen brtse ye śes phun sum tshogs ||
raṅ bźin lhun grub ṅo bo gsal ||

[22a] ḥdod chags ṅo bo sbyin pa ñid ||
gaṅ la ma chags rnam par dag ||
chags med dri bral sprul paḥi sku ||
gaṅ la chags par mi ḥdzin źiṅ ||
gaṅ la źen pa mi ḥchaḥ bas ||
gaṅ dag ḥgro ba ma lus pa ||
de yis spoṅ[a] bar mi ḥgyur bas ||
thams cad kha lo bsgyur baḥi phyir ||
mtshan maḥi dkyil ḥkhor kloṅ du gsal ||
sprul pa snaṅ baḥi tiṅ ṅe ḥdzin ||
lha sku yig ḥbru thig le sogs ||
sna tshogs mtshan ma ñams su blaṅ ||
mtshan maḥi rdzas la goms paḥo ||
yaṅ dag don la zuṅ ḥbrel skye ||
dbyiṅs śes mkhaḥ kloṅ thabs śes sogs ||

[a] span

The essence of Wrath is Voidness.
It is empty and selfless, this Body of *Bon*,
Measureless in its extent, its depth, its characteristics,
without width, range, and changeless.
'This' means lacking fixation, activity and goal.
It is the celestial sphere of primeval essence,
abiding in the *maṇḍala*-sphere of supreme *Bon*,
the contemplating of 'Suchness'.
Absorb this uncontrived non-diversity.
This is the selfless empty Knowledge-Body.
Uncontrived, immaculate, perfectly pure,
it shines as the essence of primeval buddhahood.

The essence of Mental Torpor is Knowledge,
the Perfect Body whose nature is clear light,
whence divinities and their realms spread forth in all directions,
immaculate knowledge pouring forth rays of light,
possessing the nature of wisdom and love.
It abides in the primeval measureless mass,
with the nature of the perfect *maṇḍala* in space,
as the contemplating of universal manifestation.
Absorb it, for it comprehends the four immeasurable virtues.
It is the Body of Clear Knowledge, unmoving, invariable,
The perfect knowledge of wisdom and love,
the clear essence of self-manifestation.

The essence of Desire is Generosity,
perfect purity which is nowhere attached,
the unattached, immaculate Phenomenal Body,
clinging nowhere in attachment,
acting nowhere from desire.
But it avoids no being whatsoever,
and that it may direct them all,
it shines in space as the *maṇḍala* of recognizable signs,
as the contemplating of manifest appearances.
These gods, buddha-bodies, seed-syllables, heart-essence and so on,
absorb these various recognizable signs.
Even such is the art of recognizable characteristics.
They arise in pairs in the pure absolute,
celestial sphere and knowledge, sky and space, method and wisdom, etc.

zuṅ ḥjug lha sku phyag rgya thob ||

snaṅ srid sbyor sgrol rol par bsgyur ||
phyi snod naṅ bcud gcig tu sbyor ||
sbyor baḥi mchod pa dpag tu med ||
ñid la ñid rol mṅon par dag ||
dug gsum[a] sku gsuṅ thugs su bsgral ||
dug lṅa ye śes lṅa ru bsgral[b] ||
rnam rtog bon ñid dbyiṅs su bsgral ||
dgra bgegs bar chod tshogs su bsgral ||
sgrol baḥi mchod pa dpag tu med ||
ñid la ñid rol mṅon par dag ||
dbyiṅs śes dbyer med bde bar rol ||
mkhaḥ kloṅ dbyer med gcig tu rol ||
thabs śes zuṅ ḥjug sñoms par rol ||
rol paḥi mchod pa dpag tu med ||
ñid la ñid rol mṅon par dag ||
sbyor sgrol rol pa ñams su blaṅ ||
sbyor ba bon ñid bde baḥi ṅaṅ ||
sgrol bas dus gsum ḥkhor ba ḥjoms ||
rol pas zuṅ ḥjug phyag rgya che ||
sku gsum lhun grub saṅs rgyas thob ||

thabs śes mi spaṅ gzuṅs ma ḥdzin ||
u ya dam tshig snod du bya ||
lha mo mdzes ldan yid ḥoṅ grogs ||
klu mo mdzas ldan dṅos grub grogs ||
mi mo yid ḥoṅ mthu rtsal grogs ||
mtshan ldan rgod lcam mchog gi grogs ||
sñoms ḥjug bde baḥi phyag rgya sbrel ||
thabs śes thig le dkar dmar [22b] spro ||
rkyaṅ cha ya bral don mi ḥgrub ||
gñis mthun gra bsdeb kun nas mdzes ||
gsaṅ sṅags gsaṅ la snod gcig dgos ||
thabs śes zuṅ ḥbrel ñams su blaṅ ||
rtsa rluṅ thig le zuṅ du chud ||
bde stoṅ ye śes rgyud la skye ||
dgaḥ chen rol mo dpag tu med ||
ñid la ñid rol mṅon par dag ||
gñis su med paḥi phyag rgya thob ||

[a] dus gsum [b] sgrol

One gains the divine body and the symbol of the Two-in-One.

The phenomenal world is transformed into union, release and play.
The outer vessel and the inner essence are united in one.
Immeasurable is the worship of union.
Delighting one in another, they are completely purified.
The Three Evils are released as Body, Speech and Mind.[48]
The Five Evils are released as the Five Wisdoms.
Doubts are released in the celestial sphere of Absolute *Bon*.
Enemies, adverse influences and hindrances are released as the circle of offerings.
Immeasurable is the worship of release.
Delighting one in another, they are completely purified.
Celestial sphere and knowledge play happily together indistinguishably.
Sky and space play as one indistinguishably.
Method and Wisdom play together as Two-in-One.
Immeasurable is the worship of this play.
Delighting one in another, they are completely purified.
Absorb this union, release and play.
Union has the nature of absolute happiness.
Release overcomes the phenomenal world in past, present and future.
Play gains the Great Symbol of Two-in-One
and the triple-bodied spontaneously effected buddhahood.

Do not avoid Method and Wisdom. Take your partner.
Make her a worthy recipient of the secret vow.
A beautiful goddess is a pleasing companion.
A beautiful mermaid is a companion of perfect achievement.
A pleasing woman is a skilful companion.
An excellent *ḍākinī* is the best of companions.
Entering into union, the seal of happiness is fixed.
The 'drop' of Method and Wisdom flows white and red.
Alone and without a partner, no result is achieved.
One requires someone suitable and adapted and very beautiful,
who is worthy of the secret of secret spells.
Absorb this union of Method and Wisdom.
Bring together channels, breath and the 'drop',
And the knowledge of bliss and voidness will arise in your 'soul-series'.
Immeasurable is the play of this great joy.
Delighting one in another, they are completely purified
and gain the symbol of non-duality.

lta ba spyi rgya rlabs kyis chod ||
sgom pa mdor bsdus thig le ḥbrel ||
spyod pa bon ñid la chen dor ||
dam tshig rnam dag gźi ma gzuṅ ||
ḥphrin las rnam bźi tshags[a] su bsdam ||
dṅos grub gsaṅ ba thabs źags kyis ||
ḥgro baḥi sñiṅ po dbaṅ du bsdud ||
gsaṅ sṅags don ldan gsaṅ ba ḥdus ||
gsas mkhar gsaṅ ba sgo dgu yi ||
phyi naṅ gsaṅ ba gaṅ spyod kyaṅ ||
don dam ñams su len tshul lo ||
gsaṅ baḥi man ṅag thugs la choṅs ||
sems can ḥgro la sman par mdzod ||

ces gsuṅs so / yaṅ ston pas bkaḥ stsal pa /

ñon cig dbaṅ ldan gtsug phud gśen ||
gsaṅ ba sṅags kyi theg pa la ||
bsñen daṅ sgrub paḥi go rim ni ||
gsas mkhar gsaṅ ba sgo dgu la ||
so sor bye brag maṅ lags kyaṅ ||
tshur bsdus rnam pa gsum du ḥdus ||
bsñen sgrub las gsum go rim mo ||

thog mar bsñen paḥi rim pa la ||
bsñen paḥi gźi ma sgo dgu daṅ ||
gñis pa sgrub paḥi rim pa la ||
sgrub paḥi yan lag bco brgyad daṅ ||
tha ma las kyi mthaḥ bsgyur las[b] ||
gźuṅ las gud kyi mchoṅ dgu ste ||
yan lag sum cu rtsa drug gis ||
bsñen sgrub las gsum go rim dbye ||

de yaṅ so sor bstan pa ni ||
bsñen paḥi gźi ma sgo dgu la ||
sṅon ḥgro phyi yi bsñen pa gsum ||
ñe ba naṅ gi bsñen pa gsum ||
bcaḥ gźi las kyi bsñen pa gsum ||

[a] tshigs [b] nas

Insight is determined as a smooth wave.
Contemplation is concentrated upon the 'dot'.
Practice attains to supreme *Bon.*
The Vow holds one to the basis of purity.
The fourfold Activity is bound up together.
By perfect achievement, the 'Noose of Secret Method'
the essence of living things is controlled.

O *Guhyasamāja*, who comprehend secret spells,
whoever practises the outer, inner or secret ways
of the nine doors of the secret *gSas*-palace,
this is the manner to absorb absolute truth.
Keep this secret instruction in mind
and benefit living beings.

Thus he spoke. Then again he said:

Listen, powerful *gTsug-phud-gśen*!
In the vehicle of secret spells
there are the stages of reliance (invocation) and performance (conjuration).[63]
In respect of these there are many divisions
in the nine compartments of the secret *gSas*-palace,
Compressing them, we reduce them to three kinds,
Reliance, Performance and Acts.

Firstly for the stages of reliance
there are nine compartments or bases of reliance.
Secondly for the stages of performance,
there are eighteen branches of performance.
Lastly for the supererogatory acts,
there are nine subsidiary sections from the basic texts.
These make thirty-six branches in all.

As for distinguishing the stages of these three, Reliance, Performance and Acts,
we now explain them separately.
As for the nine compartments or bases of Reliance,
there are three outer reliances concerned with preliminaries,
the three inner reliances concerned with proximity,
the three reliances of the actual practice.

thog mar phyi yi [23a] bsñen pa la ||
dpon gsas lha la bsñen pa daṅ ||
rigs ldan gnas la bsñen pa daṅ ||
mtshan ldan grogs la bsñen pa gsum ||
ñe ba naṅ gi bsñen pa ni ||
yo byad rdzas la bsñen pa daṅ ||
thar glud bskaṅ la bsñen pa daṅ ||
phyi rten skos kyi bsñen pa gsum ||
bcaḥ gźi las kyi bsñen pa gsum ||
sruṅ ba mtshams bcad phyi ru bsñen ||
dkyil ḥkhor dal bri naṅ du bsñen ||
sgo dbye bsre bsnan gsaṅ ba bsñen ||
bsñen paḥi gźi ma sgo dguḥo ||

sgrub paḥi yan lag bco brgyad la ||
thog mar gźi yi yan lag drug ||
ṅo mtshar lam gyi yan lag drug ||
mthar phyin ḥbras buḥi yan lag drug ||
bco brgyad dag tu śes pa ste ||
de yaṅ so sor bstan pa na ||
bar mtshams bdag ñid don du bsgrub ||
phyag rgya dgod pa bdag tu bsgrub ||
dug lṅa raṅ grol gdan[a] du bsgrub ||
spyan draṅ ye śes gñis med bsgrub ||
phyag ḥtshal mos ḥdun gus par bsgrub ||
ñes ltuṅ ñams bźag gus pas bsgrub ||
gźi yi yan lag drug tu śes ||
gsaṅ ba ñon moṅs tshar gcad bsgrub ||
ye śes byin dbab loṅs spyod bsgrub ||
ḥphro ḥdu gsaṅ ba ḥdzab tu bsgrub ||
phyag rgya gsaṅ ba gar du bsgrub ||
sku mdog phyag mtshan gdan khri bsgrub ||
źi khro gnas ḥgyur rtags su bsgrub ||
lam kyi yan lag drug tu śes ||
dṅos grub yaṅ sñiṅ bcud du bsgrub ||
dus gsum ḥbral med dam bcar bsgrub ||
bdud rtsi zad med gter du bsgrub ||

[a] gnad

First as for the outer reliances, there is reliance on the master-sage, reliance on a suitable place, reliance on an excellent companion.

As for the inner reliances of proximity, there is reliance on the ritual items, reliance on atoning ransoms, reliance on the symbolic arrangement (of the *maṇḍala*).

As for the reliances of the actual practice,
there is the outer reliance on protecting divinities who cut off (the profane world),
the inner reliance on the mystic circle which must be drawn,
the secret reliance on the revelation (of the mystic circle), the uniting (of divinity and practiser) and the addition (of extra consecrations).
These are the nine compartments or bases of Reliance.

As for the eighteen branches of Performance,
first there are the six branches of the Basis,
then the six branches of the Way,
and finally the six branches of the Result.
Thus they are known as eighteen.

As for explaining them each in turn,
(1) effecting for oneself a demarcation (of protection),
(2) effecting for oneself the established symbols (viz. the symbols of the divinities in the *maṇḍala*),
(3) effecting as thrones the Five Evils in their self-released state.[33]
(4) effecting the invitation (of the divinities) and unity with the gods of knowledge,
(5) effecting salutations and devotions,
(6) effecting respectfully a confession of sins.

These are the six branches of the Basis. Next come:
(7) effecting the cutting off of secret hindrances,
(8) effecting the enjoyment of the grace of the gods of knowledge,
(9) effecting the 'outflow' and the 'in-gathering' by the reciting of magic spells,
(10) effecting the secret symbols in dance,
(11) effecting (by descriptive praises) the forms, colours, symbols, characteristics and thrones (of the divinities),
(12) effecting by signs the transposition of gentle and fierce divinities.

These are the six branches of the Way. Then come:
(13) effecting the real essence of perfect achievement,
(14) effecting the vow of remaining inseparable (from one's divinity) in past, present and future,
(15) effecting (the change of) the elixir (the offerings) into inexhaustible treasure (for deserving sprites, etc.),

dmar lam sbyor sgrol rol par bsgrub ||
gzir nan drag po stobs su bsgrub ||
dbye bsdu ye śes don du bsgrub ||
mthar phyin ḥbras buḥi yan lag go ||

gsum [23b] pa las kyi mthaḥ sgyur la ||
las kyi tha ma ḥchoṅ dgu ni ||
theg pa dgu yi don daṅ sbyar ||
gsal byed me loṅ pra yi ḥchoṅ ||
phyva gśen theg paḥi don daṅ sbyar ||
snaṅ srid rab ḥbyams skoṅ gi ḥchoṅ ||
snaṅ gśen theg paḥi don daṅ sbyar ||
ye śes dbal mo srog gi ḥchoṅ ||
ḥphrul gśen theg paḥi don daṅ sbyar ||
thugs rje źags pa ḥdur gyi ḥchoṅ ||
srid gśen theg paḥi don daṅ sbyar ||
las bźi rgyun lṅa sgrib sbyaṅ ḥchoṅ ||
dge bsñen theg paḥi don daṅ sbyar ||
ḥbum sde sa ya dam tshig ḥchoṅ ||
draṅ sroṅ theg paḥi don daṅ sbyar ||
bdud rtsi gsaṅ ba sman gyi ḥchoṅ ||
a dkar theg paḥi don daṅ sbyar ||
thig le dbyiṅs chen dgoṅs paḥi ḥchoṅ ||
ye gśen theg paḥi don daṅ sbyar ||
kun khyab yaṅs pa lta baḥi ḥchoṅ ||
bla med theg paḥi don daṅ sbyar ||
de ltar yan lag gsum cu drug ||
gsas mkhar gsaṅ ba sgo dgu yi ||
bsñen sgrub las gsum go rim mo ||
gsaṅ sṅags don ldan gsaṅ ba ḥdus ||
gsaṅ baḥi man ṅag thugs la choṅs ||
sems can ḥgro la sman par mdzod ||

ces gsuṅs so /

(16) effecting union, release and play in the red way (viz. making offerings of flesh and blood to fierce demonesses, *dbal-mo*, etc.),

(17) effecting the suppression of power (foes),

(18) effecting knowledge as the result of opening (the circle for the departure of the divinities) and gathering up (the implements).

These are the branches of the Result.

Thirdly as for the supererogatory acts,
there are nine sections of such intentional acts,
which fit together with the subjects of the Nine Vehicles.

(1) There is the section on prognostics called 'The Clear-making Mirror',
which accords with the Way of Prediction.

(2) There is the section on atonement called 'Pervading the Phenomenal World', which accords with the Way of the Shen of the Visual World.

(3) There is the section on life-force called '*dBal-mo* of Knowledge', which accords with the Way of the Shen of Appearances.

(4) There is the section on funeral-rites called 'Noose of Compassion', which accords with the Way of the Shen of Existence.

(5) There is the section for cleansing defilements, called 'Four Rites and the Flow making Five', which corresponds with the Way of Virtuous Adherers.

(6) There is the section on vows called 'One Million sets of One Hundred Thousand', which corresponds with the Vehicle of the Great Ascetics.

(7) There is the section on medicine called 'Secret Elixirs', which corresponds with the Vehicle of Pure Sound.

(8) There is the section on thought, called 'Great Expanse of the Drop', which corresponds with the Vehicle of the Primeval Shen.

(9) There is the section on insight, called 'Vast Pervasion', which corresponds with the Supreme Vehicle.

Thus in all there are thirty-six branches, and this is the order of Reliances, Performances and Acts of the nine compartments of the secret *gSas*-palace.

O *Guhyasamāja*, who hold the meaning of secret spells,
keep this secret instruction in mind
and benefit living beings.

This is what he said.

VIII. YE GŚEN THEG PA

[vol. *ṅa*, f. 61a[7] onwards]

de la yaṅ ye gśen gtsug phud kyis gsol pa /
ston paḥi sgron ma ḥgro baḥi dpal daṅ mgon ||
rnam pa thams cad mkhyen paḥi thugs can lags ||
ston [61b] paḥi źal nas bden paḥi bcud phyuṅ źiṅ ||
bdag cag ḥkhor la ṅes par bstan pa yi ||
theg pa brgyad pa ye gśen bon sgo la ||
daṅ po byaṅ chub sems kyi ḥbyuṅ tshul daṅ ||
gñis pa bkaḥ rgyud luṅ gi che ba daṅ ||
gsum pa rgyud luṅ so soḥi bye brag rnams ||
bdag cag ḥkhor rnams thugs kyi dkyil du phog ||
da yaṅ phyi rabs rnams kyi don ched du ||
dug lṅa rnam dag mtshan bcas thabs kyi rgyud ||
ye śes ṅaṅ gnas mtshan med śes rab rgyud ||
rtsa baḥi rgyud gñis yan lag bco brgyad de ||
ñiṅ lag brgyad cu gya gcig rnam graṅs bcas ||
ṅes par gcig tu dril ba sñiṅ poḥi don ||
mdo ru bsdus paḥi ñams len go rim źig ||
bdag cag ḥkhor la ston pas bkaḥ stsal ḥtshal ||

ces gsol to / de la yaṅ ston pas bkaḥ stsal pa /

ñon cig ye gśen gtsug phud gus pas ñon ||
ḥdi la go rim rnam pa gñis su bstan ||
bskyed[a] pa⟨ḥi rim pa⟩ bsñen[b] źiṅ sgrub pa daṅ ||
rdzogs paḥi rim pa sgom źiṅ goms pa gñis ||
don dam kun rdzob mtshan bcas mtshan med blta ||
thabs daṅ śes rab zuṅ ḥbrel rgyu ru bstan ||
don la gñis su yod pa ma yin źiṅ ||
de yaṅ ṅes paḥi don du gcig tu bsdu ||
kun gźi byaṅ chub sems su gcig lags kyaṅ ||
sems can bkri draṅ so sor bstan pa tsam ||
deḥi phyir bskyed daṅ rdzogs pa gñis su bstan ||
de la thog mar bskyed paḥi rim pa la ||
sṅon ḥgro dṅos gźi rjes kyi bya ba gsum ||

[a] bskye   [b] sñen

VIII. THE WAY OF THE PRIMEVAL SHEN

Then *Ye-gśen gTsug-phud* said:

O Light of Teachers, Guardian and Splendour of living beings!
Your mind is quite omniscient!
The essence of truth proceeds from your mouth, O Teacher,
and you teach us, your following, with precision.
In the matter of the eighth vehicle, the *bon* way of Primeval Shen,
our minds have been instructed in:
firstly—the way of the arising of the Thought of Enlightenment,
secondly—the importance of canonical, traditional and inspired teachings,
thirdly—the various kinds of *tantras* and inspired teachings.

Now for the sake of future generations we beg you, O Teacher, to tell us
the *tantra* of Method of the characterized which will purify the Five Evils,
the *tantra* of Wisdom of the non-characterized which abides in the state of knowledge,
the eighteen branches of the two basic *tantras*,
together with an inventory of the eighty-one minor branches,
(teach us these as) essential matter summed up together and with precision, well-ordered teaching reduced to a brief form.

So they asked, and the Teacher replied:

Listen, *Ye-gśen gTsug-phud*, listen!
This must be taught in two ordered stages,
the Process of Emanation (consisting of) reliance and performance,
the Process of Realization (consisting of) contemplative practice and habit.
Absolute truth must be viewed as relative truth and the characterized as the non-characterized.
Method and Wisdom are taught as being united as a pair.
In effect they do not exist in duality, for although they are one in the Thought of Enlightenment, the universal basis, they are only taught separately for the guidance of living beings.
Thus in reality they are united as one.
But for that reason (viz. the guidance of living beings) they are taught as the Process of Emanation and the Process of Realization.
Now in the first place the Process of Emanation has three stages, namely preliminaries, the real basis and the final acts.

daṅ po sṅon du ḥgro baḥi rim pa la ||
brgyad khri bźi stoṅ theg pa rim dgu daṅ ||
sgo bźi mdzod lṅa bon sgo gaṅ spyod kyaṅ ||
kun gyi ḥbyuṅ gnas bla ma dam pa yin ||
deḥi phyir [62a] mtshan ñid ldan paḥi bla ma btsal ||
lus ṅag yig gsum mos ḥdun gus par bskyed ||
ji sñad mchod yon bla ma rje la ḥbul ||
lus srog rgyan la sogs pa thams cad kyaṅ ||
chags med blo yis bla ma mchod byas na ||
bskal stoṅ saṅs rgyas thams cad mñes daṅ mtshuṅs ||
bsod nams bsags paḥi ḥbras bu rgyun mi ḥchad ||
bskal pa stoṅ gi saṅs rgyas de dag kyaṅ ||
bla ma dag la brten nas byon pa ste ||
da ltaḥi ston pa bdag daṅ mtshuṅs paḥo ||
deḥi phyir mtshan ldan bla maḥi thugs bzuṅ nas ||
dbaṅ daṅ byin rlabs luṅ gi man ṅag gi ||
źu don gsol ciṅ khas blaṅ dam bcaḥ ste ||
sems la dam bcaḥ yod na dge ba ḥgrub ||
dam bcaḥ med na le lo g·yeṅ baḥi phyir ||
tshe gcig dge ba spyod bsam loṅ khom med ||
deḥi phyir dge ba dbyar dam bcaḥ ba ste ||
źiṅ sa gśin la sa bon btab pa ḥdra ||
nam yaṅ lo thog myu gu ḥkhruṅs par byed ||
de la ḥbras bu brtson ḥgrus stobs la rag ||
brtson ḥgrus stobs ni źiṅ paḥi so nam ḥdra ||
deḥi phyir dam bcaḥ rnam par dag pa gces ||

dam bcaḥ rnam par dag pa sṅon soṅ nas ||
dge baḥi sdoṅ la mtshan ldan grogs gces pas ||
mtshan daṅ ldan paḥi lha sras lcam dral ni ||
rigs[a] bzaṅ khuṅs btsun mi rgyal rgyud maḥi bu ||
gźon nu dal ḥbyor dpag bsam ljon pa ḥdra ||
yon tan kun ḥbyuṅ lo ḥbras me tog ltar ||
gaṅ du ḥdod paḥi don rnams rab ḥgrub ciṅ ||
yid ḥoṅ ṅag ḥjam bran gyi tha ma ltar ||
ci bcol las la bskos pa de bźin ñan[b] ||
mi dge las spaṅ dge bcuḥi las la brtson ||
sems dkar bcos sla khrel daṅ ṅo tsha śes ||
dad pa ḥgyur med dge [62b] sems gtoṅ phod che ||
gtsaṅ maḥi tshul sruṅ bram ze tshaṅs par spyod ||
g·yo sgyu zol zog[c] ḥdod pa gtiṅ[d] bas spaṅ ||
sñiṅ rje sems ldan ḥgro la byams paḥi phul ||

[a] rig [b] ñin [c] sog [d] gtaṅ

First as for the stage of preliminaries, whatever one practises among the Nine Vehicles with their 84,000 teachings, and among the Four Portals and the One Treasury as Fifth,[64] the source of everything is a holy lama.
So one must look for an accomplished lama.
With body, speech and mind one should arouse feelings of devotion,
and one must offer this lordly lama whatever offerings one can.
If you worship your lama and offer him everything, body, life and fine things, your mind will be quite free from attachment, and it will be like giving pleasure to all the buddhas of the thousand world-ages.
The fruits of your accumulated merit will appear continuously.
Even the buddhas of the thousand world-ages depended on their lamas, when they appeared in the world,
and it is the same with me, the teacher of the present age.
So hold close to an accomplished lama, ask him for consecrations, blessings and inspired teachings, and promise to observe them.
If you keep your vow in mind, you will do good.
If you keep no vow, you will be indolent and unsettled, and there will be no opportunity to practise virtue in this life.
So this making a vow to cleave to virtue is like planting seed in good soil.
Some time the shoots for harvesting will appear,
But the fruits depend on the force of one's effort.
The force of effort is like the farmer's husbandry.
So a pure vow is of great importance.

With a pure vow as precondition the important thing is a worthy mate as virtuous companion.
As for such a maiden, this worthy offspring of the gods, she must be of good family, of noble origin, an offspring of the rulers of men,
youthful and well endowed like a tree of paradise.
Her good qualities emerge everywhere like leaves and fruit and flowers,
producing all the things that one desires.
Ravishing and gently spoken, yet like the meanest servant
attentive to whatever work is entrusted to her charge,
eschewing evil acts, and exerting herself in the ten good acts,
pure minded, easily adapted, knowing modesty and shame,
of unchanging faith, virtuous disposition and of great generosity,
observing pure conduct and living in chastity,
altogether free from falsehood, deceit and selfish desire,
compassionate and full of love towards sentient beings,

rig daṅ śa mtshan pra ltas rnam[a] ḥgyur can[b] ||
rtse gcig byaṅ chub bsgrub paḥi grogs su bzaṅ ||
gaṅ du gnas kyaṅ thabs kyis dgug[c] la bsten ||
gsaṅ dam gñan[d] po gcig gis bsre bar bya ||
dpon gsas lha la dbaṅ luṅ man ṅag źu ||
sdig spyod ṅan ḥgro dman paḥi tshogs rnams ni ||
dge la bar du bcod pas spaṅ bar bya ||
de yaṅ mtshan daṅ ldan paḥi mi mo ni ||
dbyiṅs daṅ ye śes thabs daṅ śes rab ste ||
rtsa rluṅ thig le dbab paḥi gzuṅs ma che ||
byaṅ chub sems ñid bsgrub paḥi grogs yin kyaṅ ||
ḥjig rten dag na med ciṅ rab tu dkon ||
u dum ḥbar daṅ rnam par rgyal ba bźin ||
brgya stoṅ khri ḥbum re re srid pa tsam ||
de yaṅ rtags daṅ mtshan ma brtags byas nas ||
maṅ la ñuṅ du brtag ciṅ spaṅ blaṅ bya ||
rig paḥi rtsal gyis dkyil ḥkhor dbaṅ yaṅ bskur ||
gñis med dam tshig don gyi sñiṅ po sbyin ||
man ṅag gsaṅ spyod gab ciṅ sba bar bya ||
byaṅ chub bsgrub paḥi grogs su bstan paḥo ||

de ltar dpon gsas dag las luṅ nod ciṅ ||
mched daṅ lcam dral dam tshig tshogs nas su ||
bsgrub paḥi sa ru gsaṅ baḥi gnas btsal te ||
de yaṅ sṅon byuṅ bsgrub paḥi gnas lta bu ||
g·yu luṅ śel brag la sogs te ||
gsaṅ baḥi brag phug dgu rgyud lta bu daṅ ||
yaṅ na g·yuṅ druṅ dgu brtsegs[e] ri bo daṅ ||
de bo gaṅ chen gliṅ gi khrod la sogs ||
śel gyi brag dkar rtse rdzoṅ lta bu yi ||
dben la ñams dgaḥ yid du ḥoṅ ba ste ||
g·yaḥ ri gaṅ brag nags [63a] tshal mtsho gliṅ khrod ||
dur khrod mi med luṅ stoṅ dben sar bstan ||
dgra daṅ rkun bu mi mthun bar chod dben ||
mthun rkyen cha mthun ḥgal med so sogs[f] gnas ||
mdun rgyab ma bsnol ñin srib go ma log ||
g·yas sgron g·yon ḥbar rgyab ḥgyiṅ mdun ri gźol ||
gtsaṅ rgyal chab kyi lu ma dmig gi ltag[g] ||
rgya mtsho bdal[h] zab chu bran kun nas ḥdus ||
spyan lam śul riṅ śar lho yaṅs la bdal ||

[a] rnams [b] śiṅ [c] gkug [d] gñen [e] rtseg [f] gsog
[g] gis lta [h] dal

possessing the signs and attributes of knowledge and physical beauty,
she is good as a mate for the single-aimed producing of the Thought of Enlightenment.
Wherever such a one exists, draw her forth with skill and cleave to her.
You must unite with her with a solemn secret vow,
and seek the consecrations, inspired teachings and instructions of the sages and gods.
The mean multitudes, practisers of evil who go to evil rebirths
will obstruct your virtue and must be avoided.
So then this worthy woman,
this great 'Spell'[65] in whom space and knowledge, Method and Wisdom,
the channels, vital breath and vital fluid, all flow together,
is your mate for the producing of the Thought of Enlightenment.
Yet she is so scarce, she might be non-existent in this world.
Like the *udumbara* flower and myrobalan, she is just possible as one in a hundred, a thousand, ten thousand, one hundred thousand.
So examining characteristics and marks, you must look for the few among the many, reject (the unsuitable) and accept (the suitable).
You must consecrate her in the *maṇḍala* with the skill of knowledge,
and bestow upon her the substantive essence of an unambiguous vow.
The instructions and the secret practice must be concealed and kept secret.
Such is the description of a mate for the realization of enlightenment.

Having thus received the inspired teachings from the sages,
the brethren and their sworn maidens gather together
and seek for a secret place as the site for their practice,
a site such as was used for this practice in former times,
the Crystal Crag of the Turquoise Vale and the rest,
such as the Secret Set of Nine Linked Caves,
the Nine Stage Swastika Mountain
and the island ranges of the great snow mountains,
the Peak Citadel of the White Crystal Crag,
solitary, ravishing, a delight to the spirit,
rocky mountains, snowy crags, forests, lakes and island ranges,
cemeteries, empty uninhabited valleys, all such are described as solitary places,
free from enemies and thieves, adversities and obstructions,
places that are favourable and harmonious, such places as do not thwart (intentions),
untrammelled to front and rear, and the sun's shadow correctly positioned,
well-covered on the right, hilly on the left,
raised up to the rear and falling away in front,
a spring of good pure water above a well,
a lake wide and deep, gathering in streams from all sides,
a distant unobstructed view, broad and wide to east and south,

byaṅ g·yor nub bskyor dgra lam mi mthun med ||
rtsi śiṅ nags tshal me tog ḥdam[a] buḥi tshal ||
ḥdab chags skad sñan gcan gzan ri mo bkra ||
śa rkyaṅ gtsod rgo ri dvags g·yuṅ dvags ḥdzom ||
byaṅ chub sems ldan sprel buḥi tshogs kyi gliṅ ||
mi min yid gzugs lha srin dregs tshogs ḥdu ||
lta dman skye ḥjigs[b] sgrin bu ya ṅa tsha ||
lta ba can rnams bag dro[c] byiṅ ba gsiṅ ||
gaṅ du yod kyaṅ dkaḥ ba spyad la btsal ||
ma dag yul daṅ mthaḥ ḥkhob kla klo daṅ ||
groṅ daṅ groṅ khyer groṅ bdal la sogs ste ||
gnas rñiṅ mi gtsaṅ dman[d] paḥi ḥtshog ra[e] daṅ ||
mtshan daṅ mi ldan gnas yul spaṅ bar bya ||
yid ḥoṅ ñams dgaḥ mtshan daṅ ldan paḥi gnas ||
byaṅ chub bsgrub paḥi gnas su bzaṅ bas btsal ||

de ltar mtshan daṅ ldan paḥi gnas mchog tu ||
phun sum tshogs paḥi yo byad rdzas bsag ste ||
dar dkar bla bre dar dmar yol ba daṅ ||
mi nub rgyal mtshan phye ma ḥphur ma daṅ ||
mdaḥ daṅ me loṅ tsa kra ha la daṅ ||
rin chen chag śiṅ yo gal draṅ śiṅ daṅ ||
rṅa gśan rol mo mchod paḥi bye brag daṅ ||
rin chen bum pa stobs ldan man dzi daṅ ||
mtshan ldan yol [63b] chen ña phyi phud źal daṅ ||
rin chen snod bzaṅ ḥbru snaḥi phye ma daṅ ||
dkar mṅar śa khrag tshogs kyi yo byad daṅ ||
g·yu ḥbraṅ phud mchod bdud rtsiḥi rgya mtsho daṅ ||
me chu śiṅ daṅ mkho mthun rdzas cha daṅ ||
rin chen sna lṅa ḥbru yi baṅ mdzod daṅ ||
dṅos grub laṅ tsho khams gsoḥi rdzas rnams bsag ||
gaṅ dgos yo byad phun sum tshogs par bya ||
de nas rdzas daṅ yo byad kun tshogs nas ||
thog mar sṅon du ḥgro baḥi rim pa ste ||
theg pa rim dguḥi bon sgo gaṅ spyod kyaṅ ||
ḥjig rten bdag po mṅaḥ dbaṅ can rnams la ||
dkar mchod gtsaṅ maḥi gtor ma ma btaṅ nas ||
bder gśegs pho braṅ gźal yas ma bslaṅ na ||
mṅaḥ dbaṅ bdag po sa bdag klu gñen rnams ||
bstan pa ci ltar bsruṅ yaṅ ko loṅ dam ||

[a] dham [b] ḥjig [c] gro [d] dmen [e] raṅ

but blocked to the north and enclosed to the west, so there is no adverse
way for enemies,
a grove of fruit trees, a thicket of flowers and rushes,
sweet sounding with the cries of birds and colourful with spotted beasts,
where deer, wild asses, antelopes, wild goats, wild and domestic animals
all come together,
a land with troupes of monkeys whose Thoughts are on Enlightenment,
and where non-human ghostly creatures and hosts of proud gods and
demons foregather.
Mean-spirited men would be afraid and the foolish would be in terror,
but those whose views are right are happy, for indolence is removed.
Wherever it may be, make effort and seek it out.
Impure countries, wild and barbarous,
villages, towns and markets and the like,
used unclean sites, the meeting places of common folk,
such unworthy places must be avoided.
You must look for a ravishing, delightful and worthy place,
for this will be good as a place for producing the Thought of Enlightenment.

Thus in this excellent and worthy place
you must bring together the very best implements,
a canopy of white silk and curtains of red silk,
the unfailing banner of victory and pleated hangings of fine cloth,
an arrow, a mirror and a sword,
the precious sceptre, the rod which straightens crooked things,
the drum, the flat-shaped bell, the various kinds of acoustic offerings,
the precious vase, the sturdy tripod,
the skull-cup and the offering-dish of mother-of-pearl,
the fine jewelled vessel and flour from various kinds of grain,
milk offerings, sweet offerings, flesh and blood, and such sacrificial items,
an offering of consecrated *chang*, an ocean of ambrosia,
fire, water, wood, and all necessary items,
the five kinds of precious stones, a store of grain,
the items for the realization of perfection and for preserving one's health.
One must gather together whatever is required of the very best things.
Then when all the items and implements have been gathered together,
the order of the preliminaries is like this.
Whichever *bon* way of the Nine Vehicles you practise,
if you fail to give milk-offerings and pure sacrificial cakes to the powerful
lords of this world,
if you do not ask them (for a site for) your palace of the Blessed Ones,
these powerful lords, the lords of the soil, the serpents and the furies
are irascible, however much they may still protect the doctrine.

śes rgyud ci ltar ḥjam yaṅ lha min rigs ||
deḥi phyir sa bdag klu gñen dkar gyi mchod ||
rtsi śiṅ źugs daṅ gser skyems yas stags rdzas ||
rgyal baḥi bden pa smraṅ gis bkrol la dbul ||
ḥjig rten mṅaḥ dbaṅ can rnams dgyes bar bya ||
dgyes mdzad sṅon gyi tha tshig dam du bdar ||
brten paḥi gźi bslaṅ ḥdug sa bslaṅ ||
bstan pa bsruṅ baḥi tha tshig dpaṅ du bsgo[a] ||
phyin chad gaṅ yaṅ dgos paḥi sñan gsan dbab ||
de ltar ḥjig rten źi bde sa la rag ||
źiṅ khams bde daṅ lo thog legs pa daṅ ||
rgyal khams dar daṅ mṅaḥ ris ḥphel ba daṅ ||
phyed tsam sṅon gyi[b] las kyis bskos lags kyaṅ ||
phyed tsam sa gźi mṅaḥ dbaṅ rnams las byuṅ ||
ḥdi la thabs daṅ bstun par ma śes na ||
mi dge ñes paḥi rtsa ba ḥdi las ḥbyuṅ ||
deḥi phyir sa bdag klu gñen bcos par bya ||
de ltar [64a] sṅon ḥgroḥi cho ga tshar nas su ||
bder gśegs gźal yas pho braṅ gnas brtsig ste ||
dkar snum mñen la ḥbol baḥi sa blaṅ la ||
ḥdom gaṅ khru bźi mdaḥ gaṅ gru bźi daṅ ||
khru[c] gaṅ la sogs che chuṅ skabs daṅ sbyar ||
khru gaṅ chag gaṅ mtho gaṅ dpaṅs gi tshad ||
rgyas ḥbriṅ bsdus gsum gaṅ byed skabs daṅ sbyar ||
dbyibs legs ḥjam bde me loṅ sbub ḥdraḥi tshul ||
gtsaṅ maḥi tshan daṅ dri bzaṅ sman spos kyis ||
kun nas yoṅs su sñoms paḥi chag chag gdab ||
śi śon tshon thag dkar dmar rtsi yis byug ||
thabs daṅ śes rab gñis med byin gyis brlab ||
dkar dmar ḥod zer thig gis stoṅ khams khyab ||
mthaḥ daṅ tshaṅ thig skor thig zla gam bcad ||
ḥgrus daṅ ḥgrus steṅ pho braṅ byed thig daṅ ||
sgo daṅ gduṅ thig bźi brgyad skabs daṅ sbyar ||

[a] bgo [b] sṅon nas [c] gźu

However gentle their disposition, their lineage is still that of the titans.
So this white offering to lords of the soil, serpents and furies,
the ritual items of aromatic wood, sacrificial fire and sacred libations,
must be offered to the accompaniment of an exposition of the buddhas' truth.
You must give pleasure to the powerful ones of the phenomenal world,
and having made them happy, you can hold them to their former vows.
Ask them for a site for your worship and a place for you to stay,
and hold them before witnesses to their oath to protect the doctrine.
Afterwards you can make them attend to whatever you want,
Thus happiness in phenomenal things depends on (the lords of) the soil.
Fertile fields and good harvests,
extent of royal power and spread of dominion,
although some half (of such effects) is ordained by previous actions,
the other half comes from the powerful lords of the soil.
If you do not know how to act methodically in this matter,
a root-cause of evil and harm springs from this.
So you must attend to the lords of the soil, the serpents and furies.
Having thus completed these preliminary rites,
one must construct the place for the temple of the blessed ones.[66]
Take light-coloured soil which is viscous, pliable and soft,
and suit the size to the occasion, either one fathom which is four cubits, or half a fathom (which is two cubits) square, or just one cubit (square),
and fit the height-measurements to these three sizes, large, medium and small, namely a full cubit, a short cubit or a span, whichever you may do to suit the occasion.
(It should have) the form of an upturned mirror, well-formed and smooth.
Sprinkle it and make it completely smooth with pure consecrated water and sweet-smelling medicinal incense.
Smear cotton threads with white and red colouring and consecrate them as Method and Wisdom possessed of no duality.
Cover the sphere of the void (viz. the space for the *maṇḍala*) with rays (viz. lines) of white and red,
(the four) bordering lines (of the square),
(the four) crossing lines (two diagonal and two straight across),
the encircling line (inside the square),
(the four) lines forming half-moons (which enclose an inner square),
(the four inner) diagonal lines and on the diagonal lines the lines which form the palace,
the four lines for doors and lintels, (drawn as double lines, viz.) eight lines (inside the palace).

mñam la ma ḥdres yoṅs su sñoms par gdab ||
thig tshon tshar nas gtsaṅ maḥi rdzas rnams bsag ||
dag paḥi lha rdzas dkyil ḥkhor rgyan rdzas daṅ ||
bla med mchod rdzas na bzaḥ chas rgyan rdzas ||
gśen mched lha sras lcam dral ḥkhor bcas rnams ||
sta gon dag la gnas paḥi rim ḥgro bya ||
tiṅ ḥdzin mi g·yo don ma bsñel[a] bar gzims ||
mi brjed dran paḥi rmi lam pra ltas brtag ||
naṅs par khrus daṅ gtsaṅ sbra chas su gźug ||
dkar ljaṅ dmar sṅo sa tshon sna lṅa la ||
ye śes chen po lṅa ru byin gyis brlab ||
theb ḥdzub lha daṅ lha mor byin gyis brlab ||
bder gśegs pho braṅ lha yi gźal yas bri ||
bum pa mdaḥ dar ral kyu me loṅ daṅ ||
rin chen chag śiṅ mi nub rgyal mtshan daṅ ||
dbal gtor brjid ldan mtshan ldan yol chen sogs ||
phun sum tshogs paḥi rgyan rdzas bkram par bya ||
dar dkar bla gur dar [64b] dmar ḥphan gdugs daṅ ||
za ḥog bla bre yol ba dbub par bya ||
thog dbab myur mgyogs ye śes tiṅ ḥdzin bsgom ||
dpon gsas bla ma dbaṅ stegs khri la bźugs ||
mched daṅ lcam dral gtsaṅ maḥi khrus nas dbyuṅ ||
gar ma mthoṅ khyab cha lugs ldan par bya ||
mdzes brjid sgeg ldan lha daṅ lha moḥi tshul ||
dgaḥ baḥi mdaṅs phyuṅ spro baḥi dbyaṅs blaṅs nas ||
gñis med dam tshig bsre baḥi źu len bya ||
dkyil ḥkhor sgo dbye yi dam lha źal blta ||
sṅags daṅ phyag rgya tiṅ ḥdzin sñiṅ po dbog ||
lo zla źag graṅs ci ḥtsham dbyar dam bcaḥ ||
sṅon ḥgroḥi rim pa de ltar śes par bya ||

źes gsuṅs so / yaṅ ston pas bkaḥ stsal pa /

ñon cig ye gśen gtsug phud gus pas ñon ||
sṅon ḥgroḥi rim pa de ltar rdzogs nas kyaṅ ||
gñis pa dṅos gźi rim pa ḥdi lta ste ||

[a] la sñel

You should place these lines quite evenly, level and unconfused.
Having completed these coloured lines, one must gather together the pure items,
the pure divine items and the items for adorning the *maṇḍala*,
the items of supreme worship, garments, accoutrements and adornments.
The Shen Brethren, brothers and sisters with their following, must perform the homage of abiding in the preparatory stage.
With unwavering contemplation they must go to sleep, unforgetful of the matter, and not forgetting their dreams, they must examine the prognostics.
The following morning one must wash and put on clean things.
Then one must consecrate the sand of five colours, white, green, red, blue (and yellow), with (the power of) the Five Wisdoms.
Consecrate your thumb and first finger as god and goddesses,
and draw the temple-palace of the blessed ones.
Place in order the excellent adorning items,
the vase, the arrow, the sword, the mirror,
the precious sceptre, the infallible banner of victory,
the glorious pointed sacrificial cake, the fine skull-cup and so on.
Arrange the finest items of adornment.
Put up the tent of white silk with its hangings and the umbrella of red silk, the canopy and curtains of brocade.
Practise instantaneously—like lightning—the contemplation of the gods of knowledge.
The Lama Master-Sage sits on the throne.
The brethren, brothers and sisters, come forth from their ablutions,
and the 'deacon' must have all his accoutrements.
They are beautiful, glorious and gay like gods and goddesses.
Having sung joyous chants, pronounced with a happy tone,
they must ask and receive the sacramental vow which mingles (giver and receiver) as one.
The door of the *maṇḍala* is opened and the face of the tutelary divinity is seen.
The spell, the gesture, the meditation and the heart-syllable are given.
The vow is made (for the period) a year, a month, a day, that one should apply oneself, whatever (period) is suitable.
The order of the preliminaries is known to be like this.

This is what the Teacher said. Then again he spoke:

Listen *Ye-gśen gTsug-phud*, listen with devotion.
Having thus completed the order of the preliminaries,
the order of the real basis is like this:

phyi snod naṅ bcud snaṅ źiṅ srid pa rnams ||
ye nas stoṅ źiṅ bdag med raṅ bźin la ||
rnam par mi rtog dbyiṅs ñid mi zad pa ||
phyi snod thams cad rgyal baḥi dkyil ḥkhor te ||
naṅ bcud thams cad lha daṅ lha moḥi sku ||
dbyiṅs daṅ ye śes ḥdu ḥbral med pa la ||
bgegs śes bya ba gdod nas med lags kyaṅ ||
dge sdig rgyu ḥbras dkar nag mun snaṅ la ||
ma rtogs log par lta ba ḥbyuṅ poḥi tshogs ||
bsñen daṅ sgrub la bar du gcod pa daṅ ||
thar lam dge baḥi gegs śiṅ byed pa rnams ||
źi bas ma thul ñon moṅs log sred can ||
thugs rjeḥi stobs kyis rgyaṅ mtshams gcad paḥi phyir ||
thugs ñid źi baḥi ṅaṅ las ma g·yos kyaṅ ||
thugs rjeḥi sprul pa ḥbar baḥi skur spyod nas ||
me ri mtshon cha ñuṅs dkar sṅags kyi mdaḥ ||
bar chod log ḥdren rgyaṅ mtshams gcad par bya ||
[65a] thugs rje khros pas log rtog tshar bcad nas ||
mi min bgegs kyi bar chod źi baḥi phyir ||
mñam ñid źi baḥi tiṅ ḥdzin bsgom par bya ||
thog mar raṅ ñid bde baḥi gdan las su ||
cha lugs lṅa ldan phyag rgya mñam sñoms kyis ||
ma bcos spros bral kun snaṅ tshad med ḥod ||
ḥgro ba yoṅs la byams[a] sems ldan par bya ||
tiṅ ḥdzin ḥod las yig ḥbruḥi rgyu spro źiṅ ||
śiṅ khams snod bcud gdos lus bag chags sbyaṅ ||
raṅ lus gdos bcas ma dag bag chags sbyaṅ ||
dag pa phyag rgya lha yi sku ru ḥjug ||
rtsa gnas źiṅ khams lha sku phyag rgyar bsgyur ||
ḥbyuṅ dug phuṅ po gnas ḥgyur ye śes sku ||
ma bsgrubs saṅs rgyas skad cig de ñid grol ||
dbyiṅs nas ye śes bsre bsnan[b] gñis su med ||
mñam ñid ye śes lha skur gyur pa ste ||
bdag ñid bskyed paḥi rim pa ldan paḥo ||

[a] byaṅ [b] bsnaṅ

The outer vessel and the inner essence, which comprise all phenomenal existence,[67]
are void from all beginning and selfless by nature,
being free of discursive thought, infinite as space.
This whole outer vessel is the *maṇḍala* of the buddhas.
This whole inner essence (corresponds with) the forms of gods and goddesses.
In this space and this knowledge which are free both of union and of separation,
so-called demons did not exist from the beginning,
but this host arose from ignorance and false views concerning good and evil, cause and effect, white and black, and dark and light.[68]
They obstruct one's reliance (invocation) and one's performance (conjuration).[63]
They are hinderers of the virtuous way of salvation.
They cannot be subdued by gentleness. They are possessed of disturbing desires.
In order to keep them far at bay using the power of compassion,
although unmoved from the peaceful state of pure thought,
one acts in the blazing manifestation of compassionate transformation,
like a mountain of fire (shooting forth) weapons, white mustard seeds and spells in the form of arrows, so hindering false guides are kept far at bay.
Having cut off false knowledge by this compassionate wrath,
in order to tranquillize the obstructions of titans and demons,
one must practise the peaceful contemplation of universal sameness.
First seat yourself where you are comfortable and assuming the five postures with bodily gestures at ease,
you experience the unaffected state of non-activity, the boundless light of universal brilliance, and feel love for all living beings.
From this light of contemplation the seed-syllables stream forth, cleansing the various realms, both 'vessel' and 'essence', from the influences of material forms,
cleansing one's own body from the impure influences of material forms,
and turning the pure (influences) into divine manifestations.
The psychic centres are transformed into (buddha-)realms with their divine manifestations.
The (five) elements, (five) poisons, (five) elements of personality are changed into the forms of the (five) wisdoms.
In that very moment unaffected buddhahood is achieved.
From space knowledge (descends and) singles and adds itself and is inseparable, and one becomes the divine being of the Wisdom of Sameness.
This is the Process of Emanation of Selfhood.

de ltar bdag ñid lha yi thugs las su ||
skye med ṅaṅ las ḥgag med raṃ yaṃ maṃ ||
bskal pa chen pos źiṅ khams rim gyis sbyaṅ ||
stoṅ ñid ṅaṅ la bum pa dkyil ḥkhor bskyed ||
ḥbyuṅ lṅaḥi sa bon ḥbru yi bźu btul las ||
ye śes lṅa ldan gźal yas raṅ ḥod ḥbar ||
rmeṅ gźi dpyam brtsigs ya gad gur thog rgyas ||
sgo bźi phyogs ḥod rta bab rim bźi mdzes ||
phyi naṅ lcog brgyad tshogs brgyad rig paḥi mkhar ||
bar ḥkhyam ḥdod yon loṅs spyod mchod paḥi źiṅ ||
phyi ḥkhyam zaṅs lcags ḥkhor yug khyud mo sbag ||
me chu rluṅ gsum bskal paḥi bu yug ḥtshub ||
gcan chen ka ba lha brgyad gduṅ ma gśib ||
tshaṅs paḥi gral[a] dpyam rgyun skar grab non spras ||
ya gad chu ḥbab ḥphyaṅ ḥphrul za ra tshags ||
ye śes dar brgyad rig paḥi [65b] ḥphraṅ ḥphrul brlab
gcan lṅa zil gnon ñon moṅs spa bkoṅ źiṅ ||
ma chags skyon bral ñi zla pad maḥi gdan ||
ḥod las rgyu bskyed raṅ raṅ sa bon gsal ||
sṅags kyis skul gdab phyag rgyas brda mtshon źiṅ ||
tiṅ ḥdzin dgoṅs pas mi dmigs gsal gdab ciṅ ||
bder gśegs dbyiṅs na bźugs paḥi lha tshogs rnams ||
raṅ raṅ gtso la ḥkhor gyis bskor ba ru ||
sku mdog phyag mtshan rgyan daṅ bcas[b] par bskyed ||
dbyiṅs nas spyan draṅ ye śes mkhaḥ la byon ||
gñis su med paḥi dam tshig kloṅ du bstim ||
dṅos ḥbyor yid sprul loṅs spyod mchod paḥi tshogs ||
lha rdzas dam paḥi loṅs spyod ci snaṅ ba ||
tiṅ ḥdzin sṅags tshig phyag rgyas byin brlabs nas ||
rgyal baḥi dkyil ḥkhor lha la ⟨mchod pa⟩ ḥbul ||
thugs dam dgyes bskaṅ dbyiṅs su mñes par mdzad ||

[a] dral [b] chad

Thus from the divine thought of your selfhood
from the state of the unborn the (three) Great Ages of Fire, Air and Water[69] gradually purify the (phenomenal) realms.
The vase[70] and the *maṇḍala* are (mentally) produced in this state of Voidness.
From the melting and forming of the seed-syllables of the five elements
the palace of the Five Wisdoms blazes forth in its own light.
It has foundations, walls and ceiling-rafters, decorative eaves and a raised roof.
It is beautiful with its four doors of the directional colours with their tiered lintels.
It has eight pinnacles inside and outside for it is the citadel of the knowledge of the eight perceptive groups.
It has a veranda which is the place for offering desirable and enjoyable things.
It has a surrounding walk in the form of a double encircling fence of copper and iron.
(All around) there rages the turmoil of the three ages of Fire, Water and Air.
There are pillars in the form of great beasts with cross-beams (adorned) with the eight gods.
The ceiling laths are adorned with *Brahmā* and the boards which lay upon them with the constellations.
There are decorative eaves, water-spouts, garlands and other decorative devices.
The eight silk sashes of wisdom and the garlands of knowledge wave about.
There are lotus-thrones of sun and moon, desireless and free of all defect, which press down on the five beasts and overawe all disturbance.
The seed-syllable (of each divinity) shines forth, born from light as its cause.
They are ordained (in function) by spells and they show their (conventional) gestures and signs.
One practises contemplation and brings into clarity the non-envisaged.
So one produces the companies of gods who dwell in the celestial spheres of the blessed ones, each main divinity surrounded by his entourage, all with their proper colours, gestures and adornments.
They are invited down from the celestial spheres, and (these gods of) knowledge appear in the sky.
They sink down into the mental sphere which is the bond of non-duality.
Then one offers in worship to the gods of the *buddha-maṇḍala* the accumulation of offerings of enjoyable things, both real and mentally produced, divine items of sacred enjoyment, having consecrated them by the power of contemplation, spells and gestures.
Pleasing and satisfying the thoughtful purpose (of the gods), one causes delight in the heavens.

bdag ñid thugs la ñi zla pad maḥi gdan ||
ḥod kyi[a] raṅ bźin mtshan maḥi yi ge gzugs ||
skye med A la ḥgag med OṂ du ḥgyur ||
gsal ba dgu ḥdzab dpaḥo ḥbru lṅa daṅ ||
thugs gsal sum cu spu śad sgreṅ ltar ḥkhor ||
phar ḥphros dkyil ḥkhor lha tshogs thugs la thim ||
thugs la thim źiṅ thugs la de bźin gsal ||
de ñid ḥdzab skul ḥphro ḥdu dbyiṅs su mchod ||
mkhaḥ la ḥod sprod kloṅ du byin rlabs dbab ||
gñis su med ciṅ gñis med gcig tu bsgrub ||
dbyiṅs śes dbyer med bde baḥi don ldan bya ||
ḥphro ḥdu sprul pas lha daṅ bdag gźan sbrel ||
ye gśen theg paḥi don du spyod tshul lo ||

de ltar bskyed paḥi lha daṅ gźal yas la ||
dbyiṅs nas ye śes dkyil ḥkhor spyan draṅ ste ||
thog mar raṅ grol dug lṅaḥi gdan thabs ḥbul ||
dam tshig thabs ldan gśen grogs [66a] mched lcam gyis ||
mdzes paḥi tshul ldan rgyan daṅ cha lugs gzab ||
dgaḥ baḥi mdaṅs daṅ spro baḥi dbyaṅs blaṅ źiṅ ||
pad ma ha lo me tog gdan thabs ḥbul ||
dug lṅa gnas dag chen po lṅa yi stobs ||
źe sdaṅ gnas dag seṅ ge dkar mos ḥjoms ||
gti mug gnas dag glaṅ chen ser pos ḥjoms ||
ṅa rgyal gnas dag rta mchog ljaṅ khus ḥjoms ||
ḥdod chags gnas dag g·yu ḥbrug sṅon pos ḥjoms ||
ḥphrag dog gnas dag bya khyuṅ ga rus[b] ḥjoms ||
ma rig mun pa ñi ma zla bas ḥjoms ||
rtog ḥdzin bag chags skyon bral pad mas ḥjoms ||
dug lṅa gnas su dag paḥi gdan ḥbul bas ||
ye śes lṅa rdzogs ḥkhor ba zil byis gnon ||
sri źu gus tshul gdan mchog phul nas kyaṅ ||
dbyiṅs nas spyan draṅ gdan la bźugs gsol te ||
rṅa gśaṅ rol mo sñan paḥi sgra rnams bsgrag ||
dri źim ṅad ldan spros kyis śul mtshon źiṅ ||
gduṅ baḥi dbyaṅs daṅ tshig gi brda sbyar nas ||
dbyiṅs na bźugs pa rgyal baḥi dkyil ḥkhor lha ||
raṅ bźin mkhaḥ la rdzogs paḥi źiṅ khams nas ||
sri źu gus paḥi tshul gyis spyan draṅ gi ||

[a] ḥod la [b] ka ras

In one's own heart is the lotus-seat of sun and moon.
The differently characterized letters are made to enter there, each having the nature of light.
The unborn letter A changes into uncircumscribed OṂ and the nine special syllables, the five heroic seed-syllables and the thirty letters wheel round, each standing upright as finely drawn as a hair.
Spreading outwards they sink into the hearts of the hosts of gods of the *maṇḍala*, and sinking into their hearts, they continue to shine there.
One offers up to the heavenly sphere the recitation of the formula (known as *de ñid ḥdzab skul* 'Inducing Suchness by Spell') which streams forth and returns again (to one's heart).
Light streams forth in space, and grace descends into the mental sphere.[71]
That which is already free of duality is realized as one.
One possesses the reality of bliss where knowledge and celestial sphere are indistinguishable.
Through outgoing and inward flowing transformations the divinities, oneself and all others are united in one.
This is the way of practising the real matter of the Vehicle of the Primeval Shen.

Then down into the gods and palaces which one has mentally produced, one invites from the celestial spheres the circle of the gods of knowledge (viz. divinities of buddha-rank).
First one offers them the thrones of the Five Self-Released Evils.[33]
Then the Shen Brethren, brothers and sisters, in beautiful garb, fine-looking in their adornments and accoutrements, sing joyous chants with a happy tone.
They offer lotuses and *ha-lo* flowers at the thrones.
As for the power of the five great removers of the Five Evils,
the white lion is the remover of wrath and he prevails,
the yellow elephant is the remover of mental torpor and he prevails,
the green horse is the remover of pride and he prevails,
the turquoise-blue dragon is the remover of desire and he prevails,
the *Khyuṅ* bird *Garu* is the remover of envy and he prevails.
Sun and Moon prevail over the darkness of ignorance.
The Lotus, being immaculate, prevails over the influence of fixed notions.
By offering the thrones which remove the Five Evils,
Phenomenal existence is overcome by the Five Perfect Wisdoms.
Having offered these excellent thrones with reverence and devotion, one invites down (the gods) from the celestial sphere and requests them to be seated on the thrones.
The pleasing sounds of drums, flat bells and cymbals resound, and one shows them the way with the (smoke-)tract of sweet-smelling incense.
With sombre chant and textual recitation, and with reverence and respect, one invites down the gods of the *buddha-maṇḍala* who reside in the celestial sphere, from their perfect realms in the self-existing heavens.

ḥgyur med g·yuṅ druṅ dbyiṅs nas mi g·yo yaṅ ||
ḥgro drug thugs rjes bzuṅ baḥi don slad du ||
sprul pa thaṅ tsam gnas ḥdir mṅon spyan draṅ ||
gñis su med par gdan la bźugs ḥtshal źu ||
lus ṅag yid gsum mos gus lha phyag btsal ||
lus kyi phyag bgyid gus pa lṅa ldan btsal[a] ||
ṅag gi phyag bgyid spro dgaḥ dbyaṅs bskyed btsal[a] ||
yid kyi phyag bgyid dgaḥ rab mchog bskyed btsal[a] ||
thog maḥi dus nas da lta yan chad du ||
sdig pa mi dge ci bgyis bśags pa dbul[b] ||
[66b] źe sdaṅ dbaṅ gyur byams paḥi ṅaṅ du bśags ||
gti mug dbaṅ gyur ye śes ṅaṅ du bśags ||
ṅa rgyal dbaṅ gyur źi baḥi ṅaṅ du bśags ||
ḥdod chag dbaṅ gyur sbyin paḥi ṅaṅ du bśags ||
ḥphrag dog dbaṅ gyur yaṅs paḥi ṅaṅ du bśags ||
ḥgyod ciṅ dag par ye śes lha la mthol ||
tshaṅs paḥi drin len bla med tshogs mchod dbul[b] ||
tshogs brgyad ye śes rig paḥi lha mo brgyad ||
yul brgyad mchod paḥi bye brag phyag na bsnams ||
glu gar stabs kyis ye śes lha la dbul[b] ||
ḥbyuṅ lṅa rnam dag ye śes lha mo lṅas[c] ||
rin chen sna lṅaḥi gzed źal yaṅs pa ru ||
g·yu ḥbraṅ yu ti bdud rtsi sman daṅ sbyar ||
dgoṅs pa dmigs med phyag rgyas byin brlabs nas ||
dkyil ḥkhor ye śes lha la mchod pa dbul[b] ||
thugs dam mñes bskaṅ dbaṅ daṅ dṅos grub źu ||
bdag ñid lha daṅ gsas mkhar bdag gźan sbrel ||
A dkar OṂ la ye śes chen po lṅa ||
gsal ba dgu ḥdzab thugs gsal sum cu yi ||
ḥod kyi ñag thag gźaḥ tshon lu gu brgyud ||
zer gyi raṅ bźin kun nas ḥphro ba yis ||
phyi naṅ snod bcud gźal yas lha ru bsgyur ||
dbyiṅs daṅ ye śes thabs daṅ śes rab kyi ||
sku daṅ źiṅ khams zuṅ ḥbrel bdag źal mthoṅ ||
źal mthoṅ bla med tshogs kyi mchod pa dbul[b] ||

[a] ḥtshal [b] ḥbul [c] lṅa

Although they do not move from the changeless Swastika sphere, in order to hold the beings of the six regions in their compassionate grasp, they are effectively invited here just for a moment in apparitional form.

One invites them to be seated on the thrones of unity.

One makes obeisance to the gods showing respect with Body, Speech and Mind.

One makes the five devotional gestures with one's body.

One offers joyous chants as salutation of speech.

One offers joyous thoughts as salutation of mind.

One confesses whatever evil and wrong one has done from the earliest time to the present.

Wrath is overcome and confessed in the spirit of love.

Mental torpor is overcome and confessed in the spirit of knowledge.

Pride is overcome and confessed in the spirit of tranquillity.

Desire is overcome and confessed in the spirit of generosity.

Envy is overcome and confessed in the spirit of magnanimity.

One makes confession to the gods of knowledge with contrition and purity.

With pure gratefulness one offers an excellent mass of offerings.

The (eight) perceptive groups are (represented by) the eight goddesses of knowledge,

who raise up in their hands the different offerings of the eight spheres of perception.

With song and dance one offers them to the gods of knowledge.

The five goddesses of knowledge who purify the five elements,

offer in a wide-brimmed chalice made of the five kinds of gems

the elixir of consecrated *chang* mixed with medicament.

One consecrates (the offerings) with gestures and with concentrated thought which clings at nothing,

and offers them to the knowledge-gods of the *maṇḍala.*

One fills their thoughts with happiness and asks them for the consecration and for final perfection.

One's selfhood is united with the gods, and their *gSas*-palace and self and all else are united.

Pure A and OṂ and the syllables of the Five Great Wisdoms,

the nine special syllables and the thirty letters,

as fine threads of light, as a continuous rainbow chain,

stream forth in all directions with the form of light-rays,

and the outer vessel of the world and the essence it contains are transformed into divine palaces and into gods.

Celestial sphere and (gods of) knowledge, Method and Wisdom, come together in their (divine) forms and the spheres (of apparition), so one beholds the countenance of the selfhood (of the tutelary divinity).

Beholding this countenance, one offers in worship an excellent mass of offerings.

phyi naṅ snod bcud dṅos ḥbyor loṅs spyod tshogs ||
dbyiṅs śes mkhaḥ kloṅ thabs śes gñis su med ||
yul śes lha daṅ skye ḥgro gñis med sbyar ||
dkyil ḥkhor ye śes lha la mchod pa dbul[a] ||
chag ñams ḥgal ḥkhrul gduṅ tshig dbyaṅs kyis bźag ||
ma rtogs log pa thugs rjeḥi śugs kyis bsgral ||
rnam rtog mtshan ma bon ñid dbyiṅs su bstab ||
dṅos grub laṅ tsho dmu yad bcud du rol ||
zad pa med pa gter chen [67a] dbyiṅs su sba ||
thabs daṅ śes rab phyag rgya mkhaḥ la bsgyur ||
phyi naṅ snod bcud lha daṅ lha mos gaṅ ||
glu dbyaṅs gar stabs rol mo mtshams mtsham bsgyur ||
bye ba sa ya mthaḥ yas bsam mi khyab ||
dkyil ḥkhor ye śes lha la mchod pa dbul[a] ||
gñis med rig paḥi lha la phyag ḥtshal lo ||

bon ñid dbyiṅs na gnas paḥi dkyil ḥkhor daṅ ||
raṅ bźin lhun gyis grub paḥi dkyil ḥkhor daṅ ||
mtshan ma kloṅ du bskyed paḥi dkyil ḥkhor daṅ ||
dkyil ḥkhor rnam gsum gsal baḥi lha mchog la ||
dbu yi gtsug phud źabs kyi khri gdan daṅ ||
brjid paḥi sku daṅ tshaṅs paḥi gsuṅ dbyaṅs daṅ ||
mkhyen paḥi thugs daṅ brtse baḥi dgoṅs pa daṅ ||
brnag paḥi phyag mtshan brda yi don rtags daṅ ||
mdzes paḥi rgyan daṅ lhab lhub na bzaḥ daṅ ||
dgyes paḥi yum daṅ bskor baḥi ḥkhor tshogs daṅ ||
che baḥi yon tan mdzad paḥi phrin las daṅ ||
gaṅ la mos paḥi sgo nas de bźin bstod ||
bstod ciṅ dgyes paḥi mtshan ma rtags su bsgrub ||
sku daṅ źiṅ khams gdan daṅ gźal yas daṅ ||
źi rgyan bcu gsum tshaṅ paḥi tshul dgu sogs ||
dug lṅa ñon moṅs gnas su dag pa yis ||
ye śes lṅa ldan loṅs spyod rtags su bsgrub ||
bla med rtags kyi mchod pa dbyiṅs su bstab ||
glu dbyaṅs tshom tshom gar stabs bde bsgyur nas ||
stag ḥgros siṅ stabs ye śes rol paḥi bro ||
dkyil ḥkhor ye śes lha la mchod pa ḥbul ||
ñid kyi ṅaṅ tshul bdag la gnas par źu ||

[a] ḥbul

An accumulation of enjoyable things, real things from the outer vessel of the phenomenal world and all its inner essence,
These are united in one with celestial space and knowledge, sky and mental sphere, Method and Wisdom, object of knowledge and knower, gods and living beings,
and they are offered in worship to the knowledge-gods of the *maṇḍala*.
Faults, defects, transgressions, errors are confessed with sombre words.
Ignorance and heresy are destroyed by the force of compassion.
Hesitating thought with its various characteristic definitions is passed over into the sphere of absolute *bon*.
Final perfection and the zest of youth are enjoyed in their essence.
The great treasure of the infinite is concealed in the heavenly sphere.
Method and Wisdom are transformed into symbolic movements in space.
The outer vessel of the phenomenal world is filled with gods and goddesses as its inner essence.
They turn here and there in song and dance and play in their millions, tens of millions, limitless, surpassing thought.
Thus one must make offering to the knowledge-gods of the *maṇḍala*.
Salutation to the gods of knowledge who know no duality.

The *maṇḍala* that rests in the celestial sphere of absolute *bon*,
the *maṇḍala* which is self-produced in its own nature,
the *maṇḍala* which is produced with its characteristics in the mental sphere,
to the excellent bright gods of these three kinds of *maṇḍala*
from the top of their heads to the base of their thrones
one must give them such praise as will cause them delight,
(extolling) their glorious form and their well-toned voice,
their knowledgeable thought and their loving intention,
their ferocious instruments and their meaningful symbols,
their beautiful adornments and their flowing garments,
their joyous partners and their surrounding entourage,
their great accomplishments and the acts they have performed.
Thus praising them, one must explain the meaning of these joyous characteristics,
their own forms, their realms, their thrones and palaces,
their thirteen tranquil adornments and their nine pure attributes and so on.
By cleansing away the Five Evils and the molestations (*kleśa*),
one must explain these enjoyments as possessed by the Five Wisdoms.
This worship of superlative signs is passed over into the celestial sphere.
(The process) is happily transformed into singing and group dancing,
the 'tiger step', the 'lion gait', the playful dance of knowledge,
and this is offered in worship to the knowledge-gods of the *maṇḍala*.
I beg that their nature may reside in me!

dṅos gźi rim pa yoṅs su rdzogs paḥo ||

gsum pa rjes kyi bya baḥi rim pa ni ||
tshe rabs goṅ nas sbyaṅs paḥi ḥphro can gyis ||
dus ḥdir g·yuṅ druṅ bon gyi las ḥphro len ||
bskal srid goṅ nas bsgrubs pas lha źal blta[a] ||
dbaṅ luṅ yoṅs su rdzogs [67b] paḥi dṅos grub źu ||
sgrub paḥi dam bcaḥ phud gtaḥ gnas su sbyaṅ ||
dmar chen ye śes rol paḥi dmar mchod bteg ||
bdud bźi zil gnon ye śes lha bro brduṅ ||
gsas mkhar gsaṅ ba dbye bsduḥi rgyun la gźug[b] ||
lha daṅ gsas mkhar gźal yas bdag la bsdu ||
gñis med thig le kun bzaṅ ṅaṅ la bde ||
bde chen rgyal po ḥdu ḥbral med paḥi dbyiṅs ||
ḥdi la bsñen sgrub yon tan bsam mthaḥ yas ||
ḥjig rten ḥdi daṅ ḥdi las ḥdas pa daṅ ||
ma ḥoṅs phyi mar gyur paḥi ḥjig rten sogs ||
gaṅ du gnas kyaṅ gaṅ dag rgyal baḥi źiṅ ||
rgyal baḥi dkyil ḥkhor bzaṅ źiṅ ñams dgaḥ ba ||
pad mo dam paḥi źiṅ khams bde legs na ||
ḥkhor daṅ loṅs spyod sku tshe mthar phyin źiṅ ||
gdul bya ḥphrin las yon tan bkra śis pa ||
zad pa med ciṅ ḥgrib pa med pa yi ||
rgyal ba rgya mtsho⟨ḥi źiṅ⟩ la rab gnas śiṅ ||
dpag tu med ciṅ yon tan rdzogs par thob ||
mthar[c] yaṅ dbyiṅs śes dbyer med ṅaṅ mñam nas ||
mkhaḥ mñam kloṅ bdal bon ñid dbyiṅs su bde ||
mtshan bcas bskyed paḥi rim pa bstan paḥo ||
ye gśen gtsug phud thugs kyi dkyil du źog ||
ces gsuṅs so /

de nas yaṅ ston pas bkaḥ stsal pa /
ñon cig ye gśen gtsug phud la sogs ḥkhor ||
ye gśen bon la bskyed daṅ rdzogs pa gñis ||
mtshan bcas bskyed paḥi rim pa sṅon soṅ nas ||
gñis pa mtshan med rdzogs paḥi rim pa bstan ||

[a] lta [b] źug [c] mthaḥ

Thus the order of the real basis is finished.

Thirdly as for the order of the final acts:
He who has practised continuously from former life-series,
takes up the activity in this life of Swastika *Bon*.
By practising meditation from former ages, he will (now) see the divine countenance.
He begs the final perfection with the consummation of consecrations and inspirations.
Then he must clear away the special sacramental pledge by means of which the bond was effected,
and he must offer up the 'great red offerings', the red worship of sportive knowledge,
and he must dance the divine dance of knowledge which treads under foot the four *Māras*.*
The accomplishments derived from such reliance and performance are limitless.
Wherever you reside in this world or in another, in future worlds or wherever else, (you will have) a buddha-field of some kind, a beautiful and delightful *buddha-maṇḍala*.
In this happy realm of sacred lotuses you attain perfection with regard to your entourage, your enjoyable possessions and your length of life,
and you are blessed in your accomplishments and acts of converting.
Thus abiding in the ocean-like realms of the buddhas, which are infinite and immaculate,
you gain in full perfection these immeasurable accomplishments.
Finally your nature achieves the sameness of the indistinguishable condition of celestial sphere and knowledge,
and you attain blessedness in the celestial sphere of absolute *bon* with its sameness through space and its ultimate penetration of the mental sphere.
Thus the Process of Emanation with its various characteristics has now been explained.
Ye-gśen gTsug-phud, keep all this in the centre of your mind.
So the Teacher said.

The Teacher spoke again:
Listen, *Ye-gśen gTsug-phud* and your entourage.
Concerning (the Process of) Emanation and (that of) Realization in the *bon* of Primeval Shen,
having first dealt with the Process of Emanation with its characteristics,
I shall teach the second one, the Process of Realization, which transcends all characteristics.

*See errata addition page 225.

ḥdi la spyi don rnam pa gsum yin te ||
daṅ por thabs daṅ lam la ḥkhrid tshul daṅ ||
bar du byaṅ chub sems kyi skyoṅ tshul daṅ ||
tha ma rtsal sbyaṅ bogs ḥdon la bzlaḥo ||
daṅ po thabs daṅ lam la ḥkhrid tshul ni ||
skyes bu thabs daṅ rdzu ḥphrul ldan pa yis ||
skye śir [68a] gtiṅ nas ḥjigs paḥi gaṅ zag la ||
rgyud luṅ man ṅag zab moḥi gdams pa bśad ||
thar paḥi lam la brod kha g·yaṅ sa bstan[a] ||
skye śir gtiṅ nas ḥjigs paḥi gaṅ zag kyaṅ ||
mtshan ldan bla maḥi sku la rab tu ḥkhor ||
gaṅ gsuṅ bkaḥ ñan ci bcol las rnams bsgrub ||
daṅ po thos pas phyi yi sgro ḥdogs bcad ||
rgyud luṅ man ṅag goms ḥdris ga dar bya ||
thos pa gtsor ḥdzin tshig phyir ḥbreṅ mi bya ||
sgrub paḥi grogs la dben paḥi gnas gces pas ||
g·yaḥ ri gaṅs brag chu gliṅ nags khrod daṅ ||
dur khrod mi med luṅ stoṅ dben sa ru ||
sgo gsum yid daṅ lus ṅag glod byas nas ||
ḥjig rten ḥdi bden snaṅ ba rgyab tu bor ||
pha ma śa ñe yul mkhar nor rdzas spaṅ ||
ri dvags smas ma bźin du gcig pur btsaḥ ||
pha rol yul la snaṅ ba mi ḥphren ba ||
yaṅ dag rtse gcig phyi maḥi don la ḥphreṅ ||
daṅ po sems la sdug bsṅal blaṅs nas su ||
sṅar soṅ phyir ḥoṅ da lta la sogs kyi ||
bde sdug legs ñes skyon yon bye brag daṅ ||
dgra gñen ñe riṅ byams sdaṅ le len daṅ ||
lto rgyab bu lon grags daṅ mi grags daṅ ||
ḥjig rten bya ba legs daṅ mi legs daṅ ||
skyes pa pho khyad grags daṅ mi grags daṅ ||
mkhas paḥi yon tan śes daṅ mi śes daṅ ||
bzuṅ baḥi yul daṅ brtsigs paḥi sku mkhar daṅ ||
bcad paḥi źiṅ sa bsags paḥi zas nor daṅ ||
lus kyi pha ma mchan gyi zla rogs daṅ ||
ḥgrog paḥi grogs daṅ brtse baḥi gñen ḥdun daṅ ||
yul gyi mi chen dus kyi bstan chus daṅ ||
phyi snod ḥjig rten naṅ bcud skye ḥgro daṅ ||

[a] btiṅ

Here there are three kinds of general matter:
first how to give guidance in Method and in the Way,
secondly how to nurture the Thought of Enlightenment,
thirdly exploiting the benefit of one's skill and practice.
First as for giving guidance in Method and in the Way,
a sage who possesses the means and the magical powers should give profound instruction in the *tantras*, inspired teachings and general precepts to whichever persons are frightened profoundly at (the process of) birth and death.
He shows forth the joy of the way of salvation and the abyss (of ordinary phenomenal existence).
Persons who fear profoundly the process of birth and death should sit at the feet of a renowned lama.
They should listen to whatever he says and perform what he commands.
By learning first they should afterwards remove false notions.
They should be perfectly practised in the *tantras* and inspired teachings and in general precepts.
Learning should be all-important and they should not interest themselves in words.
As a main help in practice a lonely place is essential, crags or a glacier, a cave or a vale or a forest, a cemetery or any empty place.
Having relaxed the three means (of human expression), body, speech and mind,
one must abandon the notion that this world is real.
One must abandon parents, relatives, country, house and wealth,
and nurture oneself alone as does a wounded deer,
without longing for the manifestations of worldly things,
but longing single-mindedly for that which transcends this life.
First of all one should recall suffering into one's thoughts,
(examining) the happiness and sorrow of former times, the future and the present, the good and the evil, the difference between faults and virtues,
enemies and friends, both near and far, love and the retributions of hatred,
food and clothes, debts, fame and obscurity,
worldly works both good and bad,
rivalry, fame and obscurity,
scholarly accomplishments, knowledge and ignorance,
territories seized and palaces built,
fields divided and stores and wealth accumulated,
natural parents, bosom mate,
intimate friend, affectionate relatives,
great men of one's district, contemporary religious developments,
outer vessel of the phenomenal world and inner essence of living beings,

[68b] nam zla dus bźi lo zla źag grańs dań ||
skye rga na ḥchi chu bo rgyun bźi dań ||
mdań sum rmi lam da ltaḥi las spyod la ||
brtags śiṅ dpyad nas rig ciṅ rtogs par bya ||
ma brtags ma gźig dge sbyor le loḥi rgyu ||
brtags nas sñiṅ po med par śes bźin du ||
sdug bsṅal las spyod de la sun nas su ||
mi rtag blo yis bskyed la grańs bcad bsgom ||
de la goms na ḥjig rten hrul por ḥgro ||
snaṅ ba bden med śes pa yeṅs la ḥphyo ||
gaṅ la dmigs gtad źen pa chuṅ bar ḥoṅ ||
dge la źugs kyaṅ de la ḥgyur ldog med ||
de nas lus sems bde ba skye ba ste ||
lus bde tsam na sems kyaṅ bde ba ste ||
raṅ bźin mi bźag ched kyis bcos la bsgom ||
lus ni cha lugs lṅa ldan phyag rgya bcaḥ ||
sems ni gaṅ la mi ḥphro gtad med bcaḥ ||
lus sems dril de rtse gcig mi yeṅs par ||
ri dvags sgra la ñan pa lta bu yid ||
pi waṅ rgyun thag chad pa lta buḥi ṅag ||
dpaḥ bo phub la mduṅ dril lta bu yi ||
lus ṅag yid gsum gtad med ṅaṅ la gtad ||
sṅar soṅ phyir ḥoṅ da ltaḥi rjes mi gcod ||
gar spyin rlan la sbraṅ bu chags par ltar ||
gtad med ṅaṅ la śes pa zin nas su ||
g·yo med ṅaṅ la mñam par gnas pa ḥbyuṅ ||
gal te de la gtad pas ma zin na ||
de las ma yeṅs mi zin mi srid do ||
ḥdzin rgyu ḥdzin mkhan ḥgyu byed yid yin te ||
yid kyi dran pa rnam par rtog pa ni ||
daṅ po ri gzar kha nas chu ḥbab ḥdra ||
gcig phyir gcig ḥbreṅ gcig la gcig ḥphro ḥgyu ||
gcig la gcig thim gaṅ la ṅos ḥdzin med ||
ḥdzin med ṅaṅ du gaṅ la gtad mi bcaḥ ||
gtad med śes pa khrol le śigs se gnas ||
gñis pa chu kluṅ [69a] bźin du dal ba ḥdra ||
gcig la gcig ḥbrel gcig la gcig rgyun mthud ||
rtog pa rgyun chad dran pa rgyun du chags ||

the four seasons, years, months, days, such calculations,
the fourfold course of birth, disease, old age and death,
last night's dream and today's activities,
having examined and investigated (all these things) one must know and understand them.
If you do not examine them and search them out, your pursuit of virtue will be a cause of lethargy.
Having examined them and knowing them to be lacking in essence,
one is weary of these works of misery,
and arousing thoughts of impermanence, one practises the stages of meditation.
When you are expert in that, the world goes to pieces.
Appearances become unreal and knowledge flows calmly forth.
Wherever one directs one's thought, attachment is slight.
In the pursuit of virtue there is no turning back.
From this comes a feeling of happiness both in body and mind.
With mere physical happiness there comes mental happiness too.
This does not come about naturally, but by meditating constructively.
One must adopt the five bodily postures and thought must not flow forth anywhere, but must be free from all special mental objectives.
Uniting body and mind, single-pointed and unwavering,
one's thought must resemble a deer (poised) attentive to a sound.
One's speech must be (as dead) as the broken string of a *pi-wang*.
Body, Speech and Mind should be directed to the state of non-objectivity,
like spears clustered together on the shield of a hero.
Do not hanker after the past, present and future.
Like flies stuck to damp thick glue,
hold your knowing powers to the state of non-objectivity.
The condition of universal sameness will arise in this state of imperturbability.
If you do not hold on with this non-objectivity,
there is no possibility of your not holding inattention at bay.
The mind is the one who darts between object and subject,
and as for this mental reflectiveness, this disquisitive thought:
first it is like water falling from mountain crags,
one (surge) following upon another, one flowing and darting into another.
Then one sinks into another and there is no recognition anywhere.
There is no objectivizing in this state of non-grasping.
Knowledge which does not objectivize is sparkling and free.
Secondly it is quiet like a river,
one (wave) joined with another, one linked in the flow with another.
Disquisitive thought comes to an end and mindfulness flows forth.

rgyun med ṅaṅ la śes pa rtog med dbyiṅs ||
lhod de ḥbol le śigs se mñam la gnas ||
gsum pa mi g·yo gsal baḥi mtsho gtiṅ ḥdra ||
rtog med ṅaṅ du rtog ḥdzin dri ma bral ||
ḥgyu byed mkhan po sems ñid kloṅ du stor ||
ḥgyu rgyu ḥgyu mkhan raṅ rig sems kyi ṅaṅ ||
ṅaṅ ñid kloṅ thim tiṅ ḥdzin g·yo ba med ||
lhaṅ ṅe mer re kyil le ltim me gnas ||
de gsum zuṅ ḥbrel źi gnas bde baḥi tshad ||
ñin daṅ mtshan moḥi snaṅ ba ṅo mi śes ||
lo zla źag graṅs dus tshod tshad ḥdzin bral ||
bsgom pas mi gsal ma bsgom sgrib pa med ||
dgra gñen ṅe riṅ chags sdaṅ gźi rtsa bral ||
gser daṅ boṅ ba sa rdo dbyer mi byed ||
ḥdi yin ḥdi min ḥdi źes gzaḥ gtad bral ||
draṅ sroṅ ḥgog paḥi ṅaṅ la sñoms par ḥbyuṅ ||
daṅ po thabs daṅ lam la ḥkhrid tshul lo ||

bar du byaṅ chub sems kyi skyoṅ tshul la ||
bcas bcos blo yis ma bcos sems btsal ba ||
sems ñid ma bcos mñam par bźag paḥi don ||
kun gźi byaṅ chub sems kyi kloṅ yaṅs su[a] ||
g·yo med śes pa raṅ sar gnas pa la ||
ṅaṅ la ṅaṅ gis goms pa bskyed pa yi ||
daṅ po sems ñid stoṅ pa gnas paḥi tshad ||
mtshan maḥi bon la dmigs gtad blo mi ḥchaḥ ||
bskal pa ḥkhrugs kyaṅ sems la g·yo ba med ||
saṅ ṅe yeṅ ṅe phyod de rgyaṅ ṅe ba ||
phyi stoṅ naṅ stoṅ raṅ bźin mtshan ma stoṅ ||
gaṅ la dṅos po med ciṅ ṅo bor stoṅ ||
dper na ñams snaṅ nam mkhaḥi ṅogs ltar du ||
stoṅ źiṅ bdag med ḥdi ka yin nam sñam ||
de bas saṅs rgyas logs [69b] su[b] med par ḥdzin ||
stoṅ paḥi ñams la drod daṅ tshad ḥbyuṅ ba ||
mkhaḥ la bya ḥphur chu la byiṅ ba med ||
ri bor dal phyuṅ sa rdo zan ltar brdzi ||
gaṅ la chags med ser snaḥi mdud pa grol ||
gcig skyur gcig len byis pa[c] thol ma gyu ||

[a] yaṅ du [b] log du [c] byi sba

One abides relaxed, tranquil and free in a state of repose,
the sphere of non-disquisitive knowing in a non-continuous state.
Thirdly it is like a deep lake, still and clear.
It is free from the defilement of fixed views in a state of non-discriminating thought.
The one who darts (here and there) is lost in the sphere of pure thought.
The cause of darting and the one who darts (rest) in the state of self-knowing thought,
sunk in the sphere of 'suchness', unmoving in profound contemplation,
translucent, clear, limpid, pellucid.
These three united give the measure of blissful tranquillity.
The changes of day and night go unrecognized.
One is free from the measuring of time by the numbers of years, months and days.
By meditating nothing now becomes clearer and by not meditating nothing becomes obscured.
One is free from the basic notions of enemy and friend, of nearness and farness, of attachment and hatred.
One does not distinguish gold and clods or earth or stone.
One is free from fixations: 'This is this' and 'This is not that', etc.
There arises the equanimity of the sage who practises 'total suppression'.
This is the first part, how to give guidance in Method and in the Way.

Secondly as for nurturing the Thought of Enlightenment,
By an intellect acting constructively 'non-constructive' mind is sought.
This non-constructive 'universal mind' is absolute repose.
So that the unmoving knower shall abide self-composed in the vast mental sphere of the Thought of Enlightenment which is the universal basis,
practice is effected in this condition by the condition itself.
First as for the measure of this abiding in the voidness of mind,
intellect must not be directed towards characterizable elements.
Although the world-ages (of Water, Fire and Air) are in turmoil, there must be no movement in the mind,
clear, calm, colourless and vast,
externally void, internally void, void of self-nature and characteristics,
void by nature, it lacks any substance anywhere.
For example psychic manifestations are void and selfless like the expanse of the sky and one must consider them as being just this.
In this way one cleaves directly to buddhahood.
As for the advance-grades in the psychic powers of this voidness,
one flies like a bird in the sky, and in water one is not drowned,
one passes through mountains and one kneeds earth and stone like meal.
There is no attachment anywhere, for the knot of avarice is loosed.
One casts one thing away and takes up another, like the vagaries of a child.

ḥdi yin ḥdi med spyod la ṅes pa med ||
ḥbyuṅ baḥi mtshon gyis reg kyaṅ gnod mi ḥgyur ||
skyi ḥjigs g·yaṅ za ṅo tshaḥi mthu daṅ bral ||
gaṅ yin gaṅ min lha bdud ṅos mi ḥdzin ||
smyo spyod tho cho ma ṅes rdzu ḥphrul ston ||
rtsiṅ rtsub spyod pa sna tshogs ston par ḥoṅ ||
de la dran paḥi sems kyis rtsis bzuṅ la ||
ched du mi bsgom ṅaṅ du ḥbral med bźag ||
byis pa[a] g·yaṅ sar lhuṅ dogs lta bur bskyaṅ ||
ri dvags smas ma lta bu raṅ ñid btsaḥ ||
mtho la g·yaṅ sa bral baḥi bogs skyed dbyuṅ[b] ||
smyon pa g·yaṅ lhuṅ lta buḥi skyon las grol ||
stoṅ źiṅ bdag med ma bcos ṅaṅ la bźag ||
ṅaṅ la ṅaṅ gis goms pa bskyed paḥo ||

[f. 71a[4] onwards]

tha ma rtsal sbyaṅ bogs ḥdon la bzla ba ||
byaṅ chub sems ni ka dag gźir phyin la ||
rtsal daṅ bogs bskyed ḥdon du yod ma yiṅ ||
ye nas ka dag gźir phyin yin mod kyaṅ ||
thabs daṅ lam la ma ḥgag rtsal sbyaṅ ba ||
snaṅ źiṅ srid pa ḥkhor ba myaṅ ḥdas bon ||
ma śoṅ mi śoṅ yaṅs la dogs pa med ||
dpag med nam mkhaḥ lta buḥi ñams rtsal sbyaṅ ||
ḥjig rten yon tan rdzas daṅ yo byad rnams ||
ma spaṅ ma blaṅ chags daṅ źen pa med ||
ṅes med byis pa lta buḥi ñams rtsal sbyaṅ ||
skyon daṅ yon tan bde daṅ sdug bsṅal sogs ||
mi mthun rkyen daṅ ḥgal baḥi tshogs rnams la ||
ma brtags mi brtag rtog ḥdzin dri ma bral ||
gtad med smyon pa lta buḥi ñams rtsal sbyaṅ ||
chags daṅ sred daṅ len daṅ skye ba sogs ||
ḥjig rten ḥdi bden rdzas daṅ yo byed la ||
gaṅ yaṅ [71b] ma spaṅs rgyan śar yin paḥi phyir ||
dug ḥjoms rma bya lta buḥi ñams rtsal sbyaṅ ||

[a] byi sba [b] ḥbyuṅ

There is no certainty of conduct (to which such words as) 'It is this' or 'It is not this' (could apply).
Although struck by elemental weapons, one is unharmed.
One is free of the power of fear, trepidation and shame.
There is no recognition of gods or demons, of what anything is or what it is not.
Crazily behaved and capricious, such a one reveals unpredictable powers.
He manifests all kinds of wild behaviour.
In taking the measure of all this with a heedful mind, one should not practise towards a special result, but remain naturally in a state of non-separation (from the desired result).
Be careful like a child who fears falling down an abyss.
Watch over yourself in the manner of a wounded deer.
You will make advancement in height without (fear of) a fall.
You will be like a madman who yet remains safe from the precipice.
Be relaxed in the void and selfless 'non-constructive' state.
Practice is effected in this condition by the condition itself.

Lastly as for exploiting the benefit of one's skill and practice,
there can be no question of skill and benefit with regard to the Thought of Enlightenment which exists as the pure absolute.
But although it exists from all time as the pure absolute,
this accomplished unimpeded skill in Method and Way has no doubts about the comprehensiveness of something so vast, namely the whole of existence, *bon* both physical and metaphysical.[72]
One must practise psychic skill which is measureless like the sky.
With regard to worldly accomplishments, necessaries and chattels,
there is no deliberate avoidance and no deliberate pursuit of them, for no attachment to them exists.
One must practise skill which is unpredictable like a child's.
With regard to defects and accomplishments, happiness and unhappiness and the rest,
unfavourable circumstances and opposing concatenations,
they remain uninvestigated and must not be investigated,
for one is free from the defilement of fixed views.
One must practise skill which is undirected like a madman's.
With regard to attachment, to desire, to seizing and to birth and the rest (of the twelvefold causal nexus), and the real things and necessaries of this world,
since it is the first principle not to avoid anything,
one must practise the skill of the peacock who can overcome poison,

ḥjig rten rdzas daṅ zas gos grogs rnams la ||
gtsaṅ sme blaṅ dor rnam par rtog pa ḥjoms ||
gnas daṅ bla gab gaṅ la ṅes pa med ||
khyi phag loṅ spraṅ lta buḥi ñams rtsal sbyaṅs ||
bro gar glu daṅ rol moḥi tshogs rnams daṅ ||
sna tshogs sgra skad gaṅ yaṅ ṅes med pa ||
cal col thol ma gyu ltar ñams rtsal sbyaṅ ||
legs par brjod daṅ ñes par smra ba daṅ ||
ḥjig rten mchod brjod smod paḥi sdaṅ tshig sogs ||
mthun byed sgra daṅ mi mthun sgra rnams la ||
gaṅ la rtog dpyod ṅos ḥdzin med pa ru ||
dṅos med brag cha lta buḥi ñams rtsal sbyaṅ ||
legs par brjod daṅ ñes par brjod pa daṅ ||
ḥthad pa mi mthun spyod la sogs pa ste ||
bya baḥi spyod lam rnam pa thams cad kun ||
gaṅ la ḥdi źes gzaḥ gtad med pa ru ||
ḥdzin med rluṅ po lta buḥi ñams rtsal sbyaṅ ||
gźan rkyen bskul daṅ raṅ bźin blos spyad daṅ ||
śugs las byuṅ daṅ źor daṅ stabs la sogs ||
pha rol gaṅ gis bsgyur du mi btub par ||
gaṅ byuṅ snaṅ ba thad kar gcod pa yi ||
glaṅ chen chur źugs lta buḥi ñams rtsal sbyaṅ ||
bdud daṅ mu stegs srin po la sogs daṅ ||
pha rol rgol baḥi tshogs su gyur pa daṅ ||
ḥjig rten mṅaḥ dbaṅ dregs pa che ba rnams ||
gaṅ la ñam ṅa bag tsha med pa ste ||
thams cad ma lus zil gyis gnon paḥi phyir ||
dpaḥ rtsal siṅ ge lta buḥi ñams rtsal sbyaṅ ||
brgya khri bźi stoṅ phyi naṅ gsaṅ gsum bon ||
ñag gcig rol paḥi rtsal lam cho ḥphrul la ||
gaṅ yaṅ blaṅ źiṅ dor du med paḥi phyir ||
gaṅ daṅ spyod lam mthun par ñams rtsal sbyaṅ ||

[f. $73a^2$ onwards]

ye gśen gtsug phud thugs kyi dkyil du źog ||
ye gśen theg paḥi bon gyi las gñer gtad ||
ri bo gaṅs gliṅ khrod kyi bdag por bsko ||
tshad med byaṅ chub gliṅ du bon ḥkhor skor ||
gñug ma bde chen don dam mthar phyin mdzod ||
dbu ma mchog gi lam la saṅs rgyas ḥgyur ||

With regard to worldly things, food, clothes and friends,
one overcomes scruples of purity and impurity, of acceptance and rejection.
There is no predictability concerning your dwelling or the roof over your head.
Practise psychic skill like that of a dog, a pig, or a beggar.

There is no predictability with regard to various sounds, dancing and singing and music and so on.
Practise psychic skill such as unresponsiveness to noise.

With regard to good sayings and evil sayings,
honouring words of the worldly or denigrating hateful words,
sounds pleasing and sounds unpleasing,
none must receive thought or recognition.
Practise the psychic skill that resembles the unsubstantial echo.

With regard to good action and evil action,
suitable action, unsuitable action and so on,
with regard to all kinds of behaviour,
let there be no fixation: 'This is for such a one.'
Practise the psychic skill of the wind which clings nowhere.

Unable to be diverted by causes occasioned by others or by a spontaneous decision, by the inevitable course of events, by incidental happenings or accidental occurrences,
(unmoved) by anything external, cut off at once whatever arises,
practise psychic skill like that of an elephant who has entered the water (to drink).
Having no fear and trepidation for anyone,
for demons or heretics, for monsters and so on,
for the hosts of opposing enemies,
for the powerful, the arrogant and the great ones of this world,
practise psychic skill like that of a bold lion,
so that you may overcome all without exception.

In order that there may be no acceptance or rejecting of anything
among the skills and special powers of the One Alone as he sports,
among the exoteric, the esoteric, and the secret *bon* with its 84,000 doctrines,
practise the psychic skill that brings all conduct into accord with anything whatsoever.

Ye-gśen gTsug-phud, keep this in the centre of your thought! You must be responsible for the works of *bon* of the Way of Primeval Shen.
You must take charge of the hermitage of *Ri-bo gaṅs-gliṅ*.
You must turn the wheel of *bon* in the Vale of Boundless Enlightenment.
You must perfect all in the absolute, the great bliss of the uncreate,
and you will be an Enlightened One on the Way of the Excellent Mean.

lta ba dbyiṅs śes dbyer med don la blta ||
sgom pa byaṅ chub sems kyi bdar śa gcad ||
spyod pa thabs daṅ thugs rje zuṅ ḥbrel spyad ||
dam tshig rnam dag dri med ḥchal ba spaṅ ||
ḥphrin las yoṅs su rdzogs paḥi las don bsdu ||
ḥbras bu ḥkhor ḥdas dbyer med gcig tu dril ||

ces gsuṅs nas / thegs pa brgyad pa ye gśen bon rnams gtan la phab ste / ḥkhor rnams la gsuṅs paḥo /

Your Insight must be a viewing of the celestial expanse and (the divinities of) knowledge in their undifferentiated state.
Your Contemplation must be a revealing of the Thought of Enlightenment.
Your Practice must be the unified action of Method and Compassion.
Your Vow must be pure and unsullied and you must avoid all deviations.
Your Action must unite the results of all perfect acts.
The Result must be the undifferentiated uniting of phenomenal existence and all that transcends it.

Thus he spoke to those around him, setting down in order the elements of the Eighth Way, that of the Primeval Shen.

ERRATA:

Penetrating the secret *gSas* Palace (*maṇḍala*) with its flow of separation and combination,
he unites in himself the gods with their divine abodes.
There is bliss in the state of Universal Goodness (=supreme buddhahood), the non-dual essence, the sphere of the King of Great Bliss, free of all separations and combinations.

IX. BLA MED THEG PA

[vol. *ṅa*, f. 85a⁴ onwards]

de la yaṅ tshad med gtsug phud kyis gsol pa /
rnam pa thams cad mkhyen pa yi ||
ḥgro baḥi dpal mgon ston pa lags ||
bon sgo brgyad khri bźi stoṅ las ||
tshur bsdud theg pa rim dgur gsuṅs ||
de dag naṅ nas ḥphags[a] pa yi ||
theg chen sdoṅ po dgu ḥdus bon ||
bdag la gñer du gtad pa yi ||
bla med theg paḥi bon ḥdi dag ||
ḥdi yi mtshan ñid ci ltar lags ||
spyi sgos bye brag ci ltar ḥbyed ||
źib tu phyes nas[b] bkaḥ stsol ḥtshal ||

ces gsol to / de la ston pas bkaḥ stsal pa /

ñon cig tshad med gtsug phud ñon ||
byaṅ chub sems ñid rin po che ||
gdod nas ye saṅs rgyas paḥi ṅaṅ ||
gnas lugs rig paḥi ṅo bo ni ||
ka dag [85b] chen po ḥdus ma byas ||
ḥkhor ḥdas gaṅ gi gźi rtsa bral ||
ma bcos spros bral chen po la ||
daṅ po gnas paḥi byuṅ khuṅs daṅ ||
bar du bgrod paḥi lam gnas daṅ ||
tha ma phyin paḥi sa med ciṅ ||
ḥgro ḥoṅ mtshan ma ma grub ciṅ ||
tshig su brjod paḥi don med kyaṅ ||
ḥon kyaṅ rtag chad mthaḥ gsal źiṅ ||
ma rtogs sems can bkri phyir du ||
tshig su brjod de bśad bya ba ||
theg pa kun gyi yaṅ rtse ḥdi[c] ||
spyi ru rnam pa gsum du bśad ||
gźi daṅ lam daṅ ḥbras bu gsum ||
sgos su rnam pa bźi ru ste ||
lta ba sgom pa spyod pa gsum ||
bla med don gyi ḥbras buḥo ||
bye brag so sor dbye ba na ||
phar spros brgyad khri bźi stoṅ la ||

[a] dpag pa [b] dbye nas [c] rtseḥi

IX. THE SUPREME WAY

Then *Tshad-med gTsug-phud* said:

O all-knowing teacher, the splendour and protector of living beings,
You have said that the 84,000 ways of *bon* are compressed into Nine Ways.[72]
The highest of them all,
the great Way, the *bon* which consists of nine 'trunks',
you have committed to my keeping.
As for the religious truths (*bon*) of this Supreme Way,
what are their characteristics
and how does one distinguish differences both of a general and special kind?
We beg you to tell us by explaining in detail.

So he spoke and the Teacher replied:

Listen *Tshad-med gTsug-phud*, listen!
This precious thing, the Thought of Enlightenment,
the state of primeval buddhahood,
the essence of knowledge in its natural state,
the absolute purity of the unconditioned,
void of any basis whatsoever in physical and metaphysical notions,
unaffected in any way, this Great Unmoved
has no first existing origin,
has no intermediate way and progressive stages,
and has no final attainable stage,
for it lacks characteristics of going and coming.
But although it is thus inexpressible in words,
in order to avoid the extreme notions of eternity and nihilism,
and to give guidance to ignorant beings,
it has to be explained and expressed in words.
In general this summit of all (nine) Ways is explained in three parts,
as Basis, as Way and as Result.
In a special way it is explained in four parts,
as Insight, as Contemplation, as Practice
and as the Result of supreme achievement.
Divided into its separate distinctions,
it spreads out into 84,000 parts,

tshur bsdus thig le ñag gcig go ||

źes gsuṅs so / yaṅ gsol pa /

thams cad mkhyen paḥi ston pa lags ||
de ltar theg pa bla med la ||
spyi ru rnam pa gsum gsuṅs pa ||
gźi daṅ lam daṅ ḥbras bu gsum ||
gźi yi mtshan ñid ci ltar lags ||
gźi las grol tshul ci ltar lags ||
lam gyi bgrod tshul ci ltar lags ||
ḥbras bu ḥgrub tshul ci ltar lags ||

śes gsol to / de la ston pas bkaḥ rtsal pa /

ñon cig tshad med gtsug phud gśen ||
thog mar gźi yi gnas tshul ni ||
ma srid ye srid thog ma la ||
dus gsum saṅs rgyas rgyu ma grub ||
khams gsum sems can rkyen ma bslad ||
ḥkhor ḥdas ma srid goṅ rol du ||
thog mar rig paḥi rgyal po sṅa ||
gnas lugs rig paḥi ṅo bo ni ||
kun gźi phyaḥo luṅ ma bstan ||
yod pa ma yin med pa min ||
ḥkhor ḥdas gaṅ gi miṅ ma thogs ||
dge sdig gaṅ gi ḥdus ma byas ||
stoṅ pa ma yin snaṅ [86a] ba min ||
rtag pa ma yin chad pa min ||
bde ba ma yin sdug bsṅal min ||
saṅs rgyas ma yin sems can min ||
kha dog gzugs snaṅ dbyibs ma grub ||
mu med ḥbyams yas bon gyi dbyiṅs ||
rgya chad phyogs lhuṅ mthar mi dmigs ||
ḥkhor ḥdas gaṅ gi miṅ ma thogs ||
skyon yon gaṅ gi blos ma bslad ||
dge sdig gaṅ gi rgyu ma grub ||
kha dog dkar nag che chuṅ med ||
yaṅs[a] dog mthaḥ dbus dpyod las ḥdas ||
rgya khyon dpag tshad gźal mi dpog ||
thog mthaḥ ḥgyur nub med par gnas ||

[a] yaṅ

but in its compressed form it becomes a single dot.

So he spoke, and again they asked:

O all-knowing Teacher,
You have said that in general there are three parts in the Supreme Vehicle,
the Basis, the Way, and the Result.
What are the characteristics of the Basis?
How should 'release' come from the Basis?
How should one advance along the Way?
How should one gain the Result?

The Teacher replied:

Listen, Shen *Tshad-med gTsug-phud*!
First as for the nature of the Basis,
in the prime state, timeless and unoriginated,
there is no effective cause for the buddhas of past, present and future,
there is no admixture of causal conditions (for the producing) of beings of the threefold world.
Before physical and metaphysical states originated,
at the beginning the 'King of Knowledge' is first.
This is the natural state, the state of knowledge, the universal basis, void and unpredicated.
It is neither existence nor non-existence.
No name, physical or metaphysical, applies to it.
It is unconditioned by either good or evil.
It is not emptiness and it is not manifestation.
It is not eternity and it is not nihilism.
It is neither blessedness nor misery.
It is neither buddha nor living being.
It lacks colour, form and shape.
It is the boundless infinite sphere of *bon*.
It cannot be regarded as interrupted, limited or ending.
No term, physical or metaphysical can be applied to it.
It is spoiled by no notion of fault or of virtue.
It possesses no cause for good or evil.
It has no colour, is neither black nor white, nor large nor small.
It cannot be investigated with regard to its extent or its narrowness, its limits or its centre.
Its area cannot be measured in miles.
It remains without beginning or end, without change or decline.

ḥphel ba med ciṅ ḥgrib pa med ||
zad pa med ciṅ ḥbri ba med ||
stor ba med ciṅ ḥbral ba med ||
chags pa med ciṅ ḥjig pa med ||
rgyu las ma grub rkyen mi ḥjig ||
rkyen gyis ma bslad rgyu mi mṅon ||
dper na nam mkhaḥi dbyiṅs ltar du ||
sa le phyod de rgyaṅ ṅe ba ||
ci yaṅ med paḥi ṅaṅ du gnas ||
thog mar gźi yi gnas tsul lo ||

gñis pa gźi las[a] grol tshul ni ||
kun gźi skye med bon gyi dbyiṅs ||
ye nas phyo ma luṅ ma bstan ||
ci yaṅ med paḥi stoṅ pa la ||
rtag daṅ chad mthar ma lhuṅ źiṅ ||
ma g·yos dbyiṅs chen ḥbyams yas la ||
cir yaṅ snaṅ baḥi rlabs g·yos pas ||
stoṅ paḥi bcud las rig pa ḥbyuṅ ||
dper na ñi maḥi sñiṅ po bźin ||
stoṅ rig sgrib med zaṅ thal la ||
stoṅ cha ḥgag med raṅ sgra sgrog ||
de las raṅ bźin ḥod lṅa śar ||
zer ni raṅ bźin kun tu ḥphro ||
yod par snaṅ bźin dṅos ma grub ||
med par snaṅ bźin mthar ma lhuṅ ||
ye srid rgyal po ḥgyur ba med ||
yaṅ mes[b] chen po g·yo med sku ||
dus gsum saṅs rgyas gźi las grol ||
kun [86b] tu bzaṅ po glo bur ba ||
tshig daṅ miṅ gis mtshon pa tsam ||
don du mtshon pa mya ṅan ḥdas ||
ye nas ka dag chen po ste ||
ma bcos spros bral lhun gyis grub ||
gdod maḥi dus nas ḥkhrul sgrib bral ||
daṅ poḥi saṅs rgyas rgyu med pa ||
rgyu las ma byuṅ rkyen mi ḥjig ||
saṅs rgyas thog ma tha ma med ||
sgra ni stoṅ pa bon ñid sku ||
ḥod ni ka dag chen po ste ||
zer ni sna tshogs sprul paḥi sku ||

[a] gźiḥi [b] mñis

It does not increase or decrease.
It cannot be exhausted and it does not lessen.
It cannot be lost or separated.
It does not come into existence and it is not destroyed.
It is not produced from a cause or destroyed by circumstances.
It is not spoiled by circumstances and no cause is present.
For example—like the sphere of the sky
  it is clear, blank and solitary,
  remaining in a state of nothingness.
To begin with then, this is the nature of the Basis.

Secondly as for the way 'release'[74] comes from this Basis,
this universal basis is the unborn sphere of *bon*,
void in its prime state and unpredicated,
for in this emptiness where nothing exists
there is no erring into the extreme views of eternity and nihilism,
and in this infinite unmoving expanse
waves appear somehow and by their movement
knowledge arises from this essence of emptiness.
For example it is like the orb of the sun.
In this pure 'spontaneity' of the knowledge of emptiness
there resounds the 'self-sound' of the unimpeded void
and thence there arise the five lights in their own self-nature,
and their rays reach everywhere in their self-nature.
It appears as 'being', but it is really not so.
It appears as 'non-being', but does not fall into extreme views.
It is the unchanging 'Primeval King',
the unmoving form of the 'Great Ancestor'.
The buddhas of past, present and future come forth from this basis.
It is the spontaneous 'All Good',
of whom names and terms are mere indications.
In reality what is indicated is altogether transcendent.
It is the great primeval purity,
unaffected by anything, tranquil and self-existing.
From the beginning of time it is free from delusion and defilement.
It is the causeless 'First Buddha',
not produced from a cause and not destroyed by circumstances.
It is the Buddha without beginning or end.
Its sound is emptiness, the absolute body.
Its light is the great purity.
Its rays are manifold, the body of phenomenal manifestation.

ḥod lṅa kha dog ye śes lṅa ||
gźan snaṅ pha rol ma phyin par ||
raṅ mtshan dkyil ḥkhor mkhaḥ la rdzogs ||
sñiṅ po ḥgyur med bon gyi dbyiṅs ||
ṅaṅ daṅ raṅ bźin ḥdu ḥbral med ||
gdod nas ye saṅs rgyas paḥi sku ||
saṅs rgyas tshig gis mtshon bya tsam ||
don du ma bcos spros bral ṅaṅ ||
thig le ñag gcig e ma ho ||
rtogs pas saṅs rgyas grol baḥi gźi ||
ka dag ḥgyur med ṅo bo ñid ||
raṅ mtshan dkyil ḥkhor rdzogs paḥi lam ||
raṅ bźin lhun gyis grub paḥi źiṅ ||
lha lṅa sku lṅa źiṅ khams lṅa ||
rigs lṅa stobs lṅa spyan lṅa rdzogs ||
saṅs rgyas śes kyi miṅ du btags ||
gnas paḥi gźi daṅ grol baḥi lam ||
raṅ raṅ sgos kyi gźi lam ste ||
saṅs rgyas tshig gi bla dvags so ||

ma rtogs sems can ḥkhrul tshul ni ||
goṅ ltar ma g·yos dbyiṅs chen la ||
cir yaṅ snaṅ baḥi rlabs g·yos pas ||
stoṅ paḥi bcud las rig pa ḥbyuṅ ||
rig pa ḥgag med zaṅ thal la ||
sgra ḥod zer gsum rtsal du śar ||
gźi las lam gyis cho ḥphrul bslaṅs ||
de ñid ma rig ḥkhrul par śar ||
rgyu ni[a] ma rig pa las ḥbyuṅ ||
rkyen ni raṅ bźin ḥod lṅas byas ||
raṅ mtshan dkyil ḥkhor ma rtogs pas ||
gźan ḥbyuṅ rkyen[b] la rtog pa ḥkhrul ||
rtog [87a] pas brtags[c] pas ḥkhor bar śar ||
med la yod bzuṅ ḥdzin las ḥkhrul ||
bdag las gźan med brtags pas[d] ḥkhrul ||
sems la sdug bsṅal tshor bas ḥkhrul ||
sgra la raṅ skrag ḥjigs pas ḥkhrul ||

[a] ma [b] bskyem [c] brtag [d] rtags pa

The lights of the five colours are the Five Wisdoms.
They do not have counterparts in reflection elsewhere,
for they are (already) perfected in the self-characterized *maṇḍala* sphere.
This is the unchanging essence, the sphere of *bon*,
the state and self-nature which are free from association and separation.
It is the body of primeval buddhahood,
but by the term 'buddha' it is no more than indicated.
In reality it is that unaffected state of absolute tranquillity,
The Single Dot. What wonder!
By knowing it, (one uses it as) a basis for being released in buddhahood.
The pure, the unchanging, the very essence!
The way of the perfect self-characterized *maṇḍala*!
The sphere of self-existing self-nature!
Five gods, five bodies, five realms,
five families, five powers, five eyes,
perfect in everything, and known by the name of 'buddha'.
The abiding Basis and the Way of 'release'
are Basis or Way according to each particular view
and to them is attached the appellation of 'buddhahood'.

As for the manner of ignorant beings' delusion,
it was said above that in this great unmoving expanse
waves appear somehow and by their movement
knowledge arises from the essence of emptiness.
In the spontaneity of unimpeded knowledge
Sound, Light and Rays, all three, shine by reflective power.
The Way causes magical emanations to arise from the Basis,
and these (emanations) appear as the delusion of ignorance.
As for their cause, they spring from ignorance,
and the five lights in their own self-nature act as causal conditions.
Not knowing the self-characterized *maṇḍala* (as sole origin),
the knower is deluded with regard to causal conditions (thinking the appearances) arise elsewhere.
As a result of the knower's disquisitive knowing, it all appears as the phenomenal world.
The delusion of conceiving non-being as being comes from the act of conceiving.
The delusion that there is nothing but the self comes from disquisitive thinking.
The delusion of mental suffering comes from the feelings.
The delusion of self-distrust with regard to Sound arises from fear.

ḥod la daṅ chags rmoṅs pas ḥphrul ||
zer la sems ḥphro bslus pas ḥkhrul ||
ḥkhrul paḥi rjes ḥbreṅ źiṅ du śar ||
ḥod zer kha dog dkar po la ||
daṅ po daṅ chags[a] snaṅ ba ḥkhrul ||
de nas yid rmoṅ źe la sdaṅ ||
tsha graṅ dmyal baḥi źiṅ du śar ||
byams pa chen poḥi don la sgrib ||
ḥod zer kha dog dmar po la ||
daṅ po daṅ chags snaṅ ba ḥphrul ||
de la yid rmoṅ ḥdod chags ldaṅ[b] ||
bkres skom yi dvags źiṅ du śar ||
sbyin pa chen poḥi don la sgrib[c] ||
ḥod zer kha dog sṅon po la ||
daṅ po daṅ chags[a] snaṅ ba ḥkhrul ||
de la yid rmoṅ gti mug ldaṅ[b] ||
glen lkug byol soṅ źiṅ du śar ||
ye śes chen poḥi don la sgrib[c] ||
ḥod zer kha dog ser po la ||
daṅ po daṅ chags snaṅ ba ḥkhrul ||
de la yid rmoṅ ḥphrag-dog ldaṅ[b] ||
brel phoṅs mi yi źiṅ du śar ||
yaṅs pa chen poḥi don la sgrib[c] ||
ḥod zer kha dog ljaṅ khu la ||
daṅ po daṅ chags snaṅ ba ḥphrul ||
de la yid rmoṅ ṅa rgyal ldaṅ[b] ||
ḥthab rtsod lha min źiṅ du śar ||
źi ba chen poḥi don la sgrib ||
ḥod zer kha dog cha mñam la ||
daṅ po daṅ chags snaṅ ba ḥkhrul ||
de la yid rmoṅ rtog pa ldaṅ[b] ||
pham ltuṅ lha yi źiṅ du śar ||
gñis med mñam paḥi don la sgrib ||
gzugs med rgyu las gzugs su grub ||
bdud lṅa dug lṅa ñon moṅs lṅa ||
phuṅ po lṅa poḥi sgrogs su sdom[d] ||
thar med ḥkhor baḥi drva bar [87b] chud ||
raṅ rig ye śes ḥod mdaṅs nub ||
mi śes rmoṅs paḥi sdug bsṅal sbyoṅ ||

[a] chag [b] źe la sdaṅ *in every case. See note* 76 [c] bsgrib [d] bsdem

The delusion of attachment to Light arises from perplexity.
The delusion of thought-emanations with regard to the Rays arises from beguilement.
As a result of pursuing these delusions, it all appears as the (Six) Spheres (of possible rebirth).[75]
With regard to the light of white rays
there is first attachment and delusion of appearances.
Then the mind is perplexed and *Wrath* emerges,
and it all appears as the sphere of the hot and cold hells.
So a shadow is cast over the intention of great loving-kindness.
With regard to the light of red rays
There is first attachment and delusion of appearances.
Then the mind is perplexed and *Desire* arises,[76]
and it all appears as the sphere of hungry and thirsty tormented spirits.
So a shadow is cast over the intention of great generosity.
With regard to the light of blue rays
there is first attachment and delusion of appearances.
Then the mind is perplexed and *Mental Torpor* arises,
and it all appears as the sphere of stupid beasts.
So a shadow is cast over the intention of great knowledge.
With regard to the light of yellow rays
there is first attachment and delusion of appearances.
Then the mind is perplexed and *Envy* arises,
and it all appears as the sphere of wretched men.
So a shadow is cast over the intention of magnanimity.
With regard to the light of green rays
there is first attachment and delusion of appearances.
Then the mind is perplexed and *Pride* arises,
and it all appears as the sphere of contentious titans.
So a shadow is cast over the intention of tranquillity.
With regard to the light with rays coloured in equal parts
there is first attachment and delusion of appearances.
Then the mind is perplexed and *Disquisitive Thought* arises,
and it all appears as the sphere of the falling gods.
So a shadow is cast over the intention of unity and sameness.
Form is produced with the formless as cause.
One is bound with the bonds of the Five *Māras*, the Five Evils, the Five Molestations (*kleśa*) and the Five Components of Personality,
and one enters the net of phenomenal existence where there is no escape.
The light of self-knowing knowledge loses its brilliance
and one experiences the suffering of the blindness of ignorance.

ñon moṅs ḥkhor baḥi btson rar tshud ||
sdug bsṅal ḥdod paḥi rgya mtshor ḥbyiṅ ||
skye rga na ḥchi chu bo ḥgrub ||
ris drug zo chu rgyud mar rgyud[a] ||
raṅ dbaṅ ma thob gźan dbaṅ can ||
sdug bsṅal ḥkhor bar ḥkhyam pa ste ||
ma rtogs sems can ḥkhrul tshul lo ||
grol daṅ ḥkhrul paḥi mtshan ñid ni ||
gźi las ma rig rgyu bskyed ciṅ ||
lam la ḥkhrul ṅos ma zin kyaṅ ||
sṅon du gźi yi sgra yod pas ||
ñon moṅs dug lṅa sbyaṅ du yod ||
thar paḥi lam la bgrod du yod ||
saṅs rgyas ḥbras bu bsgrub tu yod ||
rig paḥi ye śes gsal tu yod ||
grol ḥkhrul bye brag de ltar ro ||

gsum[b] pa lam gyi bgrod tshul ni ||
stoṅ źiṅ bdag med byaṅ chub sems ||
gnas lugs rig paḥi ṅo bo ḥdi ||
don du raṅ sems saṅs rgyas sku ||
kun gźi skye med bon gyi dbyiṅs ||
rol pa ḥgag med raṅ ḥbyuṅ rtsal ||
cir yaṅ snaṅ ba de bźin stoṅ ||
snaṅ daṅ stoṅ pa ka nes dag ||
bon ñid raṅ las raṅ ḥbyuṅ rtsal ||
bon can mtshan ma bon ñid dbyiṅs ||
ye nas gźi gnas mthar phyin la ||
ḥdi la bgrod daṅ ḥgro ḥoṅ med ||
ma bcos rtsol bral sems ñid ṅaṅ ||
ma g·yos khyab bdal bon ñid kloṅ ||
de la ñams su len rgyu med ||
len rgyu len mkhan raṅ rig sems ||
ḥon kyaṅ brda daṅ thabs bstan pa ||
gnas tshul steṅ du bźag tshul tsam ||
don la yin tshul śes pa tsam ||
śes tsam ñid ni rtogs pa tsam ||
rtogs daṅ ḥgrol ba zuṅ ḥjug tsam ||
kun gźi stoṅ paḥi raṅ mdaṅs[c] la ||
rig pa sgrib med ye śes gsal ||

[a] brgyud [b] gñis [c] gdaṅs

One enters the prison of phenomenal existence and all its molestations (*kleśa*),
and sinks in the ocean of suffering and desire.
The river of birth, old age, sickness and death flows on
and (rebirth in) the Six Spheres[77] goes on continuously like a circular chain of water buckets.
In the power of others without gaining power over oneself
one wanders through wretched states of existence.
Such is the way ignorant beings are deluded.
As for the characteristics of Release and Delusion,
ignorance is produced with the Basis as its cause,
and although delusion is not recognized on the Way,
it exists in the first place as the Sound of the Basis.
The molestations and the Five Evils must be cleansed.
Advance must be made on the Way of Salvation.
The Result, namely buddhahood, must be achieved.
Knowing that perceives must become clear.
Such is the difference between Release and Delusion.

Thirdly, as for how one should advance along the path,
this Thought of Enlightenment which is void and selfless,
the state of knowledge in its natural condition
is really one's own mind in the form of buddhahood.
It is the sphere of *bon*, the unborn universal basis
with unimpeded power of action and self-manifesting reflective power.
Whatever the appearance it manifests, it is correspondingly void,
for both appearance and voidness are absolutely pure.
It is the absolute *bon* with reflective power self-produced from itself,
the absolute *bon* sphere of all characterizable *bon* elements.
In this basic state which is perfect from all time
there is no advance and no coming and going.
It is the state of mind itself, unaffected and effortless,
the unmoving, all-pervading expanse of absolute *bon*.
There is nothing to be learned in its regard,
for what might be learned and the learner are both the self-knowing mind.
The teaching by signs and by methods
is merely an application referring to the absolute.
It is just a matter of knowing how it really is.
It is just an understanding of knowledge itself.
It is just a combination of understanding and release.
The knowledge of pure knowing shines translucent on the face of the emptiness of the universal basis.

ḥbyuṅ ḥjug mtshan [88a] ma sna tshogs blo ||
gñis su med ciṅ so sor gsal ||
yaṅ dag mthaḥ la gcig tu gnas ||
gnas paḥi steṅ du bźag paḥi tshul ||
don du kun gźiḥi kloṅ du bsdud ||
snaṅ stoṅ dbyer med zuṅ du ḥjug ||
bde stoṅ dbyer med rol paḥi kloṅ ||
rig stoṅ dbyer med byaṅ chub sems ||
gñis med ṅaṅ du e ma ho ||
kun gźi nam mkhaḥ lta bu la ||
rig pa sa rluṅ me chur grub ||
ḥbyuṅ ḥjug źiṅ khams rab ḥbyams chags ||
gñis su med ciṅ so sor gsal ||
yaṅ dag mthaḥ la gcig tu gnas ||
gnas paḥi steṅ du bźag paḥi tshul ||
don du ba gaḥi kloṅ du bsdud ||
snaṅ stoṅ dbyer med zuṅ du ḥjug ||
bde stoṅ dbyer med rol paḥi kloṅ ||
rig stoṅ dbyer med byaṅ chub sems ||
gñis med ṅaṅ du e ma ho ||

[f. 89b[4] onwards]

de ltar sems ñid gnas tshul la ||
raṅ bźin ṅaṅ gi bźag tshul gyis ||
gnas daṅ ḥgyu ba ḥbyuṅ thim gcig ||
snaṅ daṅ stoṅ pa kha[a] ta chad ||
sku daṅ ye śes zuṅ ḥjug rtsal ||
gdod nas bla med phar phyin la ||
bgrod bya bgrod byed mthaḥ daṅ bral ||
sems ñid raṅ sar gnas pa yi ||
ḥkhor ḥdas raṅ ḥbyuṅ rol pa la ||
bgrod tshul miṅ gis gdag bya tsam ||
gsum pa lam gyi bgrod tshul lo ||

bźi pa ḥbras bu ḥgrub[b] tshul ni ||
kun gźi skye med bon gyi dbyiṅs ||
rol pa ḥgag med raṅ ḥbyuṅ rtsal ||
gñis su med pa ñag gcig sku ||
ḥkhor ḥdas med pa ro gcig dbyiṅs ||
ye nas skye med ḥchi bral źiṅ ||

[a] ka [b] grub

The intellect with its various characteristics which emerge and return
remains translucent with (such seeming) separateness in a state of absolute unity.
It remains at one in the pure ultimate.
The manner of application referring to this state
is really comprised within the sphere of the universal basis.
It is the inseparable combination of manifestation and voidness.
It is the sphere of the play of bliss and voidness mutually inseparable.
It is the Thought of Enlightenment where knowing and voidness are inseparable.
Such is this state of unity! How wonderful!
The knower is produced in the universal basis
just as earth, air, fire and water are produced in sky.
Appearing and returning, the realms of existence come into being on a very vast scale.
They are translucent with (seeming) separateness in a state of absolute unity.
It remains at one in the pure ultimate.
The manner of application referring to this state
is really comprised in the sphere of the 'universal womb' (*bhaga*).
It is the inseparable combination of manifestation and voidness.
It is the sphere of the play of bliss and voidness mutually inseparable.
It is the Thought of Enlightenment where knowing and voidness are inseparable.
Such is this state of unity! How wonderful!

Just relax spontaneously in mind itself in its abiding condition.
'Staying' and 'darting', 'emerging' and 'sinking' are a single state.
Talk of manifestation and voidness is stopped.
The (supreme) form and knowledge are the reflective power of the 'Two-in-One'.
In that which is absolutely perfect from all time
the extreme ideas of advancement and of the one who advances just do not exist.
In the self-produced play of physical and metaphysical notions (acted) by mind itself abiding in its own condition,
the term 'manner of advancement' is a mere appellation.
This is the third subject, the manner of advancement.

Fourthly as for gaining the Result,
the sphere of *bon*, the unborn universal basis,
the non-dual single form,
of unimpeded power of action and self-manifesting reflective power,
the 'single-flavoured' sphere, neither physical nor metaphysical,
is eternally unborn and deathless.

gdod nas pha rol phyin pa la ||
snaṅ srid ḥkhor ba myaṅ ḥdas bon ||
raṅ chas lhun grub raṅ bźin gyi ||
sku daṅ ye śes zuṅ ḥbrel nas ||
yon tan ma brtsal lhun rdzogs la ||
ḥbras bu grub daṅ ma grub med ||
ḥon [90a] kyaṅ gnas lugs rig pa la ||
gnas tshul steṅ na bźag tshul daṅ ||
de dag brtan pa thob nas su ||
raṅ rig mṅon du gyur pa yis ||
raṅ mtshan dkyil ḥkhor rdzogs pa la ||
snaṅ stoṅ gñis su med pa yi ||
bde stoṅ zuṅ ḥjug rol pa la ||
rig stoṅ lhun gyis grub pa yi ||
ḥphags paḥi yon tan bsam mthaḥ yas ||
nam mkhaḥ ri rab rgya mtsho ltar ||
dpag gi mi dpog gźal mi loṅ ||
sku ñid gcig las ma g·yos kyaṅ ||
sprul pa bye ba phrag brgya ḥgyed ||
gaṅ la gaṅ ḥdul cir yaṅ ston ||
ḥbyuṅ bźi mtshan ma las su ruṅ ||
nam mkhaḥ ñid la ñid du spyod ||
ḥchi med bdud bral g·yuṅ druṅ sku ||
srog med nad dug mtshon mi ḥjig ||
mkhaḥ la bya daṅ chu la ña ||
brag la thog gśeg rtsi śiṅ sdud ||
ri rab phyag ḥdeg rgya mtsho rṅub ||
chu bo źags zlog[a] gzaḥ chen rtod ||
stoṅ gsum stoṅ gi ḥjig rten yaṅ ||
rkaṅ pa ya gcig mthil gyis gnon ||
ḥgyur ba med paḥi sku mchog ldan ||
gsuṅ ñid gcig las ma bsgrags kyaṅ ||
ḥgro ba sems can thams cad kyi ||
skad rigs mi mthun so so ru ||
raṅ raṅ sgra skad ji[b] bźin go ||
brgyad khri bźi stoṅ bon rnams kun ||
thogs pa med pa raṅ bźin śes ||
skad rigs sum brgya drug cur sgyur ||
ḥgro ba yoṅs la bkaḥ dbaṅ btsan[c] ||
bden paḥi tshig la spro ba skyed ||
tshaṅ paḥi dbyaṅs kyis mya ṅan bsaṅ ||

[a] sdog [b] ci [c] brtsan

The phenomenal world, physical and metaphysical notions,
pertain from all time to the 'beyond'.
The essential nature of this spontaneously produced self-nature,
is (absolute) form and knowledge as 'Two-in-One'.
Without striving for any qualities, it is spontaneously perfect,
so there can be no gaining or not gaining of any achievement.
But in knowing this natural state
there is a way of relaxing upon things as they are,[78]
and having got them stable,
self-knowledge becomes manifest,
so that in the self-characterized *maṇḍala*
manifestation and voidness are in unity,
and in the unified play of bliss and emptiness
knowledge and emptiness are spontaneously produced,
with superb qualities surpassing all thought.
Like the sky, like Mount *Kailāsa*, like the ocean,
it cannot be measured, it cannot be appraised.
Although unmoved from its single form
a hundred million manifestations spread forth,
showing itself anyhow, wherever anyone is converted,
and in keeping with the characteristics of the four elements
acting absolutely in absolute space.
It is the deathless Swastika body, free of *Māra*.
As it is lifeless, disease, poisons and weapons cannot destroy it.
(He who has realized this is like) a bird in the sky and a fish in the ocean.
He splits rocks as by lightning and gathers in (magically) aromatic shrubs.
He raises Mount *Kailāsa* in his hand and sucks up the ocean.
He pulls back the waters as with a noose and transfixes the planets.
He treads the whole universe under the sole of one foot.
He possesses the supreme unchanging form.
Although only one sound resounds, all living beings hear the sounds of their own languages in their different styles of speech.
He knows effortlessly and in their self-nature the 84,000 elements of *bon*,
and he translates them into the 360 styles of speech.
Firm in word and sanctifying power towards all living beings,
he causes joy to arise at the word of truth.
He removes suffering by means of the melody of *Brahmā*,

rgyal baḥi bkaḥ la thams cad ḥdud ||
bskos paḥi las la gaṅ yaṅ ñan ||
drug cuḥi yan lag tshaṅs paḥi gsuṅ ||
ḥgag pa med paḥi gsuṅ mchog ldan ||
thugs ñid gcig las ⟨ma⟩ g·yos kyaṅ ||
ḥgro ba rigs drug sems can la ||
gaṅ ḥdul dgoṅs pa re re ḥchar ||
mkhyen paḥi [90b] ye śes dgoṅs pa yis ||
ḥgro ba gaṅ la gaṅ ḥdul gyi ||
mtshan ñid bye brag so sor ḥbyed ||
sṅon daṅ ma ḥoṅs da lta yi ||
skye gnas rim pa bźin du śes ||
tiṅ ḥdzin yan lag drug cu yi ||
ḥod zer spro bsduḥi ḥdu ḥphro ḥgyed ||
ḥkhrul med mñam ñid thugs daṅ ldan ||
yon tan gcig las ma spros kyaṅ ||
gaṅ dag ḥgro baḥi dmigs lam du ||
dpag bsam ljon śiṅ rgyas pa la ||
lo ḥbras me tog ḥkhruṅs pa bźin ||
so sor ṅo mtshar che ba yi ||
nad la sman daṅ dug la rtsi ||
dbul ḥphoṅs dag la yid bźin nor ||
ḥjigs pa rnams la skyel ma go ||
rmoṅs paḥi tshogs la gaṅ dgos skyabs[a] ||
mtshan daṅ dpe byad legs paḥi rgyan ||
dpe byad brgyad cu ṅes par rdzogs ||
kun gyi mchod gnas bkur baḥi źiṅ ||
bya rgyal gtsug gi nor buḥi tog ||
ḥgro baḥi dpal mgon dpal du gyur ||
legs par ḥbyuṅ baḥi yon tan ldan ||
ḥphrin las gcig las ma mdzad kyaṅ ||
ḥgro ba gaṅ la gaṅ ḥdul gyi ||
ḥdam gyi phur pa lta bu ru ||
gaṅ dag gnas la gar bskor bde ||
źi rgyas dbaṅ drag las bźi rgyun ||
tshe nor dbaṅ thaṅ dpal skyed sogs ||
bar chod bgegs ḥdul g·yul las rgyal ||
snaṅ srid ḥkhor lo thabs kyis bsgyur ||
gdul bya źiṅ khams bsam mthaḥ yas ||
stoṅ gsum stoṅ gi ḥjig rten gyi ||
mi mjed źiṅ khams dbu ma ru ||

[a] skab

and he subdues all things to the word of the Buddhas.
They listen, whoever they are, to their directed work.
He possesses the supreme unhindered Speech with the 60 divisions of *Brahmā* sound.
Although unmoved from a single state of thought, whatever thought might convert them is produced for the living beings of the Six Spheres of existence.
With the purposeful knowledge of one who knows
he explains in detail the different characterized notions for converting whatever kind of being it may be.
He knows the order of the places of rebirth for past, present and future.
He sends forth and regathers the rays of light of the 60 divisions of contemplative thought in a process of contraction and expansion.
He possesses the Mind of Sameness free of all illusion.
Although unmoved from a single state of good quality,
in the sight of various living beings
leaves and fruits and flowers seem to be produced on the spread tree of paradise.
There are wonderful things for each case,
medicine for illness and potion for poison,
a wish-granting gem for those in want
and an escort for those who are frightened, (all) understood (as suits the case).
To the foolish crowds he is whatever protector they need.
He is adorned with the major and minor marks (of a buddha),
with all the eighty minor marks quite perfect.
He is a centre of worship for all and the object of their homage.
Like the crest gem of the king of birds,
he is the splendour of living beings, their splendid protector.
He possesses all those qualities which come out well.
Although he performs just a single act,
he converts living beings whoever they are and wherever they are,
leaning easily towards them wherever they are, like a post in the mud.
The Four Actions of pacifying, prospering, empowerment, destroying, and the 'Flow' (as fifth),
long life, wealth, good fortune, prosperity and so on,
quelling hindrances and demons, victory in battle,
acting like a world-conqueror,
the fields for acts of conversion surpass all thought.
In the central country of our suffering world, in this universe of 1,000 times 3,000 worlds

rgyal po lta bur sku ḥkhruṅs śiṅ ||
btsun mo sras daṅ ḥkhor du bcas ||
mdzad pa bcu gñis bkod pa yi ||
ḥgro ba ḥdren paḥi dpal du gyur ||
ma brtsal lhun grub ḥphrin las ldan ||
tha ma ḥbras buḥi ḥgrub tshul lo ||

de ltar bla maḥi theg paḥi bon ||
thog mar gźi yi gnas tshul daṅ ||
gñis pa gźi las [91a] grol tshul daṅ ||
gsum pa lam gyi bgrod tshul daṅ ||
tha ma ḥbras buḥi ḥgrub[a] tshul de ||
tsad med gtsug phud sprul paḥi gśen ||
ḥgro baḥi dpal du ḥgyur bar mdzod ||

ces gsuṅs so / de la yaṅ tshad med gtsug phud kyis gsol pa /

ston paḥi sgron ma ḥgro baḥi dpal ||
thams cad mkhyen paḥi thugs can lags ||
bla med theg pa yaṅ rtse la ||
gźi daṅ lam daṅ ḥbras bu yi ||
yin tshul goṅ du soṅ nas kyaṅ ||
lta sgom spyod pa ḥbras bu bźi ||
ḥdi yi mtshan ñid ci ltar lags ||
thugs kyi dkyil nas bcud phyuṅs la ||
bdag cag ḥkhor la bśad du gsol ||

ces gsol to / de la ston pas bkaḥ stsal pa /

ñon cig ḥdus paḥi ḥkhor rnams daṅ ||
tshad med[b] gtsug phud gus par ñon ||
bla med theg pa yaṅ rtse la ||
lta ba sgom pa spyod pa gsum ||
bla med don gyi ḥbras bu yi ||
thog mar lta ba bstan pa ni ||
kun gźi skye med bon gyi dbyiṅs ||
rig pa ḥgag med ye śes sku ||
gñis su med pa ñag gcig daṅ ||
bla med theg pa chen poḥi don ||
blta[c] rgyu lta byed mthaḥ daṅ bral ||
bltas pas mthoṅ med bon gyi dbyiṅs ||
ma bltas raṅ gsal sems kyi ṅaṅ ||

[a] grub [b] ye gśen [c] lta

he is born as a king with wife and son and entourage,
and performing the twelve great acts,
he is the glory of those who guide living beings.
So he possesses action which is effortlessly self-produced.
Such is the last item on how to gain the Result.

Thus in the case of the *bon* of the Supreme Vehicle,
first there is the nature of the Basis,
secondly how 'release' comes from this Basis,
thirdly how one should advance along the Way,
and lastly how one should gain the Result.
Tshad-med gTsug-phud, Shen who manifest yourself in various ways,
act as the splendour of living beings!

So the Teacher spoke, and *Tshad-med gTsug-phud* said again:

O Light of Teachers, Splendour of living beings,
whose mind knows all things!
Concerning this top vehicle, the Supreme One,
the nature of the Basis, the Way and the Result has been dealt with above,
but what are the characteristics of the (other) four,
Insight, Contemplation, Practice and Result?
Bring forth the essence (of their meaning) from the centre of your thought,
and tell us, we beg.

So he asked, and the Teacher replied:

Listen, O you who are gathered here.
Tshad-med gTsug-phud, listen with respect!
Concerning Insight, Contemplation, Practice and the Result of supreme achievement
in this top vehicle, the Supreme One,
first I shall explain Insight.
This sphere of *bon*, the unborn universal basis,
is unimpeded knowing and the very form of knowledge,
the single thing which possesses no duality,
the 'substance' of the great Supreme Vehicle.
It is free from the extreme notions of viewed and viewer.
It is the sphere of *bon* where nothing is seen by looking.
It is the unviewed state of mind in its own clarity.

gñis su med pa ñag gcig yin ||
bla med theg pa chen poḥi don ||
skye bar ḥdzin pas[a] grub pa med ||
ye nas bon ñid stoṅ paḥi kloṅ ||
ḥgag par ḥdzin pas[a] chad pa med ||
ye nas raṅ ḥbyuṅ ye śes mkhaḥ ||
skye ḥgag gñis med sems kyi ṅaṅ ||
gñis su med pa ñag gcig dbyiṅs ||
bla med theg pa chen poḥi don ||
yod par ḥdzin pas[a] grub pa med ||
ye nas dmigs med bon gyi sku ||
med par ḥdzin pas[a] chad[b] pa med ||
ye [91b] nas loṅs spyod rdzogs paḥi źiṅ ||
yod med gñis med[c] sems kyi ṅaṅ ||
gñis su med pa ñag gcig dbyiṅs ||
bla med theg pa chen poḥi don ||
rtag par ḥdzin pas[a] grub pa med ||
ye nas mi gnas mya ṅan ḥdas ||
chad par ḥdzin pas[a] phyal ba med ||
ye nas sna tshogs cir yaṅ sprul ||
rtag chad gñis med sems kyi ṅaṅ ||
gñis su med pa ñag gcig dbyiṅs ||
bla med theg pa chen poḥi don ||
snaṅ bar ḥdzin pas[a] dṅos po med ||
ye nas bon ñid stoṅ paḥi kloṅ ||
stoṅ par ḥdzin pas ṅo bo med ||
ye nas rol pa ḥgag med ṅaṅ ||
snaṅ stoṅ gñis kyaṅ sems kyi ṅaṅ ||
gñis su med pa ñag gcig dbyiṅs ||
bla med theg pa chen poḥi don ||
yod med rtag chad snaṅ stoṅ ṅaṅ ||
skye ḥgag mu bźiḥi mthaḥ daṅ bral ||
mthaḥ bral chen poḥi lta ba la ||
snaṅ srid ḥkhor ba mya ṅan ḥdas ||
bskal srid chags gnas ḥjig stoṅ daṅ ||
bde sdug legs ñes ḥbyuṅ[d] tshor daṅ ||
re dogs ḥdzin pa yod ma yin ||
dper na nam mkhaḥi kloṅ yaṅs su
me chu sa rluṅ ḥbyuṅ ba bźi ||
chags daṅ gnas daṅ ḥjig stoṅ daṅ ||

[a] paḥi [b] khyab [c] kyaṅ [d] byuṅ

It is the single thing which possesses no duality,
the 'substance' of the great Supreme Vehicle.
There is no realization of it by grasping at what comes into existence.
It is the sphere of the primeval empty absolute.
There is no denying it by grasping at what comes to an end.
It is the primeval self-produced 'sky' of knowledge.
It is the state of mind where nothing is born and nothing impedes.
It is the sphere of the non-dual single one.
It is the 'substance' of the great Supreme Vehicle.
There is no realization of it by grasping at existence.
It is the primeval unenvisaged form of *bon.*
There is no denying of it by grasping at non-existence.
It is the primeval realm of perfect enjoyment.
It is the state of mind where nothing exists and nothing does not exist.
It is the sphere of the non-dual single one.
It is the 'substance' of the great Supreme Vehicle.
There is no realization of it by grasping at eternity.
It is the primeval non-abiding 'passage from sorrow' (*nirvāṇa*).
There is no denial of it by grasping at nihilism.
Primevally a whole variety springs forth from it somehow.
It is the state of mind where there is neither eternity nor nihilism.
It is the sphere of the non-dual single one.
It is the 'substance' of the great Supreme Vehicle.
There is no real substance by grasping at appearances.
It is the sphere of the primeval empty absolute.
There is no non-entity by grasping at emptiness.
It is the state of primeval unimpeded 'play'.
It is the state of mind where neither appearance nor emptiness exists.
It is the sphere of the non-dual single one.
It is the 'substance' of the great Supreme Vehicle.
It is free of the extreme notions of existence and non-existence, of eternity and nihilism, of appearances and emptiness, of being born and being stopped, free of these four extreme pairs.
In this great insight free of all extremes phenomenal existence has passed beyond sorrow.[79]
There is no origination, continuing, dissolution, and emptiness of ages and existences,
no happiness and unhappiness, no sense of the arising of good and evil,
no seizing upon hopes and fears.
For example in the wide expanse of the sky
the four elements, fire, water, earth and air
originate, continue, dissolve and become void,

nam mkhaḥi naṅ du ḥbyuṅ[a] mi tshor ||
de bźin sems ñid kloṅ yaṅs su ||
sems ḥbyuṅ mtshan maḥi cho ḥphrul rnams ||
sems ñid naṅ du ḥbyuṅ[a] mi tshor ||
snaṅ srid sems kyi yo laṅ la ||
spaṅ daṅ blaṅ baḥi rgyu ma mchis ||
ḥkhor ḥdas bon ñid rol pa la ||
bzaṅ ṅan legs ñes gźal mi dpog ||
lha bdud sems kyi cho ḥphrul la ||
phan daṅ gnod[b] paḥi mthaḥ ma grub ||
dper na mkhaḥ la khyuṅ gśegs na ||
srid gsum spyi rgya rlabs kyis gcod ||
sder chags thams cad zil gyis gnon ||
de bźin [92a] mkhaḥ la ñi śar na ||
ḥod gźan ma lus zil gyis gnon ||
ma rig mun paḥi gliṅ khrod gsal ||
de ltar theg pa chen poḥi don ||
rtog med lta baḥi rgyas thebs na ||
rtog paḥi tshogs rnams zil gyis gnon ||
theg pa ḥog ma bag la źa ||
thams cad kun yin gaṅ yaṅ min ||
mu bźi mthaḥ bral dbus ma grub ||
khyab bdal bon ñid spros mthaḥ bral ||
ye nas ye saṅs rgyas paḥi ṅaṅ ||
gdod nas ma bcos khyab bdal ñid ||
theg chen don gyi lta ba yin ||

gñis pa sgom pa bstan pa ni ||
bla med theg pa chen poḥi don ||
byaṅ chub sems ñid rin po che ||
ka dag lhun grub ḥdus ma byas ||
ye nas ma bcos rtsol bral la ||
bsgom bya sgom byed mthaḥ daṅ bral ||
bsgom rgyu byuṅ na bon ñid bcos ||
sgom mkhan byuṅ na sems ñid bslad ||
ma g·yos ma bcos ma bslad par ||
so ma gñug[c] ma dbu maḥi lam ||
bde ba chen po bon ñid ṅaṅ ||
ṅaṅ la ṅaṅ gis ma bcos par ||
ṅaṅ la ṅaṅ du gnas pa na ||
sgom paḥi rgyal po de ka yin ||

[a] byuṅ [b] bden [c] ñug

but within the sky itself there is no sense of their emergence.
In the same way in the wide expanse of true mind
(there arise) the characterizable magical forms which emerge from mind,
but within the mind itself there is no sense of their emergence.
In phenomenal existence which is the tremulation of mind
there is no cause for avoiding or accepting anything.
In physical and metaphysical states which are the 'play' of true *bon*
there is no measuring of good and bad, virtue and evil.
As regards gods and demons, which are the magical forms of mind,
the extremes of benefit and of harm do not exist.
For example when the *Khyuṅ* appears in the sky,
he cuts smoothly through the three atmospheric levels
and subdues all creatures who have claws.
In the same way when the sun appears in the sky,
it subdues all other lights
and brightens places of dark ignorance.
Likewise if one seals the 'substance' of this Great Vehicle with the seal of non-discriminating insight,
one quells all the hosts of discriminations
and all the lower vehicles are cowed.
It is everything, and yet there is nothing.
It is free of the four extreme views, and yet it has no central position.
It is the all-pervading *bon* itself with no outward movement and no limits,
the state of primeval buddhahood, primeval unaffected pervasiveness.
Such is the insight of the 'substance' of the Great Vehicle.

Secondly as for the explanation of Contemplation,
the 'substance' of the great Supreme Vehicle
is the precious Thought of Enlightenment itself,
pure, spontaneously produced, uncompounded.
Primevally unaffected and effortless,
it is free from such extremes as an object of contemplation and a contemplating agent.
If there were an object of contemplation, it would be possible to affect the absolute.
If there were a contemplating agent, mind itself would be defiled.
Unmoved, uncontrived and unadulterated,
it is the 'ever-fresh', the natural, the middle way.
It is the great bliss, the state of *bon* itself.
Unaffected in its state by any (other) state,
it abides as such a state in just such a state.
It is the king of contemplation itself.

ḥon kyaṅ tshig gi mtshon bya la ||
byaṅ chub sems ñid rin po che ||
dpe don rtags daṅ gsum du bstan ||
dpe ni nam mkhaḥ lta bu la ||
don ni yoṅs la khyab pa ste ||
rtags ni phyogs ris med par gnas ||
mthaḥ skyon bral baḥi sgom pa yin ||

[f. 93a[6] onwards]

gsum pa spyod pa bstan pa ni ||
bla med theg pa chen poḥi don ||
byaṅ chub sems ñid rin po che ||
ḥkhor ḥdas dbyer med mñam pa ñid ||
spaṅ daṅ blaṅ baḥi mthaḥ ma grub ||
bon ñid ṅaṅ la raṅ ḥbyuṅ sku ||
thig le ñag gcig mṅon rol spyod ||
spyad rgyu spyod mkhan raṅ gi sems ||
spyad kyaṅ raṅ ḥbyuṅ [93b] sems kyi rtsal ||
ma spyad ñag gcig don la gnas ||
de dag spyad paḥi rgyu ma mchis ||
spyod ces bya ba mtshan maḥi tshig ||
ḥon kyaṅ tshig gi mtshon bya la ||
sems ni nam mkhaḥ lta bu la ||
snaṅ ba me chu sa rluṅ grub ||
nam mkhaḥi ṅaṅ du mṅon rol spyod ||
spaṅ blaṅ med paḥi spyod pa yin ||

[f. 94a[2] onwards]

bźi pa ḥbras bu bstan pa ni ||
byaṅ chub sems ñid rin po che ||
bla med theg pa chen poḥi don ||
bdag med lta ba rtog med dbyiṅs ||
dmigs med sgom pa bon ñid ṅaṅ ||
byar med spyod pa raṅ ḥbyuṅ rtsal ||
re dogs med pa ḥbras buḥi mchog ||
gdod nas śes rab pha rol phyin ||
mi skye mi ḥgag bon gyi dbyiṅs ||
mtshan ñid so so ye śes spyod ||
ye nas ye saṅs rgyas pa la ||
bsgrub rgyu sgrub byed mthaḥ daṅ bral ||

But in order to explain it by words,
the precious Thought of Enlightenment
is taught as a set of three, example, substance and sign.
For example, (it is said to be) like the sky.
As substance, it pervades everywhere.
As sign, it abides free of all partiality.
It is contemplation free of the defect of extremes.

Thirdly I shall explain the Practice.
The 'substance' of the great Supreme Vehicle
is the precious Thought of Enlightenment,
that Sameness which does not distinguish physical and metaphysical states.
It is free of the extremes of avoidance and acceptance.
It is self-produced form in the state of the absolute,
the single dot, of which 'practice' is playfulness.
What is practised and the practiser are both self-thought.
Although practised, it is the reflective power of self-produced mind.
Unpractised, it abides as the Single One,
There is no cause for anything practised.
The term 'practice' is a word (referring to) characteristics.
In terms of such verbal reference, thought is like the sky,
where appearances are produced like fire, water, earth and air.
In the self-nature of the sky all practice is playfulness.
It is practice without avoidance or acceptance.

Fourthly I shall explain the Result.
The precious Thought of Enlightenment
is the 'substance' of the great Supreme Vehicle,
the non-discriminating sphere of selfless insight,
the absolute state of non-directed contemplation,
self-produced reflective power acting in non-action,
the supreme achievement free of hopes and fears,
the primeval 'state beyond wisdom' (viz. *Perfection of Wisdom*),
the absolute sphere where nothing is born and nothing stops.
Its characterizing quality is the action of Discriminating Wisdom.
In this primeval buddhahood there is absence of the extreme notions of achievement and achiever.

bsgrub rgyu byuṅ na bon ñid bcos[a] ||
sgrub mkhan byuṅ na sems ñid bslad ||
bcos bslad maṅ na rgyu rkyen ḥbyuṅ ||
byaṅ chub sems ñid rin po che ||
bla med theg pa chen poḥi don ||
rgyu las ma byuṅ rkyen mi ḥjig ||
ye śes rgyu med rkyen bral źiṅ ||
srog med bdud bral g·yuṅ druṅ sku ||
ḥgyur ba med paḥi ḥbras bu ḥchaṅ ||
byaṅ chub sems ñid rin po che ||
bla med theg pa chen poḥi don ||
ḥkhor ba źes kyi spaṅ du med ||
myaṅ ḥdas śes kyi blaṅ du med ||
ḥkhor ḥdas dbyer med mñam pa ñid ||
re dogs med paḥi ḥbras bu ḥchaṅ ||
byaṅ chub sems ñid rin po che ||
bla med theg pa chen poḥi don ||
dug lṅa źes kyi spaṅ du med ||
ye śes śes kyi blaṅ du med ||
skyon yon dbyer med mñam pa ñid ||
du ma ro gcig ḥbras bu ḥchaṅ ||
byaṅ chub sems ñid rin po che ||
bla med theg pa chen poḥi don ||
bdag tu bzuṅ baḥi ṅes pa med ||
gźan du ḥdzin paḥi rtog pa med ||
bdag gźan dbyer [94b] med mñam pa ñid ||
gñis med mñam paḥi ḥbras bu ḥchaṅ ||
byaṅ chub sems ñid rin po che ||
bla med theg pa chen poḥi don ||
gcig tu ḥdzin paḥi grub pa med ||
du ma ḥdzin paḥi dbye ba med ||
ma bcos rtsol bral mñam pa ñid ||
thig le ñag gcig ḥbras bu ḥchaṅ ||
byaṅ chub sems ñid rin po che ||
bla med theg pa chen poḥi don ||
saṅs rgyas thog ma tha ma med ||
gdod nas ye saṅs rgyas paḥi ṅaṅ ||
ṅo bo ḥgyur med bon gyi dbyiṅs ||
sñiṅ po ḥgyur med rig paḥi mkhaḥ ||
ṅaṅ ñid ḥgyur med sems kyi kloṅ ||
ṅaṅ daṅ raṅ bźin ḥdu ḥbral med ||

[a] bslad

If there were anything to be achieved, the absolute would be contrived.
If there were anyone to do the achieving, mind itself would be adulterated.
If there were much contriving and adulterating, causes and conditions would arise.

This precious Thought of Enlightenment,
the 'substance' of the great Supreme Vehicle,
has not sprung from a cause and is not destroyed by conditions.
It is Knowledge without cause and conditions,
the Swastika body which is both lifeless and deathless (free of *Māra*),
and it holds the unchanging Result.

This precious Thought of Enlightenment,
the 'substance' of the great Supreme Vehicle,
has nothing to be avoided under the name of physical states,
has nothing to be accepted under the name of metaphysical states.
It is that Sameness where the physical and the metaphysical are indistinguishable.
and it holds the Result which is free of hopes and fears.
The precious Thought of Enlightenment,
the 'substance' of the great Supreme Vehicle,
has nothing to be avoided under the name of the Five Evils,
has nothing to be accepted under the name of the Five Wisdoms.
It is that Sameness where faults and virtues are indistinguishable,
and it holds the Result of the 'single-flavoured much'.

This precious Thought of Enlightenment,
the 'substance' of the great Supreme Vehicle,
has no authenticity which can be conceived of as a self,
has no discriminating power which can conceive of others.
It is that Sameness where self and others are indistinguishable,
and it holds the Result in the Sameness of non-duality.
This precious Thought of Enlightenment,
the 'substance' of the great Supreme Vehicle,
has no effective form which can be conceived of as a unity,
has no distinctions which can be conceived of as many.
It is that Sameness which is unaffected and effortless,
and it holds the Result which is a single dot.
This precious Thought of Enlightenment,
the 'substance' of the great Supreme Vehicle,
is buddhahood without beginning and end,
the state of primeval buddhahood,
the changeless selfhood, the sphere of *bon*,
the changeless essence, the sky of knowing,
the changeless state, the sphere of thought,
state and nature with no joining and no separation,

ḥkhor daṅ myaṅ ḥdas dbye ma med ||
bde daṅ sdug bsṅal tshor ba med ||
skyon daṅ yon tan blaṅ dor med ||
bdag daṅ gźan du ḥdzin pa med ||
thabs daṅ śes rab ḥgag pa med ||
sñiṅ po ḥgyur med ye śes sku ||
snaṅ ba rin chen gser gyi gliṅ ||
ṅo mtshar yid bźin ḥdod yon nor ||
yon tan dpag bsam ljon paḥi śiṅ ||
ḥphrin las dbaṅ phyug ḥkhor lo sgyur ||
don gñis ḥbras bu bcud kyi gter ||
thogs pa med paḥi ḥbras bu ḥchaṅ ||
bla med theg paḥi don dam mo ||
tshan med gtsug phud sprul paḥi gśen ||
bla med theg pa chen poḥi don ||
lta sgom spyod gsum ḥbras buḥi don ||
sems can ḥgro la sman par mdzod ||
ces gsuṅs so /

indistinguishable as physical or metaphysical,
imperceptible as happiness or misery,
no acceptance and no rejection of virtues and faults,
inconceivable as self or other,
unhindered as Method and Wisdom,
changeless essence, body of knowledge,
whose manifestation is the land of gems and gold,
wondrous gem that grants all wishes,
tree of paradise (laden) with good things,
in action like a universal monarch,
whose twofold effect is a treasury of elixir.
It contains the unimpeded achievement.
It is the absolute truth of the Supreme Vehicle.
Tshad-med gTsug-phud, all-manifesting Shen,
bring to perfection for all beings
the 'substance' of the great Supreme Vehicle,
the 'substance' of Insight, Contemplation, Practice and Result.

Thus he spoke.

NOTES

1. *bslu* for *blu* 'to ransom'.

2. The *ju-thig* or *cu-thig* consists of a long thread and six short ones which are knotted together. An alternative name is *moḥi skud-pa* 'thread of prediction'.

3. Diagram XIX represents a horoscope (*gab-rtse*) as drawn conventionally on a tortoise. The outer circle gives the names of the years in their sixty-year cycle. Next are the twelve animals of the twelve-year cycle. Then the circle of the eight *sPar-kha*, and at the centre the set of the nine *sMe-ba*. See *The Buddhism of Tibet, or Lamaism*, London, 1895, Waddell, L. A., pp. 456 ff.

4. The meaning of *ju-źag* remains unknown to us.

5. 'Harrying' is merely a conventional translation. *thun* properly refers to various small items which are believed to be unpleasant to demons. Thus one harries them by hurling these items at them. T. N. lists twelve: *mkhar-sgon* (small white stones of some kind), *yuṅs-dkar* (white mustard), *lgaṅ-śag* (split pods), *ske-tshe* (black mustard), *śaṅ-tshe* (a plant of some kind which from T. N.'s description might be wild rhubarb), *zi-ra* (caraway), *mtshe* (a plant of some kind), *btso* (a *bonpo* bomb—in the story of *Lig-mi-rgya* as told in the *rnam-thar* section of the *Źaṅ-źuṅ sñen-rgyud* such 'bombs' are made of gold and worked upon by spells), *me* (fire), *chu* (water), *mdaḥ* (arrow), and *dug* (poison).

Here *thun* may be a manuscript error for (*b*)*snun*. Later on (page 34^{33}) this rite is referred to as the *bsnun paḥi gto* or 'stinging rite'. The two terms also appear together on p. 110^{17}: *thun daṅ sna tshogs mtshin chas bsnun* 'Sting them with *thun* and various other weapons'.

6. T. N. suggests we read *gzo* for *gzod*, which would improve the meaning: 'Where no one is grateful continue to act kindly.'

7. The four lower ways of *bon* are known as the 'Bon of Cause', because if practised properly, i.e. with the 'Thought of Enlightenment' as the primary intent, they will result in the higher religious progress as envisaged in the five higher ways. These higher ways are referred to as the 'Bon of Effect'.

8. Tenzin Namdak, supported by Samten Gyaltsen Karmay, understands *sgrub-gśen-dbal-bon* as a single term referring to the officiating priest, interpretable presumably as 'the *Bon* (in its ancient meaning of priest who invokes) of the *dBal* divinities (a class of "warrior-gods") who officiates (*sgrub*) as sacrificial priest (g*Śen*)'. I have not seen this long title elsewhere, and I would have preferred to have translated this line as: 'the officiating priest (*sgrub gŚen*) makes a recitation (*bkrol*) with the "exposition" (*smraṅ*) of the *bon* (traditional chant) pertaining to the *dBal* divinities.'

9. *smraṅ*, quoted from Csomo de Körös in Jäschke's *Tibetan–English Dictionary*, p. 429, is an interesting term. It is clearly connected with *smra-ba* 'to speak'. It seems to occur as a *bon* technical term referring to the 'exposition of the archetype'. Such an exposition of how a certain god first established the rite and the circumstances of the establishment guarantee the efficacy of the rite. (Such an idea is a well-known religious phenomenon. The rules of the Buddhist *Vinaya* are regularly guaranteed by the same method, viz. a story recounting how the Buddha came first to make the rule. Similarly in Christian practice the consecration of the host and the wine is properly effected by an 'exposition of the archetype' by the officiating priest. He tells the story and repeats the words of Christ.)

See also references to *dpe-srol* 'archetype' in the glossary.

10. This term is regularly spelt *sruṅs-rta* in the manuscript, and I have simply deferred to T. N. in emending it regularly to *kluṅ-rta*, which is certainly the regular *bon* spelling for this term. The effigy is well known from Tibetan prayer-flags, where it is represented by a horse carrying a wish-granting gem. See Waddell, p. 411 ff. The more usual spelling is *rluṅ-rta*, translatable as 'wind horse'. As Waddell has pointed out, the term is of Chinese origin and the Tibetan spellings *kluṅ* or *rluṅ* are really phonetic representations of Chinese 龍 (lung) 'dragon'.

For range of meaning see the Glossary: *kluṅ-rta*.

11. *mdos* seems only to be known in the specialized meaning of a 'thread cross'. (Concerning these see R. de Nebesky-Wojkowitz, *Oracles and Demons of Tibet*, The Hague, 1956, pp. 369 ff.) It also occurs as *mdos-cha* which T. N. glosses as *gto la gdos paḥi chas* 'things necessary for the rite'.

The thread-cross is here referred to as *nam-mkhaḥ*. Later on (p. 77 onwards) *mdos* refers to a form of ransom, and I have there translated it as 'quittance'.

The various items listed here, the sky symbol, tree symbol, etc., are illustrated in the Glossary.

12. The four portals of the 'Black Waters', 'White Waters', '*ḥPhan-yul*', and 'Master Sage' were discussed in the Introduction (pp. 16 ff.). The whole of this section, 'The Way of the Shen of the Visual World', represents the portal of the 'Black Waters'. We are told now that there are four types of practice involved in this section, and these four types are here named after the four portals. This is unsatisfactory and confusing. T. N. can give no explanation for this and no explanation is provided within the text. It seems likely that the compiler of this chapter has simply confused the terminology, and since there are four types he has erroneously applied the names of the four portals to them. We have added numerals in the text to clarify its various parts:

(1) 'Black Waters', the portal of exorcism: pp. 43–69
- A. The great exposition of existence pp. 43–51
- B. The *Thug-khar* Furies (*gñan*) pp. 51–57
- C. The hero-gathering of the Genies (*sgra-bla*) pp. 57–65
  - (i) Genie Furies, pp. 59–61
  - (ii) Wer-ma Lords, pp. 61–63
  - (iii) *Caṅ-seṅ* Furies, p. 63
  - (iv) *Śug-mgon* Furies, pp. 63–65
- D. The stream of existence pp. 65–69

(2) 'White Waters', the portal of demons and vampires pp. 69–77

(3) '*ḥPhan-yul*', the portal of ransom pp. 77–87

(4) 'Master Sage', the portal of fates and furies pp. 89–97

This whole section, 'The Way of the Shen of the Visual World', is concerned with propitiating or overpowering the 'gods and demons' of this world. A large number of kinds of indigenous Tibetan divinities are mentioned, especially in (C), and it is not always possible to distinguish between them. Nor does the compiler of this chapter always do so. I have regularly translated *gñan* as 'Fury' and *sgra-bla* (= *dgra-lha*) as 'Genie'.

13. *ba-gar* remains uncertain. It may represent Skr. *bhaga* (as on p. 238[16]) with Tibetan locative ending *-r*.

14. *byur* and *mi-la* are different kinds of sprites which cause harm. *byur* occurs in the dictionaries with the meaning of 'misfortune'.

15. The name of this unidentified bird also occurs in a list of bird names in *gZi-brjid*, vol. *kha*, 41b[6]. Is it meant to be the phoenix?

16. 'Black Waters' here refers properly to the whole 'Way of the Shen of the Visual World', where the use of 'exposition' (*smraṅ*—see n. 9) is typical. The 'White Waters', of which spells are typical, refers to Ways III, VII, and VIII.

17. *Thug-khar* is variously spelt. This and *thugs-dkar* are the most regular spellings.

18. An unknown term.

19. This term *bya-rdaṅ* (lit. 'bird-rack') is a curious term. It refers here and at p. 64[16] to an article of ritual. T. N. suggests that it is a kind of summit-cairn sacred to this divinity 'Great Runner', who is otherwise unknown to him (see Fig. XVIII). Nevertheless the reference to the 'Thirteen Birds of *Bon*' in the same context on p. 64 encourages me to keep to the literal translation. Elsewhere at 58[1] and 64[5] the actual divinity is named 'Bird-Rack'.

There may be a connexion between the second part of this term (*rdaṅ*) with the term 'mendang' which is of uncertain literary spelling and refers to prayer-walls built of stones on which the OṂ MA ṆI PAD ME HŪṂ formula is carved. It should probably be spelt *maṇ-rdaṅ*.

20. In *bon* literature this term is regularly spelt *sgra-bla* and this could be an earlier spelling than the now more familiar *dgra-lha* which may be only an attempt at giving sense to an unknown name. (In this respect compare *rluṅ-rta* in n. 10, above.) This term is certainly pronounced 'd^{r}apla' and this would favour the *bon* spelling. Also the meaning of *dgra-lha* 'enemy god', for a divinity whose protection one expects, seems rather unsatisfactory. There is a chapter on this class of divinities in Nebesky-Wojkowitz, *Gods and Demons*, pp. 318 ff.

21. There is a brief reference to the *lam-lha* 'Road God' group of these *Caṅ-seṅ* in ibid., p. 334. T. N. knows the term but nothing else about them.

22. The thirteen birds of *bon*, as listed in vol. *kha*, 47b[1] onwards, are: *khu-byug* (cuckoo), *lco-ga* (lark), *khruṅ-khruṅ* (crane), *the-ba* (?), *khug-ta* (swallow), *pha-waṅ* (bat), *khyim-bya* (house-martin), *bya-waṅ* (? bat or crow), *goṅ-mo* (partridge), *duṅ-khra* (?), *phu-shud* (hoopoe), *bye-ma-brel* (flying squirrel or bat), *ne-tso* (parrot).

23. Here 'Black Waters' explicitly refers to the whole 'Way of the Shen of the Visual World' and the confusion is self-confessed. See n. 12 above.

24. Again the term refers to the whole of Way II.

25. See Fig. XX.

26. Literally 'the afflictions of grasped (object) and grasper (subject)'. This is familiar Buddhist terminology.

27. According to T. N. the 'others' are the possessing demons who do not know what harm they are doing.

28. Concerning *mdos* translated as 'quittance' see note 11 above.

29. See Fig. XXI.

30. Only six are listed.

31. 'Calling down slaughter' (*gsad-gcad-dbab*) upon foes and demons is a well-known Tibetan (Buddhist and *Bon*) ritual. It is elsewhere referred to as the 'Circle-of-Life Practice' (pp. 107 and 111) and the *Liṅga* Practice (p. 109), where the 'Circle of Life' and the *liṅga* both refer to the magic circular design or the quasi-human effigy which represents the foe during the rite. See the important article by R. A. Stein, 'Le *liṅga* des dances masquées lamaiques et la théorie des âmes' in the *Liebenthal Festschrift*, *Sino-Indian Studies*, Santiniketan, 1957, vol. v, nos. 3–4.

'Enforced release' translated the verb *sgrol-ba* / *bsgral*. To 'release' the consciousness from the body is a tantric euphemism for 'slaying by ritual'.

32. The 'Family Defenders' are according to Tenzin Namdak the animals of the four quarters, viz. Tiger, Tortoise, Red Bird (? for Phoenix), and Dragon. For more on this subject see R. A. Stein, *Recherches sur l'epopée et le barde au Tibet*, Paris, 1959, p. 456, and *Les tribus anciennes des marches sino-tibétaines*, Paris, 1961, p. 7. The regular *Bon* set of five animals, developed later under Buddhist influence, comprises lion, elephant, horse, dragon, and *khyuṅ* (*garuḍa*), as listed on p. 207.

The 'Family Signs' are Swastika (east), Wheel (north), Lotus (west), Gem (south), and the sign of good fortune known as *dPal-dbye* or *dPal-beḥu*. For the actual design of the last item see Jäschke's dictionary, p. 326.

The 'guardian divinities' referred to below on page 103 are the Four Kings of the Quarters according to *Bon* terminology.

33. The 'Five Evils Self-Released' are the 'Five Wisdoms' as represented by the 'Five Buddhas'. For all these symbolic equations, see pp. 173-81 and the references given in note 48. The thrones are symbolized by the set of five animals, listed in n. 32 and on p. 207. They are the supports of the Five Buddhas, and thus represent the power which removes the Five Evils.

34. One supposedly raises the position of the slain (human) victim by transferring his consciousness to a higher condition of rebirth. This is a Buddhist tantric notion.

35. This term *źiṅ chen g·yaṅ gźi*, lit. 'the (antelope) skin of the great field' is a tantric euphemism for a human skin.

36. We may attempt to distinguish *bla* (spirit), *yid* (thought), and *sems* (mind). The *bla* (spirit) is that part of consciousness that may be said to wander, moving by power of the imagination and the memory. In T. N.'s words: 'My *bla* goes here and there, staying perhaps for a while at my old monastery of *sMan-ri*, brooding unhappily and then returning.' The *bla* can easily be seized by demons, and then a man may appear deranged. The *yid* (thought) represents the active powers of consciousness, and interpretation of this term is affected by its regular use to translate Sanskrit *manas*. *Sems* is the mind itself (corresponding to Sanskrit *citta*) and is in effect equated with consciousness itself. Hence the Tibetans translated Sanskrit *sattva* by *sems-can* (lit. 'mind-possessor') meaning 'sentient being' as applied to men, animals, birds, fishes, insects, etc.

37. The terms god and demon are used in the absolute sense of the Force of Divine Good and the Force of Devilish Evil which seem to control existence. This idea continues to exist in Tibetan religion (whether *Bon* or Buddhist) side by side with the Indian notion of Good and Evil resulting from one's own past acts. In the higher ways of *Bon* this is not forgotten. For example, in the VIIIth Way (p. 199): 'Extent of royal power and spread of dominion, although some half (of such effects) is ordained by previous actions, the other half comes from the powerful lords of the soil' (*sa gźi mṅaḥ dbaṅ* = *sa bdag*).

38. The meaning of *smraṅ* 'exposition' emerges very clearly from the context of this passage. See n. 9 above.

39. We can make no good sense of this line. The first part of it is certainly corrupt. The amendment gives a possible solution.

40. *ḥdur* appearing in the dictionaries as *dur* (as in the well-known term for cemetery, *dur-khrod*) might seem to mean 'death rites'. *Dur-bon* certainly refers to religious traditions concerned with death and the departed. (The term is in S. C. D.'s dictionary, p. 631.) In our text *ḥdur* clearly appears as a verb (at p. 118[29]) and I have translated it as 'consecrate (for burial purposes)'. The same idea occurs in l. 34 (same page) and so *ḥdur* is effectively glossed by *cho gas bcos* 'prepare by means of ceremony'. *ḥdur ba* occurs again in a seemingly verbal form at p. 120[21], but the context permits me to translate it nominally.

41. This is the *byaṅ-bu*, the 'name-card' essential for these ceremonies. See my *Buddhist Himālaya*, Cassirer, Oxford, 1957, pp. 262 ff., where the corresponding *rñiṅ-ma* ceremony is described.

42. *ḥbum* 'one hundred thousand' is used here as often to refer to the 'Perfection of Wisdom' literature in general, of which the version in 100,000 (meaning simply a vast number of) verses is the most renowned. The *bon* version entitled *bon ñid sñiṅ po bdal baḥi ḥbum* is a plagiarism of the Tibetan translation of the *Śatasāhasrikaprajñāpāramitā*.

The set of four quoted here does not quite correspond with the 'Four Portals' as explained in the Introduction (pp. 16–19). There *sūtras* including 'Perfection of Wisdom' literature are all classed as *ḥphan yul*. 'Spells' as listed here cover both *chab nag* and *chab dkar*. 'Wise lore' corresponds to *dpon gsas*.

43. *gZi-brjid* itself, like *gZer-mig*, is classed by *bonpos* as a *sūtra*. Thus the compiler, who is concerned here with the special virtues of the Vth Vehicle, which might certainly claim to be based on the teaching of the *sūtras* (understood in a normal Buddhist sense), merely attempts to claim the pre-eminence of the *sūtras*.

44. According to T. N. these four kinds of 'thought-raising towards enlightenment' refer to one's resolution to help others as their (i) shepherd, (ii) boatman, (iii) guide, and (iv) king.

45. *Tsha-tsha* are miniature reliquaries or *stūpas*, normally made of baked clay. See G. Tucci, *Indo-Tibetica*, Rome, 1932. vol. i, pp. 53 ff.

46. The term *g·yuṅ-druṅ sems-dpaḥ* 'Swastika Being' is the expression coined by the *bonpos* to correspond to *byaṅ-chub sems-dpaḥ* 'Enlightenment Being' (viz. *bodhisattva*).

47. Receiving and bestowing refer here to the receiving and bestowing of the vows of monkhood. The three 'officials' present on such an occasion are the officiating 'abbot', the novice's teacher, and the witness. Compare similar references in my *Four Lamas of Dolpo*, pp. 87, 133.

48. The three basic evils (or poisons) are Wrath, Ignorance (or mental torpor), and Desire. With the addition of Pride and Envy they are increased to a set of five. The various equations that occur in this text between the Evils, the Buddha-Bodies, the Five Components of Personality, the Five Wisdoms, etc., accord with normal tantric theory. See my *Hevajra-Tantra*, vol. i, pp. 28 ff. and pp. 127 and 129. See also my *Buddhist Himālaya*, pp. 65 ff.

49. I have guessed the meaning of 'tiger' for *gcan-chen*. As this word appears elsewhere (p. 204[13]), I have not amended it to the more usual *gcan-gzan*.

50. Eleven, not eight, are listed. Some names are repeated from the earlier set of five, but without epithets.

51. *bya-waṅ* is presumably an alternative form of *pha-waṅ*, although it is given various other meanings in the dictionaries as well as 'bat'. *Bya-waṅ*, *pha-waṅ*, *bya-ma-byel-bu* are listed among the thirteen birds of *bon*, so 'bat' would seem to occur three times. See n. 22.

52. As well as the highly valued cross-breed, the *mdzo*, which is produced by an ox and a *ḥbri* (female of the yak), two inferior breeds, *ḥgar* and *rtol*, are listed, both offspring of the *mdzo-mo* (the female *mdzo*).

53. We have cut just over one whole folio from the extract. The text continues with a list of evils which 'arise with *chang* as their cause'.

54. This is the only mention of honey in the present context. To eat it is evil, because getting it involved (and still involves in Tibet) killing the bees.

55. We can make no sense of *ḥtsho ba byad len*.

56. *u-dug* here referred to a sound, refers to drunkenness elsewhere (p. 146[15]).

57. To obtain this meaning I have taken *rbad dan* as a corruption of *rbad-rbol*. But it is possible that *rbad* stands for another animal.

58. Each Way (Vehicle) tends to praise itself at the expense of its predecessors. The way of *transformation* is so called because it claims to transmute good and evil and all other opposites into a single essence in accordance with regular tantric theory. The previous Way of the Great Ascetics manifestly corresponds to the Buddhist Way of the *śrāvakas* 'simple disciples', referred to as the 'Lesser Way' from the point of view of the 'Great Vehicle' (*Mahāyāna*), because their practice was said to be self-centred. Our *bonpo* writer in this VIIth Way now says that the Vth and VIth Ways do not belong to the 'Great Vehicle', not only because they are self-centred, but because by their teachings of rejecting (evil) and accepting (good) they fail to act in accordance with the tantric theory of the 'identity of opposites'. In the three highest Ways (Vehicles) the *bonpos* reveal themselves quite naïvely as tantric Buddhists in all but name.

59. All these fivefold sets are either modelled upon or taken directly from Buddhist lists. The Five Wisdoms (occurring on p. 179) and the Five Powers (knowledge, generosity, magnanimity, wisdom, and compassion) are totally Buddhist in terminology. The Five Family-Signs are listed in n. 32. The Five Gods are *gSal-ba raṅ-ḥbyuṅ* (east), *dGe-lha gar-phyug* (north), *Bye-brag dṅos-mad* (west), *dGaḥ-ba don-grub* (south) and *Kun-snaṅ khyab-pa* (centre). They correspond to the Five Buddhas of Buddhist terminology (see n. 48 for references). The Five Buddha-Bodies are the 'Phenomenal Body' (*sprul-sku*), 'Perfect Body' (*rdzogs-sku*), 'Body of *Bon*' (*bon-sku*), 'Body of the Absolute' (*ṅo-bo-ñid kyi sku*), and the 'Body of Real Enlightenment' (*mṅon-par byaṅ-chub kyi sku*). It seems scarcely necessary to quote Buddhist equivalents for the last set. Replace *rdzogs* by *loṅs-spyod* (*saṃbhoga*) and *bon* by *chos* (*dharma*), and they are identical.

60. As one progresses through these Ways (Vehicles), all the previous ones become inferior by comparison with the one immediately under discussion. These lines look forward to the IXth Vehicle (referred to as 'the way of Release', *grol-baḥi lam*), where the VIIth Vehicle ultimately leads. From this very highest point of view neither 'Avoidance' nor 'Transformation', viz. all the Vehicles from V to VIII, achieve anything.

61. For the whole theory of 'transformation' and the equation of opposites see the references given in n. 48. The various 'sets' which are transformed are listed here as the Five Evils (Wrath, Mental Torpor, Pride, Desire, and Envy), the 'eight perceptive groups' (see Glossary item *tshogs*), the 'four bodily elements' (*rgyu-bźi-phuṅ-po*), and the 'five sacred items'. These last five, appearing under their secret names on p. 179, are semen, human flesh, dung, uterine blood, and urine. All these sets are Indian Buddhist in origin, even the last, for which see my *Hevajra-Tantra*, vol. i, pp. 99–100. The set of Three Evils given on p. 181 consists of the three basic items, Wrath, Mental Torpor, and Desire, from the larger set of Five.

62. This dual Process is described in detail in the VIIIth Vehicle. It represents the whole theory of 'Two-in-One' as realized in the practice of meditation which seeks to produce existence as a formal mental image (this is the 'Process of Emanation', *utpattikrama*) and then realize its illusory nature as the creation of one's own mind identified as a kind of universal mind (this is the 'Process of Realization', *saṃpannakrama*). See my *Hevajra-Tantra*, vol. i, pp. 22 ff.

63. One of the main difficulties in preparing the present translation arises from the subtle ranges of meaning which the same Tibetan term assumes in the different contexts of different Ways (Vehicles). *bsÑen* and *sGrub* provide very good examples of this, and I refer my readers who know Tibetan to the Glossary without more ado.

These two terms often occur as a compound meaning 'invoke and conjure', referring to the process of recitation of spells and concentrated thought, by which a divinity is induced to manifest himself to his devotee. (The Sanskrit term is *sādhana.*) But *bsÑen* means also 'getting near' in a more general sense. Thus it occurs in another context with the meaning of 'veneration' (see p. 101), and in the present context it refers to the 'means whereby one get near' and for this notion I have used the term 'reliance'. The use of different translations for the same Tibetan word has the most unfortunate effect of destroying the unity of what still remains in Tibetan a single concept despite its wide range of meaning, but there is clearly no solution to the problem, when no one English word will fit the various contexts. The range of meaning of *sGrub*, 'to effect, perform, work upon, conjure', is also very wide, but the connexion between the various English words used is close enough perhaps for us to comprehend them as a single concept.

64. Concerning the 'Four Portals and the One Treasury' see the Introduction, pp. 16–19.

65. Concerning the term 'Spell' (representing Skr. *vidyā*) as a title of the feminine partner, see my *Buddhist Himālaya*, p. 288.

66. For a diagram of the *maṇḍala* as drawn here, see Fig. XVII.

67. The (outer) vessel and the (inner) essence are a simple recurring cliché for the whole of existence. The 'vessel' is the physical support of the world, and the 'elixir' comprises the beings that inhabit it. The *maṇḍala* itself (often with a ritual vase, *bum-pa*, in the centre) is the 'vessel', and the 'gods of knowledge' who symbolize and cleanse all the sets which go to make up the life of living creatures (see n. 61 above) become the elixir.

68. An attempt is made in the IXth Vehicle to explain how they arose. See p. 233.

69. The three basic elements are represented in the text by their 'seed-syllables'. They provide the basis for the *maṇḍala* and schematically they are represented by an outer ring of three colours which encloses the whole circle.

70. The vase (*bum-pa*) represents the 'vessel', viz. the physical world. See n. 67 above.

71. *kloṅ* defies simple translation. It refers at one and the same time to the translucent expanse of space and the purity of the meditator's own mind, which by its very purity ceases to be his own and becomes universal like the expanse of space.

72. Translated literally without any textual emendment, this line might mean: 'no doubt about anything so vast that there has not been room and won't be room', viz. it contains everything. Such an interpretation fits the context well. S. G. K. suggests, however, an improvement, viz. emending to: *śoṅ daṅ mi śoṅ yaṅs daṅ dog pa med* = 'there is no idea of there being room or not being room, of wide extent or of narrowness'. This is certainly a literary improvement.

73. I draw attention to my inconsistency in the translation of *theg-pa* (Skr. *yāna*) as both 'vehicle' and 'way'. I have normally translated it as 'way' (as in the title of the whole work) because this is the only word which suits Tibetan understanding of *theg-pa*. Although this word is cognate with the verb *ḥdebs-pa* 'to support', etc., it is used only as a translation of Skr. *yāna*, and Tibetans, however well educated, cannot conceive of its use in any other context. Now with all its modern connotations the term 'vehicle' has become quite unsuitable, especially when one is working with Tibetans whose English is continually improving so that they argue against the use of a term, with which one might (for want of a more satisfactory one) rest content oneself. Thus Tenzin Namdak insists that 'way' is the only suitable translation for *theg-pa*. Unfortunately 'way' is required as an equivalent for other terms as well (e.g.

lam and *sgo*), and when I need to distinguish *theg-pa* from these I have fallen back upon the word 'vehicle' for *theg-pa*.

74. 'Release' here is used in the sense of the 'self-release' of the fivefold manifestation of buddhahood from the unpredicated 'basis'. From pure 'spontaneity' come Sound, Light, and Rays, which are at the same time the substance of the delusion of ignorance.

grol (Release) and *ḥkhrul* (Delusion) are thus essentially the same. The difference consists in how one views them. This again is basic tantric theory.

75. Delusion is the origin of phenomenal existence, conceived as the *bar-do* state. The consciousness seeking rebirth in the 'Intermediate State' is identified with the universal origin of things.

76. The Text repeats 'wrath' (*źe-sdaṅ*) five times over, whereas it is clear from the whole context that it should occur only once. We are concerned here with the 'Five Evils' increased to six by the addition of 'disquisitive thought' (*rtog-pa*) as typifying the evils of the Six Spheres of Existence. Compare *Buddhist Himālaya*, p. 271, where the equivalent sets are arranged a little differently.

77. The text reads *ris drug* 'six regions' which may be an error for the more usual *rigs drug* 'six classes'.

78. The two terms 'staying' (*gnas-pa*) and 'putting' (*bźag-pa*) have a quasi-technical significance. Other examples may be found under *bźag-pa* in the Glossary. Here *gnas-tshul* means the ways things are in an absolute and ultimate sense; *bźag-tshul* refers to the way the meditator disposes his mind (viz. 'in a state of evenness', *mñam-par bźag-pa*) so that he may rest in things as they ultimately are.

79. The range of translations used for *ḥkhor-ḥdas*, the Tibetan abbreviation of their very long term for *saṃsāra* and *nirvāṇa*, is illustrated by the references in the Glossary. The problem of translation arises because this dual term has changed its meaning so radically throughout the history of Buddhism. According to earlier teachings *nirvāṇa* was itself the ultimate, which a sage might gain by releasing himself from *saṃsāra*. According to the later theories, with which we are almost entirely concerned here, both *saṃsāra* and *nirvāṇa* have to be transcended so that final enlightenment may be realized for what it is. In this later context such a translation as 'physical and metaphysical' would seem to fit very well. This particular passage, however, on p. 247 provides a rare instance in these texts, where *saṃsāra* and *nirvāṇa* may be rendered by the conventional Tibetan translations of 'phenomenal existence' and 'passing from sorrow'.

LIST OF ILLUSTRATIONS BY TENZIN NAMDAK

In this collection of pen-drawings Tenzin Namdak has illustrated the types of clothes and varied equipment that a religious practiser might need throughout the range of the Nine Ways of *Bon*. He has also included some items not mentioned in our texts, but which *bonpos* take for granted as the normal possessions of their high dignitaries and scholars. Please note in this respect Figures VI and VII and my observations on page 12 of the Introduction.

I express my acknowledgements and thanks to Tenzin Namdak for this pleasing and useful addition to all the literary work which we have done together.

D. L. S.

MONK'S CLOTHES AND EQUIPMENT

I. (a) *rmad-gos* (patched cloak)
(b) *gliṅ-snam* (patches)
II. (a) *stod-gos* or *ḥgag-riṅ* (upper garment)
(b) (c) (d) *pad-źva* (lotus-hats—various types)
(e) *stod-gos* or *ḥgag-thuṅ* (upper garment—short)
(f) *śams-ḥjug* or *smad-g·yogs* (under garment)
(g) *dgun-źva* ('winter hat')
(h) *thaṅ-źva* ('summer hat')
III. (a) *smad-śams* or *śams-thab* (cloth for lower part of body)
(b) *pad-lham* (lotus-boots)
(c) *phyam-tse* (long wrap)
(d) *phyar-bu* (short overcoat)
IV. (a) (b) *chu-tshag* (strainer)
(c) (d) (e) *pad-gdan* (lotus-mats—various sizes)
V. (a) *pad-khug* (a book cover for travelling)—front
(b) ditto—back
(c) *gźi-bskur* or *lhuṅ-bzed* (begging bowl)
(d) *mkhar-gsil* (mendicant's staff)
(e) *khrus-bum* (jar for ablutions)
(f) *khab-śubs* (needle-case)
(g) *pad-phor* (lotus-cup)
(h) *skra-gri* (razor)
(j) *ḥphreṅ-ba* (beads)
VI. (a) *gser-theb* (hat worn by high ecclesiastical dignitaries)
(b) *rta-źva* (hat worn when riding)
(c) *gzan-sdom* (metal strap for binding clothes when riding)
(d) *kha-skris* (scarf bound around head and neck when riding)
(e) *gos-stod* or *stod-ḥbog* (rich coat made of brocade silk, otter-skin, etc.)
(f) *rta-ber* (a shawl)

VII. (a) *gos-ber* (special cloak worn by a high dignitary—when seated on a throne)
(b) *gos-ber* (as seen from behind when standing) & *rgyab-dar* (pendant) which is attached separately
(c) *rtsod-źva* ('debating hat')
(d) *ras zom* (cloth boots)
(e) *chab-blug* (wallet made to contain a flask of water. The bottle no longer contains anything, and the embroidered wallet is simply one of the marks of a monk)
(f) *stod-ḥgag* ('waistcoat' made of brocade silk)
(g) *gzan* (cloak as worn every day)

TANTRIC DRESS

VIII. (a) *dbu-rgyan* or *rigs-lṅa* (Five-Buddha crown)
(b) *ske-rgyan* or *mgul-chu* (pendant)
(c) *sñan-cha* (ear-ornaments)
(d) *lag-gdub, phyag-gdub* (bracelets)
(e) *stod-g·yogs* (upper garment)
(f) *smad-śams* (lower garment which is simply wrapped around the body)
(g) *dar-dpyaṅs* (special scarf—worn around the shoulders when performing the rites of *dbaṅ, sbyin-sreg,* etc.)

IX. (a) *stag-źva* ('tiger-hat')
(b) *stag-ber* ('tiger-cloak')
(c) *ḥgyiṅ-thod* (turban)
(d) *bon-źva* (*bon* hat, named *dkar-mo rtse-rgyal*)
(e) *ḥphreṅ-ba* (beads)
(f) *dar-dbyaṅs* (same as VIII g above)
(g) *phur-pa* (dart)
(h) *hom-khuṅ* (the special cavity for the *homa* (*sbyin-sreg*) rite; = *thun-khaṅ* or *e kloṅ ḥbrub-khuṅ*)
(j) *lcags-kyu* (metal hook)
(k) *sta-re* (axe)
(l) *ḥkhor-lo* (wheel)
(m) *ral-gri* (sword)
(n) *spar-śad* (claw—for lifting the *liṅga*)
(o) *lcags-thag* (chain)
(p) *źags-pa* (noose)
(q) *tho-ba* (hammer)
(r) *mduṅ* (spear)
(s) *mdaḥ* (arrow)
(t) *gźu* (bow)
(u) *kha-ṭam* (Skr. *khatvāṅga*—trident)
(v) *thun-rva* (special horn for hurling *thun*—see note 5 to text)
(w) *skam-pa* (tongs) for *liṅga*

MAṆḌALA

X. (a) *gdugs* (parasol)
(b) *ḥkhor-lo* (wheel)
(c) *ri-dvags* (deer)
(d) *g·yuṅ-druṅ ba-dan* (swastika ensign)
(e) *bya-ḥdab* or *khyuṅ-gur* (roof)
(f) *śar-bu* (gutter)

X. (g) *za-ra-tshags* (criss-cross decorations)
(h) *śam-bu* (frill or pelmet)
(j) *ḥphan* (pendants)
(k) *yol-ba* (curtains)
(l) *dkyil-ḥkhor* (*maṇḍala*) drawn here in colours on the top of a table.
On the *maṇḍala*
centre: (m) *bum-pa* (sacrificial vase) resting on a *rkaṅ-gsum* (tripod) against which rests a *tsa-ka-li* (a card with a sacred symbol)
left: (n) *źi-gtor* (sacrificial cake of the tranquil divinities) and in front of this *gtaḥ-chen* (skull-cap) covered with a cloth
right: (o) *khro-gtor* (sacrificial cake of the fierce divinities)
(p) *gźi* (the basis, *viz.* a table)
(q) *mar-me* (butter lamp)
(r) *rgyun-gtor* ('reserved sacrificial cake'). It is difficult to make out on the diagram. It is the small *gtor-ma* standing at the foot of the central *mar-me*
(s) *ka-pa-li* (skr. *kapāla*—skull-cup) containing *sman* (medicament)
(t) *ka-pa-li* containing *rak-ta* (Skr. *rakta*—blood)
(u) a whole row of *yon-chab* (sacrificial water) in bowls
(v) a whole row of *źal-zas* (sacrificial food—in the form of sacrificial cakes)
(w) a whole row of *me-tog* (flowers)
(x) a whole row of *spos* (incense)
(y) *mchod-khrid* (altar)

SACRIFICIAL CAKES

XI. (a) *źi-baḥi gtor-ma* (sacrificial cake for the tranquil divinities—see Fig. X n)
(b) *dbaṅ-gi-gtor-ma* (s. cake used in the rite of 'empowerment')
(c) *drag-poḥi gtor-ma* or *dbal-gtor* (s. cake for fierce divinities)[1]
(d) *tshe-gtor* (s. cake offered in the 'life-consecration' ceremony)[2]
(e) *zlog-gtor* (s. cake for hurling against foes)

RITUAL ITEMS

XII. (a) *dgaṅ-gzar* or *hom-gzar* (sacrificial ladle for holding liquids)
(b) *blug-gzar* or *ḥbyams-gzar* (sacrificial ladle for holding solids)
(c) *gśaṅ-chen* (flat *bonpo* bell—large size)
(d) *gśaṅ-chuṅ* (the same—small size)
(e) *ḍa-ma-ru* (Skr. small drum)
(f) *sbug-chol* (cymbals)
(g) *rṅa* (drum)
(h) *duṅ-chen* (great trumpet—extendable)
(j) *rgya-gliṅ* (shawm)
(k) *duṅ-dkar* (conch—drawn monstrously out of scale)
(l) *mkhar-rṅa* or *rgya-ṅa* (large drum)
(m) *sil-sñan* or *sil-chol* (small cymbals)
(n) *rduṅ-chas* (drum-stick)
(o) *ko-yo* (a pair of trumpets)

[1] Concerning these fierce rites see *Buddhist Himālaya*, pp. 258 ff.
[2] Concerning the rite of 'life consecration' see *Himalayan Pilgrimage*, pp. 141 ff.

HERMIT'S REQUIREMENTS

THRONE (*bźugs-khri*)

VARIOUS ITEMS

MONK'S CLOTHES AND EQUIPMENT

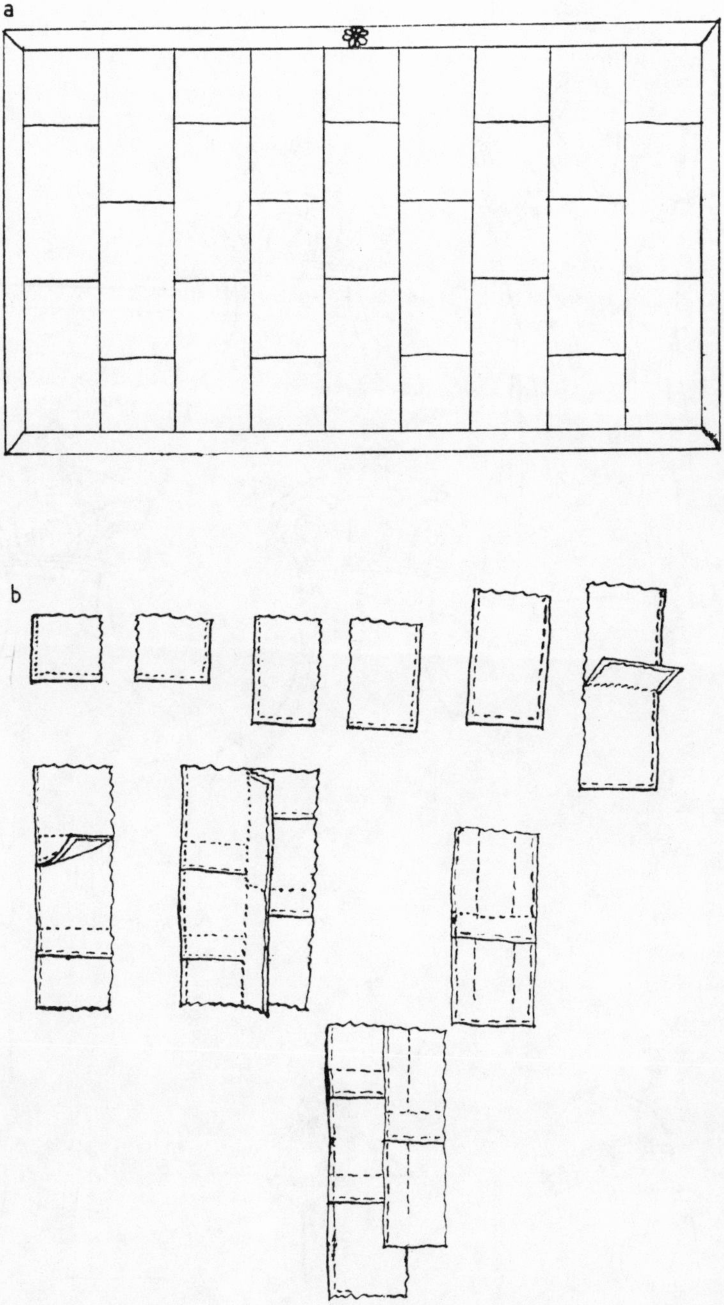

I. (*a*) *rmad-gos* (patched cloak). (*b*) *gliṅ-snam* (patches)

MONK'S CLOTHES AND EQUIPMENT

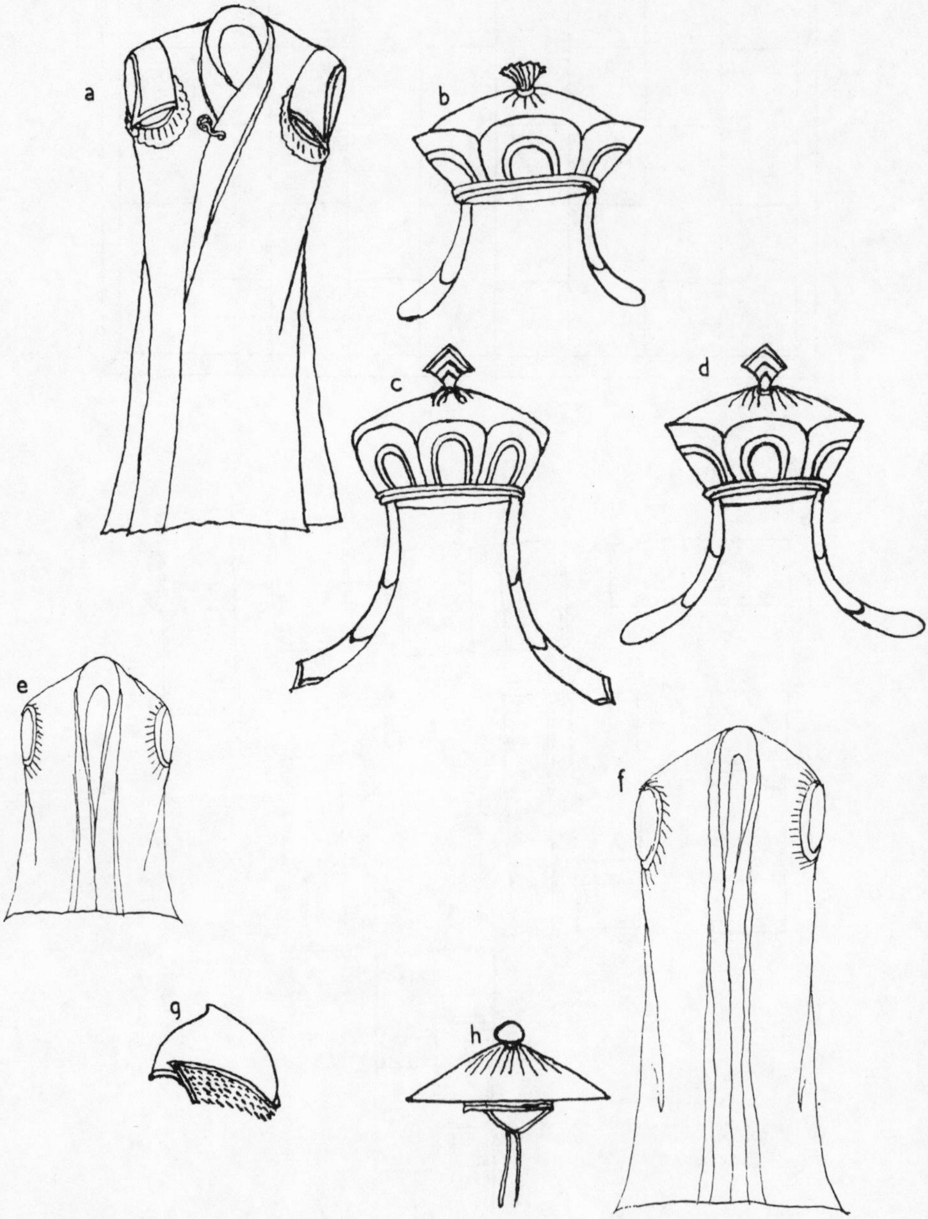

II. (*a*) *stod-gos* or *ḥgag-riṅ* (upper garment). (*b*), (*c*), (*d*) *pad-źva* (lotus-hats—various types). (*e*) *stod-gos* or *ḥgag-thuṅ* (upper garment—short). (*f*) *śams-ḥjug* or *smad-g·yogs* (under garment). (*g*) *dgun-źva* ('winter hat'). (*h*) *thaṅ-źva* ('summer hat')

MONK'S CLOTHES AND EQUIPMENT

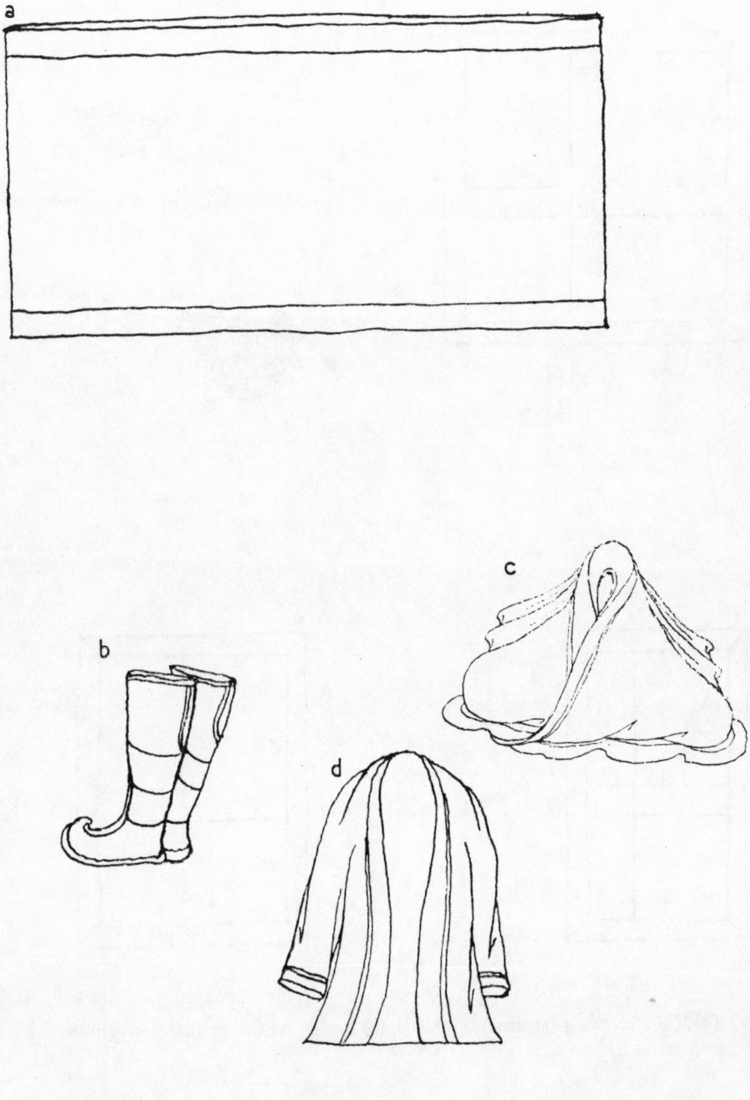

III. (*a*) *smad-śams* or *śams-thab* (cloth for lower part of body). (*b*) *pad-lham* (lotus-boots). (*c*) *phyam-tse* (long wrap). (*d*) *phyar-bu* (short over-coat)

MONK'S CLOTHES AND EQUIPMENT

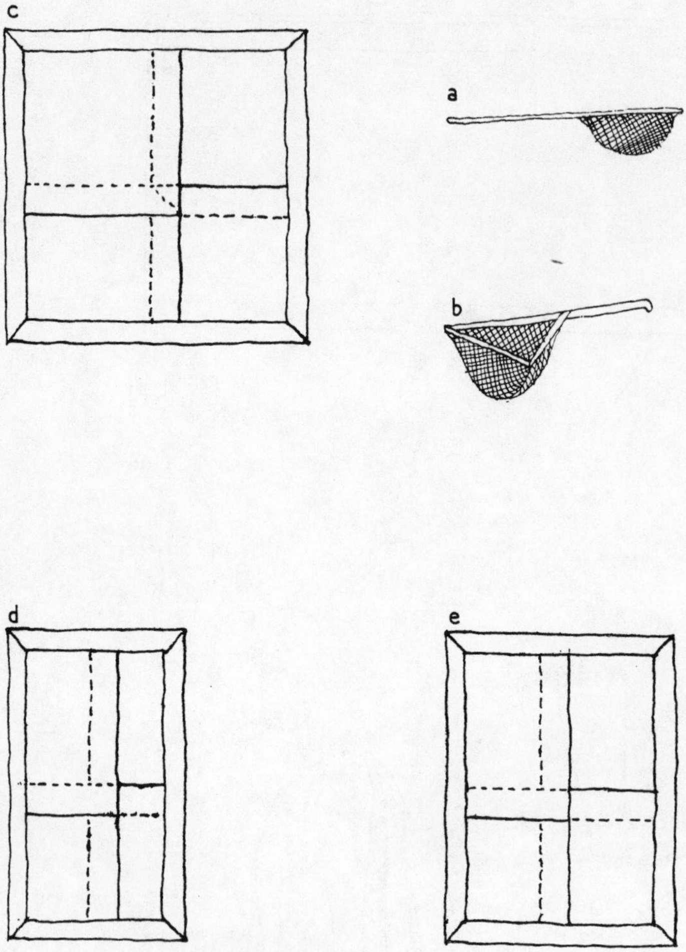

IV. (*a*), (*b*) *chu-tshag* (strainer). (*c*), (*d*), (*e*) *pad-gdan* (lotus-mats—various sizes)

MONK'S CLOTHES AND EQUIPMENT

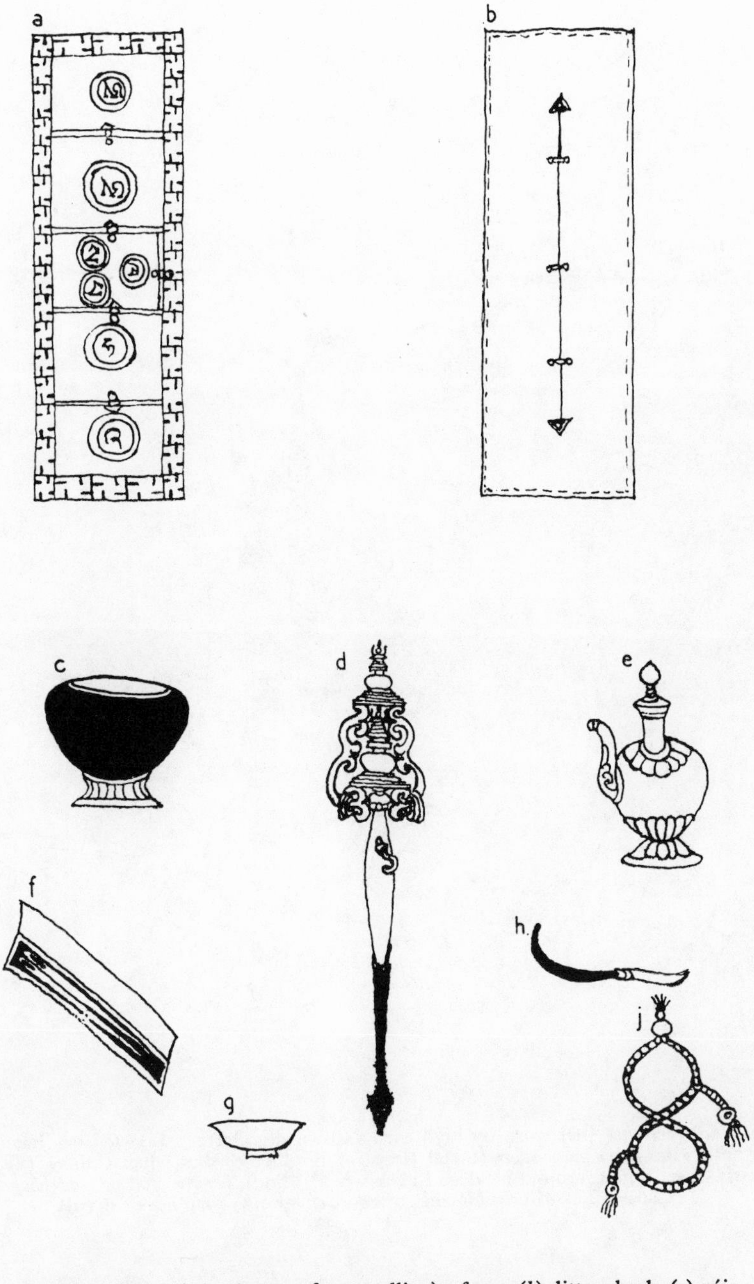

V. (*a*) *pad-khug* (a book cover for travelling)—front. (*b*) ditto—back. (*c*) *gźi-bskur* or *lhuṅ-bzed* (begging bowl). (*d*) *mkhar-gsil* (mendicant's staff). (*e*) *khrus-bum* (jar for ablutions). (*f*) *khab-śubs* (needle-case). (*g*) *pad-phor* (lotus-cup). (*h*) *skra-gri* (razor). (*j*) *ḥphreṅ-ba* (beads)

MONK'S CLOTHES AND EQUIPMENT

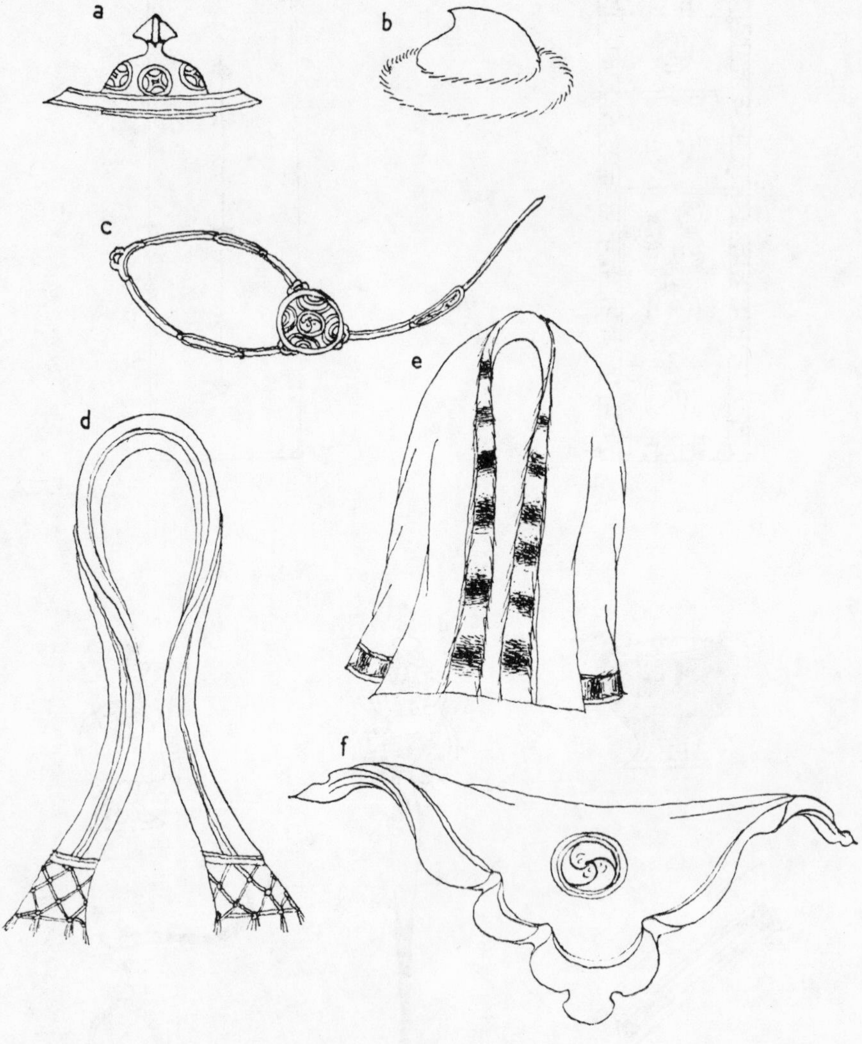

VI. (*a*) *gser-theb* (hat worn by high ecclesiastical dignitaries). (*b*) *rta-źva* (hat worn when riding). (*c*) *gzan-sdom* (metal strap for binding clothes when riding). (*d*) *kha-skris* (scarf bound around head and neck when riding). (*e*) *gos-stod* or *stod-ḥbog* (rich coat made of brocade silk, otter-skin, etc.). (*f*) *rta-ber* (a shawl)

MONK'S CLOTHES AND EQUIPMENT

VII. (*a*) *gos-ber* (special cloak worn by a high dignitary—when seated on a throne). (*b*) *gos-ber* (as seen from behind when standing) & *rgyab-dar* (pendant) which is attached separately. (*c*) *rtsod-źva* ('debating hat'). (*d*) *ras zom* (cloth boots). (*e*) *chab-blug* (wallet made to contain a flask of water. The bottle no longer contains anything, and the embroidered wallet is simply one of the marks of a monk). (*f*) *stod-ḥgag* ('waistcoat' made of brocade silk). (*g*) *gzan* (cloak as worn every day)

TANTRIC DRESS

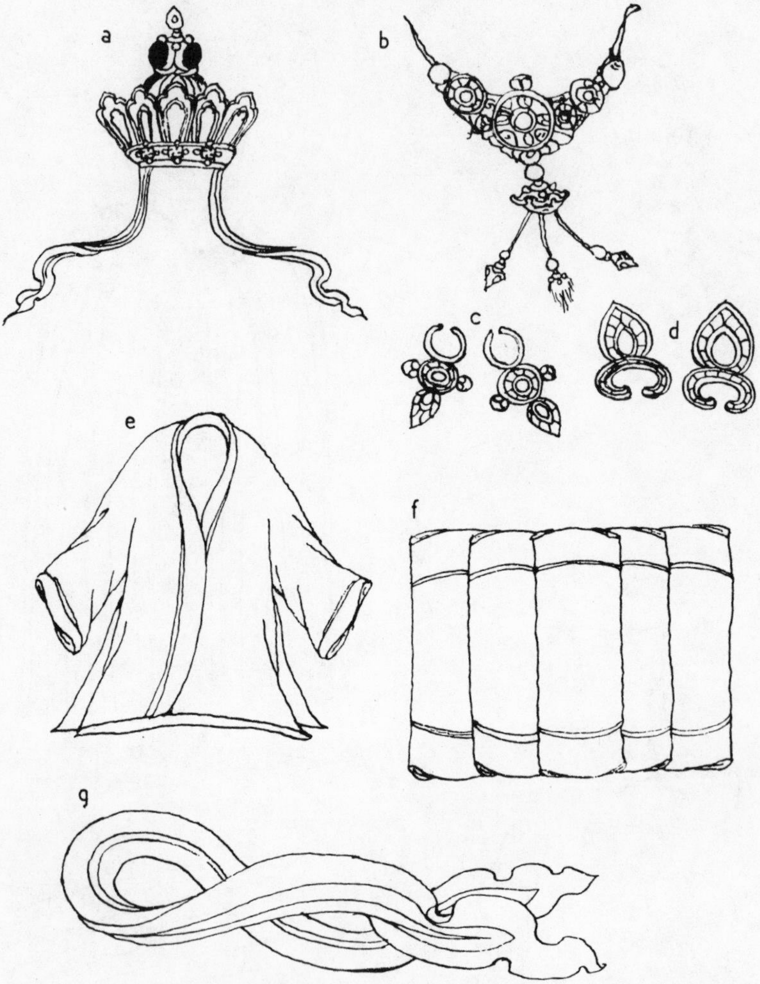

VIII. (*a*) *dbu-rgyan* or *rigs-lṅa* (Five-Buddha crown). (*b*) *ske-rgyan* or *mgul-chu* (pendant). (*c*) *sñan-cha* (ear-ornaments). (*d*) *lag-gdub*, *phyag-gdub* (bracelets). (*e*) *stod-g·yogs* (upper garment). (*f*) *smad-śams* (lower garment which is simply wrapped around the body). (*g*) *dar-dpyaṅs* (special scarf—worn around the shoulders when performing the rites of *dbaṅ*, *sbyin-sreg etc.*)

TANTRIC DRESS

IX. (*a*) *stag-źva* ('tiger-hat'). (*b*) *stag-ber* ('tiger-cloak'). (*c*) *ḥgyiṅ-thod* (turban). (*d*) *bon-źva* (*bon* hat, named *dkar-mo rtse-rgyal*). (*e*) *ḥphreṅ-ba* (beads). (*f*) *dar-dbyaṅs* (same as VIII (*g*) above). (*g*) *phur-pa* (dart). (*h*) *hom-khuṅ* (the special cavity for the *homa* (*sbyin-sreg*) rite; = *thun-khaṅ* or *e kloṅ ḥbrub-khuṅ*). (*j*) *lcags-kyu* (metal hook). (*k*) *sta-re* (axe). (*l*) *ḥkhor-lo* (wheel). (*m*) *ral-gri* (sword). (*n*) *spar-śad* (claw—for lifting the *liṅga*). (*o*) *lcags-thag* (chain). (*p*) *źags-pa* (noose). (*q*) *tho-ba* (hammer). (*r*) *mduṅ* (spear). (*s*) *mdaḥ* (arrow). (*t*) *gźu* (bow). (*u*) *kha-ṭam* (Skr. *khatvāṅga*—trident). (*v*) *thun-rva* (special horn for hurling *thun*—see note 5 to text). (*w*) *skam-pa* (tongs—for *liṅga*).

MAṆḌALA

X. (*a*) *gdugs* (parasol). (*b*) *ḥkhor-lo* (wheel). (*c*) *ri-dvags* (deer). (*d*) *g·yuṅ-druṅ ba-dan* (swastika ensign). (*e*) *bya-ḥdab* or *khyuṅ-gur* (roof). (*f*) *śar-bu* (gutter). (*g*) *za-ra-tshags* (criss-cross decorations). (*h*) *śam-bu* (frill or pelmet). (*j*) *ḥphan* (pendants). (*k*) *yol-ba* (curtains). (*l*) *dkyil-ḥkhor* (*maṇḍala*) drawn here in colours on the top of a table.

On the *maṇḍala*

centre: (*m*) *bum-pa* (sacrificial vase) resting on a *rkaṅ-gsum* (tripod) against which rests a *tsa-ka-li* (a card with a sacred symbol)

left: (*n*) *źi-gtor* (sacrificial cake of the tranquil divinities), and in front of this *gtaḥ-chen* (skull-cup) covered with a cloth

right: (*o*) *khro-gtor* (sacrificial cake of the fierce divinities).

(*p*) *gźi* (the basis, *viz*. a table). (*q*) *mar-me* (butter lamp). (*r*) *rgyun-gtor* ('reserved sacrificial cake'). It is difficult to make out on the diagram. It is the small *gtor-ma* standing at the foot of the central *mar-me*. (*s*) *ka-pa-li* (Skr. *kapāla*—skull-cup) containing *sman* (medicament). (*t*) *ka-pa-li* containing *rak-ta* (Skr. *rakta*—blood). (*u*) a whole row of *yon-chab* (sacrificial water) in bowls. (*v*) a whole row of *źal-zas* (sacrificial food—in the form of sacrificial cakes). (*w*) a whole row of *me-tog* (flowers). (*x*) a whole row of *spos* (incense). (*y*) *mchod-khrid* (altar).

SACRIFICIAL CAKES

XI. (*a*) *źi-baḥi gtor-ma* (sacrificial cake for the tranquil divinities—see Fig. X*n*). (*b*) *dbaṅ-gi-gtor-ma* (s. cake used in the rite of 'empowerment'). (*c*) *drag-poḥi gtor-ma* or *dbal-gtor* (s. cake for fierce divinities).[1] (*d*) *tshe-gtor* (s. cake offered in the 'life-consecration' ceremony).[2] (*e*) *zlog-gtor* (s. cake for hurling against foes)

[1] Concerning these fierce rites see *Buddhist Himālaya*, pp. 258 ff.
[2] Concerning the rite of 'life consecration' see *Himalayan Pilgrimage*, pp. 141 ff.

RITUAL ITEMS

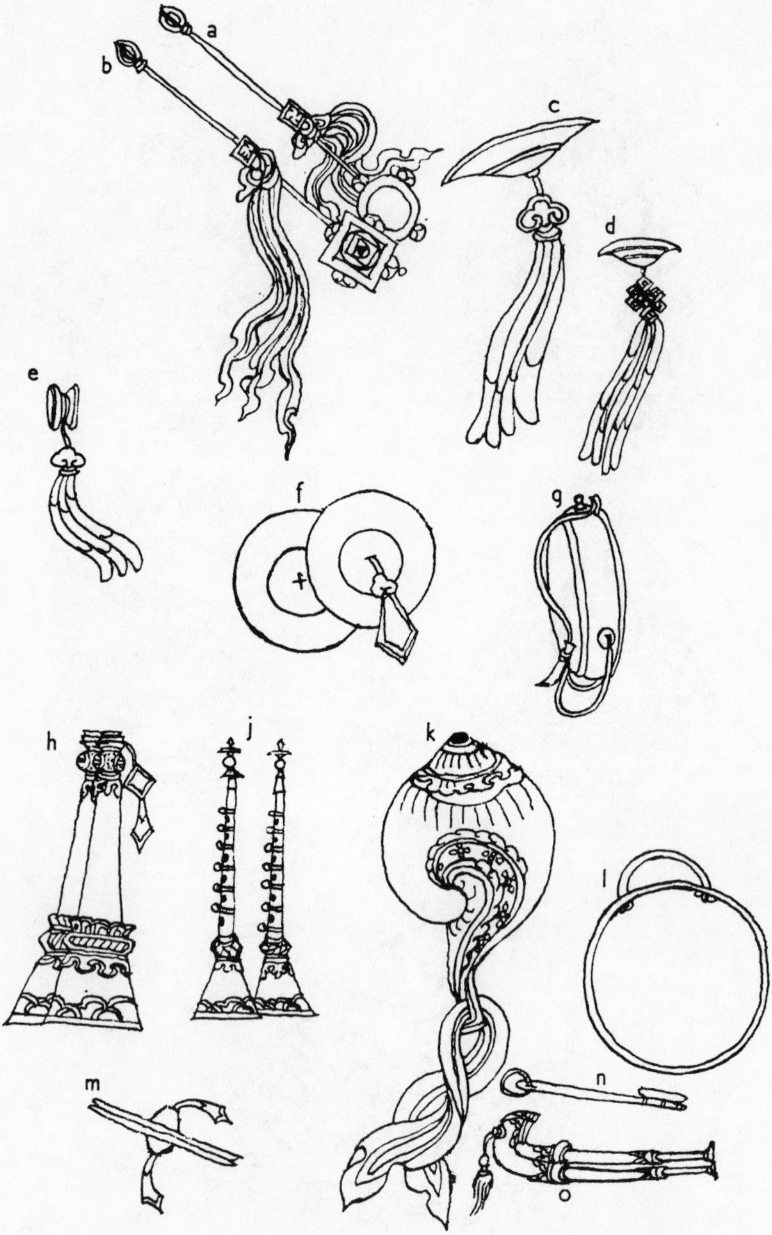

XII. (*a*) *dgaṅ-gzar* or *hom-gzar* (sacrificial ladle for holding liquids). (*b*) *blug-gzar* or *ḥbyams-gzar* (sacrificial ladle for holding solids). (*c*) *gśaṅ-chen* (flat *bonpo* bell—large size). (*d*) *gśaṅ-chuṅ* (the same—small size). (*e*) *ḍa-ma-ru* (Skr. small drum). (*f*) *sbug-chol* (cymbals). (*g*) *rṅa* (drum). (*h*) *duṅ-chen* (great trumpet—extendable). (*j*) *rgya-gliṅ* (shawm). (*k*) *duṅ-dkar* (conch—drawn monstrously out of scale). (*l*) *mkhar-rṅa* or *rgya-ṅa* (large drum). (*m*) *sil-sñan* or *sil-chol* (small cymbals). (*n*) *rduṅ-chas* (drum-stick). (*o*) *ko-yo* (a pair of trumpets)

RITUAL ITEMS

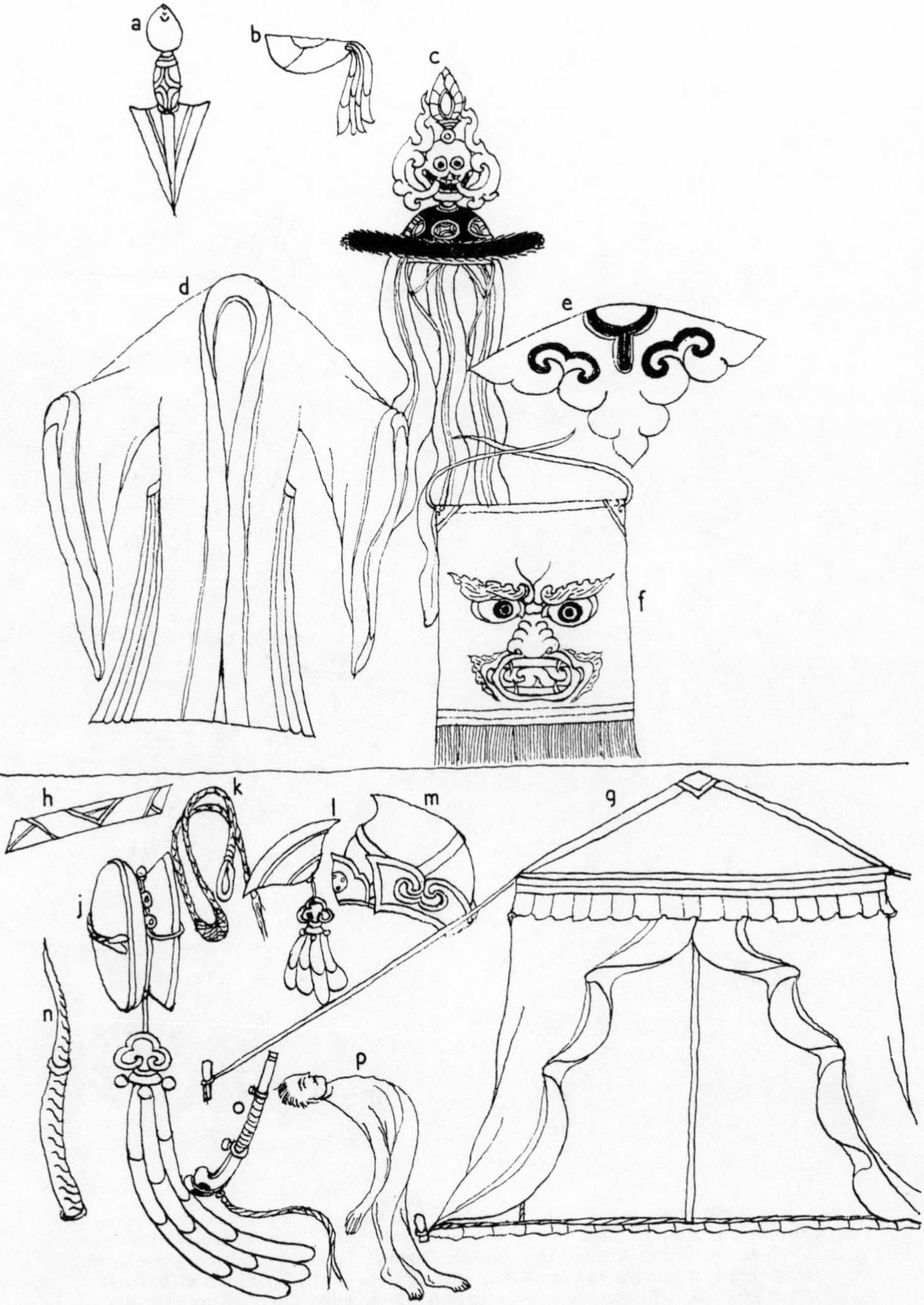

XIII. (*a*) *phur-pa* (dart). (*b*) *thod-źal* (skull-cup). (*c*) *źva-nag* (black hat). (*d*) *ber* (cloak). (*e*) *stod-khebs* (chasuble). (*f*) *paṅ-khebs* (ritual skirt). (*g*) *gur* (tent). (*h*) *be-ḥbum* or *po-ti* (book). (*j*) *ḍa-ma-ru* (small drum). (*k*) *ḥur-rdo* (sling). (*l*) *gśaṅ* (flat bell as used by *bonpos*). (*m*) *bon-źva* (*bon* hat). (*n*) *gtsod-ru* (antelope horn). (*o*) *rkaṅ-gliṅ* (thigh-bone trumpet). (*p*) *źiṅ-chen g·yaṅ-gźi* (human skin)

HERMIT'S REQUIREMENTS

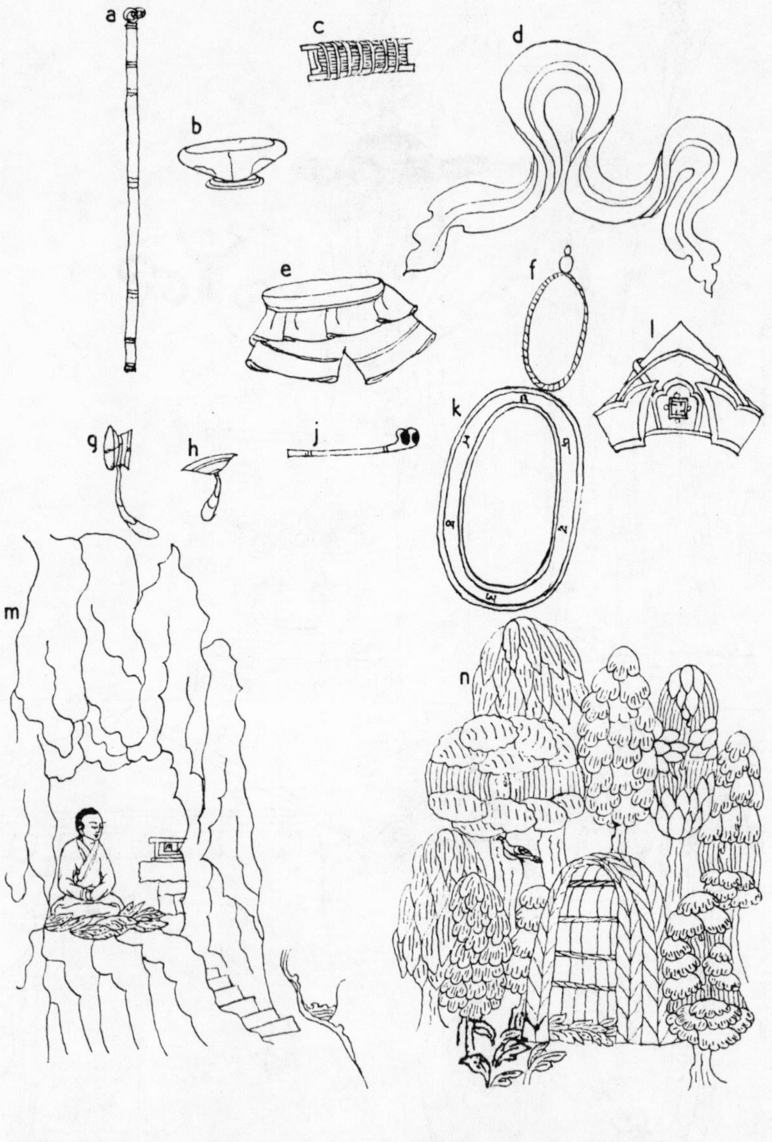

XIV. (*a*) *sba-ḥkhar* (a cane). (*b*) *thod-źal* (skull cup). (*c*) *be-ḥbum* or *po-ti* (book). (*d*) *rluṅ-ras* (a binding scarf). (*e*) *aṅ-ga-ra* (underpants). (*f*) *ḥphreṅ-ba* (rosary). (*g*) *ḍa-ma-ru* (small drum). (*h*) *gśaṅ-chuṅ* (small flat *bon-po* bell). (*j*) *rkaṅ-gliṅ* (thigh-bone trumpet). (*k*) *sgom-thag* (meditation cord). (*l*) *bon-źva* (*bon* hat) (*m*) *sgrub-phug* (meditation cave). (*n*) *spyil-po* (meditation hut—in a forest)

THRONE

XV. (*a*) ***khri-gdan*** (throne-mat). (*b*) ***bla-bre*** (canopy). (*c*) ***rgyab-yol*** (back-piece)

VARIOUS ITEMS

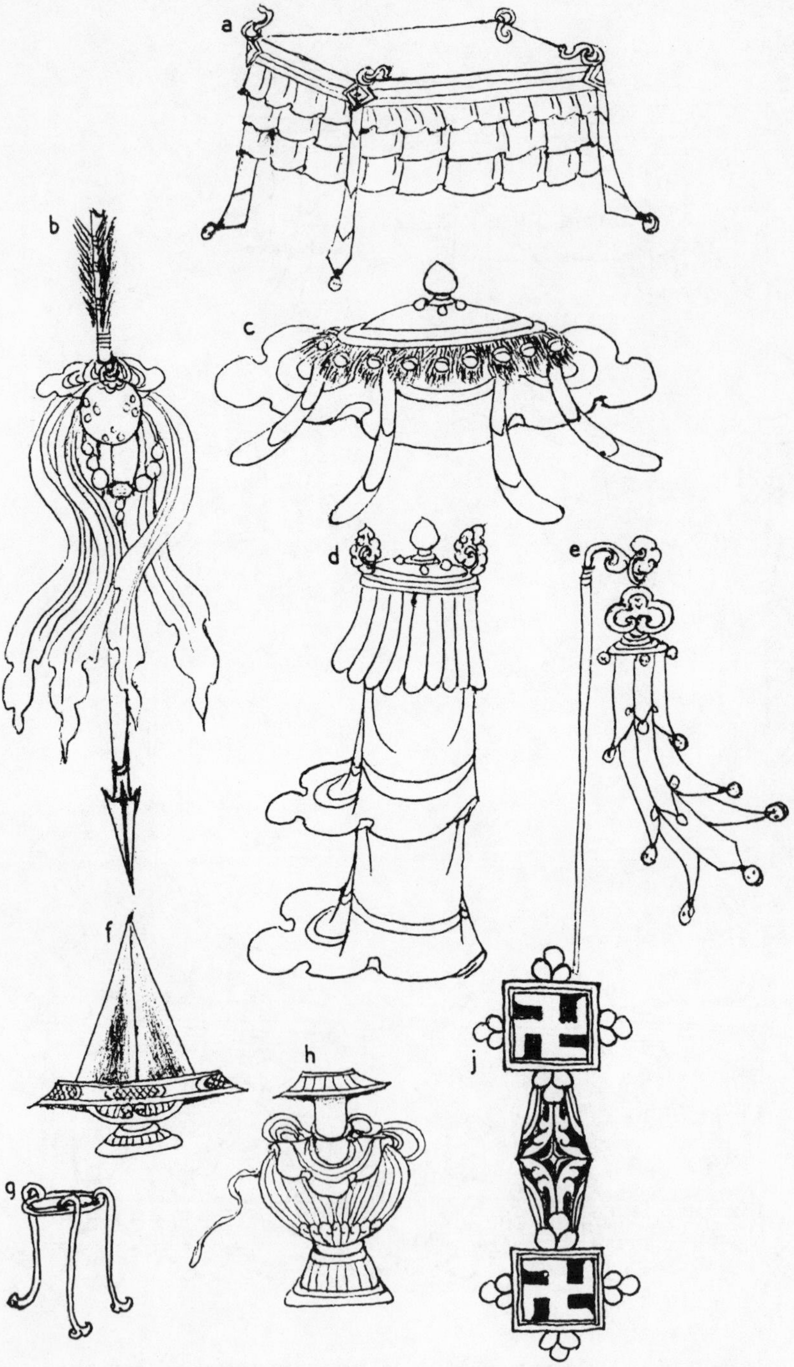

XVI. (*a*) *bla-bre* (canopy). (*b*) *mdaḥ-dar* (garlanded arrow). (*c*) *gdugs* (parasol). (*d*) *rgyal-mtshan* (banner of victory). (*e*) *ḥphan* (pendant). (*f*) *dbal-gtor* (fierce sacrificial cake). (*g*) *rkaṅ-gsum* (tripod). (*h*) *bum-pa* (sacrificial vase). (*j*) *chag-śiṅ* (a *bon-po* 'powerbolt')

VARIOUS ITEMS

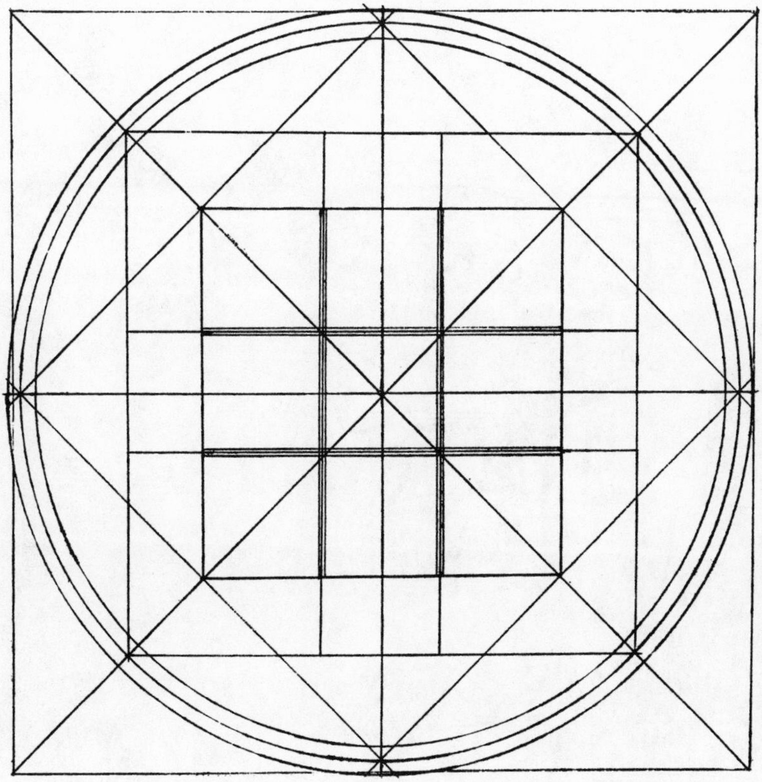

XVII. Drawing the *maṇḍala* (see p. 198[30–33])

VARIOUS ITEMS

མི་ནོར་ཡུལ་མཁར་འདོད་ཡོན་རྫས།

XVIII. The offering of a man's wealth (see pp. 36[11] and 90[34])

VARIOUS ITEMS

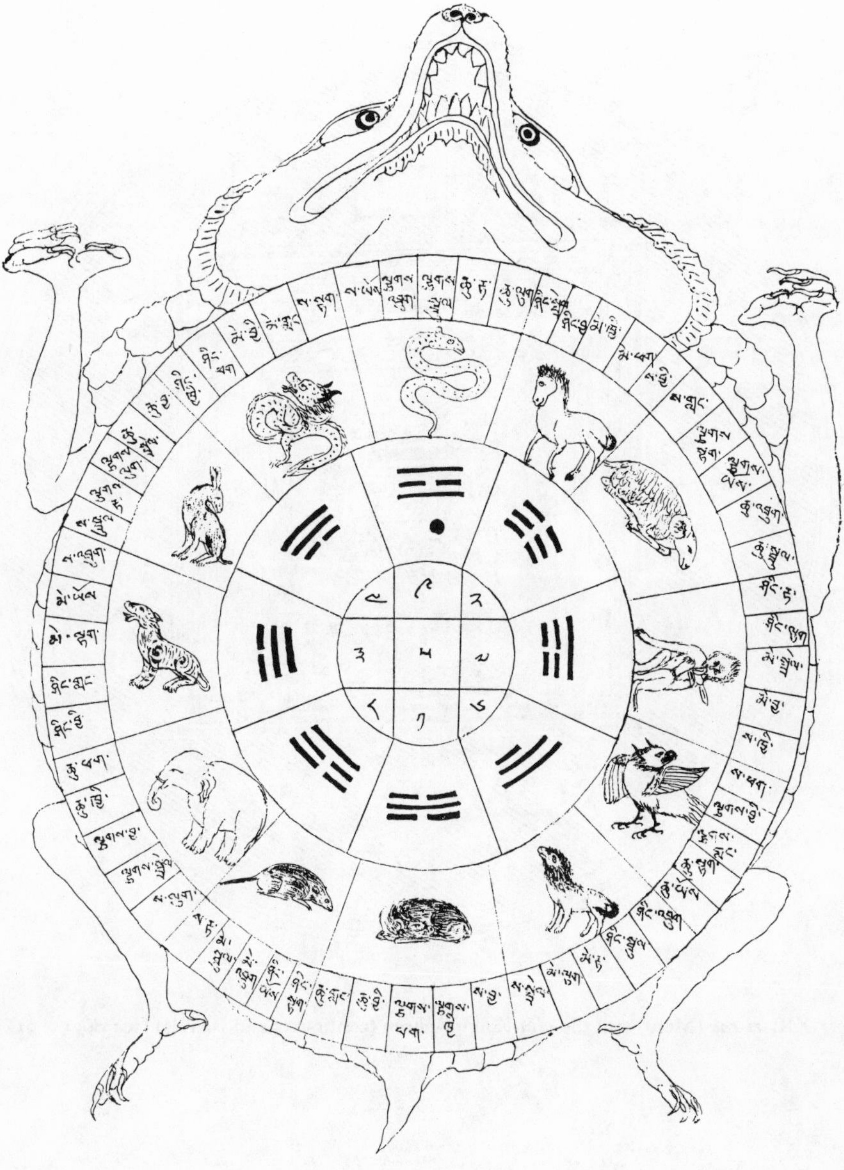

XIX. *gab-rtse ḥphrul-gyi me-loṅ* (horoscope) (see Way I)

VARIOUS ITEMS

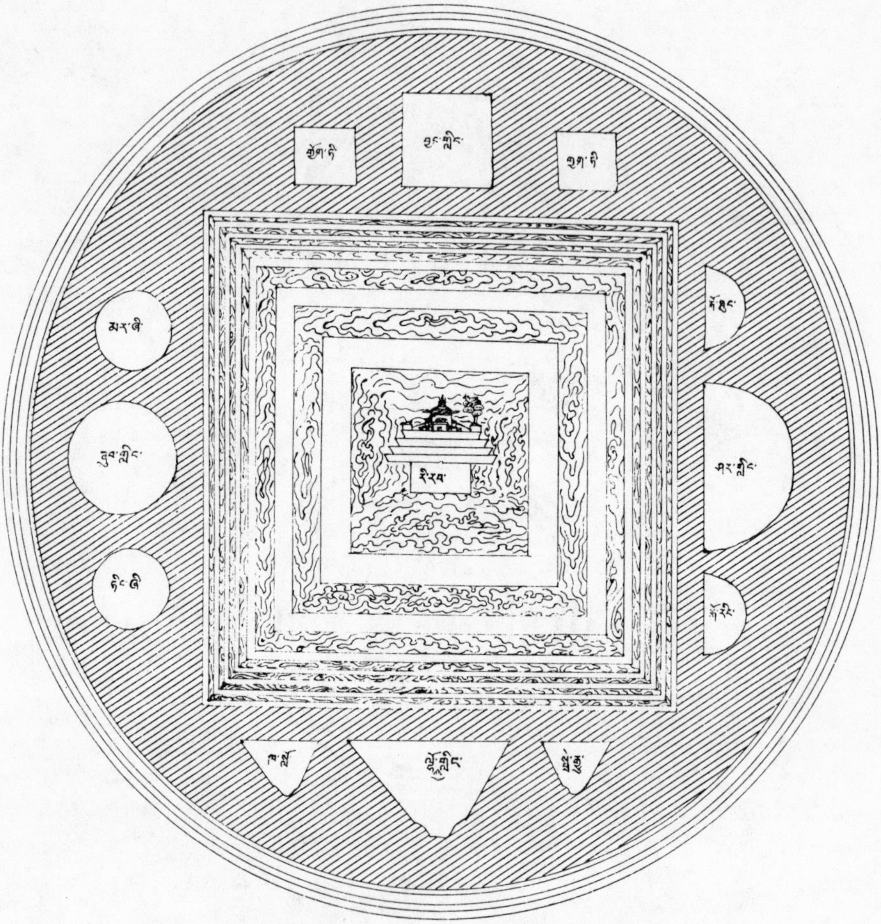

XX. *ri-rab* (Meru) and the *gliṅ-bźi gliṅ-phran* (continents and islands) (see pp. 90–91)

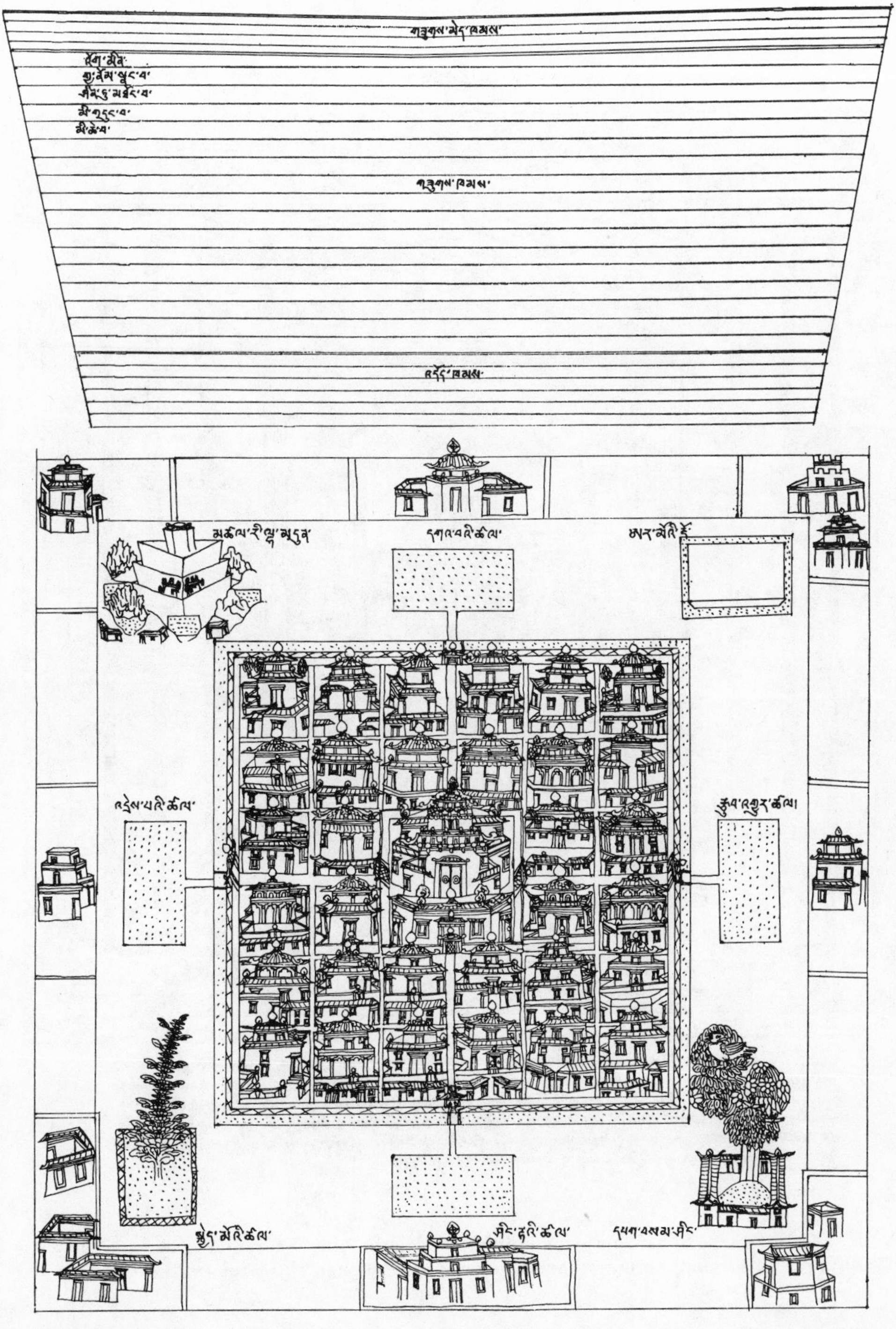

XXI. *lha sum-cu-so-gsum gyi gźal-yas-khaṅ*—the palaces of the 33 gods, the bird *khyuṅ* and the parks, as described on pp. 90–91.

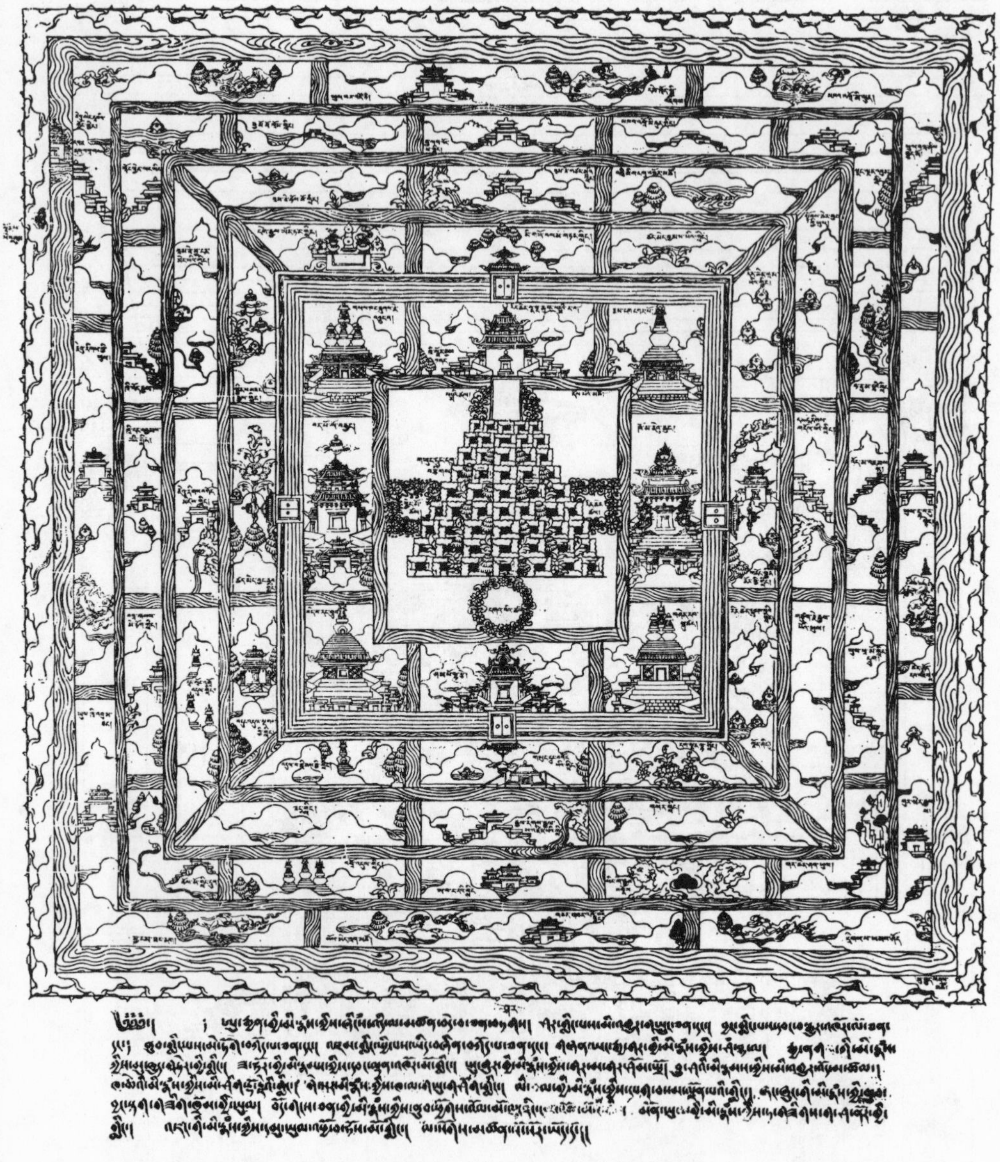

XXII. The Nine-Stage Swastika Mountain (representing the Nine Ways of *Bon*) surrounded by its eight royal palaces in the country known variously as *sTag-gzigs*, *'Ol-mo-luṅ-riṅ*, *Śambhala*, etc.

Two *rNying-ma-pa* lamas of Tarap (Dolpo) performing a *sbyin-sreg* ('fire-oblation') ceremony. (Photograph by Corneille Jest)

Samling of Dolpo, the source of our manuscript of *gZi-brjid*. This monastery (about 15,000 feet above sea-level) is built on a high 'alp' above the gorge illustrated on the frontispiece, where the same main corner shrine (*mchod-rten*) has been photographed from the monastery side. (DLS 1961)

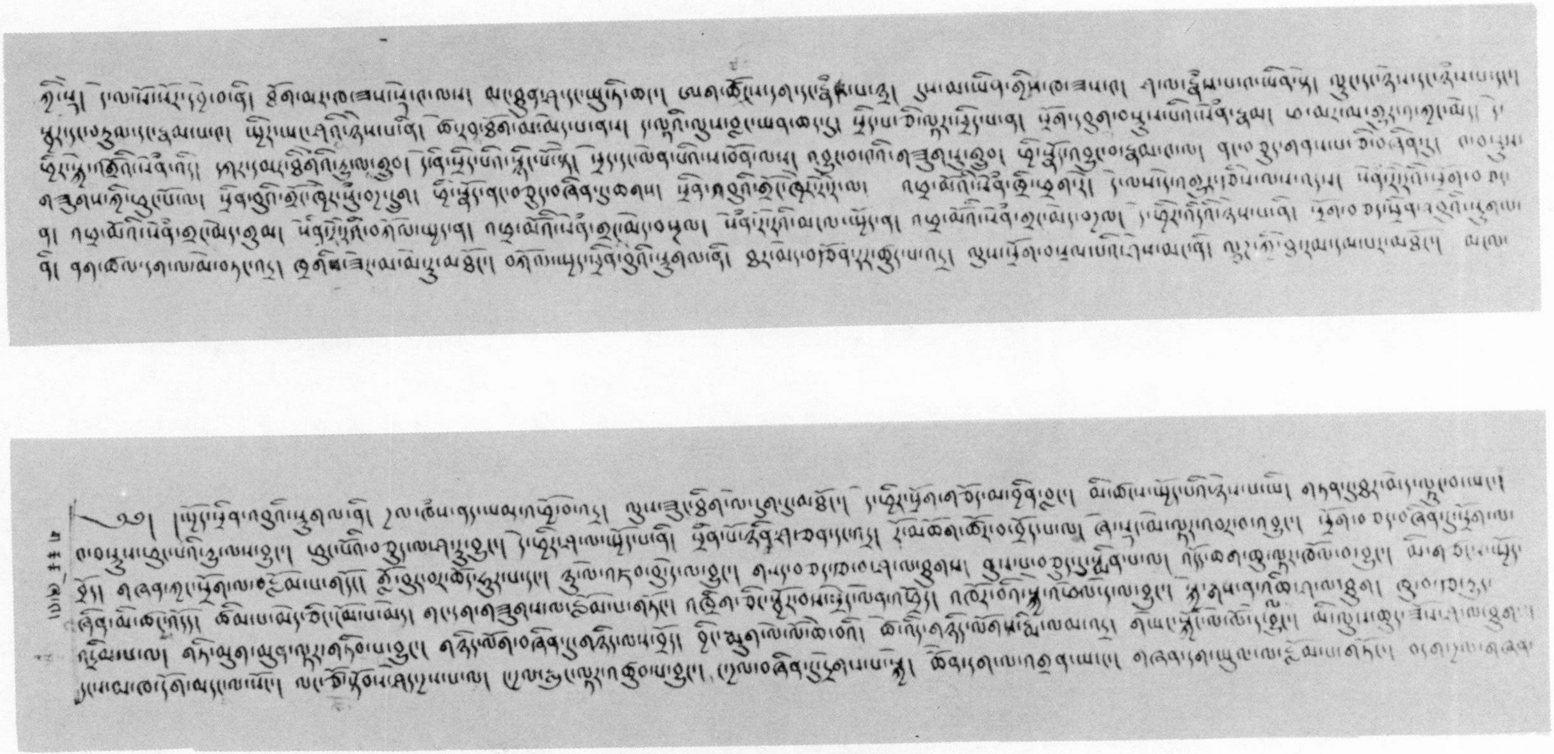

Vol. GA, folios 243b and 244a (see p. 138)

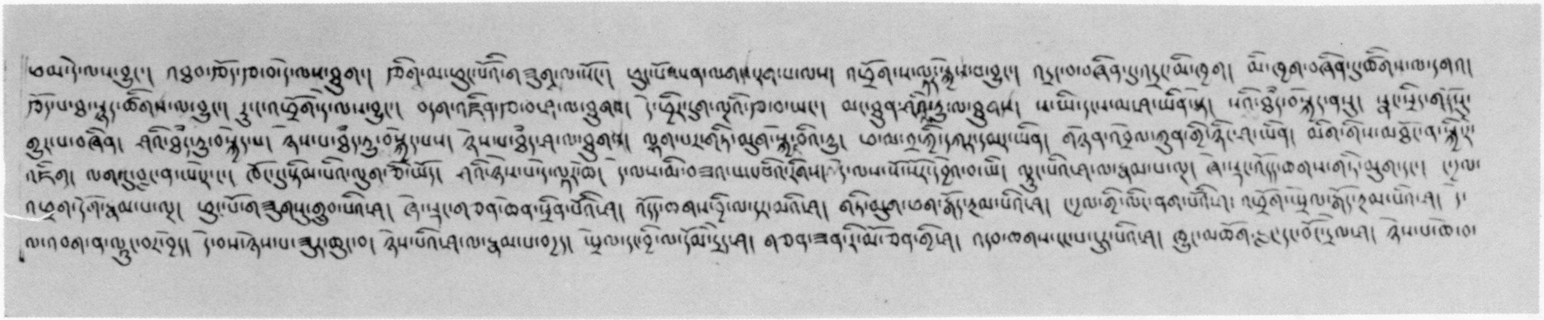

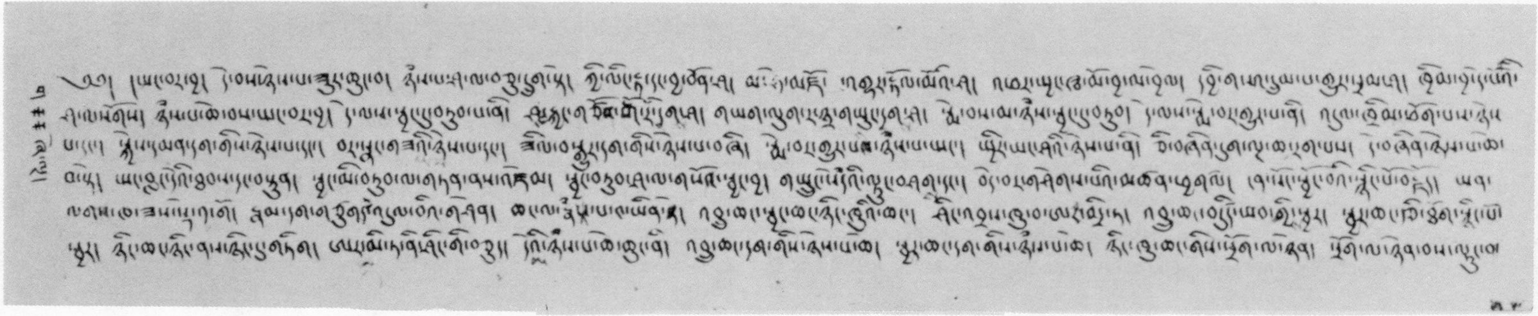

Vol. GA, folios 244b and 245a (see p. 142)

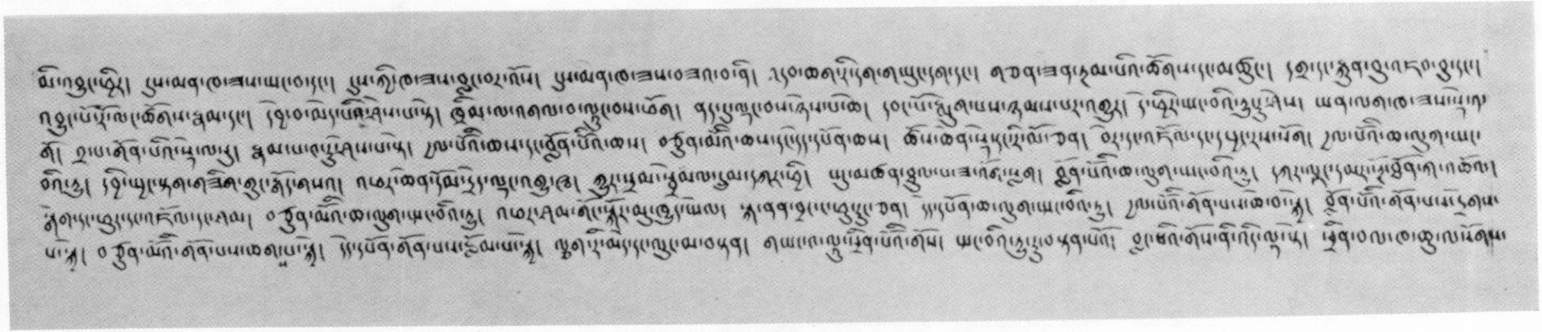

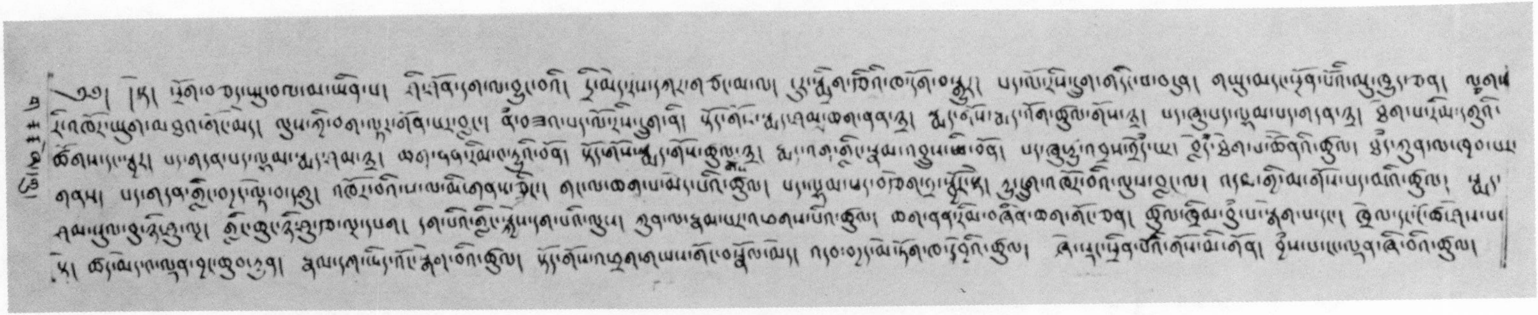

Vol. GA, folios 248b–249a (see p. 152)

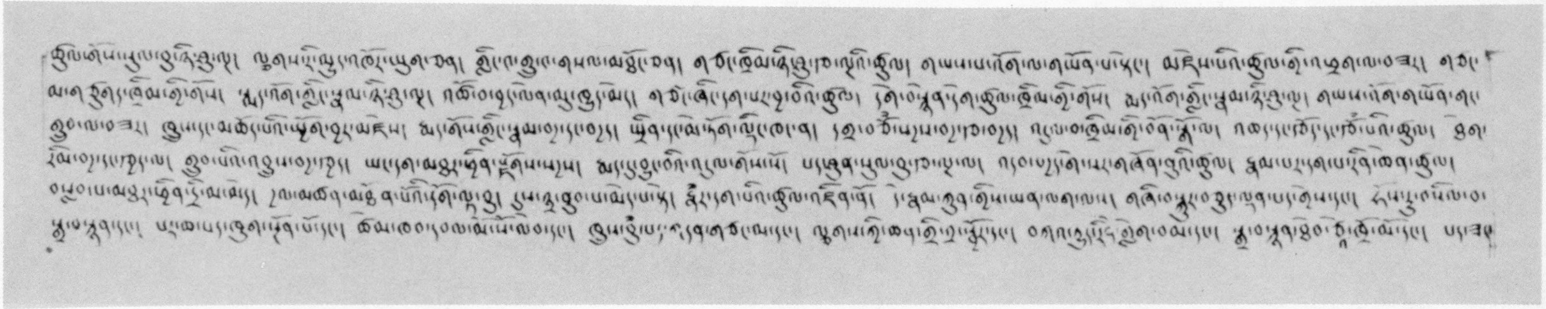

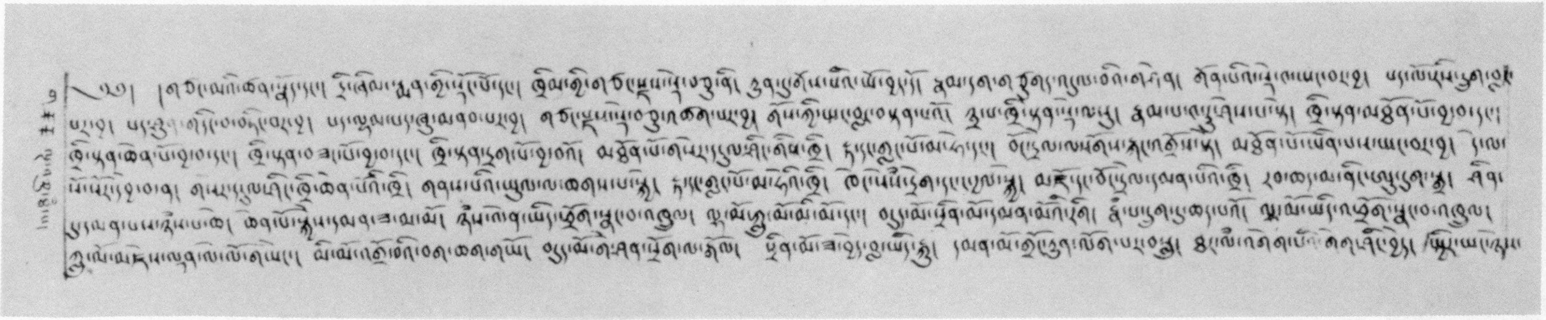

Vol. GA, folios 249b–250a (see p. 156)

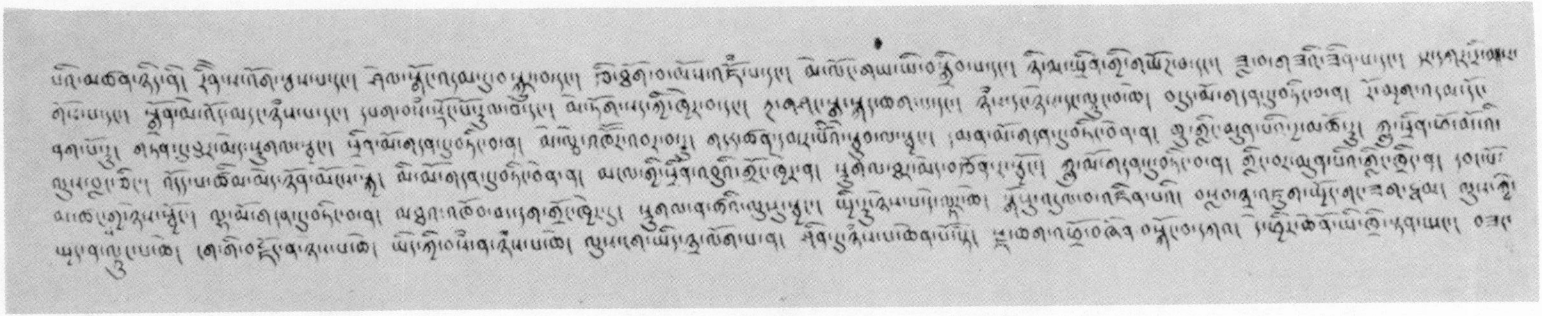

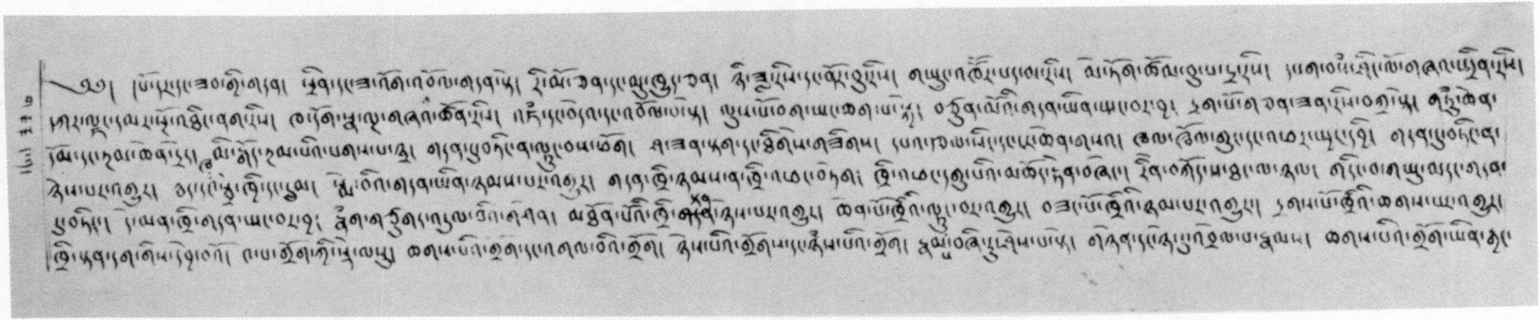

Vol. GA, folios 250b–251a (see p. 160)

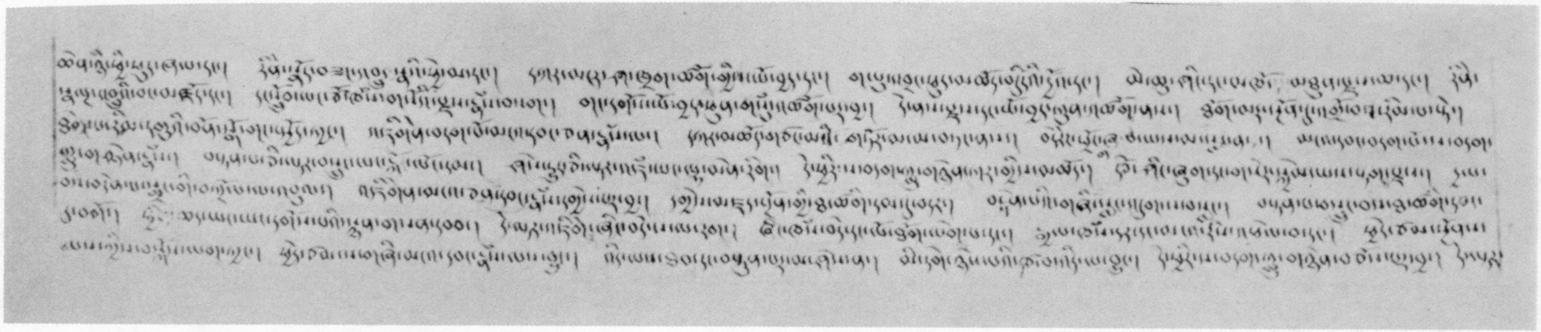

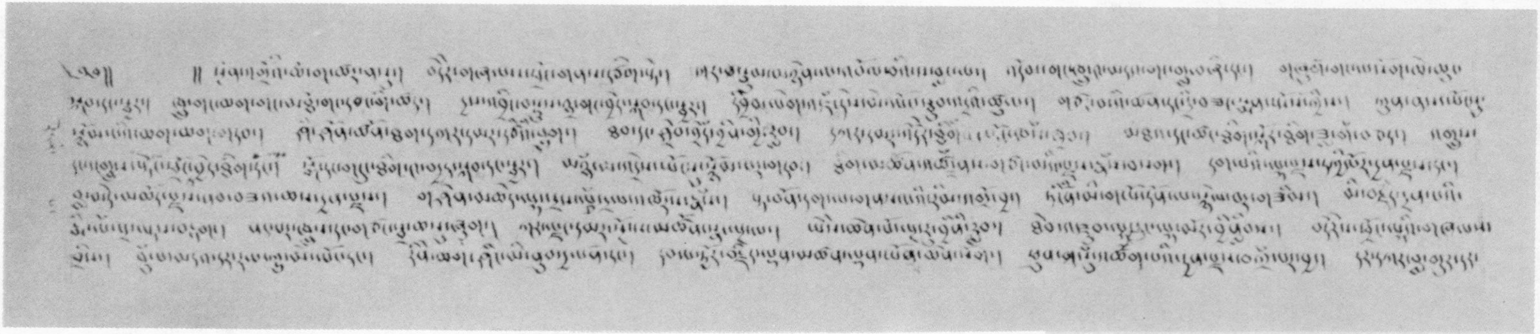

Vol. NGA, folios 63b–64a (see p. 196)

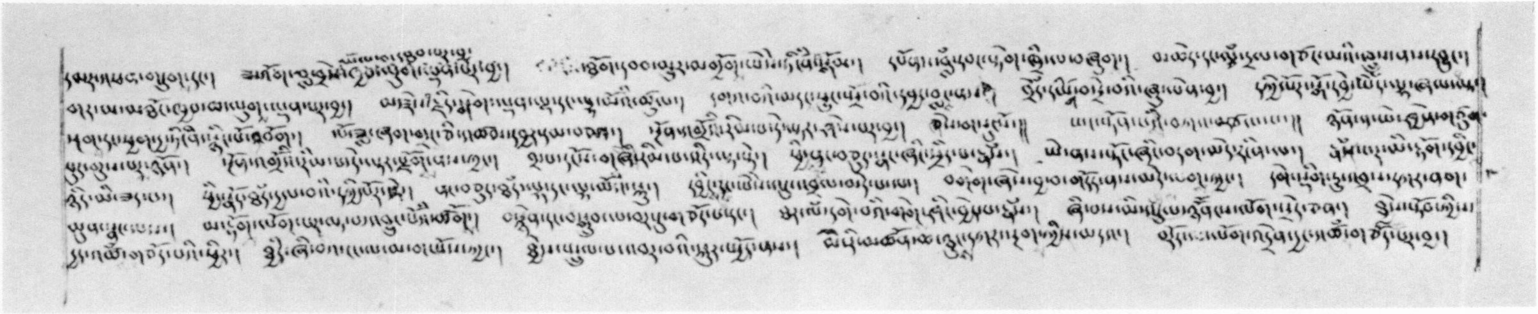

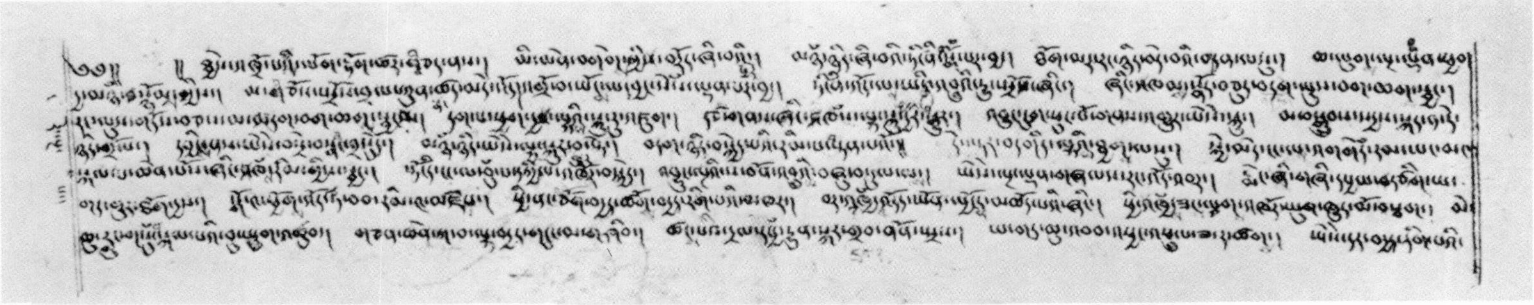

Vol. NGA, folios 64b–65a (see p. 200)

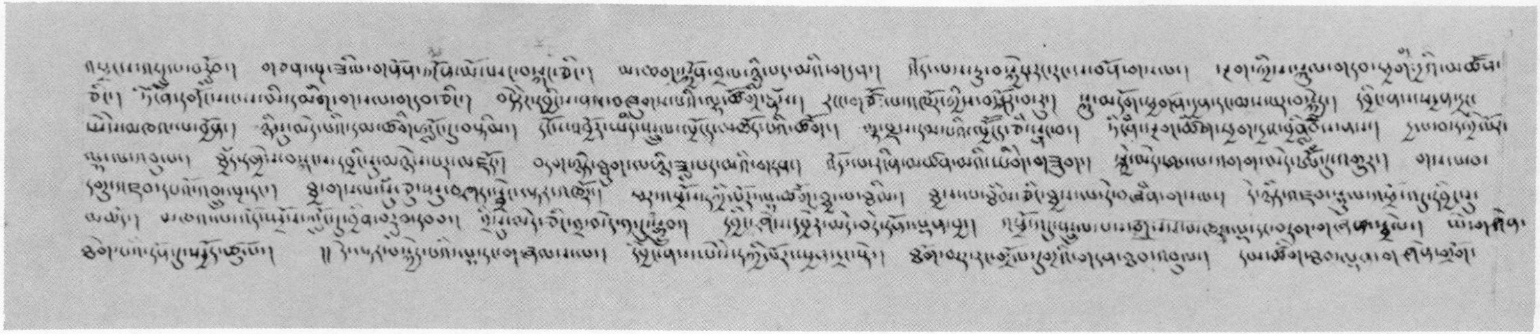

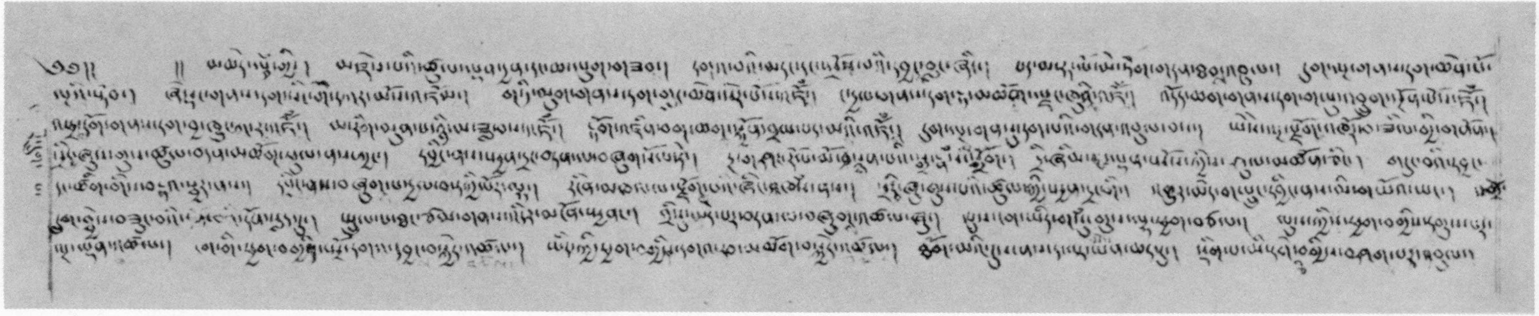

Vol. NGA, folios 65b–66a (see p. 204)

NOTE ON THE GLOSSARY

THIS glossary has been drawn up to include (i) rare words and rare meanings, (ii) words with special technical meanings, (iii) words which cover in translation a wide range of meaning, and (iv) some well-known Tibetan Buddhist terms of which I have found it useful to keep track. As my standard work I have taken the *Tibetan–English Dictionary* of H. A. Jäschke, whose long labours in the service of Tibetan lexicography have recently received their proper recognition in an important article by Professor Walter Simon.[1] There is little doubt that when one turns to indigenous Tibetan literature, this dictionary is of incomparably greater value than any other that has since been produced. Having taken it as my standard, I have marked with an asterisk all terms (single or compound) and all meanings in my glossary which do not occur in Jäschke's work. My brief references to new and unusual meanings can only be completed by turning to his dictionary, and except on the rare occasions when I have written MD ('meaning doubtful'), against the reference to his work, my new meanings are not meant to supplant those he has already given. In some cases I have written NM against my reference to his entries, to indicate that I regard as 'normal meanings' the ones which he has already given.

I have tried to be as consistent as possible in my translation of technical terms, but as all translators of such literature know, to translate consistently and at the same time produce a comprehensible translation is a well-nigh impossible task. As the next best thing I have used in some cases a variety of carefully controlled translations in order to suit different contexts (e.g. see *rgyud* and *bsñen-pa*).

Words for animals, precious stones, plants, etc., are for the most part uncertain, in whatever dictionary or word-list they occur, and having only recently tried (rather doubtfully) to identify with precision the Tibetan rock-plant known as *mTshe*, I know how difficult this task can be. It can only be done when we can bring together a Western botanist, a Tibetan really skilled in the names of plants, and an example of the plant itself. This is far more difficult to arrange than might seem to be the case, and the same kind of academic proficiency is required on both sides in the case of animals, precious stones, and all the rest. Very precise terms exist for a surprising variety of such things, but few Tibetans (just like ourselves) are capable of making accurate distinctions unless it is their business to know just these things. Thus, I have translated *guṅ* as 'caracal' for no better reason than that Tenzin Namdak observed that a stuffed caracal in the Natural History Museum in Tring seemed to be just this creature; neither of us claims special zoological knowledge. Fortunately, most of the terms in this glossary are concerned with religious practices of one kind and another, and there is no doubt of his mastery of this kind of technical vocabulary. The use of 'single inverted commas' indicates a provisional translation or one devised to suit the context where the term occurs; the use of "double inverted commas" indicates a straight translation, e.g. of a title or place-name or of an extract from a Tibetan dictionary.

[1] 'Tibetan Lexicography and Etymological Research', *Transactions of the Philological Society*, London, 1964.

ABBREVIATIONS

adj.	adjective
abbr.	abbreviation, abbreviated
BH	D. L. Snellgrove, *Buddhist Himālaya*, Cassirer, Oxford, 1957
ChGr	*Tibetan–Chinese Dictionary* of Geshey *Chos-kyi grags-pa*, Peking 1952
Cs	S. Csoma de Körös, *Tibetan–English Dictionary*, Calcutta, 1834, as quoted by J
cp.	compare
D	*Dictionaire thibétain–latin–français par les Missionaires Catholiques du Thibet*, ed. by A. Desgodins, Hongkong, 1899
DC	deduced from context
Ency. Br.	*Encyclopaedia Britannica* 1961
hon.	honorific
HT	D. L. Snellgrove, *Hevajra Tantra*, OUP, 1959
imp.	imperative
instr.	instrumental
item	a detailed item to be found under the quoted reference
J	Jäschke's *Tibetan–English Dictionary*, Kegan Paul, London, 1881, and subsequent reprints
Lex	indigenous Tibetan dictionaries and word-lists
lit.	literally
MD	meaning doubtful
MVP	*Mahāvyutpatti*
n.	noun
NM	normal meaning
NS	normal spelling
NW	René de Nebesky-Wojkowitz, *Oracles and Demons of Tibet*, Mouton, The Hague, 1956
SCD	*Tibetan–English Dictionary* by Sarat Chandra Das, Calcutta, 1902
Sch	I. J. Schmidt, *Tibetisch–Deutsches Wörterbuch*, as quoted by J
SGK	Samten Gyaltsen Karmay
Skr.	Sanskrit
TN	Tenzin Namdak
vb.	verb

GLOSSARY

ka-źu (J: ka-gźu) = pillar capital 132[29]

ka-gdan = pillar base 132[29]

kag (J/Cs: kag-ma) *also* gag q.v. = impediment 34[31, 32, 39], 48[14]

kag-ñen (= kag) 56[33], 74[11]

*kag-sri = 'demon of impediments' 34[35]

*ku-hraṅ (TN: = rkyaṅ) = 'wild ass' 116[30]

*kun-snaṅ-ḥod = 'Universal Shining Light' (11th stage towards buddhahood) 96[14], 114[1, 2]

*Kun-śes ḥphrul gyi draṅ-mkhan, name of a god 26[8]

ko-loṅ-dam (J/Sch: ko-loṅ-ba) (TN: = bzod-pa med-pa) = 'irascible' 196[39]

*kor-tshe-ba (ChGr: = ñi-tshe-ba = phyogs-re-ba) = 'self-centred' (TN) 170[20]

*kluṅ-rta (J: rluṅ-rta) *see note* 10, = symbol of well-being, god of well-being, *or just meaning* well-being 32[34], 44[24], 56[36], 88[21]

klu-mo = 'mermaid' 182[25]

kloṅ *see note* 71 = spacial sphere, mental sphere 88[8, 13, 30], 90[7], 92[17, 19], 104[1, 25], 108[2], 120[8], 170[27], 204[26], 206[9], 210[2, 18], 218[5, 21], 238[5]; sa-gźiḥi kloṅ = 'face of the earth' 70[37]

*kloṅ-grum = ? a kind of badger (grum-pa) 48[25]

dkar-dmar (*see* J: thig-le) = 'white and red essence' 142[27]

dkar gsum = 'three white products', viz. milk, curds and butter 64[6], 196[26]

dkyil-ḥkhor = mystic circle (*distinguished in Tibetan usage from* maṇḍala; *see* ma-ḥdal *below*) 102[22, 26], 134[10], 204[30]

bkas-sa = shelter 164[21]

bkaḥ-gñan (J/Lex MD; ChGr: bkaḥ-btsan *probably same meaning but different one given*) = 'coercion' 82[18]. *See below* gñan-po

bkaḥ-bab (J: bkaḥ ḥbab-pa) = 'soothsaying' 24[20], 32[7]

bkol (J: ḥkhol-ba) = committed 124[17]

*bkyag (J: ḥkhyog-pa) = to present or make offerings 52[23, 35], 56[39], 64[16], 72[31], 90[16]

bkyon (J: = to beat, scold) = *'causing harm' 88[13]

*ska-nan (J: rked-pa & sked-pa 'waist'; nan 'pressing') = 'fitted to the waist' (*compare* ska-rags 'belt') 154[25]

sku-mkhar = 'palace' 214[33]

skoṅ-ba / bskaṅ, *nominal form* skoṅ; also *kha-skoṅ-ba*, = *lit.* to fill up, *used in special meaning of* to make good deficiencies in one's debts to the gods, *hence* to satisfy, to make atonement 76[37], 78[8], 86[23], 88[7, 12, 29], 90[11, 15, 16], 92[2, 37], 102[31], 104[5], 110[19], 204[31]; to fulfil (hopes) 94[31]

*skya-yas (*probably* = skyas) = an offering (to demons) 74[7]

*skyas / bskyas (J: skya-ba, skyas & skyes) = a departing gift in the special sense of ransom-offering to demons; *used with* ḥdebs-pa: to dispatch with a ransom offering 68[27], 70[35]

skyems = draught (of concentrated *chang*) 32[1], 50[1], 92[3]; *see also* gser-skyems

*sKyoṅ-ma-khram, name of a god 78[12]

bskos (J: sko-ba) = to set up, to bring into order, to authorize; *the same form used as imperative* 48^{30}; *as verbal participle* 64^{39}, 124^{5}; *and as noun* 54^{15}, 94^{24} (*in combination with* ḥdebs-pa), 64^{39}

bskyal-ba (J: skyel / skyol) = to dispatch, send away 74^{9}

*bskyor (J: skyor-ba II 'enclosure') = 'enclosed' 196^{1}

kha-ta (J: = advice NM) = 'talk' 238^{24}

kha-drag (J: = mighty; ChGr: = "harsh speech") = 'might' 54^{15}, 62^{35}

kha-bad (J: = humidity [p. 36] & projecting ends of beams which support the roof [p. 37] NM) = 'eaves' 52^{1}

*kha-bo (ChGr: = kha-drag tsha-bo) = 'big talk' 30^{8}

*kha-mi-ya (ChGr: kha-ya = "affectionate") = 'do not reply' (TN) 28^{17}

*kha-ḥdzin (ChGr: = rogs-ram byed-pa) = 'overseer' $60^{4, 5}$

*Kha-la-gaṅs-dkar, name of a god 78^{13}

*kha-yo (*tentative emendment of* kha-lo *which may, however, be preferable*) (J: yo-ba = crooked) = 'crookedness' 64^{20}, 92^{12}

kha-lo bsgyur-ba (J: kha-lo; ChGr: kha-lo-ba) = to guide 42^{15}, 108^{32}

khams = appearance, disposition 26^{3}, 36^{36}, $38^{29, 31}$, 120^{5}; = realm *as in* khams gsum, threefold world 96^{10}, 112^{37}

*khas-ñan (ChGr: khas-źan = "weak") = 'weakness' 44^{23}, 56^{3}

*khu-ḥphrig (ChGr: = rnam-rtog za-ba; J/Sch: ḥphrig 4) = 'erroneous views' 116^{7}

*Kho-ma-ne-chuṅ, name of palace on the north side of the Nine-Stage Swastika Mountain (*see* Fig. XXII) 114^{15}

*khoṅ-ḥkhyul = 'patience' (TN) 166^{15}

Khyuṅ = 'king of birds' 58^{13}, 60^{36}, 62^{13}, 74^{1}, 80^{5}

*Khyuṅ-nag ral-chen $58^{13, 14}$, 108^{25} name of a god

khyud (J/Sch: khyud-mo = rim): sgo-khyud = door-way 134^{1}; khyud-mo = rim 204^{1}

khram (J: khram-kha) = 'tally-stick' 76^{38}, $78^{12, 13}$

khri-ḥphaṅ = steps (of platform serving as basis of a shrine or a throne) 44^{26}, $164^{19, 20}$

*Khri-smon-rgyal-bźad, name of palace on the west side of the Nine-Stage Swastika Mountain (*see* Fig. XXII) 96^{29}

khrol-le (J: khrol-khrol) = 'sparkling' 216^{35}

*mKhaḥ-ḥgyiṅ-dbal, name of a god $108^{12, 15}$

*mKhaḥ-gsal-ye-śes = "Knowledge of the Clear Sky", name of a ritual 104^{11}

mkho (J: mkho-ba) = 'requirement' 26^{24}

mkhon (J: ḥkhon = quarrelling) = 'animosity' 46^{35}, 88^{10}

ḥkhor-ḥdas (ḥkhor-ba daṅ myaṅ-ṅan las ḥdas-pa). *See note* 79. = *saṃsāra* & *nirvāṇa*, the 'wheel of existence and the transcending of sorrow', 'phenomenal existence and its transcendence', 'physical and metaphysical' 170^{34}, 224^{7}, $228^{22, 31}$, 238^{29}, 240^{2}, 246^{34}, 248^{7}, 250^{11}, 252^{12-13}, 254^{1}

ḥkhyil (J: ḥkhyil-ba) = *'mountainous amphitheatre' (TN) $48^{19, 20}$

*ḥkhra-ba / ḥkhras = *as verb* to resort to; *as noun* place of home 60^{27}, 80^{19}, 172^{15}

*ga-dar = 'perfect' (TN) 40^{2}, 102^{7}

gag *see* kag 46^{1}, 78^{27}, 120^{2}

gab-rtse (? Chinese 甲子) = horoscope $24^{9, 24}$, $32^{15, 23}$ (*see* Fig. XIX)

gar (J: gar-ba) = 'strong' 44^{21}

*gar-ma-mthoṅ-khyab = 'deacon' (TN) 200^{23}

*Gar-ma-li-śo, name of 'Grand Master of Arts and Crafts' in *'Ol-mo-luṅ-riṅ* (TN) 132^{24}

*Gar-gsas-btsan-po *also* Gar-gsas-dbal, name of a god $72^{32, 34}$, 74^{39}, 76^{10}, 86^{20}, 90^{12}, 94^{17}

*guṅ (D: guṅ / dguṅ) = 'caracal' (MD) 154^{16}, 164^{15}

gur-thog (J/Sch) = tent roof, raised roof (like a tent) 204^{7}

ge-sar (J/Cs 1) = a flower of a kind (MD) 158^{19}

*ge-śan (J: śan-pa) = 'murderous' (DC) 160^{31}

go (& go-cha) = armour 10^{12}, 60^{24}, 130^{37}

*goṅ-skor (J: goṅ-ba & skor) = 'collar' 154^{24}

*gon-na gñan-pa (*see* gñan-pa) = 'superior in dignity', *lit. those who are grave in their superiority, e.g. father vis-à-vis son, king vis-à-vis minister* (TN) 118^{32}

*gyi-liṅ = a much prized breed of horse (TN) $144^{2, 14}$

gyer (J: dgyer-ba) = incantation, to intone $42^{9, 20}$, 46^{18}, 48^{17}, 52^{35}, 68^{22}, 84^{11}, 96^{21}, 104^{6}

gyoṅ-po (J: = rough, rude NM) = 'stern' 28^{4}

*gra-bsdeb 'fitted to one another' (TN & DC) 182^{31}

*grab-non (ChGr: drab = lcam-śiṅ, *where* lcam *represents our* dpyam, *q.v.*) = light boards forming a ceiling fixed between and above the ceiling laths (*gral-dpyam*) in costly buildings 204^{14}

*gram-khrod (J: gram-pa & khrod) = lit. heap of shingle (TN), 'heap, sparkling heap' (DC) 90^{26}, 106^{29}

gral-dpyam (J: gral-phyam; ChGr: dral-lcam) = ceiling laths 204^{14}

*gri-bdud = 'demon of murder' (TN: gri = murder, not necessarily by knife) 72^{12}, 116^{12}

grum-pa = badger 48^{25}, 144^{17}, 154^{18}, 164^{17}

grol (J: ḥgrol-ba) = *as vb.* to be released, *in special sense of* to be derived, to emanate; *as n. technical term* 'release' (*also meaning* 'emanation') 66^{8-18}, $66^{24, 27}$, $170^{12, 33}$, 228^{8}, $230^{11, 28}$, $232^{10, 17}$

*gliṅ-snam (*abbr.* gliṅ) = patches *of which* rmad-ḥog *and* rmad-gos *are made* (TN) $156^{13, 17, 24}$, $158^{2, 7, 9}$ (*see* Fig. I b)

glud = ransom 34^{37}, $36^{12, 16}$, 70^{32}, $76^{21, 28}$, $78^{5, 18, 19, 28, 34, 36}$, $80^{9, 12, 20}$, $82^{33, 40}$, $86^{10, 24, 34}$, 94^{26}, 122^{1}, 186^{7}; *also* tshe-bslu 34^{36}

*dGaḥ-baḥi tshal, place-name: 'Park of Joy' on the west side of the 'Palace of Victory' (*see* Fig. XXI) 90^{21}

*dguṅ-sman (J: dguṅ & sman-mo) = 'celestial goddess of medicine' 52^{21}

dgoṅs-pa = 'thoughtful purpose' 242^{8}; (*see* thugs-dam *which serves as an honorific of this word*)

*dgra-gśed (J: gśed-ma 2) = 'antagonistic' (DC) 34^{9}

ḥgar (J: ḥgar-ba) = low-grade mixed breed of cattle, viz. a cross of a bull (*glaṅ*) and a *mdzo-mo* 144^{15}

*ḥgur-chu = 'decorative garlands' (TN) 132^{35}

*ḥgog-pa (J: ḥgogs-ka; ChGr: ḥgog-pa la sñoms par źugs) = 'total suppression', viz. of all external impressions (*a technical term in meditation*) 218^{16}

ḥgyiṅ (J: ḥgyiṅ-ba = to look down upon) = *'raised up' (TN) 194[36]; *'lordly mountain' (TN) 48[19, 20]; *also in* *ḥgyiṅ-thod 'turban' 48[39] (*see* Fig. IX c)

*ḥgram-bcos (J: ḥgrams-pa & bcos) = (ceremony for) curing hurt (TN) 92[33, 36]

ḥgras-pa (J: = to hate) = 'at enmity' 44[37], 88[9]

*ḥgrus = 'diagonal lines' (TN) 198[32]

ḥgreṅ-bu = 'upright creature', viz. man, ape, etc. 86[6]

ḥgres (J: ḥgre-ba 2; ChGr: ḥgres-pa) repeated *or perhaps* continued (TN) 92[18]

rgo 'wild goat' 144[21], 154[16], 196[4]

*rgod-lcam (J: rgod & lcam) = *ḍākinī* (TN) 182[27]

rgya (J: rgya 3 = net; ChGr: rgya = "trap") = *trap (TN) 116[29]; net 90[28]

*rgyaṅ-ṅe-ba (*probably connected with* rgyaṅ 'afar') = 'solitary' (TN) 230[8]

*rgyaṅ-bu & rgyaṅ-ḥphan = 'tree symbol' (TN) 36[6], 90[30] (*see Illustration*)

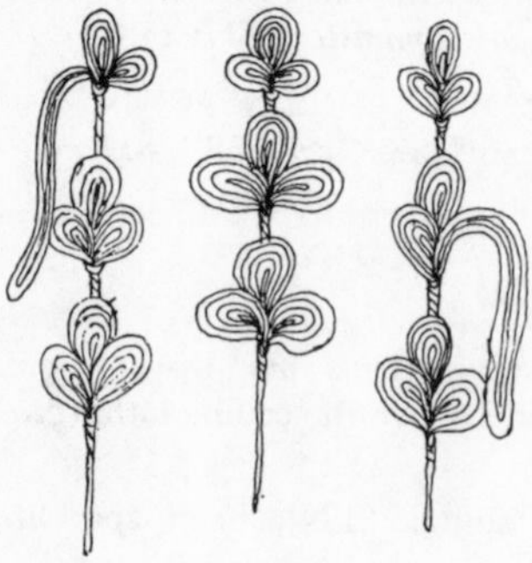

rgyan-śar (J: rgyan *item* rgyan-du ḥchar = it proves a blessing or benefit) = *'first principle' (TN) 172[27], 174[4, 15, 26, 37], 176[10, 21, 32], 220[32]

rgyal *unusual use describing water*, ? = good 194[37]

rgyu-mthun-srid = 'species' (lit. 'coming into existence in accordance with things') 66[26]; *see* srid-pa *below*

rgyu bźi phuṅ-po = 'four bodily elements' (viz. flesh, blood, warmth, breath) 176[26]

rGyug-chen, a guardian divinity 'Great Runner' 52[23], 64[16]

rgyud *basic meaning*: sequence, series, line, etc.: stream 44[9], 48[6], 64[35], 66[35], 68[7]; species 66[1, 26, 33]; tradition, traditional teachings 82[37, 39], 104[12], 118[16], 158[32], 190[8]; *tantra* 102[6], 190[9, 12, 13, 14], 214[8, 14]; soul-series (*referring to the* series *of rebirths of the consciousness of sentient beings*), *and since every living creature embodies such a* soul-series, *the term comes to mean in some contexts* soul *or simply just* mind 126[26], 128[12, 18], 182[35]; *used as a postposition* rgyud(-nas): in the line of *hence* in accordance with 90[11], 104[5]; dgu-rgyud 'nine-fold link' 194[26]; *see also* śes-rgyud *below*

rgyun *in special meaning of* the 'Flow', a ritual which belongs with the set of 'Four Acts' (*for which see BH pp.* 257–8) 188[16], 242[35]

sgam (J: sgam-pa Cs & Sch; ChGr: = profound, wise) 'bat' (creature noted for its cleverness) 86[12]

*sgo-skyes (ChGr: = sgoḥi ru-śiṅ ṅam them-pa lta-bu) TN: = door (*as distinct from* sgo *properly meaning* doorway) 134[2]

*sgoṅ-pri = skin around yoke of egg (TN) 60[27]

*sgra-bla (= ChGr: dgra-lha NS) = 'genie' 24[18], 44[8], 56[30, 38], 58[5, 8], 64[3, 13], 66[34]

*sgrin-bu (*contrast with* J & ChGr: sgrin-po 'clever') = 'foolish' (TN & SGK/Lex) 196[7]

sgrib-pa (J: NM) 'inner anguish' *of a* yi-dvags (*preta*, tormented spirit) 148[4]

sgrub-pa / bsgrub = *as vb.* to perform, to effect, to work upon, *especially in meaning of* to coerce, conjure, bring a divinity to one's presence, *also* to produce, to realize; *as n.* coercion, performance, realization 52[35], 62[2], 74[28], 98[14], 100[5], 102[14], 104[26], 110[1], 112[33], 184[17], 186[14], 188[3], 190[22], 194[23, 24], 212[14]

*sgrub-rten 'ritual articles' (lit. 'supports for the performance') 102[35]; *see* rten-pa *below* *sgrub-gśen-dbal-bon (*see note* 8) = 'officiating priest' 32[2]

sgron (J: sgron-pa 'to cover *or* lay over'; ChGr: 'to lay as one lays bricks') 'well-covered' (TN) 194[36]

sgrol-ba / bsgral (J: sgrol-ba 3) 'to slay' 98[11, 20] (*see note* 31)

*ṅa-bo (= ṅa-rgyal) 'pride' (TN) 28[10]

ṅaṅ-gis *special use of* ṅaṅ *with instr. meaning* 'of one's own accord' *hence* 'naturally' 92[27]; ṅaṅ-gis bźag 'be indifferent' (lit. 'let things be in a natural way') 28[9] (*see* bźag-pa)

*ṅaṅ-thag (bsriṅ) = to keep going, to persevere, to be long-suffering, 28[8, 36], 128[8]

ṅaṅ-riṅ (J: ṅaṅ *item* ṅaṅ-rgyud riṅ-ba) = forbearing 166[15]

ṅar-chu (J: ṅar-ba & chu) = 'strength-potion' 60[26]

ṅar-mi = figurine (TN) 36[8], 86[25]

ṅes-med & ma-ṅes = 'unpredictable' 220[5, 25], 222[3, 6]

*ṅo-loṅ (J: ṅo & len-pa, *imp.* loṅ) = 'undertake' 52[36]

ṅogs (J: = slope *or* bank) nam-mkhaḥi ṅogs = 'expanse of the sky' 218[30]

ṅos ḥdzin / ṅos zin = identify / identification 26[1], 34[1], 36[34]

dṅos-grub = perfect achievement, realization of perfection, final perfection, 'special powers' 90[12], 92[25], 104[19], 182[25], 186[34], 196[30], 208[26], 210[8]

dṅos-ḥbyor = 'real wealth' (*as opposed to what is mentally produced* yid-sprul) 204[27]

*mṅan-sems (J/Cs: mṅan-pa) = 'accursed thought' 148[20]

mṅaḥ-ris = *'sphere of influence' 56[4]

mṅaḥ-gsol-ba (J/Cs: MD) = *to beseech 32[21], 64[13]

mṅar gsum = "three sweet products", *viz. sugar, molasses, and honey* 196[26]

mṅon-cha *for* brṅan-cha *q.v.*

mṅon-rtogs = 'delineation' (of a divinity) 74[35]

mṅon-śes = 'clairvoyance' 24[18], 32[5]

mṄon-śes phyaḥu g·yaṅ dkar, name of a god 26[9]

brṅan-pa (J: rṅan-pa II) = to requite 32[20], 50[20], 52[35], 58[2]

*brṅan-cha (*also written as* mṅon-cha) = 'requital', sacred offerings intended as payments to the gods 34[25], 92[21], 94[20]

*caṅ-seṅ, a class of divinities 58[2, 6], 62[29, 32], 64[4]

*gcan-chen (J: gcan-gzan & chen-po) = 'tiger' 142[39], 204[13]

gcun (J/Lex) = subduing 78[1], 110[10]

gces-ḥdzin = attachment 80[35]

gcoṅ (J: gcoṅ-skad Sch/Lex) = *'ululation' 42[10, 22], 46[14, 17, 19, 23], 50[3], 72[37], 74[1, 3], 86[31], 94[22, 25, 28], 96[22]

bcaḥ sgyur, *technical terms for two different hand-gestures* phyag-rgya, *q.v.* 102[40]

*bcaḥ-gźi (J: ḥchaḥ-ba 1 & gźi) = arrangement *or* disposal of sacred items 48[16]; bcaḥ-gźi-las 'the actual practice' (of the ritual) 184[34], 186[9]

bcas = 'subsidiary matters' 108[37]

bcol (J: ḥchol-ba 'to entrust' NM) = 'urge' 54[10–17]; *see also* gtad-bcol

bcos (i) (J: bcos-pa 1) = 'remedy' 38[16], 92[31–37]; (ii) (J: bcos-pa 2) = 'constructive' 'contrived' 216[15], 252[1, 3]; *also* bcas-bcos *same meaning* 218[19]; ma-bcos 'unconstructive' 'uncontrived' 218[19], 220[13], 248[35] lcags: *special kind of* iron *designated by* *sṅo-mñen-lcags 'iron which is blue and subtle' ? = steel 50[38]

lcags-ri = border 154[31], 156[3, 37]

*cha-rags-pa (J: cha & rags-pa) = 'gross' (DC) 144[31]

*cha-las = 'supplementary' (DC) 64[22]

cha-lugs (J: = clothing / costume [MD], appearance); NM = style, fashion; *special meaning in* cha-lugs-lṅa = 'five bodily postures', viz. (i) *źabs-skyil-kruṅ* 'cross-legged' (ii) *phyag-mñam-bźag* 'palms upwards on lap' (iii) *dpuṅ-pa gzeṅ* 'shoulders up' (iv) *mgrin-pa an-tsam ḥgug* 'neck bent slightly forward' (v) *mig sna rtser phab* 'eyes concentrating on the tip of the nose' 202[22], 216[16]

chag-gaṅ (J: chag 5 MD) = *'one length from elbow to clenched fist' (TN and SGK) 198[23]; (*compare* khru-gaṅ 'one length from elbow to tip of extended fingers')

*chag-goṅ = 'strap' (DC) 156[27]

*chag-nan & chag-non (J: chag 3 & *probably* nan) = 'sandals' 134[25], 156[6, 11, 27]

*chag-tshad (ChGr: = cha-tshad 'size') = 'estimate' (DC) 32[36]; *also:* chag-la gźal 'make an estimate' 26[13, 14], 32[22]

chag-śiṅ (J: 'splint' MD) *a *bonpo* sceptre 196[21], 200[15] (*see* Fig. XVI j)

chan-gri (J: chan-pa; ChGr: chan-gri) = scissors 158[31]

*chab-dkar = "White Waters" (*see the Introduction, pp.* 16–17) 42[6], 50[7], 68[23], 92[18]

*chab-nag = "Black Waters" 42[5, 31, 33], 44[10], 46[6], 50[6, 9], 68[7, 15, 22], 72[29], 76[20, 26], 82[39]

cham-la-ḥbebs (J: cham Lex & Sch NM; ChGr: MD) = 'suppress' (TN) 54[17], 98[17]

*chib *occurring in* rtse-ru chib 'to be perfect' (TN), ? lit. 'to reach the top' 56[24]

chu-gri (J: = a sort of knife) = 'sabre' 60[35]

*chu-ḥbab = 'roof-gutter', normally made of wood or copper in Tibet 204[15]

chu-sram (J: sram) *emended in our text from* kyur-sram *and* khyur-sram, = otter 144[17], 154[18]

chud, **one of the 33 classes of* 'titans' (*lha-min*) 78[7]; *note also* ma-bla-chud

*chun-ḥphyaṅ (J: chun-po 2 & ḥphyaṅ-ba) = 'hanging in intertwined loops' (TN) 90[27]

chus (J: jus C. 'strategy' & jus-legs Sch & Cs) *occurring in* bstan-chus 'religious developments' *or more exactly a programme for these* (TN), 214[37] (TN: groṅ-chus *also exists meaning* 'domestic budget', *viz. crops to be planted, house and land improvements, estimate of income and expenditure*; SGK *also notes* srid-byus 'politics' *as used in modern newspapers*)

*cho-rabs (D: cho-rabs 'parenté' NM) = 'parental lineage' 92[7], 64[2], 66[2, 30], 92[7] (TN: phaḥi cho = phaḥi rigs; maḥi braṅ = maḥi rigs; cho-ḥbraṅ = khyo-śug 'husband & wife'; ChGr: cho-ḥbraṅ MD)

mchoṅ (J: choṅ & mchoṅ) = 'chalcedony' (*tentative identification by TN from among gems illustrated in Ency. Br.*) 58[38]

*mchoṅ *or* ḥchoṅ = a section *or* chapter (TN) 184[27], 188[6–24]

mchod-rten = 'shrine' (*stūpa*), lit. 'support for worship' 136[15] (*see* rten-pa)

ju-thig (J: = 'drawing lots by threads of different colours' NM) = 'knot-sortilege' 24[17], 32[4]

*ju-źag, an unidentified method of astrology (*rtsis*) 24[26], 32[26]

ḥjab-bu (J: ḥjab-pa 'to sneak') = 'thief, thieving' 140[26], 154[1] *ḥjug-sgo = 'introduction' 66[12]

ḥjum (J: ḥjum-pa Lex & Sch) = 'contracted' (TN) 58[30]

ña-phyi (J: ña-phyis NM) = mother-of-pearl 196[24]

ñag-gcig (J: ñag-ma 3 NM) = 'single one, undifferentiated' 60[15], 170[35], 222[30], 228[1], 232[9], 244[33], 246[1], 250[14], 252[33]

*ñams-snaṅ (ChGr: = brtag dpyad yid la śar ba = "thoughtful reflections" & sgom las skyes-paḥi yon-tan = "accomplishments of meditation"), 'psychic manifestations' (DC) 218[30]

ñams-rtsal (J: = skill) = 'psychic skill' (DC) 220[22], 222[4, 7, 12, 17, 22, 28, 32]

*ñiṅ-śa (J: ñiṅ-khu & śa) = 'flesh-essence' 142[28]; ñiṅ-śa-can = 'eating their own kind' 140[20]

ñid *in sense of* 'self alone, absolute' *as in* nam mkhaḥ ñid la ñid du spyod 240[22]

ñu-le (J: ñul-ba) = 'mean' 140[26]

ñen (J: ñen-pa) = 'trouble' 34[39]; *also* ñen-gto 'Trouble Ritual' 74[11]

ñes-dmigs (J: ñes-pa 3; MVP 7309) = 'disadvantage' 122[13]

gñan / gñan-po (*in our MS. regularly occurring as* gñen / gñen-po) (J: gñan 1 'plague' & gñan-pa 'gods of vengeance') = 'furies' 44[7, 37], 50[23, 27], 58[2, 6], 62[11, 29, 33], 88[4, 9, 31], 118[26]

gñan-pa / gñan-pa (J: gñan-pa *as above but with additional meaning* 'cruel, rigid, solemn') = 'rigid, solemn, serious', 82[18], 84[34], 118[32], 194[4]

gñen-pa / gñen-po (J: gñen 2) = aid, antidote 48[30], 56[12], 62[27], 64[9], 130[16]

*sñiṅ-phur ḥkhrugs-pa = 'complete disarray' (TN) 34[17] (ChGr: sñiṅ-phur-thebs = yid-ches-pa "trusting")

bsñen-pa = getting near *in the special sense of* getting near a divinity by the continual recital of his particular spell, *hence* 'invocation'; *also*: 'holding to' (*compare* rten-pa) *and hence* 'veneration' *and* 'reliance' (*used here as a technical term*); *see note* 63; *'invocation' 74[28], 98[14]; 'veneration' 100[5, 6, 32, 37], 102[1, 13], 105[5, 6], 110[1]; *'reliance' 184[17, 32], 186[1–13], 190[22], 212[14]; (*also note my translation of* dge-bsñen 'virtuous adherer' *not included in Glossary*)

bsño-ḥbog (J: smyo-ḥbog) = 'crazy' 164[36]

gtad [1] (J: gtod-pa) = 'commit to the care of' 118[26], 124[8]

gtad [2] (J: brtad) = harmful rite, imprecation 78[3]

gtaḥ (for gtaḥ-chen), *a ritual bowl made from a skull and called 'the great pledge' (*see next item*); 212[7] (*see* Fig. X n)

gtaḥ-ma (J/Lex & Cs) = pledge 34[35], 110[11]

gtar-ba = 'bleeding' 38[17]

gto = 'ritual' 24[1, 10, 11, 29], 26[5, 21], 28[1], 30[18, 33], 34[6, 10, 21, 33], 36[19, 21], 38[34], 40[6], 42[8], 70[29], 74[9–13], 82[4, 33], 88[26, 31], 92[31], 94[26], 118[26]

gtod (J: gtod MD), *local divinities living in rocks*, 'lords of the rocks' 88[5, 10], 92[36], 94[5]

gtor-ma (J: NM) = (i) holy water 130[36]; (ii) sacrificial cake (torma) 200[16] (*see* Figs. XI *and* XVI f)

gtos (J/Lex) = 'vastness' 90[7]

rta-dbab (J: rta-babs MD), *steps around a shrine (*mchod-rten*) and the step-like tiers of a roof built up as a shrine 132[33], 204[8]

rten-pa / brten (J: rten & rten-pa NM) = to hold to, to rely on, to trust, *used here with reference to ritual articles, etc., on which the worshipper and the presence of the divinities depend, hence* 'supporting, symbolic' 34[24], 88[30], 102[3, 35], 110[11], 186[8], 198[7]

rtol (J: Lex/Sch/D; ChGr: rtol-gog = mdzo-moḥi phru-gu), an inferior cross-breed of cattle, *compare* ḥgar, *of which it may be a stage lower, viz.* cross-breed of a bull (*glaṅ*) and a *ḥgar-mo* (D) 144[15]

*ltag-śa (J: ltag-pa & śa) = 'flesh from nape of neck' 54[1]

*ltim-me = 'clear' (TN & DC) 218[8]

*lto-rgyab = 'food and clothes' 214[29]

ltos-pa lṅa = 'five related ones' (DC/MD)

*sTag-lha-me-ḥbar, name of a god 114[12]

staṅ-dbyal (TN: = khyo-śug) = husband and wife 70[4], 72[14], 80[17]

stabs-la (J: stabs) = 'by way, by chance, accidentally' 222[19]

sToṅ-gsum-sgron-me = "Light of the Universe" (viz. Buddha) 84[21]

*brten-ma (NW pp. 181–98), a group of twelve goddesses 78[11], 88[16]

bstim-pa (J: stim-pa) = directing towards, causing to sink into 94[27]

tha-tshig (J/Sch) = oath 198[8]

tha-ram (J/Sch MD) *fetter (TN) 140[10]

thaṅ (J: thaṅ 4) = potion 38[1]

than (J/Sch: ḥthan) = 'evil' 46[6, 34]

thig-pa (J: thig *item* thig-tshad Cs 'proportion') = *'to fit, to meet the case' (TN) 38[31]

thig-le (J: NM) = dot, seed, vital fluid (viz. semen virile), drop (of semen), essence 102[39], 108[14, 27], 138[25], 140[13], 164[13], 180[35], 182[29, 34], 184[2], 188[22], 194[10], 228[1], 232[9], 250[14], 252[33]

*thiṅ-ba = 'to hit the mark' (TN), to reach the objective, 74[8], 86[22], 94[30]; (*in meaning it resembles an intransitive form of* bstim-pa *q.v.*)

*thug-dkar (*or* thugs-dkar) = 'genies', *a class of* sgra-bla (dgra-lha) 44[7], 50[17, 20, 32], 52[11, 18, 24]

thug-pa = to touch upon, to be concerned with 114[11], 140[27, 35], 142[1, 9, 17, 25]

thugs-dam = (i) thoughtful purpose (= dgoṅs-pa *hon.*) 90[11], 92[24], 104[5], 110[19], 204[31]; (ii) tutelary divinity (= yi-dam *hon.*) 104[13]

thun (J: thun II) = rduṅ-chas (TN), various small items hurled at demons from a special horn (*thun-rva*, Fig. IX v) in order to harry them (*see note* 5), *'deterrents' 24[31], 108[18], 110[17]

*thun-khaṅ, a triangular iron receptacle used for the effigy of a foe (*liṅga* q.v.) against whom the rite is directed, and the harmful 'deterrents' 110[4] (*also known as* ḥbrub-khuṅ; *see* Fig. IX h)

*thun-gto = 'harrying rite' 24[31]

*theb-tse = dish (TN) 158[33]

them (as in J: thems-yig Sch) = *fixture *or* certainty (TN: them-yig *is an abbreviation of a word which at the same time fixes* (*viz. symbolizes*) *its whole meaning; e.g. the* them-yig *for the Six Spheres of Existence are listed in BH, pp.* 264–5) srog-yig them-la blaṅ viz.: 'take the Life-Letter which represents the "soul" *bla* of the foe as a valid symbol' 110[9]; (*the same idea but with a different intention occurs on* 120[30]: sa-bon dgod 'establish the seed-syllable')

*theḥu gśog = 'down feathers' (TN) 58[28]

tho-co & tho-cho (J: tho-co 'foolish joke'; ChGr: = spyi-brtol byed-pa "acting capriciously" [J/Sch: spyi-brtol MD]) = 'irresponsible behaviour' (TN), capriciousness 54[21], 220[5]

thob-rdzob = 'false ambition' 134[28]

*thob-ma-gyu = 'vagueness, vagaries, unresponsiveness' 218[37], 222[7]

*mthaḥ-bsgyur = 'acts of supererogation', viz. extra activities such as sortilege (*mo*) which are not part of the essential activities of those who follow a higher tantric way 184[26], 188[5]

mthu (J: mthu 2) = magical force 62[2], 70[32]

mthoṅ (J: mthoṅs NM) = 'vault (of the sky)' 50[34]

*daṅ-chags = 'attachment' (DC, *probably* = chags-pa) 234[1, 5, 10, 15, 20, 25, 30]

daṅs-ma (J: dvaṅs-ma) = 'vitality' 142[2, 20]

dam-can (J: dam *item* dam-can 'bound by an oath') = *'divine guarantors', *viz. gods who are bound by an oath to protect the doctrine* (*Buddhist or Bon as the case may be*); *see BH, pp.* 242–4; 88[8, 13, 17, 30], 92[10, 27]

dam-tshig (J: dam *item* dam-tshig NM) = sacrament, vow (*see BH, pp.* 287–8) 104[2], 150[18], 166[1, 13], 184[4], 188[18], 200[26]

*dam-rdzas = 'sacred items' (*see note* 61 *concerning the* 'five sacred items') 54[1], 99[20], 102[23], 106[3], 176[37]

*dar-bu-khad (J: dar & *perhaps* khad-pa 'to be stuck'), outside pelmet such as is fixed to Tibetan windows, 132[32]

dal [1] = ma-ḥdal, q.v.

dal [2] (J: dal-yams) = 'disease' (TN) 78[2]

dal-ba (J: NM) = 'careful' 32[39], 84[5]

*du = 'liquid offering' (TN), 'drink' 90[2]

duṅ-duṅ (J/Sch: = 'staggering, reeling') = *'persistently' (TN & DC) 60[9]

*Duṅ-ri-mchoṅ-luṅ, place-name 58[38]

des-pa (J/Cs: = 'noble, chaste'; ChGr: = ṅaṅ-rgyud bzaṅ-ba "good disposition"; MVP 2360) = *'gentle' (TN) 38[22]

dom = 'brown bear' 144[7], 154[17], 164[10]

*dom-chol (J/Sch: dob-dob & chol / ḥchol-pa / ḥchol-ba II. 2) = 'gossip, nonsense' (TN) 30[7], 96[27]

*Dra-ma, a group of divinities 60[11, 15, 16]

*draṅ-śan (J: draṅ-po & śan 4) = 'straight-forward distinction' 26[11], 32[11]

dri-za = parasite (*gandharva*) 70[13], 80[13]

dregs-pa (J: NM) = 'the proud ones', viz. local gods 98[9]

dred = 'yellow bear' 144[7], 154[17], 164[10]

*drod-tshad (J: drod & tshad) TN: indications of advance in meditational practice (lit. 'measure of warmth') = 'advance-grades' 74[34], 218[33]

*gdag-sgo (J: ḥdogs-pa & sgo) = 'terminology' (DC) 126[16]

*gdar-tshan = 'hot metal' (TN) 162[12]

*gdar-so = 'bottom of hell' (TN) 86[5]

gdiṅ-ba = 'monk's mat' 156[1]

gduṅ-ma (J: NM) = cross-beam, lintel 132[28], 198[33], 204[13]

gdon (J: NM) = evil spirits, demons 70[13, 20, 33], 116[8], 140[24], 164[36] gdos-pa (J: gdos NM) = gross substance, material elements, 116[4], 120[1]

bdar-ba (J: bdar-ba 3) = to invoke or pray to a divinity (TN) (*used only in the two lowest Ways of Bon, this would seem to be a pre-Buddhist term which was later supplanted by* bsñen-pa, *q.v.*) 32[4], 52[32], 60[8], 86[20], 94[17]

*bdar-thag-gcad = 'cut off completely' (DC & TN) 136[24]

bdar-śa (J/Sch: = nerves, sinews?) = *'tegument inside egg-shell' (TN) 60[25], 70[12]; bdar-śa-gcad = 'revelation' (TN), ? lit. 'remove the tegument or veil' 224[2]

bdud-rtsiḥi śiṅ, any aromatic wood used for burning as incense (TN) 30[39]

*mdaṅ-sum = 'last night' 216[3]

*mdaṅs-ḥbyin-pa (J: mdaṅs & ḥbyin-pa) = 'to temper' (DC) 172[33]

mdaḥ, *a measure equalling half a 'fathom' (ḥdom), viz. about three feet, literally 'an arrow-length' 198[21]

mdud = *'cross-roads' (TN) 48[18, 19, 21]

mdos (J: = 'thread-cross') = *'ritual device' and 'quittance' (*used by us in technical sense; see note* 11) [TN: *mdos ni lha ḥdre la dgaḥ baḥi rdzas / mdos la glud zer thub / glud la mdos mi zer* = "*mDos* refers to items which are pleasing to gods and demons; a ransom (*glud*) may be referred to as a *mdos*, but a *mdos* is not referred to as a ransom (*glud*)". Thus *mdos* is a general term for 'ritual devices' of various kinds.] 36[7], 76[33–38], 78[1–27], 84[8–14], 86[1]

*mdos-cha = 'ritual items' 24[30], 34[21, 24]

ḥdu-ba = 'mixture (of bodily humours)' 80[34]

*ḥdun-pa (cp. J: mthun-pa) = 'to agree' (TN & DC) 28[5]

ḥdur / ḥdur-ba (J: dur) = death rites, funeral rites 118[7], 120[18, 20, 21]; **as vb.* 'consecrate (for funeral rites)' 118[29] (cp. 118[34]) (TN: ḥdur-ba = ḥdul-ba *in special sense of suppressing troublesome spirits that return from the dead, especially those who have been murdered; for this purpose there is a ritual known as* gri ḥdur byed-pa. DLS: *I prefer to see the two verbs as separate.*)

*ḥDur-gsas-rma-bo, name of a god 120[18]

*ḥdus-so = 'a concentration' 24[4, 15]

ḥde-gu (J/Cs: = syrup?) = syrup 36[40]

*ḥDres-paḥi-tshal, a place-name: 'Park of Intermingling' on the south side of the 'Palace of Victory' 90[21] (*see* Fig. XXI)

rdug-pa (J: MD) = *to fail, to be of no use (TN & SGK) (SGK: present-day Amdo: ṅaḥi tshoṅ rdug-soṅ = 'my business has failed') 38[34]

lda-ldi (J/Lex: NM) = 'pleat' (TN) 90[27]

*lda-byad = 'special malevolence' (DC MD) 108[19]

*ldaṅ-ḥgyu (MD) ? a kind of animal (J: ldaṅ-sgo-gka = *Skr.* śarabha) 154[17]

ldem (J: ldem-pa III) = 'excitability' (DC MD) 152[30]

ldem-me-ldem & lhems-se-lhem (J: lhem & lhems-kyi MD) = 'how gay' (DC MD) 86[10, 17]

*brdeg-gto = 'Striking Rite' 24[30], 34[21]

nan-tar (J/Lex: MD; ChGr: = ṅes-par) = *'certainly' 38[35]

nam-mkhaḥ (*or just* nam) = *'sky-symbol', viz. thread-cross (*see* J: *mdos*) 39[9], 90[28]; khaṅ-bzaṅ nam-mkhaḥ = Thread-cross designed as a divine palace 90[28]

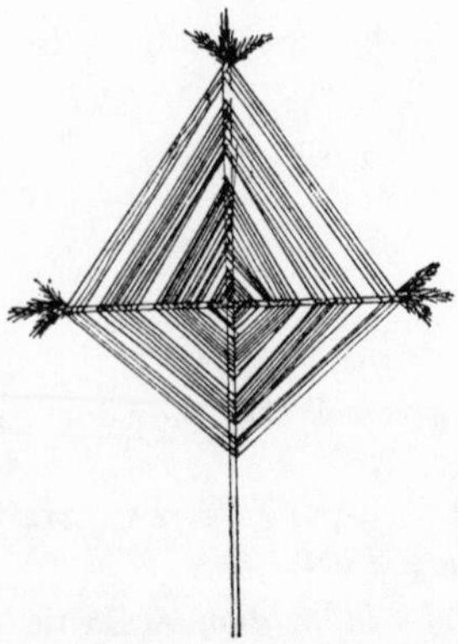

nam-mkhaḥ

khaṅ-bzaṅ nam-mkhaḥ

nal (J/Cs NM) = incest (and other kinds of forbidden intercourse) 46[4, 33]

nus-pa (J: nus-pa 3 NM) = potency (effect) of a medicine 38[21], 50[6, 7, 8], 74[21, 24]

gnas-pa *see* bźag *below*

*gnas-ris chen-po bźi = 'four great realms' (viz. the four heavens next below the top one [*ḥog-min = akaniṣṭha*] in the World of Form [*gzugs-khams = rūpa-dhātu*]) 150[9] (see Fig. XXI)

mnol (J/Cs: = mnal; ChGr: = btsog-pa) = 'impurity' 46[3, 37, 38], 48[10], 52[8]

*rnam-dag-mchod-gtor = 'pure offering of water' (*see* gtor-ma) 130[36]

rnam-par-rgyal-ba (ChGr: rnam-rgyal 2 = a-ru-ra) = *myrobalan 194[13]

bsnun-pa (J: snun-pa NM) *in* bsnun-paḥi gto 'Stinging Rite' 34[37], 110[17]

brnag-pa (J 3 'full of corrupt matter' Cs; ChGr: = źe-sdaṅ) (TN: = drag-po) = *ferocious, ferocity 98[15, 19], 104[28, 34], 106[9, 16], 108[10, 21, 32], 110[20, 25], 210[23]

pa-tra (J: pa-ta) = 'criss-cross design' 132[31, 34], 164[2]

*pad-khug (J: padma & khug-ma) = 'carrying case' for monks 158[28] (*see* Fig. V a, b)

*pad-źu (J: padma & źva), a special kind of religious hat 156[8], 158[18] (*see* Fig. II b, c, d)

*pad-lo (= pad-maḥi lo-ma), the set of six garments of a *bonpo* monk, *referred to in full as* pad-lo ris-drug 156[1], 158[40]

pra (J/Cs & Sch) = prognostic 24[6, 7], 26[10], 34[33], 46[5], 68[35], 110[5], 188[8]

*dpaḥ-khrom (J: dpaḥ & khrom 2) = 'hero-gathering' 56[30, 38], 62[17], 64[18]

dpaḥ-bo ḥbru lṅa = 'five heroic seed-syllables', viz. A OṂ HŪṂ RAṂ DZA 206[4]

dpal = *'a good place' 48[19, 21]

*dpe-srol = 'archetype' (*see the Introduction, p.* 20) 46[10, 11], 62[37], 92[7], 118[37]

*dpon-gsas = 'Master-Sage' (TN) 42[8], 50[8], 88[26], 94[23], 100[6], 102[1], 124[27], 186[2], 194[21]

dpyad (J: dpyod-pa) = 'diagnosis' 24[1, 12, 13, 34], 26[5, 26], 28[1], 30[18, 33], 36[22, 25, 33–36], 38[29, 34], 40[6], 70[28], 82[4]

*dpyam (*also* gral-dpyam & dpyam-gduṅ) = ceiling laths 132[29], 204[7, 14]

spa-bkoṅ-ba (J: ḥgoṅ 2 & sgoṅ-ba 2, spa-sgoṅ-ba 'to despond' Lex.) = *'over-awed' (TN): 'as are the stars by the sun and lesser animals by the lion' 204[17]

spar-kha (*see note* 3) 24[24], 32[24], 34[8], 94[6]

spyan lṅa = 'Five Eyes', viz. of knowledge (ye-śes-kyi spyan), divine (lha-yi), of wisdom (śes-rab-kyi), of *bon* (*bon*-gyi) and fleshly (śa-yi) 174[6, 17, 28], 176[1, 12, 23]

spyan-gzigs (J: = 'costly offerings') = *'display' 72[35], 128[8]

*spyi-rgya-rlabs = 'smooth' (TN) 184[1], 248[12]

phu-duṅ (J/Cs) = sleeves 154[25]

*Phu-wer-dkar-po, name of a god 32[3]

*phud-źal (J: phud & ChGr: źal-bu) = 'offering vessel' (cp. thod-źal, bzed-źal, sman-źal) 196[24]

*pho-khyad (J: pho & khyad) (TN: = ḥgran-zla byed-pa) = 'rivalry' 214[31]

*pho-rgo (ChGr: pho-sgo = "pride") = 'insolence' (TN) 30[3]

*pho-thong *or* pho-toṅ = 'male figure' 36[10], 90[35]; *for illustration see* śiṅ-ris (p. 290)

phon (J: = 'bundle, bunch, etc.') = 'mass' 52[8]

phya & phyva 'fates', 'prediction' 34[26], 42[8]

phyva-rten, implements used in rites of prognosis (*see* rten-pa) 34[24]

phyag-rgya = 'hand-gesture', *see also HT* vol. i, *pp.* 136–7; *the fivefold process of making a hand-gesture*; hands at rest (*bcaḥ*), turning the hands (*sgyur*), holding the hands in the actual gesture (*ḥchiṅ*), releasing the hands with a click of the fingers (*bkrol*), bringing hands together in a supplicatory manner (*sprad*) 102[40]

*phyag-gñen (ChGr: phyag-brñan = ḥkhor-g·yog) = 'religious office or service' 88[26], 94[23, 27]

phyaḥo & phyo-ma = 'void' (TN & DC) 228[20], 230[13]

*phyar-bu = 'short overcoat' (TN) 134[25] (*see* Fig. III d)

phyar-g·yeṅ (J/Lex?; ChGr: = rnam-g·yeṅ) = *'relaxation' (TN) 30[2]

*phyal-ba = (TN: = stoṅ-ba) 'denial' 246[19]

*phyi-rten-bsos (*see* rten-pa & bskos) = 'symbolic arrangement (of the *maṇḍala*)' *with special reference to the 'outer symbols', those of lesser guardian divinities, as distinguished from those of the main (and therefore 'inner') tutelary divinities; the items used are decorated spears and arrows, small quantities of gold, silver and lesser metals, shells, turquoises, etc.* 186[8]

phye-ma phur-ma (J: phur-ma *item*) = 'pleated hangings' 196[19]

phyo-ma, *see* phyaḥo

phyogs-ltuṅ (J/Lex: phyogs-lhuṅ) = partial 228[30] (cp. mthar-ma-lhuṅ 230[25])

*phyod-de (J/Cs: phyod-pa 'progress') = 'blank, colourless' (TN & DC) 218[27], 230[8]

*ḥphen-pa (J: phan-pa) = to prosper 44[19], 56[1], 72[3]

*ḥphar-śam (J: śam-bu & ? J/Sch: ḥphar-ma) = 'trimmings' (TN) 154[24]

ḥphar-ba (phar-ba) = 'red wolf' 144[16], 154[17], 164[15]

ḥPhan-yul (*see the Introduction, p.* 17), 42[7], 76[21], 86[34]

ḥphen-pa (for spoṅ-ba?) 34[35]

ḥphyaṅ-ḥphrul (J: phyaṅ-ṅe-ba *item* phyaṅ-phrul Lex.) 'decorations in loops' 204[16]

ḥphyo-ba (J: NM) = flow, meander 72[19], 216[10]

ḥphrin-las (J: NM) = act, task 54[10], 104[15] (*for the* 'Four Acts' *see BH, pp.* 257–8)

*ḥphred-ñal (J: phred & ñal-ba), *lit.* lying athward, *referring to such creatures as* birds *and* fish *who move in this way* 86[6]

ba-ga (*Skr.* bhaga) = 'universal womb' 44[22], 238[16]

*ba-le-duṅ (J: duṅ) type of shell 50[39]

*bag-dro-ba (ChGr: = 'to be happy') 196[8]

*bag-yaṅs (ChGr: = 'mind relaxed') = 'at ease' 164[7]

*bag-la-źa = 'cowed' (TN & DC; *cp.* spa-bkoṅ-ba *of similar meaning*) 248[20]

*baṅ-ṅe, a kind of sacrificial cake (gtor-ma), 90[2]

*bar-ḥkhyams (T: bar & ḥkhyam-pa) = veranda round a house 134[4], 204[10]

*bar-snaṅ-gzaḥ (J: bar-snaṅ & gzaḥ) = 'celestial bodies'; — — yis ñes-pa, 'the harm they cause, viz. a nervous stroke' 144[27]

bar-sa (= bar-do) 'intermediate state' 118[10], 122[4]

*bu-yug: (J: NM) = storm *or* turmoil *of water, fire, snow, etc.* 204[12]

Be-du-dya-ḥod = "Light of *Vaiḍūrya*", name of the God (or Buddha) of Medicine 36[31], 148[10], 150[38]

bogs (J/Sch: = 'profit, advantage') = benefit, advancement (*combined with vbs.* ḥdon-pa *and* skyed-pa) 214[4], 220[11, 15, 17]

boṅ-ba (J: boṅ 3 Cs MD; ChGr: = 'lump of earth') = *clod 218[14]

bon (*see the Introduction*, pp. 1 & 20) (i) 'priest' 32[2], 62[5]; (ii) 'chant' 54[22]; (iii) 'absolute truth, religious truths and doctrines 28[31, 35], 44[17], 46[29], 82[12, 15], 112[1], 124[24], 172[23], 226[9], 236[25]; (iv) phenomenal elements, philosophical and ethical notions 34[27], 110[32], 170[34], 172[11], 218[25], 240[2]

*bon-can mtshan-ma (= bon iv) = characterizable elements and notions 172[24], 236[26]

bon-po = a follower of *bon*, a *bonpo* 52[30], 64[15], 82[37], 88[33], 94[2], 118[16]

*bya-rdaṅ (J: bya & gdaṅ/rdaṅ; SCD p. 658) = 'bird-rack'?, *see note* 19; TN: 'a mountain shrine' 52[23], 58[1], 64[5, 16]

bya-bon bcu-gsum = "the thirteen birds of *bon*" (*see note* 22) 64[14]

bya-ma-byel-bu (J/Sch: bya-ma-byi 'flying squirrel') 'bat' (TN), *but is a bat good at keeping watch day and night?* 48[26], 144[16] (*gZi-brjid, vol.* kha, *f.* 48b: *bya-ma-byel gyis khos nus zer-ba-las / khyod kyaṅ ñin-mtshan gyi bya-ra la mkhas te bya daṅ byi la ḥtshos* (= *bśos*) *paḥi bu yin pas / phug tu nal yod* = "*when the 'bat' spoke of his competence,* (*he received the reply:*) *you are clever at keeping watch day and night, but since you are the offspring of a cat and a bird, you are impure from the very start*")

bya-waṅ (*emendment of* bya-bon) (J: pha-waṅ 'bat'; ChGr: bya-waṅ = bya-rog che-ba "large crow") = 'bat' MD 144[14]

byaṅ-bu (J: NM) = 'indications' 108[31]; miṅ-byaṅ = 'name-card' 110[15]

byaṅ-(chub-)sems = 'Thought of Enlightenment' 178[1] (= semen), 190[7, 28], 194[2, 11], 196[15], 214[3], 218[18], 220[11], 224[2], 226[15], 236[18], 238[8], 248[29], 250[2, 10, 26], 252[4, 10, 22, 27], 252[34]; *see also* sems bskyed

byams-chen-lṅa = "five great acts of love" 130[20]

byad (J: byad II) = 'malediction' 108[16, 17, 18, 19]

byiṅ-ba (J: ḥbyiṅ-ba 2) = 'indolence' 120[5], 196[8]

byur (J: = 'misfortune') = *a kind of demon (TN: = mi-kha byed mkhan ḥdre 'a demon who spreads defamatory talk') 44[33], 46[34], 72[17]

*bye-sri (J: ḥbye-ba & sri) = 'divorcing demons' 72[17]

*byol-kha = 'attack' (TN & DC) 36[5]

*braṅ-ṅa (J: braṅ) = 'fitting the chest' (TN & DC) 154[25]

brug (J/Cs: brug-pa) = 'flow' 78[38]

bre (J: bre-ba), TN: square piece of masonry resting on the dome of a *stūpa* and serving as base for the spire-like rings; the same word as *bre* which is a square measure about this size 132[35]

brel-phoṅs-pa (J: brel-ba 2 NM) = poor 234[22]

*bla-gab = 'ceiling' (DC) 222[3]

bla-dvags (J/Sch MD) = *'appellation' (TN) 232[19]

bla-bre & bla-(re-)gur = canopy 54[3], 90[30], 200[18, 19] (*see* Fig. XVI a)

*bla-bzuṅ-nas = 'relying on' (TN) 26[19]

bla / yid / sems = 'spirit, thought and mind' 120[4, 11, 32], 116[15], 160[32]

*dBaṅ-chen-bdag-po, name of a god 32[21]

dbaṅ-thaṅ (J: NM) = 'influence' 56[36], 88[21]

*dbaṅ-ris = 'importance' 84[20]

*dbar (J: ḥbar-ba 3) = anger 46[35]

dbal (J/Lex 'point') = (i) point, extreme 60[36], 62[23], 88[38], 200[16]; (ii) *a whole class of warrior-divinities, of whom the chief is *Gar-gsas-dbal* 60[20], 62[20, 23], 74[39], 76[1, 2], 88[7, 12], 90[10]

*dbal-mo = (i) a point 158[29], (ii) a class of powerful flesh-eating goddesses 88[29], 108[28–31], 110[12]

*dBal-gsas, leading *Bon* tantric god 108[13, 21], 110[6]

dben-pa (J: NM) (used as vb. = med-par byed-pa) = *'to remove' 106[16]

*dbyar-dam-bcaḥ (TN & SGK: = dam-bcaḥ; DLS: dbyar *may be an unrecorded root connected with* ḥbyor-ba / ḥbyar-ba 'adhering') = vow 192[21], 200[29]

dbyiṅs = celestial sphere, heavens 88[6, 11], 92[17], 104[8, 15, 21, 23], 122[17], 150[11], 170[27], 188[22], 206[11]

dbyen (or g·yen) (J: dbyen-pa), **alternative name for the* lha-ma-yin (titans), presumably meaning '(beings of) discord' 44[38], 78[30], 102[31]

*ḥban-tshogs = 'general offerings' (ḥban *untraced*) 194[23]

ḥbar (J: ḥbar-ḥbar) = 'hilly' (TN) 194[36]

ḥbod-pa = call, invoke 54[5]

ḥbyuṅ-po = spirits 80[13]

ḥbrid-pa (J: = 'deceive, impose upon') to impose (in a good sense) 126[37]

*ḥbrug-pa (*see* brug-pa) = to flood 44[4]

*ḥbrub-khuṅ (TN: ḥbrub-pa = rduṅ-ba) = thun-khaṅ *q.v.* 108[1] (*see* Fig. IX h)

rbad / rbad-pa (J: NM) = to excite 60[10] *and* doubtfully 164[17]

sbag (J: sbag-pa 2) = double 204[11]

sbub (J: ḥbub-pa) = 'turned downwards', *viz. epithet for* animals *who move with their head down* 86[6]

sbyaṅ / sbyaṅs (J: sbyoṅ-ba) = to practise 74[21]; to purify, to remove 34[24], 120[30], 122[2, 26], 150[24, 31]

sbyoṅ / sbyaṅ (= myoṅ-ba) = to experience 116[13, 24], 148[4], 150[26, 28], 234[39]

sbyor / sgrol / rol = 'ritual union, ritual slaughter and magical manifestation' 106[2], 182[2, 17]

sbran-ma (J: sbron-pa) = sprinkling, libation 30[36], 48[35], 72[30, 31]

sbreṅ-ba (J/Cs: = 'to play an instrument') = *to waft 30[39]

ma-ḥdal (*abbr.* dal) (J: maṇḍal) = 'magic circle', dish of offerings symbolizing the universe (*Representing Skr.* maṇḍala, *this term is used in the lower* bon *vehicles with a slightly different range of meaning from the proper Tibetan term* dkyil-ḥkhor *which is used for* maṇḍala *in the higher tantric sense, that of the sacred sphere of the 'gods of knowledge'. The two terms* maṇḍal *and* ḥkhyil-ḥkhor *continue to be used with distinct meanings in present-day Tibetan usage.*) $34^{11, 12}$, 36^{29}, 94^{3}

*ma-bla-chud = a sort of demon (TN) 70^{39}

ma-mo (J: ma-mo 3) = 'she-demon', 'mother-goddess' 34^{34}, $78^{8, 10}$, 88^{15}, 108^{18}

*ma-yam-rgyal-mo, name of a *ma-mo* $78^{9, 19}$

*Ma-saṅs, a special class of 'furies' (gñan); *see* NW, p. 224 $88^{4, 9}$

*maṅ-thun (maṅ = *Skr.* maṃsa 'meat'; *see* thun *above*) = 'flesh' as a sacrificial offering 90^{2}, 138^{11}, 142^{19}; maṅ-sa 106^{25}

man-dzi (J: = 'sacrificial tripod') = tripod 196^{23} (*see* Figs. XVI g & X m)

*mi-la, a kind of demon, unidentified (TN) 44^{33}

*mug = defilement of child born after father's death, 'fatherless child' (TN) $46^{4, 33}$, 48^{11}

*me-btsaḥ (ChGr: me-btsaḥ & me-tsa; D: me-tas bsreg) = branding 38^{17}

med (*cp.* yod) = 'wrong' 48^{32}, 54^{32}, 70^{7}, 72^{1}; med-khams = bdud-khams 'Demon Realm' 148^{17}

mer-re (J: mer-pa 4) = clear 218^{8}

mo = sortilege $24^{1, 15}$, $26^{5, 6, 19}$, 28^{1}, $30^{18, 33, 34}$, 40^{6}, 80^{39}

*mo-thoṅ (*cp.* pho-thoṅ) = 'female figure' 36^{10}, 90^{35}; *for illustration see* śiṅ-ris

mod-pa = 'too much' 28^{29}

mos-par-spyod-pa = 'devotional practice' 96^{11}; name of stage towards buddhahood $112^{28, 38}$, $122^{26, 36}$

*dmar-chen = 'great red offerings', a sacrificial offering of blood, medicament and a cake (*rgyun-gtor*), kept as a kind of 'reserved sacrament' 212^{8} (*see* Fig. X r, s, t)

*dmar-gsum = 'three red products', viz. flesh, blood and bones 64^{7}

dmig (= chu-mig) = 'a well' 194^{37}

*dmu, one of the thirty-three sections of the 'titans' (*g·yen-khams*) 78^{1}

*dmu-thag = 'life-cord' 92^{26}

*dmu-yad (TN: = dṅos-grub / bcud / g·yaṅ) = 'zest' (TN & DC) 210^{8}

dme, *see* sme

*rmaṅ = feeble (TN) $44^{19, 28}$, 56^{1}, 72^{3}

*rmad-gos (J: rmad-pa & gos) = 'special monastic cloak' viz. a garment made of patches for formal wear *on top of* rmad-ḥog (TN); *see also* gliṅ-snam 134^{25}, 156^{7} (*see* Fig. I a)

*rmad-ḥog = 'ordinary cloak', viz. a garment made of patches for daily wear (TN) 134^{25}, 156^{7}

rmeṅ (J: rmaṅ) = foundation 50^{36}

sman-pa (J: sman III) = to benefit 56^{14}

*sman-mar = 'butter-moulded medicine' 38^{1}

*sMan-mo-gzed, name of a goddess 78^{14}

sme / sme-ba / dme (J: rme-ba II) = filth, impurity, defiling $46^{3, 4, 16, 31, 33}$, $48^{9, 10, 11}$, 52^{38}, 78^{24}, $144^{23, 24, 29}$, 164^{18}, 166^{21}; sme-mnol / dme-mnol 46^{3}, 48^{10}, 52^{38}, 166^{1}

sme-ba (or rme-ba), *see note* 3, a set of nine horoscope signs 24[24], 32[24], 34[8], 60[14], 92[35], 94[6]

smra-ba (J: smar-ba) = *'to produce understanding, to provide the sense, to make an exposition' (TN *claims this as the basic meaning and not just* 'to speak'; *cp.* smraṅ) 66[21], 92[5]; *also* smra-chen 50[1]

smraṅ (*see note* 9) *'exposition' 32[2], 34[16], 42[34], 44[6], 46[12, 18], 50[5, 6, 9], 64[2, 15], 66[3], 72[33], 74[4, 9], 78[38], 82[17], 84[11], 86[21, 28], 92[5], 198[4]

*tsa-kra-ha-la (*Skr.* cakrahala) = 'sword' (TN) 196[20]

*gtsaṅ-ma gtsug-phud = 'top pure ones' (SGK: *the four stages of oblates and monks in bonpo usage are*: (i) bsñen-gnas *involving light fasting rules*, (ii) dge-bsñen *involving five rules* [*see p.* 130], (iii) gtsaṅ-gtsug *involving twenty-five rules* [*corresponding to Buddhist* dge-tshul] *and* (iv) draṅ-sroṅ *involving about 250 rules* [*corresponding to Buddhist* dge-sloṅ]) 158[1]

*gtsaṅ-ris-lha = 'gods of the Pure Abode' 46[37]

gtsod = 'antelope' (MD) 144[21], 196[4]

btsan = 'fiend' 34[34], 76[36], 78[2], 88[15]

*btso = 'bomb' *Introduction, p.* 14[20], *p.* 256 *n.* 5

rtsa = 'channel' (*see HT*, vol. i, *pp.* 36–37) 44[13, 14, 16, 27], 52[26], 78[27]

*rtsaṅ, small stakes shaped like weapons (arrows, swords, spears) which are placed around the 'magic triangle' (*thun-khaṅ* / *ḥgrub-khuṅ*) after the liṅga has been placed in it (TN) 108[3]

rtsal (J: NM) = 'reflective power' (TN: *rol-pa rtsal las ḥbyuṅ* = *'magical play arises from reflective power'*, *e.g. mchod-rten byin-rlabs kyi gźi* / *byin-rlabs mchod-rten las ḥbyuṅ-ruṅ-ba ni rtsal* = *a* stūpa *is a source* (*lit. basis*) *of grace; grace is the magical play of a* stūpa*; reflective power is the virtuality of grace from a* stūpa) 232[25], 236[22, 25], 238[25, 34], 250[16]

rtsal-ba (J: rtsol-ba) = to make effort, to try 130[10, 24]; *see* brtsal

rtsi-thog = 'berries' 146[6]

rtsi-śiṅ = 'aromatic shrubs' 198[3], 240[26]

*rtsiṅ-rtsub-spyod-pa (J: rtsiṅ & rtsub-pa II) = 'wild behaviour' 220[6]

rtsis = astrological calculation 24[1, 8, 22], 26[5, 19], 28[1], 30[18, 33], 40[6], 74[13]

*rTsub-ḥgyur-tshal, a place-name: 'Park of Fierceness' on the north side of the 'Palace of Victory' 90[21] (*see* Fig. XXI)

rtsed-ḥjo = 'to play' 86[17], 90[36]

brtsal (J: ḥtshol-ba): ma-brtsal = 'effortlessly' 82[21]

tshags (J: tshags 5) *in* tshags-su bsdam = 'bound up together' 184[5]

*tshaṅ-rgyuṅ = 'universe' (TN) 80[2, 15], 86[1]

*tshaṅs-paḥi tshul dgu = 'nine pure attributes' 210[30]

*tshan = 'water' (TN) 198[26]

*tshig-bśad = 'liturgy' 54[7], 102[17], 104[6]

*tshul-gos = 'cope' 156[7, 11, 36]

tshogs = 'mass (of offerings), general offerings' 88[28, 34], 208[17]; 'a host' 88[28, 32], 90[14], 92[9]; 'heap' 136[20]; 'accumulation (of merit and/or knowledge)' 130[37]

tshogs brgyad (J: tshogs 3) = 'eight perceptive groups', viz. those of eye, ear, nose, tongue, body, mind (yid), 'defected mind' (ñon-moṅs-paḥi yid) and 'universal basis' (kun-gźi) 176[10], 204[9], 208[18]

*tshod-mdaḥ = 'precipitancy' (TN & DC) 28[28]

tshom-bu (J/Cs: tshom-pa 'bundle, bunch') = 'heap' (TN) 88[37]

*tshoms-tshom (J/Sch: tshoms-rṅams 'noise, clatter'), mode of religious dancing (? coming together in groups) 210[34]

tshor-ba rags-pa = 'insensitivity' 150[16]

*mtshal-bu, name of a bird: 'Red Bird Vermilion' 46[2] (*see* gZi-brjid, *vol.* kha, *f.* 41b[6])

*mTshal-ri-lha-ḥdun, a place-name: '(Park of) the Red Mountains where the gods gather' on the south-west side of the 'Palace of Victory' 90[23] (*see* Fig. XXI)

*mtshe, a Tibetan rock-plant used from early times in religious ceremonies and well known by Tibetans, who use the dried leaves as snuff. (It seems to be *Ephedra*, probable species *girardiana*, according to Major George Sherriff) 36[10]

*mtsho ru & mtsho ro (TN: = g·yu) 'turquoise' 30[37], 52[1]

*ḥtshag-pa (*cp.* tshogs) = to assemble, collect 160[3]

ḥtshaṅs (J: ḥtshaṅ-ba) = 'to treat' 28[29]

*rdzu-ḥphrul-lha = 'gods of illusion' 98[13]

rdzoṅs-ḥdebs (J: rdzoṅ-ba & ḥdebs-pa) = to dismiss, dispatch 68[33], 72[28], 74[6]

*Dzo-dbal-thigs, a group of divinities (TN: dzo = btso) 108[16]

*wal-wol = 'restive' (TN) 164[15], 168[28]

*Wer-ma dpaḥ-khrom = 'the hero-gathering of the Wer-ma genies' 44[8], 56[38], 60[19], 62[8-28], 64[3] (*a group of warrior-gods*; *see* gZi-brjid, *vol.* kha, *f.* 26b[2] *where the terms refers to one of 81 ways of fighting taught to the young* gŚen-rab)

*źi-rgyan bcu-gsum = 'thirteen tranquil adornments', viz. crown (*dbu-rgyan*), ear-ornaments (*sñan-cha*), pendant (*mgur-chu*), necklace (*do-śal*), low-hanging necklace (*se-mo-do*), shoulder-ornaments (*dpuṅ-rgyan*), bracelets (*phyag-gdub*), anklets (*źabs-gdub*), upper garment (*stod-g·yogs*), lower garments (*smad-śams*), seat-mat (*khri-gdan*), back-piece (*rgyab-yol*) and *bla-gur* (canopy) 210[30]. (*For most of these items see* Figs. VIII and XV)

*źiṅ-chen g·yaṅ gźi = 'human skin' *see note* 35; 106[31] (*see* Fig. XIII p)

*źugs-śaṅ = 'mixture of roasted and unroasted barley used as offering' (TN); *see also* śel-tshigs 198[3]

źor-la (J: sbyor-ba 3) = 'incidentally' 222[19]

*gźi-bskur (TN: = lhuṅ-bzed) = begging-bowl 158[26] (*see* Fig. V c)

*gźi-gnas (= gźi-bdag) = 'lords of the soil', local gods 46[38], 94[7]

gźuṅ (J: NM) = *'lore' 42[33], 44[6, 7, 8, 9, 10], 46[7, 12], 50[17, 22, 24, 25], 52[34], 54[20], 58[7], 60[11, 19], 62[8, 29], 64[35], 66[31, 34], 68[8], 92[18]

gźol-ba = effort, application 130[23]

bźu-ḥdu (*emendment of* bźu-bdul) (J: źu-ba 2 & ḥdu-ba) = 'dissolution' (TN) 102[39]

bźen-ḥdebs (J: gźen *with* ḥdebs-pa 'to admonish') = urging, exhorting, coercing 46[16], 72[40], 74[2, 37], 86[30, 32]

bźag / gźag (J: ḥjog-pa) = lit. 'be placed'; 'let things be' 28[9, 12], 220[8, 17], 238[22]; raṅ-bźin mi bźag 'things are not disposed naturally' 216[15]; mñam-par bźag-pa 'to be put at ease, to be reposed' 34[18], 238[22]; *cp.* bźag-pa (to be put) *with* gnas-pa (to stay) 218[2, 22], 238[21, 28]

*za-kha-sdaṅ-ba = 'hating and consuming' 36[4]

*za-ma-mo (ChGr: za-ma = "[1] grain, something castrated or neuter, and likewise popular religious beliefs which are just as ineffectual, and [2] woman *and* time") = 'feminine creature' 160[23]

*za-ra-tshags 'criss-cross decorations' = 132[31, 35], 204[15] (*see* Fig. X g)
za-lam = 'consuming way' 104[22]
*zaṅ-thal = 'immediacy, spontaneity' (TN) 230[20], 232[24]
zil-bsgyur (cp. J: zil-bun-pa) = 'frenzy' 116[25], 144[28]
zuṅ-ḥjug = 'two-in-one' (*see HT*, vol. i, *pp.* 22–24) 172[7], 182[1, 14, 20], 238[25]
*zuṅ-thub (J: ḥdzin-pa & thub-pa) = 'of quick comprehension' 166[13]
*zur-ḥdeg (J: zur & ḥdeg-pa) = 'subsidiary help' 64[23]
zegs-ma *see* gzeg-ma
zor (J: zor 2) = 'hurled offerings' 108[18] (*see* zlog-gtor, Fig. XI e)
gzab-pa (J: gzabs-pa) = to take care of 168[2, 14]
*gzaḥ-gtad & bzaḥ-gtad = 'fixation' (TN & DC) 180[5], 218[15], 222[16]
gzi-mdos (J: gzi 2) = 'banded agate' 78[12]
gzu-dpaṅ (J/Sch: = witness, mediator) = advocate, mediator (TN) 72[33]
*gzuṅ-so (J: gzuṅ-ba & so II) = 'field of study' 126[16]
*gzuṅs-ma (**Skr.* vidyā; *see BH, p.* 288) = 'feminine partner' 106[5], 182[22], 194[10]
gzeg-ma & zegs-ma (J: gzeg(s)) = drops, small particles 70[25], 140[6]
*gzed-źal (J: gźed I & źal) = 'chalice' 208[22]
*ḥod-gsal-lha = 'Gods of Pure Light' 66[27]
*ḥol-kon, a dish heaped with *rtsam-pa* (ground roasted barley) and butter as a ceremonial offering (TN) 30[41]

*ya-gad (ChGr: = "stairs" MD) = 'decorative eaves' (TN) 132[31], 204[7, 15]
ya-ṅa (J: NM) = 'how terrible!' 142[6, 30]; ya-ṅa-tsha 'to be in terror' 196[7]
*yag-ka and ya-ka = 'a blessing' (TN) 34[28], 50[10], 52[21]
*yaṅ-dag-mthaḥ (J: yaṅ-dag-don; ChGr: yaṅ-dag-mthaḥ = stoṅ-pa-ñid) (TN: = don-dam) = the 'pure ultimate' 238[3]
yar-ba (J/Sch: = 'to be scattered') = 'to be lost' (TN) 116[32]
*yas-stags (*cp.* J: stag-chas; ChGr: yas-stag = "*bonpo* ritual items"; TN: = mchod-sbyin-gyi-rdzas) 'ritual items' 30[5], 36[7], 50[4], 74[5], 198[3]
yi-dam, tutelary divinity 74[35]; *cp.* thugs-dam
*yu-ti (TN: = chaṅ) = *chang*, 'ale' 90[1], 106[35], 138[11], 208[23]
yug (J: yug-sa) = 'widowhood'): *byur-yug = 'misfortune' (TN DC MD) 46[34]
yul-mkhar = '(model of) the property' 36[12], 90[36], 94[10] (*see* Fig. XVIII)
yul brgyad (*corresponding to the* tshogs brgyad *q.v.*) = 'eight spheres of perception', viz. form, sound, smell, taste, touch, ornament (*rgyan*), *bon* and treasury (*gter*); 208[19]
*Ye-mkhyen-sgra-bla, name of a god 24[18], 32[5], 58[15]
*ye-ṅam (TN: = lha-bdud) = 'gods and demons' 92[34]
*Ye-rje-smon-pa, name of a god 24[19], 32[6], 58[10, 34], 60[6]
*Ye-dbaṅ-mthu, name of a god 58[11], 60[18]
*Ye-dbaṅ-lha, name of a god 24[20], 32[7]
ye-ḥbrog (J/Cs) = 'injuries' 70[14, 30, 38], 116[13]
*Ye-smon-rgyal-po, name of a god 66[30]
*ye-śes gźal-yas = 'palace of wisdom' = *dkyil-ḥkhor* 90[28]
*ye-śes-lha (*also* ye-śes *in same special sense*) = 'gods of knowledge' 104[8], 186[23, 28], 210[4]

*Ye-gśen-dbaṅ-rdzogs, name of a divine sage 60^{7}, 62^{2}

ye-srid (*see* srid-pa) = timeless, primeval 228^{14}, 230^{26}

*Ye-srid-ḥphrul-gyi-rgyal-po, name of a god 24^{17}, 26^{7}, 58^{9}

*Ye-srid-lha-dbaṅ-rgyal-po, name of a god 32^{19}

yeṅ-ṅe / yeṅs (J: g·yeṅ-ba 1) = 'calm' (TN) 216^{10}, 218^{27}

yo (J/Sch: yo-ba 2) = all (TN) 168^{31}

*yo-gto (J: yo-ba 1 & gto) = 'Awry Rite' 24^{29}, 34^{10}

*yo-ma = (TN: = rgod-ma) 'mare' 52^{28}

*yo-laṅ = 'tremulation' (DC MD) 248^{5}

yod = being, existence 48^{31}, 52^{10}, 54^{31}, 70^{7}; 'right' 72^{1}; *cp.* med *and* srid-pa (iv)

*yol-chen (J: yol-kha) = 'skull-cup' 106^{38}, 196^{24}, 200^{16}

*g·yaṅ-rten (J: g·yaṅ 1 & rten) = 'talisman' 34^{24}

g·yaṅ-gźi, animal skin, especially that of the antelope 154^{32}; *see* źiṅ-chen g·yaṅ-gźi

g·yaṅ-za (J: g·yaṅ 2) = abyss 100^{15}; 'hesitation, trepidation' (TN) 168^{13}, 220^{3}

*g·yu-ḥbraṅ bdud-rtsi = 'concentrated *chang*' (TN) 32^{1}, 72^{36}, $92^{3, 22}$, 106^{36}, 196^{27}, 208^{23}; *also* g·yu-mṅon *same meaning* 94^{20}

*g·yu-ris, 'a blue design' (TN) 120^{28}

*gYu-luṅ-śel-brag, a place-name: 'Crystal Crag of the Turquoise Vale', *a cave in the realm of the thirty-three gods* 194^{25}

*g·yuṅ-dvags (ChGr: = miḥi sgo zog gi phyugs thams-cad NM) = 'domestic animals' 90^{32}, 94^{9}, 196^{4}

g·yuṅ-druṅ (*Skr.* svāstikā) = swastika 54^{11}, 62^{26}, 82^{12}, $96^{12, 13}$, 98^{26}, 112^{40}, 114^{9}, 144^{36}, 165^{1}, 208^{1}

g·yen *see* dbyen

*g·yor = 'blocked' (DC MD) 196^{1}

rag-ta (*Skr.* rakta) = blood 106^{27}, 178^{22} (*see* Fig. X t)

rags-pa *see* tshor-ba rags-pa

*raṅ-chas (TN: 'special characteristic, *e.g. heat is the* raṅ-chas *of fire*) = 'self-nature' 240^{3}

rabs-chad (J: = 'issueless'; ChGr & D both refer to "woman without issue") 'impotent' (TN & DC) 160^{21}

ral (J: ral 2) = 'high vale' 48^{31}

ri-rab = 'best of mountains' (*Meru*) 90^{16}

rigs-lṅa = 'Five Families' *see note* 59; 102^{20}, 170^{30}

ru-ma (J: = curdled milk, leaven) = leaven *in special meaning of* 'causing to rise up (into existence)', viz. 'source' $58^{32, 36}$

ru-mtshon (J/Sch) = pennant 94^{19}

ro-myags (*Skr.* Kuṇapa) = 'Hell of Putrefaction' 150^{26}, 162^{8}

rla-rdol (J: rdol-ba *item* bla-rdol Lex = bab-chol; ChGr: *idem*) = 'excitable' 164^{36}

rlob-pa / brlab = to wave about, to be hung with 132^{32}, 204^{16}

la dor (? ḥdor-ba *for* ḥdaḥ-ba; *see next entry*) lit. 'to cross the pass', viz. 'to attain to one's objective' 184^{3}

la bzla-ba (J: zla-ba II 4) bogs-ḥdon la bzla-ba, lit. 'attaining the benefit' 220^{15}

*lag-len (J/Sch: 'practice, dexterity') = skill, techniques 28^{38}, $30^{10, 23}$, 84^{10}, 108^{37}

*lag-riṅ (J: lag-pa & riṅ-ba) = 'to be mean' (DC) 88^{5}

lan-chags (J: NM) = 'debts of evil, demonish retributions' 34[37], 90[25], 116[8]
las-mkhan (J/Cs) (TN: = g·yog-po) = 'expedients' 108[34]
*las-sbyor = 'application' (DC) 100[5], 110[21, 25]
li-mar (J: li I) = (? red) bronze 30[38]
liṅ-ga = 'effigy of foe against whom the slaying ritual is practised', *Skr.* liṅga; *see note* 31; 108[5]
liṅ-phyiṅ (J: liṅ-ba? & phyiṅ-pa) = felt 30[35]
lu-gu (J: lu-gu 2) = chain 208[30]
lu-ma = a spring of water 44[3], 194[37]
luṅ (J: luṅ 2) = 'inspired teachings' 54[29], 102[6], 112[22], 124[27], 190[8, 9], 192[16], 194[5, 21]
luṅ (J: luṅ-pa 1) = valley 48[32]
lus-gzuṅs (J: gzuṅs 2 *q.v.*) = (seven) elements of the body 140[13]
le-len (J/Cs & Sch) = retribution (TN) 214[28]
*lo-phrom-bse = 'pure copper' (TN) 50[37]
logs-su med-pa = 'direct', lit. 'not in other directions' 218[32]

*śa-mtshan (ChGr: = sme-ba nag-thig "mole") = 'physical beauty' (DC) 194[1]
*śi-śon = 'cotton' (TN & DC) 154[37], 198[28]
śigs-se (J: śigs-se-śigs 'rocking') = 'free' (TN & DC) 216[35]
*Śiṅ-rtaḥi-tshal, a place-name: 'Park of Riding' on the east side of the 'Palace of Victory' 90[21] (*see* Fig. XXI)
śiṅ-rtsi (J/Cs: = resin) TN: 'aromatic shrubs', *cp.* rtsi-śiṅ *and* bdud-rtsi 94[13]
*śiṅ-ris = 'ritual stake' 36[9], 90[29] (*see Illustration*)

*śim-phod = (TN: = spos) 'incense' 178[15]
*Śugs-mgon or Śug-mgon, a class of Genies (sgra-bla) 58[2, 6], 62[35, 36], 64[1, 4]
śugs: śugs-kyis = 'by force' 74[25]; śugs-las byuṅ = 'come about by the inevitable course of events' 222[19]
śe-maṅ (J/Sch: śe-moṅ) = 'wretchedness' 140[9]
*śel-tshigs TN: = 'sacrificial barley', viz. mixture of over-roasted (blackened) barley and normal roasted barley (*yos*) 48[23]
*śes-rgyud (TN: = gśis-ka 'character') = 'disposition' 198[1]; 'experience' (DC) 68[36]
*śo-rdo (J: śo) = dice (the actual numbered pieces) 32[18]
*śo-gźi-khra-bo = dice-board (as used for sortilege) 32[17]

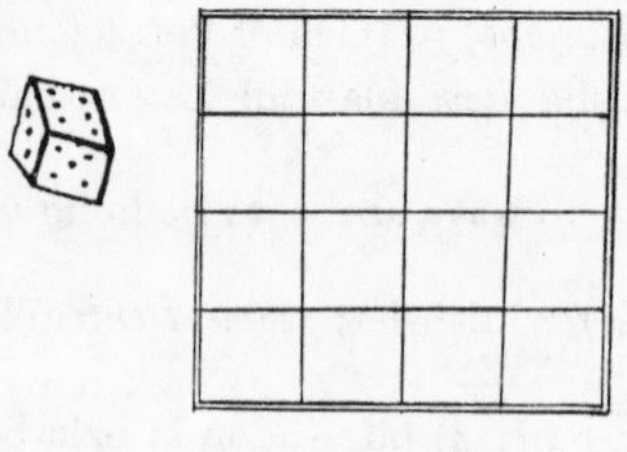

gśaṅ = flat-shaped *bonpo* bell 54[5], 92[4], 162[5] (*see* Fig. XII c, d)

gŚin-rje = 'spirits of death' 34^{34}, 76^{38}, 88^{15}; 'Lord of Death' 116^{24}

gśed (J: gśed-ma 2) = 'minions of hell' 120^{31}

*gśen-po = a (sacrificial) priest 82$^{13, 17}$, 84^{24}; gśen-grogs / gśen-mched 'Shen Brethren' 200^{5}, 206^{17}

gŚen-rab = 'the best of Shen' (viz. a good priest) 54^{12}, 101^{8}, 120^{22}, 122^{22}; *probably = the Teacher* gŚen-rab 87^{21}, 98^{25}, 132^{3}

bśos-bu (J: bśos) = a sacrificial cake (= źal-zas; *see* Fig. X v) 54^{4}, 88^{38}, 94^{8}

sa-bcu = 'ten stages (towards buddahood)' 96$^{12, 13}$, 122$^{15, 38}$, 126^{28}

sa-bdag = 'lords of the soil', local gods 44^{21}, 78^{23}, 92$^{30, 35}$, 94^{33}, 196^{38}, (198^{14}); *see also* gźi-gnas

*sam = 'sweet offering made of *rtsam-pa*, molasses, butter, etc.' (TN) 90^{2}

sul-bu (J: sul) = gathering (made in cloth) 156^{36}, 158^{18}

sems-bskyed (*see* byaṅ-chub-sems) = 'Raising the Thought (of Enlightenment)' 26^{40}, 28$^{26, 32}$, 50^{14}, 68^{3}, 96$^{4, 5}$, 100^{34}, 102^{5}, 110^{33}, 112$^{3, 17}$, 126^{38}; *see also note* 44

sel (J: sel 2) = purification, removal, 'exorcism' 42$^{5, 31}$, 44^{4}, 44^{12} to 46^{18}, 48$^{7-14, 37}$, 48^{38}

sel-ba / bsal (J: sel-ba) = to purify, to remove, to exorcize 46^{26}, 48$^{7-14}$, 98^{16}, 120^{2}

*sel-ra = 'exorcizing ring' 48^{30}

so-ma (J: so-ma 2; TN: = ma-bcos-pa) = 'ever fresh' 248^{36}

*sog-khrig *or just* sog (*cp.* J: sog-pa 2 & khrigs) = complete set of ritual items, viz. thread-crosses, arrows, stakes, etc. (TN) 84$^{10, 14, 37}$

sri = 'vampire' 42^{6}, 44^{29}, 68$^{26, 28}$, 70$^{24, 33, 34}$, 72$^{11-17}$, 74$^{2, 10}$, 78^{19}; kag-sri 34^{35} *see* kag

srid-pa (J: srid & srid-pa) = *vb.* (i) to come into existence, to originate, to happen, to be produced 32^{29}, 46^{10}, 52^{12}, 58^{17}, 64^{38}, 66$^{15, 25}$, 70$^{7, 8}$, 72^{9}, 74^{12}, 120^{9}, 138^{20}, 228^{14}; (ii) to be changed into (= ḥgyur-ba) 54$^{31, 35, 39}$, 56^{1}, 60$^{24-27}$, 66^{26}; (iii) to be possible 66^{36}, 68^{40}, 194^{14}. *n.* (iv) being, existence, existing world, existing things 44$^{20, 22, 31}$, 46^{8}, 58$^{33, 35}$, 64^{35}, 66$^{24, 31, 35}$, 68$^{7, 39}$, 72^{9}, 80^{6}, 86^{4}, 90^{17}, 108^{4}, 120^{9}, 138^{25}, 220^{20}; (v) origins 64^{38}, 138^{20}; (vi) phenomenal existence (*usually occurring as* snaṅ-źiṅ-srid-pa) 72^{38}, 74^{36}, 76$^{6, 9, 23}$, 78^{10}, 86^{23}, 90$^{8, 15, 17}$, 92$^{12, 15, 31, 37}$, 94$^{24, 29, 32, 35, 37}$, 96^{4}, 98^{5}, 142^{22}, 170^{34}, 182^{2}, 188^{10}, 202^{1}, 240^{2}, 248^{5}; (vii) a living being (= ḥgro-ba) 86^{6}; (viii) generation 62$^{35, 37}$, 64^{1}. *adj.* (ix) 'original' 44^{9}, 46^{12}, 48$^{6, 30, 38}$, 52^{30}, 60^{8}, 64^{15}, 66^{36}, 70$^{1, 2, 24}$, 72^{10} (*note especially*), 82^{37}, 88^{33}, 94^{2}, 118$^{16, 35-38}$. *Special meanings*: (x) (J: srid 2) srid mi-bskyaṅ 'don't assume responsibilities' 168^{26}; (xi) srid-gsum 'three atmospheric levels' 248^{12}; (xii) srid-pa gsum-po 'three spheres of being' *viz. under, on and above the earth's surface* 92^{11}

srin (*for* srin-bal; *see next item*) = silk 162^{37}

*srin-bal kha-chu = lit. 'insect-wool-saliva' = silk (TN) 154^{35}

sruṅ-ma = defenders, guardians 92^{27}, 102$^{20, 34}$, 150^{19}

sruṅs-rta = kluṅ-rta

*sreg-ḥphaṅ-mnan = 'burned, hurled, suppressed', viz. the threefold process of destroying the *liṅga* (q.v.), part burned, part let go on an arrow, part buried under ground 108^{7}, 110^{22}

*srog-mkhar = 'life-force citadel', viz. an arrow representing a male (a distaff for a woman), 30^{38}; a symbolic drawing used as an amulet (= *sruṅ-maḥi rten-ḥkhor*) 34^{36}, 36^{1}, or as a *liṅga* (q.v.) 110^{11}

*srog-gi ḥkhor-lo = 'circle of life', viz. a symbolic drawing used as a *liṅga* (as in item above) 106^{23}, 110^{8}

*srog-dbugs-mchod-pa = 'blood sacrifice' (lit. offering of the breath of life) 106[33]

*srog-yig = 'life letter', viz. a single syllable representing the life-force of a god or demon; in higher religious practice *sa-bon* (Skr. *bīja*) is used in this sense 110[9]

*gSaṅ-ba-thabs-źags, a book-title: 'Noose of Secret Method', one of the six sections *of the* Khro-ba-rgyud-drug, *an important* bonpo tantra (*in our collection*); 184[6]

*gsad-gcad (J: gsod-pa & gcod-pa) = slaying, slaughter 98[21], 140[27]; *see note* 31

gsaḥ = 'snow-leopard' 144[17], 154[16], 164[16]

gsal-ba-dgu-ḥdzab = 'the nine special syllables', viz. A Ā DKAR SALE ḤOD A YAṂ OṂ ḤDU (*as in our MSS. of* źi-ba a-gsal gyi cho-ga, *f.* 9a *and* thos-grol *f.* 8b) 206[4], 208[29]

*gsas, high-ranking divine beings (*bonpo* usage only) 60[20], 62[19], 72[32, 34], 90[10], 104[1]

*gsas-mkhar = '*gSas* Palace', viz. a shrine or a mystic circle (*dkyil-ḥkhor*) 64[17], 184[9, 18], 208[27]

*gsas-mthoṅ (*see* mthoṅ *above*) = 'divine vault of the sky' 50[34]

*gsiṅ-ba (*cp.* J: siṅs-po) = 'to dispense, to clear away' (DC) 38[5], 120[5], 196[8]

gser-skyems (*see* skyems) = 'libation' 34[25], 94[20], 198[3]

*gSer-ri-g·yu-luṅ, a place-name: 'Turquoise Vale by the Golden Mountain' 58[37]

*gsor-ba & bsor-ba = 'to transpose' (TN) 24[32], 36[6, 13], 44[15, 36], 78[25], 82[36]

hur-pa (J: hur-ba) = 'trickster' 140[25]

*hos-ru (TN: = mkhar-gsil), a staff surmounted by a miniature double *mchod-rten* and fitted with twelve jingling metal rings, 'jingling mendicant's staff' 158[27] (*see* Fig. V d)

hrul-po[r] (J: hrul-ba) 216[9] '[in] fragments'

*lha-gźi = mat (for religious purposes) 48[34], 72[30]

lhab-lhub (J: NM) = 'flowing loose (of garments)' 90[27], 92[2], 210[24]

lhems-se-lhem *see* ldem-me-ldem

aṅ-drag, *unknown word describing a conch* 148[33]

Ar-moḥi rdo, a place-name: 'Park of Fine Stones' on the north-west side of the 'Place of Victory' 90[23] (*see* Fig. XXI)

u-dug = 'unpleasant' (TN & DC) 146[15], 160[21]

u-ya (? *skr.* guhya) = 'secret' 182[23]

e-kloṅ (TN: = thun-khaṅ & ḥbrub-khuṅ *q.v.*) 108[1], 110[4]